The Atlantic as Mythical Space

An Essay on Medieval Ethea

Alfonso J. García-Osuna
Hofstra University

Series in World History

Copyright © 2023 Vernon Press, an imprint of Vernon Art and Science Inc, on behalf of the author.

All rights reserved. No part of this publication may be reproduced, stored in a retrieval system, or transmitted in any form or by any means, electronic, mechanical, photocopying, recording, or otherwise, without the prior permission of Vernon Art and Science Inc.
www.vernonpress.com

In the Americas:	*In the rest of the world:*
Vernon Press	Vernon Press
1000 N West Street, Suite 1200,	C/Sancti Espiritu 17,
Wilmington, Delaware 19801	Malaga, 29006
United States	Spain

Series in World History

Library of Congress Control Number: 2022941598

ISBN: 978-1-64889-777-1

Also available: 978-1-64889-173-1 [Hardback]; 978-1-64889-627-9 [PDF, E-Book]

Product and company names mentioned in this work are the trademarks of their respective owners. While every care has been taken in preparing this work, neither the authors nor Vernon Art and Science Inc. may be held responsible for any loss or damage caused or alleged to be caused directly or indirectly by the information contained in it.

Every effort has been made to trace all copyright holders, but if any have been inadvertently overlooked the publisher will be pleased to include any necessary credits in any subsequent reprint or edition.

Cover interior's image: commons.wikimedia.org. Public Domain.

Cover design by Vernon Press.

Cover image: commons.wikimedia.org/wiki/File:BLYatesThompson26LifeCuthbertFol26r CuthSails.jpg (Public Domain).

Background image by aopsan / Freepik.

Table of contents

List of figures	v
Foreword	vii
Introduction	xi
Portolan chart, or the routes of myth	1
The problem of myth as framework for the acquisition of knowledge	1
Myth and history	12
Myth and water	19
Myth and its domains: the Atlantic's exceptional reality	27
Myth and syncretism: *immrama, echtrai,* and visions	41
Myth and the identity politics of medieval travel	53
Medieval sight and perception vs. modern practical judgment	60
Chapter 1 North	71
The Greeks' northern Atlantic	71
The *Norse* Atlantic: Niflheim	74
The symbol	77
Inis Glora: truth, syncretism and collective subjectivity	89
Merlin: society and the self	104
Chapter 2 South	111
The Canary Islands: fantasy and the imagination	111
The Spanish discovery of Ireland, or the polarization of reality	121
Isla Encubierta: the function of mystery	124
The *Periplus* of Amaro and the Celtic cultural orbit	128

Chapter 3 **East**   139

   Greek underpinnings of medieval mythology regarding the Atlantic   139

   Myth as agent in exploration and in the interpretation of reality   148

   The Bible and geographical uncertainty   153

   Brân: of heads and the composite ethos   160

Chapter 4 **West**   169

   Atlantis: a panoptic reflection   169

   Ireland, the "other" Atlantis   174

   The early navigations into the Atlantic   177

   Magical ships and the esoteric substance of travel   184

   U sheen in the Island of Youth, or the trappings of identity   193

   St. Brendan: verisimilitude as social covenant   201

   Prince Madoc of Wales, discoverer of America: the medieval myth that crossed the Atlantic   208

   The Voyage of Máel Dúin: The Legacy of Syncretism   213

   Hy-Brasil (Uí Bhreasail), naughty aliens and the logistics of syncretism   219

Conclusion   227

Works Cited   233

Index   249

List of figures

Figures

0.1. Circe turns Odysseus's companions into animals.	53
1.1. Hecataeus's Map. c. 480 BCE.	72
1.2. The Herodotus Map. c. 450 BCE.	72
1.3. The Map of Crates. 180-150 BCE.	74
1.4. The Norse Worldview.	75
1.5. From Olaus Magnus's *Carta Marina*. 1539.	77
1.6. Full View of Olaus Magnus's Carta Marina. 1539.	79
1.7. From Robert de Boron's *Merlin en prose*. c. 1200.	104
2.1. Hieronymus Bosch's "Garden of Earthly Delights." c. 1500.	111
2.2. *Lebor Gabála Érenn*. Fol. 53. Twelfth Century.	121
3.1. Prester John's Kingdom.	148
3.2. Sebastian Münster's Map of the Americas. 1561.	150
3.3. Martin Waldseemüller's "Carta Marina." 1516.	150
3.4. The 11th Asian regional map from Ptolemy's *Geographia*. 150 CE.	151
3.5. Ptolemaic World, by Hartmann Schedel. 1493.	153
3.6. Jephthah's sacrifice - Maciejowski Bible. c. 1250.	160
4.1. Athanasius Kircher: *Mundus Subterraneus*. 1678.	169
4.2. Black-figure Cup Painting of a Greek Vessel. c. 520.	177
4.3. The first known representation of a sailor consulting a compass on board a ship. 1403.	184
4.4. St. Brendan and the Whale. c. 1460.	201
4.5. Christ Enthroned. *Book of Kells*. Ninth Century.	213
4.6. Ortelius Map of Europe. 1601.	219

Foreword

What was the Atlantic to ancient and medieval people? How did this immense body of water buttress or disturb their assumptions regarding reality, life and the afterlife? Is it possible to capture the cultural importance of this indefinite, chimeric, protean space that confused primitive intuition and undermined common-sense perspectives on the world? Why was the Atlantic the site of a concealed, preternatural cosmos where ancients had access to the most bizarre, ecstatic dreamscapes? The endeavor to answer these questions is the essence of Dr. Alfonso J. García-Osuna's *The Atlantic as Mythical Space: An Essay on Medieval Ethea*.

Herein, the author covers an impressively extensive range of topics, myths and legends, and while he confesses, with a tinge of apologetic remorse, that he did not have a preconceived strategy when configuring this book, it is obvious that its heterogeneity and diversity of perspectives not only speak to the wide scope of his interests, but also gives the text much of its manifest value.

The texts analyzed in this book verify that the Atlantic, savage and splendid, hostile and magnificent, was a space full of unknown dangers, spiritual uncertainty, and a paramount source of wonderment, fear and curiosity. The ocean generated that anxiety which is usually provoked by unfathomable mysteries and, as the author skillfully demonstrates, this disquiet both troubled and utterly fascinated the medieval mind. In the *immrama* and *echtrai*, be they Irish or Galician, this fascination was conjugated into a literary aesthetics dominated by the objective of making the readers/listeners participate in a journey into a vast unknown. Most importantly, this space was unanticipated by their holy book, and because of it, these stories offered the delights of venturing into murky spaces in the collective imagination, into speculative recesses not well-shielded from extraneous influences by the faith's dogmatic prescripts.

As a consequence of this objective, the language used to describe mythical Atlantic journeys, with its methodical descriptions of monsters and aberrations, is built upon that anxiety and that fascination, so that the enjoyment of reading or listening to the stories can be considered analogous to the delight of transgressing, of going beyond limits, of subverting, of seeing beyond statutory horizons. As the author shows, a story of sailing into the unknown is, by definition, a subversion of the status quo order, a journey that propels the listener/reader towards a place of danger, towards a mindscape where the imagination can overwhelm the ordered common beliefs upon which authority systems build consentient awareness.

Therefore, and as the author eloquently informs the reader, the Atlantic is an exotic place of wonder that beckons the medieval mind towards a heteromorphic reality; upon arrival, it can rid itself of intransigent dogma and imagine new worlds among the metamorphosed creatures it finds there. Such monsters, in a way, symbolize the power of the human spirit to break shackles and transform the world. Accordingly, the medieval Atlantic voyage represents the flight of the suppressed, intimidated imagination to a place where the shortcomings of daily existence fade away.

In the light of it, and as we delve into this book, we verify that a crucial objective is to show that for ages the Atlantic has been contested space, an unrestrained mental geography that needed to be controlled or occupied by uneasy authority establishments, especially the Church. The danger posed by these uncontrolled jaunts would have been palpable: they had the power to seriously undermine those substantial collective identity patterns that underpinned that authority's doctrinal claims.

An upshot of García-Osuna's analyses is that Atlantic myths and legends are the result of that particular character that is common to the broad cultural community that developed along the ocean's European shores. The idea of Atlantic cultural cohesion is substantiated by the manner in which the ocean became a "mythical space," a "relevant metaphor" for profound anxieties and a providential geography where the unencumbered medieval imagination could roam.

This text demonstrates García-Osuna's vast knowledge of his subject, a knowledge aided and abetted by his Canary Islander origin, which must have exposed him since childhood to Atlantic lore (I might be excused for declaring that origin is relevant here, as the Canaries are a focal point of so many myths and legends regarding the Atlantic). Consequently, he embarks us on an intense journey through the many and sundry places along the ocean's shores that have contributed to its myths.

Far from feeling overwhelmed, we can turn that long journey into a profound learning experience across multiple myths and cultures. Through his erudite as well as entertaining prose, the author invites us to imagine the world that created those myths and to recreate the cultural contexts in which they were fashioned. These contexts include more recent interpretations and leaky analyses. As the author explains, the overly enthusiastic "research" that accompanies the discussion surrounding myths, especially investigations conducted in more recent centuries, can be cloaked in a shroud of absurdity—at least in the view of modern academics—yet these scholars are included here not as researchers, but as contributors to the myth. In other words, in their own way, they've added interesting fictional dimensions to the mythologization of diverse islands and places along the ocean's shore.

Foreword

Myths have a long lifespan, and many are still in vogue. All epochs, including our current one, need myths, and on many occasions, cultures reframe old myths to fit new environments. Besides naughty aliens pointing the way to Hy-Brasil for dumbfounded US soldiers in recent news stories, we might recall that the island of San Borondón (St. Brendan's Isle), in the Canary Islands, still pops up through the waves when it feels like surprising the locals. On our screens, the always-popular Merlin still haunts Hollywood productions, Arthurian legends proliferate in contemporary television shows, and many other ancient myths materialize in film and literature.

The author has put an enormous amount of work into this book and provided a wealth of data. Admirable is the interdisciplinarity that is evident in the research and the depth of his global vision, one that embraces the diverse and complex traditions united by this ocean. For those of us that have an interest in Atlantic cultures, there are many passages of pure enjoyment in these pages. I would recommend reading this book slowly and with an open mind, one ready to learn, reflect upon and assess those mythological energies that shaped the societies and cultures of Europe's western fringes, creating a very broad network of knowledge that cohered and helped to "reinforce and share models for communal cohesion."

It has been a pleasure to read this book, and I am grateful for having had the opportunity to contribute these comments. Moreover, I am proud to share with the author our origin, the Fortunate Islands, the Canary Islands, a condition that gives us an intimate familiarity with that thunderous Atlantic, an ocean captured in the verses of that famous Canary Islander Tomás Morales in his "Ode to the Atlantic" (1920):

> Thunderous Atlantic! With robust spirit,
> Would my voice once more acclaim your ardor.
> Be ye, Muses, favorable to my quest:
> Blue sea of my homeland, sea of Dreams,
> sea of my childhood and my youth... sea of mine!

Isabel Pascua-Febles, University of Las Palmas de Gran Canaria, 2020.

Introduction

O Gilgamesh, there has never been a way across,
nor since olden days can anyone cross the ocean.
Only Shamash the hero crosses the ocean:
apart from the Sun God, who crosses the ocean?
The crossing is perilous, its way full of hazard,
and midway lie the Waters of Death, blocking the passage forward.
     (Shiduri's counsel to Gilgamesh, tablet X, lines 79-84, in George 2000, 78)

The idea for writing this book sprang from the gracious invitations extended to me by Professors Patricia Navarra (Hofstra University Irish Studies Program), Isabel Pascua Febles and Elisa Isabel Costa Villaverde (University of Las Palmas de Gran Canaria), Minni Sawhney and Taruna Chakravorty (University of Delhi, India) requesting that I deliver end-of-semester seminars in their respective institutions. Furthermore, its realization was made possible by the gracious support and encouragement of Provost Joanne Russell, at the City University of New York. Imparted to diverse and international groups of students, these seminars all hinged upon my interest in cultures that have flourished on Atlantic islands and coasts. Frankly, it is an interest whose origin is not easy to understand. Perhaps the circumstances of having been born on an island in the Atlantic (Cuba), of having been raised on another island in the Atlantic (Gran Canaria), of having traveled extensively for academic reasons in two other Atlantic isles (Ireland and Great Britain) and of being presently living in yet another Atlantic isle (Long Island, NY), has predisposed me to the development of an intellectual curiosity that has been focused on the cultural life of groups around that great body of water. I can, however, give a more coherent reason for why the Atlantic has continued to draw my attention: historically, that immense, unstructured space has provided those groups' popular imagination with the latitude to colonize it with whatever their unrestrained imagination could conceive. This gives researchers wide-ranging analytical vistas that never cease to yield new insights.

Because the ocean was a preferred location for spiritual *essentia*, another noteworthy aspect of the Atlantic that has captured my attention is its peculiarity of being a contested space. I mean contested not only in the sense that nations and empires have fought over its sea-lanes, islands, ports, and coastlines for centuries, but also, and more importantly because cultures have clashed for the right to colonize its metaphysical space with their particular ethea. For many centuries, pagan Celtic cultures had placed their most basal beliefs, those regarding paradise, the afterlife, otherworldly beings, and the like firmly in the Atlantic Ocean. Thus, when the Christianization of Ireland began in the early Middle Ages, it was not simply the incursion of a new religion into a pagan island; the invasion needed to include the pagan Atlantic next to it, an ocean filled with mythical matter that had to be subsumed into the new faith's ethos if its dogmas were to succeed.

This entailed the modification and reorientation of pagan legends and myths focusing on the Atlantic, stories that had been transmitted orally and were firmly ingrained in the pagan culture of the Celtic Crescent. Such an effort has a strong analog in the conversion of pagan shrines into Christian churches, a practice that was common throughout Christendom.

Accordingly, Christianity populated pagan Atlantic myths and legends with its own heroes, generating distinctly syncretic versions that would be centaurs if they had material substance. Symbolic spaces like the Atlantic imprint customs, rituals and traditions of the past, so Christian proselytizers were not entering an empty space that could be bought or requisitioned. To me this gave rise to questions of how erstwhile pagans might have experienced the newfangled dogmatic aura that intruded new meaning into their deep-rooted symbolic space, imposing an unfamiliar functionality onto protagonists and events.

It is to be assumed from my observations in this work that the Atlantic, as symbolic space, is considered an "otherworld." Medieval descriptions of mythical places in the Atlantic betray ancient existential yearnings and angst; such feelings can only be portrayed through the depiction of spaces that lie beyond the confines of common human experience and understanding. Thus, the "otherworld" is the product of subjective solutions to a spiritual bewilderment for which there are no commonsense answers. These solutions attend the primaeval need to reach a place that validates human intellection regarding transcendence.

Such places have been produced by the human imagination, most likely, ever since we came down from the trees and started being conscious of our feelings, thoughts and perception, wondering why we are here, why we *are* and why we die. We began by fashioning deities that were associated with places that were unique or at the very least infrequent, such as an unusually large tree, a remarkably tall mountain, a cave that stretched far into the womb of the life-giving ground and places with life-sustaining water like a spring or a lake. These were places where interaction with supernatural beings was believed to be possible; they were removed from commonplace reality (temple, from the Latin *templum*, has the same root as the Greek τέμενος, which means detached or separated space), they were "other" worlds. One can only imagine the overwhelming emotional and notional associations experienced by the first human groups that reached the shores of the Atlantic and found that they could

Introduction xiii

not sail across to other places as they were accustomed to doing in the Black Sea or the Mediterranean. The Atlantic was believed to be endless, separated in every conceivable way from commonplace reality; the Atlantic was the ultimate "temple," the quintessential "otherworld."

As a result of my interest in many of the varied analytical possibilities offered by the Atlantic, this work reflects a myriad of insights and, as a result, its parts are as diverse as the imagination of peoples and cultures that have prospered on the ocean's shores. I think of this as an asset: hopefully, the heterogeneous character of my work will mitigate against the prospect of having its conclusions be applicable only to a specific type of text or context.

For these reasons, *The Atlantic as Mythical Space: An Essay on Medieval Ethea* might seem a euphuistic title for a collection of ideas recorded on various occasions and for different reasons. I will not profess to have had a particularly articulate design in mind when I began to put them together to form this book, and this will be evident in the wide range of topics and diversity of cultures that, as mentioned, are considered in its pages. To illustrate this point: the reader might be a bit unsettled by the way in which I swerve at will from early medieval Ireland to the pre-Hispanic Canary Islands to courtly-love France. But there is one obvious and consequential ligature that runs throughout the different sections of this text, the Atlantic Ocean, a bewildering expanse of mythical substance that for centuries has fueled the imagination of ocean-side peoples. From time immemorial the ocean has been a stage upon which Europe's imaginative genius has represented abstract anxieties and transcendental yearnings. The Atlantic is a great font of myth.

Among the agents that drive the human will to overcome the indifference of an apathetic universe, myth is critically important, and myths with the Atlantic as a preferential stage are especially relevant in pagan and early Christian western Europe. To elaborate on the significance of myth, it should be noted that, especially during the period in question, myth served to forge and propagate assumptions that fashioned the way communities thought about reality. An important stimulus for the activity of myth-creation was the fact that those societies were not disposed to view natural phenomena as the outcome of processes that could be understood through experimentation; consequently, they were not overly anxious about *natural* causality. Thus, in the fabulous realm where the sun sank enigmatically into the waters, prescientific societies fashioned an alternate cosmos where events, beings and places existed in harmony with communal mental structures whose most eloquent representative is the druid. In that contrived watery domain, these societies' angels and monsters were able to materialize with wonderful profusion.

The faculty to create worlds that challenge the blind dictates of what we call "reality" has allowed human beings to explain what is essentially unknowable:

the origins of the universe and the reason for our existence in it. Myth, the communal reorganization of a "reality" that is otherwise chaotic and meaningless, is therefore an instinctual creation that characterizes our will to *be* purposefully and, moreover, exposes our need to overcome the distressing suspicion that we are here accidentally. For this reorganization, intended to reconstruct reality in accordance with the designs of human will, the Atlantic has been a privileged environment.

But the need to reorganize the world in which we seem fortuitously inserted is not limited to the physical reality of *this* world. There is at the end of life an inexplicable emptiness the thought of which causes overwhelming dread, an angst that must be overcome if human beings are to live in harmony with their environment. The process to overcome begins with filling that void with anthropocentric concepts such as that of a "created" world, one where life has a purpose and leads to another, more significant existence. Such concepts demand substantiation, and lacking a scientific underpinning to their constructs, premodern societies used language to produce alternate realities that populated the emptiness with places and beings that linked the otherworld with the world of the living. The undefinable was thus defined in concert with the needs of the individual and the community.

Any activity geared towards the creation of an alternate reality, one more in tune with human spiritual needs, must be metaphysical, intimately connected with antithetic or "sacred" spaces. For ancient and medieval communities, the Atlantic, site of the Isles of the Blest, the Celtic Otherworld, the Green Isle, Hy-Brasil, the White Island of Atala, the Great Isle of the Solstice and sundry other mythical/sacred places, has been habitually endowed with compelling metaphysical traits and has acted as an important agent in the genesis and evolution of spiritual assumptions. Here it is important to note that metaphysical thought emerges from the depths of human consciousness, promotes the formation of communal mental objects and fuels the evolution of the traits that distinguish human beings from the rest of creation. Evidently, when a significant part of this foundational activity is enacted in a particular geographical space, the importance of that space for the development of normative structures of cognition and social cohesion cannot be understated.

In view of the scopic nature of the subject, and to structure my arguments in a reasonably coherent manner, I offer the premises for my assertions regarding myth and its metaphysical and social scope in this "Introduction" and in the "Portolan." As a reminder, portolan charts were "characterized by rhumb lines, lines that radiate from the center in the direction of wind or compass points and that were used by pilots to lay courses from one harbor to another. The charts were usually drawn on vellum and embellished with a frame and other decorations" (*Encyclopaedia Britannica*, s.v. "Portolan"). Understanding the special place that metaphor has in medieval thought, I use the portolan metaphor as an aesthetic expedient, but also because I trust that the section's content, acting as a portolan, will give an initial sense of direction to the reader.

Consistent with the nautical trope, the rest of the book is divided into four major chapters named after the four cardinal points. Given that our mythological heroes' general direction of travel will almost always be due West, this nomenclature denotes the general environment of the myth's source. Consequently, "North" deals with Atlantic myths originating around Scotland and Scandinavia; "South" is devoted to the Iberian Peninsula, the Canary Islands and Africa's Atlantic coast; "East" embarks upon an analysis of myths regarding the Atlantic from biblical lands and the eastern Mediterranean in general, and "West," the bulkiest chapter for obvious reasons, analyzes Irish and Brittonic myths.

I can think of no period in the history of human cultures that does not offer distinct signs of the constitutive impact of myth in the formation of communal mental structures. For the ancient and medieval inhabitants of the western shores of Europe, the experience of living in close proximity to the Great Mystery, that immeasurable *alia natura*, generated certain social and cultural attitudes that were shaped by that specific environmental circumstance, one that clearly accounts for many of their teleological narratives and for the distinguishing features of their mythical worlds.

Even while laying in a different course in the analysis of the medieval Atlantic, I am guided by the insights of researchers like d'Arbois de Jubainville, Patch, Eliade, Campbell, Lavezzo, and Byrne, whose influential work has guided the way for future studies. I am confident that the analysis of the function and features of medieval Atlantic myths, despite the diverse social and cultural contexts, will pull all the different sections of this book in the same thematic direction, will make them coalesce in chorus around the theme of the Atlantic as mythical space, and will give this text whatever rational symmetry it may have.

Alfonso J. García-Osuna, Hofstra University, May 23, 2022.

Portolan chart, or the routes of myth

The problem of myth as framework for the acquisition of knowledge

Myth is a lie that speaks the truth.

In a work that includes the word "Mythical" in its title, it is almost compulsory to propose a coherent summary of what is meant by the word "myth." I offer my version of Picasso's famous remark "art is a lie that makes us realize truth" as a broad-spectrum guide to the way I understand and categorize the value and meaning inherent in myth. This approach may give the idea that opaque reasoning must follow, but the fact is that self-styled coherent summaries have proven perilously unstable in the past. Even Joseph Campbell "is often criticized for presenting oversimplified versions of myths and ignoring glaring inconsistencies to support his theory" (Beaumont 2009, 170).

Perhaps that instability can be rationalized by the fact that myth cannot be scientifically explicated. A scientist that explains the features of gravity can use mathematical truths to support his rationalizations. The validity of such reasonings is available because of the unchallenged link between the explanation and observed reality, a link that is sustained by the exceptional descriptive coherence offered by numbers. It is important to note that this explanation is formulated not in terms of the direct observation of a physical object called "gravity," but by referring to interactions between physical objects that are influenced by it. In short, we cannot see it, but we quantify its influence by using numbers.

Let us attempt an explication of myth by looking through a materialist–of sorts–lens (bear with me here). Myth, like gravity, is not a directly quantifiable phenomenon, but it can be measured by its causal relationship with reality in the sense that, as a deontic system, it can regulate the physical movement of people and objects and synchronize their motions in line with concerted interpretations of contextual reality. Myths drive us to conquer, migrate, build megastructures within which to worship, tear others down, hate, and show compassion. Consequently, the truth value of theoretic assumptions regarding myth would depend on how well they were able to define the ability of myth to configure the world, to move its objects like gravity. Like gravity, myth is not observed to act upon the world of objects directly: Myth's influence on physical objects originates in its capacity to provide us–its accessories–with explanations that propose moral contours for an otherwise unstructured and unresponsive universe.

I make use of a scientific analogy here with good reason. For much of the recent past, most academic disciplines have been influenced substantially by positivist ideas and materialist theories. Under this influence, the social sciences were designed to analyze what one might call the "human experience." Yet from a humanist perspective, research that is based strictly on positivist, materialist, or physicalist approaches requires a subservient dedication to an integrated view of knowledge and the use of canonical methodologies, culled from the physical sciences, to explain the discursive megacosm of the social domain.

Such integration presupposes the acceptance of a closed, compulsory set of materialist postulates (e.g. consciousness is the outcome of material processes, an ordinary product of biochemistry) that tends to suppress more open exchanges on the nature of the *human* experience of the world and that experience's agency in the imaging and interpretation of "reality." This imaging, often manifested as myth, has been consequently consigned to the dark storeroom of pre-scientific human folly, as modern dictionary descriptions of the word "myth" amply demonstrate. Albeit true that a distinguishing aspect of more recent criticism (post-modern, feminist, post-structuralist...) is the tentative dismissal of premises that may be generally classified as positivist or materialist, it is also true that many professors still find themselves rationalizing the relevance of myth because the worlds it generates cannot be scientifically verified nor can they survive the test of logical or historical proof.

While Western materialism can be traced back to ancient Greek atomists like Democritus (c. 460–c. 370 BCE), who speculated that everything in nature consisted of only two elemental principles (atom and void), it can be said that materialism's positivist sequels first seeped into the humanist disciplines during the second half of the nineteenth century, and that it arguably happened as an upshot of Émile Durkheim's (1858–1917) theoretical principles. The intellectual attractiveness of Durkheimian methods (using objective indicators like the natural sciences to describe social experience) served to legitimize the idea of a social *science* that could be endowed with competence over every branch of the humanist endeavor. Scientific models began to be devised in the humanities and "laws" of how people behaved within social structures were formulated by analyzing sets of observed invariables. Myth, as a product of collective and individual consciousness, came to be interpreted and explained by using the positivist prescriptions of new disciplines like sociology and psychology:

> For Durkheim, myth serves to provide collective identity and an emotional bond among a people. [...] For Durkheim, myths fall into a larger category of socially transmitted symbolic structures that he calls collective representations. [...] He argues that through these collective

representations society is infused with value (and indeed, in some cases, sacred qualities). (Twing 1998, 13-14)

Yet, if one were to judge by the confusion generated by this process, one might be justified in thinking that science, and the social sciences in particular, were not the most suitable analytical instruments for the description of myth. Freud and Jung, for example, were at odds in their assumptions regarding myth:

> Where for Freud myth in particular is a way of venting unconscious wishes without becoming aware of them, for Jung myth is the opposite: it is a way of becoming aware of unconscious sides of the personality, albeit never fully. [...] For Freud, myth perpetuates neurosis. For Jung, myth helps preclude neurosis. (R. Segal 2014, 423)

Clearly, the social sciences' inadequacy is largely due to the fact that science is inherently objective, while myth, the result of a process whereby human consciousness arbitrates reality into meaningful patterns, is subjective by nature. Thus, to better understand myth we must be aware of the probable shortcomings of modern research methodologies regarding myth, all the while keeping in mind that science has not come up with a sound explanation for consciousness; such an explanation is very likely well beyond its capabilities.

The questionable adequacy of social science models becomes apparent when one considers that much of the speculation revolving around myth rarely considers the ancient mental landscapes where the production and reception of myth actually took place. Strictly speaking, adequate consideration is seldom given to the active participation of those flesh and blood individuals involved in the production and reception of mythical texts, people that were thoroughly implicated in the construction of meaning; evidently, such deliberation would have sobering consequences for the understanding of myth.

To illustrate this point, let us say that when reading the stories of ancient seafaring heroes like Bran, Madoc, or Máel Dúin (Maelduin), a modern reader is consuming myth; on the other hand, it is unlikely that a person on the coast of Ireland in the year 600 CE would interpret those stories in the same manner. Ancient myths were generated by social contract, that is to say, societies in particular environments provided the collective mental structures that produced the myth's unique character. It follows that if a distinct society is involved in constructing its meaning, so its elucidation must necessarily be contextual. If a thousand years separate different sets of myth interpreters, the altered context and the dissimilarity in the strategies used to construct meaning will be considerable and will inevitably lead to confusion as to the true nature and purpose of myth, as Freud and Jung's conflicting judgments clearly illustrate.

Talking *methodically* about myth presupposes that one can access an accretion of circumstantiated concepts and ideas about myth and its distinctiveness. But if what today we receive or read as *myth* is the product of a very distant insight, of an ancient interpretive system that is incompatible with modern modes of discernment, then whatever we affirm about myth can only be the product of our modern, idiosyncratic reception. The concept of myth that we might derive from Joseph Campbell or Mircea Eliade, for example, has no counterpart in a world of druids. So it can be said that speculation and assumptions about these ancient narratives, as introduced by modern thinkers steeped in positivist methodology, generated the thoroughly modern meanings that are now attached to the word "myth."

For over a century myth has been subjected to formal scientific scrutiny, analyzed through a microscope by detached, impartial researchers. *Prima facie* this might seem commendable, but it also reminds one that science, firmly attached to its positivist foundations, has remained in many ways estranged from the real life of flesh and blood individuals, its savants forming a detached class that Michael Bakunin (1970, 56) likened to a priesthood. As such, science has replaced druidic gods and attained a kind of divinity, becoming a positivist deity that suppresses that unique and intuitive individuality of human existence commonly addressed by myth. Presumably, this abrogation of the subjective traits inherent to individuality is due to the fact that science must move within the realm of generalization and abstraction. While it could be argued that myth moves in the same realm, the abstractions created by myth differ in their essential nature: they talk directly to human individuality, human uniqueness, human exceptionality, and to the imagination that assembles and sustains them. Myth, then, puts abstractions at the service of the individual imagination, while science immolates the imagination in the pyre of rational systematic abstractions.

I have made science a sort of antithesis to myth because, contrary to myth, science is as ineffective in comprehending human individuality and imagination as it is effective in understanding the atomic structure of ice cream. Social scientists approach this individuality in systematic ways that are subordinated to sanctioned methodological designs; in their endeavors, human individuality is reduced to a principle, to an abridgment devised by intellectual agencies that are incapable of grasping the idiosyncratic reality of each one of an indeterminate number of flesh and blood individuals. Science's ineptness in this respect is explicable when one considers that each individual imagination is capable of conceiving a unique social and private persona and its own distinctive microcosm. On the other hand, myth's proficiency hinges on the fact that it is adaptable to private microcosms; it is compliant with subjective needs because its material has the power to transmogrify and integrate into personal narratives, especially those that touch upon existential anxieties and fortuity. Myth, unlike science, confidently propels the imagination against the inscrutable essence of existence.

Less methodical speculation on the nature and function of myth has come down to us from classical antiquity. For Plato, dialogue and myth "used their linguistic beauty, their appeal to the emotions, and their unquestioned authority to transmit a dangerously false image of man and the world" (Most 2012, 18). Yet, despite this less-than-enthusiastic assessment, any perceptive reader of Plato will note that he used dialogue and myth to his advantage, employing their authority as a means to convey moral doctrine and philosophical truths.

Plato derived his notion of the "authority" of myth from earlier literature: in Pindaric epinician poetry, the essential function of myth was to speak to the individual and interface their personal experience of apathetic reality with an archetypal narrative that gave it meaning. In this sense, its function was the same as in most high Greek and archaic poetry: "to set the particular, nonrecurrent event [...] in relation to an event in the permanent, paradigmatic world of the gods and heroes which makes it understandable" (Carne-Ross 1985, 18). Furthermore, by promoting the convergence of personal experience with archetypal narratives, myth has the power to cohere individuals into powerful identitary assemblages.

This potential to create communal coherence endows it with a wide range of cultural and political relevance: Herodotus, for example, uses myth as a paradigm of authority in order to "problematize or unravel ideological claims, puncturing dominant models by pressing other possibilities" (Baragwanath 2012, 290). But his relationship with myth was conflicted: on a different occasion, he commented that improbable stories, such as the one explaining that the Nile floods because it is connected to the great river Okeanos, are the invention of poets like Homer and are in the realm of *mythos* (Morgan 2004, 19).

In more recent contexts, the assumptions that generally buttress academic conjecture on myth can be classified for practical purposes into two main theories: the first explains that myth is an allegory for philosophical truths, while the second has myth as an actual history of persons and episodes of communal importance, an account that has undergone a process of amplification and dramatization intended to enhance its social impact. The former theory has received more attention than the latter, with books by prominent intellectuals like Natale Conti (*Mythologiae sive explanationis fabularum libri decem*, 1568) and Francis Bacon (*De sapientia veterum*, 1609) elucidating its main attributes. The latter theory was defended by such writers as the abbé Antoine Banier (*Mythologie et la fable expliqués par l'histoire*, 1711). The more tendentious Bernard de Fontenelle, in his *De l'origine des fables* (1724), presents myth as a sort of catalog of the blunders to which the human intellect is prone. As Fontenelle's attitude illustrates, by the early eighteenth century mythology is becoming the science that explains a chaotic world, one presently being overcome by reason and the Enlightenment. It is interesting to note that Fontenelle is expanding the reach of a critical tradition that maligned many of the most notional characteristics of myth (exemplified by Plato and Herodotus); he is an example of the way this tradition is refurbished and augmented by the Enlightenment.

To a considerable measure, contemporary social science has derived its concepts regarding myth from unfavorable assessments such as Fontenelle's. Marcel Detienne explains it clearly: modern conceptualization of myth has been inherited from a critical tradition that goes back to the Greeks; as a concept, myth has always been defined as antithetical to truth (myth is false, deceitful), to rationality (myth is irrational), and to verifiable experience (myth is fiction) (Detienne 1981, 47).

But it is useful to point out that there has been a contrasting intellectual discussion, originated by Giambattista Vico (1668–1744), that has aimed to include myth in the systems that are valuable and necessary to organize culture and consolidate social coherence. Creator of the modern philosophy of language, Vico recognized that an authentic description of human culture (*cose umane*) must include language, art *and* myth, and famously stated that "the first science to be learned should be mythology or the interpretation of fables" (Mali 2012, 101) if one is to understand the beginnings of science and of nations. Vico's design attained comprehensive systematized classifications afterward, when the Romantics, dauntless in their rejection of Enlightenment constraints, fashioned what today we call cultural science.

Working within its parameters, a young Friedrich Wilhelm Joseph Schelling (1775–1854) would call for a merger of formerly exclusive categories: "polytheism of the imagination conjoined with a monotheism of reason" (Farrel-Krell 2005, 3), very likely as a response to philosophers like Henri de Saint-Simon (1760–1825), Pierre-Simon Laplace (1749–1827) and Auguste Comte (1798–1857), who believed the scientific method, that is to say, the categorical link between theory and observation, must replace metaphysics in the progress of thought. This last system of thought produced the notable positivist excesses of Ernst Mach (1838–1916), who in his *Contributions to the Analysis of Sensation* (1885), subtitled "Antimetaphysical," resolved all sensations into individual elements and contended that everything could be constituted by combinations of their unvarying components.

But, as demonstrated by Schelling, these positivist formulations had considerable and continuous rebukes. A generation after Vico, Schelling was echoing Vico's preoccupation that orthodox scientism of this sort would obstruct the path to a complete description of human culture. Moreover, Schelling shared with Vico an assessment of myth as crucial to the elucidation of the transcendental domain, that is to say: essential in revealing the purposes of Divine Providence (in Vico's words); fundamental in unveiling the workings of the Absolute Spirit (as described by Schelling). Schelling also advocated for a marriage of sorts between philosophy and mythology, which he saw as a complementary pair: "Mythology must become philosophical, and the people rational, while philosophy must become mythological, in order to make philosophers sensuous. The eternal unity will prevail among us" (Farrell Krell 2005, 25).

Although Johann Gottlieb Fichte (1762–1814) was largely indifferent to myth, Schelling's ideas are influenced by Fichte's endeavors to discover the objective underpinnings that he believed were inherent to metaphysical truth. Such endeavors to link the world outside with the world of the mind also motivated philosophers like Friedrich Schlegel (1772–1829), who in his work "Rede über die Mythologie" (published in his *Gespräch über die Poesie*, 1800) saw mythology as a symbolic substance, a reservoir of inventiveness that could help to kickstart German creativity, and Novalis (Georg Philipp Friedrich, Freiherr von Hardenberg, 1772–1801) who saw myth as an example of the human ability to transform and synthesize reality.[1] In an indirect way, they also contributed to Friedrich Hölderlin's (1770–1843) privileging of poetry over philosophy, as is evidenced in his epistolary novel *Hyperion* (1797; 1799) and in his practical views on mythology:

> First, I will speak here of an idea which, as far as I know, has not occurred to anyone. We need a new mythology, however, this mythology must be at the service of ideas, it must become a mythology of reason. Until we render the ideas aesthetic, that is, mythological, they will not be of any interest to the populace, and vice-versa: until mythology has become reasonable, the philosopher has to be ashamed of it. (Hölderlin 1988, 155)

But Schelling's philosophical investment in myth is perhaps more comprehensive than that of the rest: for him, myth could explain "the theologic reasons of human civilization [and] the divine causes for the rise of nature and of human consciousness" (Feldman and Richardson, Jr. 1972, 316).

Notably, German Romantic myth theorists such as Joseph Görres (1776–1848), Johann Arnold Kanne (1773–1824), and the Grimm brothers (Jacob Ludwig Carl 1785–1863 and Wilhelm Carl 1786–1859) were sincerely interested in promoting the social importance of myth, while Swiss philologist Johann Jakob Bachofen (1815–1887) saw myths not only as chronicles of the cultural life of past civilizations, but also as evidence of a shared and incontestable

---

[1] For a relevant discussion on Novalis's mythopoesis, see Burton Feldman and R. D. Richardson, Jr., *The Rise of Modern Mythology*, 335.

Truth, as he "presupposed a unified mythical *Weltanschauung* among all peoples, epochs, and generations that evidenced objectively knowable and legitimate Truth" (Figueira 2008, 517). Contributing to the discussion, Ernst Cassirer (1874–1945) was clearly influenced by Vico when he stated that "No longer in a merely physical universe, man lives in a symbolic universe. Language, myth, art, and religion are parts of this universe. They are the varied threads which weave the symbolic net, the tangled web of human experience" (Cassirer 1944, 25).

Keeping in mind that myth creates a symbolic universe through language, Jacques Lacan (1901–1981) offers a truly radical interpretation of the relationship between that universe and reality. Reality, in a manner of speaking, is absorbed by the symbols used to describe it (language) and is destroyed in the process:

> Canceling out the real, the symbolic creates "reality," reality as that which is named by language and can thus be thought and talked about. The "social construction of reality" implies a world that can be designated and discussed with the words provided by a social group's (or subgroup's) language. What cannot be said in its language is not part of its reality; it does not *exist*, strictly speaking. In Lacan's terminology, existence is a product of language: language brings things into existence [...] The real, therefore, does not exist... (Fink 1997, 25)

From Lacan's perspective, then, the object of so much scientific interest (that is, the raw reality that predates words) is annihilated by myth's most distinct characteristic, symbolic language. In Lacan's view, one cannot speak consensually of a categorical reality, as it does not have existence outside our language-generated cosmos.

Moving on to the present moment, in my own classroom I find a general reluctance to divorce myth from its negative connotations: myth is "untruth" and "fabrication." As most of my students are habituated to the positivist approach to knowledge, I find myself having to direct their attention to the fact that dutiful adherence to positivist or materialist thinking will restrict our conceptualization of what is specifically human, will reduce human insight and intuition to mechanistic description, and will replace consciousness with simple variables. We cannot be so indentured to positivist discipline that we reject that rich, subjective cosmos that refuses to be collapsed into the standardized receptacle of efficient causation.

By this, I am not advocating an explicit return to unscientific analysis, and trust that my admonition does nothing to summon it. Leaning upon Lacan, I generally assert that, in its role as *human* perceptual phenomenon, the physical world is *socialized* through the operations of a set of communal codes that are conceived in language and are buttressed by myth. Put simply, myth has a functional implication in the way individuals experience ambient reality.

This means that, while historical proof that Brendan's voyage took place would be quite significant to historians, it is just as important to probe the manner in which that myth became integral to the perception of reality in the mindscapes of those who consumed it. It seems more productive to investigate the purpose for which human thought deployed mythological structures, stories, and individuals like the intrepid Irish saint; these served to explore, order, and categorize the world that was perceived, postulating along the way an abstract supreme entity to superintend each feature of the human environment and each facet of the human experience. Moreover, proceeding in this manner allows us to see how myth is a critical aspect of communal cognitive strategies, how it identifies and illustrates the knowledge that needs to be shared by its constituents, and how by its workings it sustains structured communal life. Accordingly, researchers and educators must keep working towards a deeper understanding of how myth offers substantial human collectives a conceptual grid, a stable framework with which to organize the assimilation of their social and physical environment and formulate shared assumptions regarding reality.

On this subject, scholar Yuval Noah Harari explains that a human conglomerate of more than 150 individuals is too large and complex to work in a concerted manner toward a common goal. And yet humans managed to gather in numbers much greater than 150 and cooperate closely and effectively:

> How did *Homo sapiens* manage to cross this critical threshold [of 150 individuals], eventually founding cities comprising tens of thousands of inhabitants and empires ruling hundreds of millions? The secret was probably the appearance of fiction. Large numbers of strangers can cooperate effectively by believing in common myths.
>
> Any large-scale human cooperation–whether a modern state, a medieval church, an ancient city or an archaic tribe–is rooted in common myths that exist only in people's collective imagination. Churches are rooted in common religious myths. Two Catholics who have never met can nevertheless go together on crusade or pool funds to build a hospital because they both believe that God was incarnated in human flesh and allowed Himself to be crucified to redeem our sins. States are rooted in common national myths. Two Serbs who have never met might risk their lives to save one another because they both believe in the existence of the Serbian nation, the Serbian homeland and the Serbian flag. (Harari 2011, 33)

Consequently, myths have very tangible real-world applications and may be–as Harari suggests–responsible for the onset of widespread human cooperation. We should keep in mind that those societies that produced the early medieval myths pre-date the obligatory cynicism that, nowadays, has made the plausible a proviso for the allocation of value. For those early societies, myths were neither real nor unreal: they existed beyond the requirements of scientific verification. Moreover, they served to consolidate large, otherwise unconnected populations and inspire concerted action; myths created realms where the individual could access a contrived collective imagination.

In the Atlantic context, the realms of myth through which Brendan-like characters ventured were vast, hazy expanses of drama and mystery; they were found beyond the horizon in the vast western ocean upon which the mind's eye sailed, like Brendan's coracle, in its flight from prosaic reality. The exceptional vastness of the ocean's enigmatic geography made it a stage for myths that offered demiurgic images of the nature of existence. Moreover, they proposed a privileged view of the universe that preserved our subjective, physiognomic perceptions and safeguarded the personal, human significance of information about reality that positivist approaches, since the Enlightenment, have attempted to eradicate.

Consequently, I would propose that information provided by myth is just as valid as that offered by science in the sense that, as a human social construct, "reality" (as Lacan suggested) is effectively intertwined with human experience. Furthermore, myth is primarily the ambit where *personal* events unfold and a symbolic universe is generated, one that offers "a general theory of the cosmos and a general theory of man [that] orders history [and] locates all collective events in a cohesive unity that includes past, present and future" (Berger and Luckmann 1966, 103). The legitimacy of myth, then, flows from its ability to supply human beings with a coherent, qualitative method of interpreting reality through metaphorical patterns and symbolic archetypes.

Evidently, myth is not expedient as a tool for describing the universe in positivist terms, as positivist rationalism, inherently peripheral to the human being, is unreceptive to our wishes and blind to our visceral existence. But for pre-modern societies, myth has value to the extent that it articulates reality in terms of human prospects, and as such, it affords truths whose diagnostic value differs in no significant way from those offered to modern individuals by purely "objective" experiences. Consequently, one must speak of the nature of myth with a special focus on its social *function*, which is to merge individual, private experience with archetypal narratives that socialize reality and articulate it in understandable terms.

Returning to Ernst Cassirer (1874–1945), in *The Myth of the State* the German philosopher explains that myth's function is essentially social: it encourages feelings of harmony within societies and of unity with the whole of nature (1946, 37). So as Cassirer moves beyond considerations of particular cultures and considers this "whole of nature," it becomes evident that, for him, mythological thought does not observe nature in theoretical or practical terms, but is rather *sympathetic* in that it is permeated by the profound conviction that an elemental and indelible *solidarity of life* fuses together the multiplicity and diversity of all its forms (1946, 82). There can hardly be a more direct dismissal of the relevance of positivist analyses regarding myth.

Recognizing that an essential function of myth is social must, concomitantly, cause us to address the underlying question of who assembles–and profits from–the truth cosmos constructed in mythological narratives. An easy answer would be to say that, as often happens with historical narratives, those in power are responsible for its main features, but this would be at least misleading and would promote myth as just one more cog in the social mechanisms of domination. Cultural devices with agency in the direction of social life are always the site of contention, and those who prevail are almost always those who wield social, military, religious, or political power. So it follows that proceeding to "uncover" those who profit would prove unimaginative.

A more befitting task than that of identifying them (they are certainly obvious to scholars) is to seek to recognize and understand the basal spiritual and psychological needs that produce the codes, formulas, and precepts whereby myth narratives are devised and framed, and only afterward try to ascertain the connection between these precepts and the economic, political and social contexts within which they were conceived and nourished. This will surely yield a more comprehensive panorama of societies and of individuals for whom myth provides the conditions and the motivation for tangible, material activity. Such material activity depends on the concrete, geographical properties of the physical environment as much as on the internalizing mechanisms that are ingrained and instinctive in societies that inhabit that environment. For Western European societies, a salient physical environment that drove myth-construction activity was a vast, perplexing span of water that stretched endlessly to the west; its mere presence, moreover, generated and framed many of those internalizing mechanisms' fundamental patterns.

Evidently, as modern individuals, we are unable to appreciate the Atlantic Ocean with the aesthetic intrepidity of our forebears. Nowadays we can get from New York to London in six hours while we sleep, watch a film, or have dinner in the relative comfort of an airplane seat. For most of us, the Atlantic has dissipated as a metaphysical *lusus naturae*. This is because in order to project mythical substance onto a specific environment, its features must be enigmatic; if that enigma seems unfathomable, so much the better.

Plainly, medieval imaginative projections are not likely to thrive in modern technological societies, where the vital bond between myth and everyday life has largely dissipated. Moreover, Enlightenment rationalism and subsequent positivist thinking coached us to believe that only discourses based on logic and rational thought lead to viable truth claims. At a glance, myths relate stories about hazy beings, events, and places, promoting beliefs that are often unquestioned; they tell of origins, explain aspects of culture and buttress religion and ritual. Yet for earlier societies, serious belief in mythical individuals, communities, and places often mixed with a dismissal of superstition and irrational behavior. To them, the foundations of myth were not unreasonable: they were based upon the unbroken connection between human beings and the remote sacred. Myths, then, were an important component of their intellectual constructs, of their "truth."

This naturally leads us to a discussion of the nature of "truth." If we consider truth from postmodern perspectives, as something that does not exist as an eternal, transcendent reality, medieval understanding of the universe can come into better focus. When we think of societies in the early Middle Ages as communities that decode the universe in particular ways in order to consign sense and meaning to existence, we will be able to see how their "truth" is a socially negotiated consensus, much like ours is today, one that was as legitimate to them as ours is to us. For them, as for us, truth exists in a sacred space of recognized legitimacy. The only difference between them and us is the descriptive criteria with which that space is circumscribed.

Something should be clarified before we proceed: Because of the variety of narratives that can be *mythical*, the term "myth" can lend itself to confusion. For our purposes in this text, when speaking of mythical Atlantic spaces in the fabulous geography of the Middle Ages I require that the texts involved have elements of description, anecdote, and yarn, and that they tell stories with a supernatural component that not only entertains but also makes available a design with which people can confirm and systematize conventional beliefs about the universe in which they live. In this sense, and as we will see in the narratives studied herein, the critical relevance of the Atlantic was that it provided the transcendental environment wherein pagan and early medieval Europeans could contrive allegories that helped them to identify and validate their place in Creation.

Myth and history

These two ports of call on our conceptual portolan chart are so close to each other, that in some charts they seem indistinguishable. They are history and myth, and the analysis of their complex affinity is indispensable if we are to understand the Atlantic as a "mythical space." I will analyze their kinship here in general terms.

As we plot the course of our voyages into the mythical Atlantic, we must first understand how myth is a practical tool for generating communal identitary reflection and social cohesion. We must first acknowledge that myth, like history, serves to cohere the community through a dramatized past that is more practical than analytical. Myth is built upon the adventures of heroes that we will consider in subsequent chapters. In Wales, they are heroes like Brân (in Welsh mythology, Brân the Blessed, king of Britain, is a giant that appears in several of the Welsh Triads and in the Second Branch of the *Mabinogi, Branwen ferch Llŷr*), and Madoc (a Welsh prince who–it is said–sailed to America in 1170). In Ireland, they are voyagers like Bran mac Febail and exemplary individuals like U sheen (a.k.a. Oisín, the greatest poet of Ireland, warrior of the Fianna in the Ossianic or Fenian Cycle of Irish mythology, and the narrator of many of the poems that are associated with him). In Spain, they are faithful men like Trezenzonio (a monk from Galicia who lived in times of the Asturian monarchy [est. c. 718 C.E.] and whose story is extant in the twelfth century *Trezenzonii de Solistitionis Insula Magna*, relating how he sailed the Atlantic to the Island of Paradise), and Amaro (Spanish abbot and sailor whose story details his voyage across the Atlantic Ocean to an earthly paradise).

Their myths reflect some of the deep-seated attitudes and concepts that originated in pagan Celtic culture and informed the early medieval worldview. Additionally, these myths originate in the search for stability, meaning, and structure in a decidedly unpredictable world. Composing a story to explain the world and at the same time structure a community's identity can be the task of both myth and history; in premodern times, the differences between them are oftentimes blurred.

Contributing to that blurring is the fact that, in the pagan mind, the past is an inconsistent mass of stories consigned to memory. These are told and retold, experiencing the unavoidable accretions and expunctions that attend such processes. Hence, the importance that past circumstances or incidents may have had in their original context collapses into a new pattern of priorities, one governed by the exigencies of current frames of reference. Thus, the longevity of a story that originates in Europe's pagan past may reflect archetypal frames of reference in terms of plot, environment, and characters, but it may not necessarily reflect the stability of its original message; it is more likely that its message has proven malleable and thus submissive to the demands of new social, religious, and political contexts.

It is important to bear this in mind when we engage in discussions regarding the Christian appropriation of pagan stories in the process of propagating the faith. This appropriation also reflects the fact that pagan stories were still very current in early medieval societies on the Atlantic shore, and because of that currency, their annexation and modification by the church became an imperative undertaking.

When the past is a malleable commodity, it does not exist in the hallowed realm of books whose reliability is regarded as unquestionable. The past is not inviolable. This means that when pagan and early medieval narrators tell the story of a past event, they don't follow a sacrosanct version that disallows improvisations, but rather generate a cognitive space of mutual interest where the audience's frames of reference are anticipated. In this way, the narrator will emphasize some details and downplay or ignore others, making the past fit certain expected myths that enhance community coherence and promote its values. Historical events become amenable to those who have identitary, religious, or social investment in their "proper" interpretation, so history and myth are conflated and exist in a symbiotic relationship. The past, then, has a social purpose, and texts like Geoffrey of Monmouth's *Historia regum Britanniae* (c. 1136) and epic literature illustrate this point very well.

Ancient peoples were more concerned about natural forces than about a human past the precise knowledge of which was not a practical asset. Judging by the astonishing efforts of the early inhabitants of the British Isles, Brittany, and the Iberian Peninsula to build megalithic structures that would record and predict the natural cycles of nature, there seems to have been an urgency to preserve the uninterrupted operation of natural rhythms that were responsible for the continuation of the cosmos. Their enduring accomplishments tell a story of their engagement with the enigmatic forces that rule the universe and their endeavor to integrate human life with a coherent macrocosm. As such, the great monoliths are mythical energies embodied in stone, erected to withstand time and overcome the limitations that an insubstantial and transitory medium like language placed on their communal truths.

They also reveal two important details that separate myth (a product of a community's collective conscience), from history (a compilation of names and dates filtered through manifold truth claims) as we understand the terms today: the first is myth's straightforward assumption that concealed and enigmatic powers influence human destiny, and the second, the idea that interaction with these powers is entirely possible. Ancient and early medieval voyages (like those of Brendan, U sheen, Máel Dúin, Trezenzonio, Madoc, etc.) into the Atlantic–mythical or factual–were journeys into the medieval collective conscience, journeys that, for pagan and proto-Christian communities, have been one of the preferred ways of bringing about interaction with those enigmatic powers.

I portray them as journeys into the collective consciousness because myth is as important to a community as the imagination is to a person. Imagination is an essential component of a human being's consciousness, as it helps one travel into a reality beyond the observed material world; without the imagination, the superficial world of objects would be the measure of "all there is," apathy would follow and life would be meaningless. Myth is communal imagination, providing the community with a shared, more profound reality, where the struggles, successes, and setbacks of not the "I," but the "we," are transmuted into a concerted set of metaphors. The immram hero, sailing into the Atlantic in his insubstantial currach, enters that space where medieval collective consciousness blossoms.

Such journeys were not whimsical: pagan and early medieval natives of the "Celtic Crescent" regarded the universe as an integrated totality, as there was no intractable boundary between this world and the otherworld. A favored setting for their otherworld, to judge by their mythical journeys, was their next-door neighbor, the Atlantic Ocean, so the use of the word "otherworld" to characterize these precincts is problematic and must be understood here as an expedient. The marvelous beings encountered on Atlantic journeys and their human counterparts on dry land were all considered inhabitants of a single cosmos. These societies seemed to establish no essential division between spiritual and intellectual endeavors, as suggested by the fact that the druidic class officiated organically in both spheres. Moreover, unhindered by consequential scientific speculation, observations of the physical environment were largely motivated and influenced by myth.

What we call "history," as a method of transmitting a hierarchy of selected events in order to ensure the political stability of a community, can be regarded as a practical offshoot of myth, it being an arrangement of past events that helps to shape an opportune image of reality. But history's current image of "reality" has been filtered through a political lens: in an era that has been fully immersed in pragmatic conventionalities, history's priorities depend on the idea of human beings as *citizens*. Consequently, they are acclimated to the citizens' political behavior and habits. The communal spiritual needs that have traditionally been addressed by myth have been largely abandoned by history.

To a large extent, and unlike pagan and early Christian societies, modern people see history as a set of conclusive empirical data that reveal a past "reality" and incorporate the present moment as its manifest consequence. The modern mindset has severed the constructive link that once existed between myth and the community's present moment, replacing myth–the nexus between the present and the transcendental–with a systematic set of data whose significance to the present moment is political. It is political because it narrates the great events and important ideologies that *shaped* the present national/international situation. In short, as a maxim attributed to Sir John

Seeley declares: "History is past politics; and politics present history" (Wormell 1980, 44). But nowhere does it speak to the flesh and blood human being.

Given the practical, political significance of history, when comparing it to myth a devaluation of myth necessarily follows. This devaluation has been uncompromising: The revered Van Dale Dutch Dictionary describes myth as "a baseless story, a fable...a groundless representation" (2234), while *The Oxford English Dictionary* has myth as "A purely fictitious narrative usually involving supernatural persons, actions or events, and embodying some popular idea concerning natural or historical phenomena (vol. 10, 177). Withal, this is changing: postmodern analyses have allowed us to view history itself as a sort of myth, one designed to describe and validate contemporary points of view and give us a more focused perspective on the future.

On a different plane, the modern concept of "epistemic feedback" tells us that there is a factual interplay between what is being observed and the observation; that which is observed is not captured in untouched purity by the observer, as the observation "acts" upon that which is observed. In the case of history, that which is observed is past, lifeless, only re-animated after being infused with the observer's dynamic, value-laden glance. Likewise, if we see history as resulting from the limited observation (carried out by human beings) of a virtually limitless organism (the past and all its events), designed in the interests of interpreting and describing rationally the general progress of humankind that leads to the moment of the observer's description, we can understand how it will of necessity be infused with subjectivities inherent to the act of observing. What's more, scholarship in the critical philosophy of history, such as that of Lionel Rubinoff, has been actively discussing the nature of historical "truth" and questioning whether historical knowledge, value-laden as it is, can be said to result from objectivity (van der Dussen and Rubinoff 1991, 135). Ultimately, this recognition of history as design will allow us to breach the fissure that moderns have opened between myth and history: modern societies, having divorced myth from history, still exploit myth to advance political agendas. This new mythology is an element of the subjectivities that percolate into history, so that the body of value-laden texts we now call history is not an improvement that displaces myth, but in an ambiguous way, its persistence.

Several factors have played a part in the modern split between myth and history. Returning to the origins of modernity, we find that humanism itself has, to some extent, divorced history from myth, forcing us to look at time as a linear progression that leads from a well-defined beginning to an apocalyptic or utopian end. Because the *philosophes* of the Enlightenment were attempting to reassemble mankind's view of its world and society, their interest in myth, as source of information on the past and on origins, was intense. But they never stopped regarding it as a usable tool that, nevertheless, was hostile to rational and lucid ways of experiencing the world. Voltaire, for example, "firmly and caustically rejects myth as patent superstition and historical distortion. But Voltaire everywhere touches on myth, for it is a problem rooted deeply in at least three of his central concerns" (Feldman and Richardson 1972, 151). Those concerns–the past; origins; religion–were critical for the coherent alignment of his fundamental hypotheses.

For pre-modern peoples, myth was nothing like an analytical tool because they viewed the past, first and foremost, in mythical/religious terms. Thus, myths were the preeminent way of looking back in time, as their edifying content helped establish the individual's place in the present moment and assign value to his actions and to those of the community. In short, they made available an ethical blueprint and provided a cosmos where time had amorphous features, one where past and present events coalesced in relative atemporality and where mythical stories and reality existed within analogous spheres of intellection. As a result, past events were rendered in mythical terms; they were contoured to encourage social cohesion, frame collective identity patterns, and establish codes of conduct according to which people could guide their endeavors in the present, such that every step of a person's social experience and spiritual edification could be explained through an analogous episode in the past.

History as we know it is a genre, containing the organized, dated, and assessed deeds of individuals and groups; consequently, it is quite unlike the concept of history that is had in traditional cultures. In the Middle Ages, history had a more ample latitude, as it needed to incorporate substance that was locally *consequential*, that is to say, important to the community's coherence. This is not to say that medieval chronicles are fiction, but the fact is that history had some traits of a persuasive chronology: it rendered the community an inheritor of a cultural and intellectual legacy that legitimized its identitary logic and justified its place in the world.

King Alfonso X of Castile's *General Estoria* (1260-1284) is a case in point. The first parts of Alfonso's history identify Spain as heir to an explicitly biblical legacy, as they recount distant origins (Creation; Abraham; David; Babylonian Captivity, etc.). Subsequently, the *Estoria* begins to relate events–that we could somewhat accurately define as "historical"–from primitive and Roman Spain to thirteenth-century Castile and León, although many Greco-Roman myths "are incorporated into the *General Estoria* text" (Cristóbal 2015, 66).

As seen in this example, and in many ways, myth had a significant import in medieval history narratives. This is proven by the fact that medieval scholars relied heavily on myth when attempting to decipher the past, something that is often misunderstood by modern scholarship. For example one could point to the centuries-old debate surrounding the value of Geoffrey of Monmouth's

History of the Kings of Britain (c. 1136) as true *history*, beginning with Polydore Vergil's scornful observations in his 1534 *Anglica Historia* (Vergil 1844, xxiv).

As has been well established, in his account of the foundation of Britain Geoffrey seems to be emulating Virgil (*Aeneid*) and Livy (*Ab Urbe Condita*) among others, using all the mandatory tropes: undeserved exile, wandering through distant lands, divine prophesy, and the arrival at the promised land of Britain (Geoffrey of Monmouth 2008, 22). But such discussions as to the factual validity of the *History of the Kings of Britain* often miss the point: Geoffrey made his *History* "mythical" precisely because of myth's value as purveyor of information that was necessary to his community's identity, coherence, and continuance. Such material was a functional accessory that infused his history with symbolic data; that data contributed to *his* "truth," to a truth that was as legitimate to him as ours is to us.

It is evident even today that, while modern rationalism and empiricism have had a momentous effect on culture, largely relegating myth to the sphere of inconsequence, in the media and in politics a new and arguably more dangerous type of mythology has appeared. Lance Bennett, for example, notes that "Myths condition the public to the powerful symbols used by politicians. Myths underwrite the status quo in times of stability and they chart the course of change in times of stress" (1980, 168). More importantly, "In the day-to-day business of politics myths set the terms for most public policy debate. When mythical themes and myth-related language are stripped away from policy discourse, very little of substance remains" (1980, 168). He ends by saying that "Most political controversy centers around disagreements over which myth to apply to a particular problem" (1980, 168).

This new mythology owes its characteristics to new technologies that bring politicians' self-serving messages to a massive audience. Thus, myths such as "We are the land of the free, the home of the brave, and our destiny is to bring freedom and our way of life to all the people of the world" bring about the acceptance of absurd conflicts by the wider public and help identify enemies, structure the nature of antagonisms and drive political action. And while to call something a "myth" today is to degrade its factual value, myth still holds the potential to evoke jingoistic national "realities," emanating from a venerated past, one that is deemed to be more important than our trivial daily concerns.

Despite the modern mishandling of myth, it still emblematizes truly universal concerns regarding our residence on the planet, depicting anxieties and truths through symbols and symbolic action: Don Quixote's excursions into the recesses of his mind, for example, do not make his adventures less truthful; they are a most valid depiction of the absurdity and the tragedy of the human condition.

Myth and water

In premodern western European worldviews, the Atlantic Ocean was the most evident–and largest–space occupied by water, but its transcendental significance was only part of an ancient, conventional set of traditions that consecrated those places where water was found:

> Hydrolatry is panhuman and sacred wells and springs of some sort can be found around the globe. [...] As such, water was surely venerated by the first people to reach Ireland in Mesolithic times, and Christina Fredengren (2002) argues that Mesolithic human remains and lithic materials found in lakes might have been votive deposits. [...] It is hardly surprising that where a body of water or spring endured as a resource, its value as such fostered ongoing veneration. Irish rivers and lakes have yielded Iron Age metalwork, and pre-Christian votives have been found around St Anne's holy well at Randalstown, County Meath [...]. Such wells remained sacred with the arrival of Christianity as early missionaries preached where people already worshipped. [...] While sacred springs are a global phenomenon, Ireland is unusual in Europe in retaining holy-well visitation as a regular part of parish life. (Ray 2013, 271)

Anthony Stevens (2001, 130) believes that water has a very comprehensive role in worldwide myth-formation:

> As an agent of purification before entering a sacred temenos, to worship or make a sacrifice, the universal symbolism of ablution is readily understandable. Dirt dissolves in water and is washed away. Immersion in water, therefore, removes contamination; it cleanses and renders pure. The symbolism holds at the individual level (baptism, lustration, the sprinkling of holy water) and at the collective level (cataclysmic deluge and flood). As a result of such events, old sins are washed away and new life (and new faith) begins: "Then will I sprinkle clean water upon you, and ye shall be clean: from all your filthiness, and from all your idols, I will cleanse you" (Ezequiel 36:25). (Stevens 2001, 130)

For Mircea Eliade, "Water symbolizes the whole of potentiality; it is *fons et origo*, "font and origin," the source of all possible existence; it precedes every form and supports every creation. [...] Water symbolizes the primal substance from which all forms come and to which they shall return." (1978, 130). Large amounts of water can symbolize creation and birth:

> One of the reasons why the flood narrative may have diffused as widely as it undoubtedly has–even to peoples who live far inland away from natural floods–could be attributable to its symbolic content. For example, inasmuch as all human neonates are so to speak delivered

from an initial flood (of amniotic fluid) when the sac breaks, it is not impossible that the creation of the world was thought to have occurred in parallel fashion. As the individual is born, so was the earth born. (Dundes 1988, 168)

Water has been traditionally an agent of the gods and a palpable example of their wrath. In the Bible it is closely aligned with cleansing the land from sinful populations before the coming of the Son of Man:

> [37] But as the days of Noah were, so shall also the coming of the Son of man be.
> [38] For as in the days that were before the flood they were eating and drinking, marrying and giving in marriage, until the day that Noah entered into the ark,
> [39] And knew not until the flood came, and took them all away; so shall also the coming of the Son of man be. (Matthew 24:37-39 KJV)

Water makes an appearance in a dialogue where Nicodemus asked how an old man can be born again, "[5]Jesus answered, Verily, verily, I say unto thee, Except a man be born of water and of the Spirit, he cannot enter into the kingdom of God" (John 3:5). It is evident that in religious thought, and perhaps as a consequence of water's factual life-giving properties, places abundant in water have always been considered unique: "[23]And John also was baptizing in Aenon near to Salim, because there was much water there: and they came, and were baptized" (John 3:23).

In Greek myth, Charon ferried the souls of the dead across the river Acheron, and in Egypt Pharaoh Tutankhamun was buried with a boat in which he'd make a safe passage to the otherworld. The Zoroastrian Avesta gives an account of the western sea Pûtika and of another, the heavenly sea called Vourukasha, created by the god Hurmuz. In Vourukasha grows Gaokerena, the tree of immortality (Patch 1970, 8). In Gilgamesh, the hero travels across the southeastern waters of death to reach the fields of the blessed. This idea of bodies of water as avenues to the otherworld traveled west and was resilient: many centuries later an Anglo-Saxon warrior would be interred at Sutton Hoo with a longboat that would speed him across the water to the afterlife.

In keeping with the ancient and widespread myths surrounding water, and as the largest bodies of water on the planet, oceans have a power of enchantment that is perhaps only equaled by great mountains. Large bodies of water are commonly associated with the otherworld, the ascent to heaven, and are present in common myths throughout the ancient world. Patch (1970, 7) maintains that the essential body of common ocean myths spread from the east to the western shores of Europe, and adds that academicians like Becker, Coli, Cox, and Landau have even identified those myths' exact points of departure.

Portolan chart, or the routes of myth

The Atlantic's power to generate mythical thought, owing to its sheer size, is considerable. Fascination with the Atlantic was extensively memorialized by the classical world, which endowed its island realms with very special characteristics. One example is Homer, whose account of the Elysian Fields in the *Odyssey* gives us an accurate idea of the ancient world's fascination with the ocean:

> As for yourself, heaven-favored Menelaus, it is not destined you shall die and meet your doom in grazing Argos; but to the Elysian Plain and the earth's limits the immortal gods shall bring you, where fair-haired Rhadamanthus dwells. Here utterly at ease passes the life of men. No snow is here, no winter long, no rain, but the loud-blowing breezes of the west the Ocean-stream sends up to bring men coolness. (39)

In *Works and Days*, Hesiod strikes the same chord:

> And they live untouched by sorrow in the islands of the blessed along the shore of the deep swirling Ocean, happy heroes for whom the grain-giving earth bears honey-sweet fruit flourishing thrice a year, far from the deathless gods, and Cronos rules over them. (Patch 1970, 17)

There can be little question that, once culture reached the western fringes of the Eurasian continent, archaic water-related myths proliferated due to the proximity of the ocean. A case in point is Ireland.

The Irish have always had an interesting relationship with water: Christian pilgrimage to Lough Derg (a place now associated with Christian devotion as "Saint Patrick's Purgatory)" repurposes the pagan pilgrimage to what was a sacred site on a lake where druidic initiations took place, and the wells dedicated to Christian saints reenact an age-old pagan ritual of visiting holy springs. (This is part of a general repurposing of pagan sites that included topography devoid of water: The pagan festival of Imbolc is now St. Brigid's Day, and the pagan goddess Brigid herself has been repurposed as a Christian saint; the barefoot climb up 762-meter high Croagh Patrick is a recycling of the pagan festival of Lughnasadh, celebrated on hilltops).

Consisting of an enormous amount of water, the Atlantic is not just another sacred site, but a whole otherworld, one to which the Irish habitually traveled and from which they could return. When mythical travelers enter this world of water, the most spiritual substance, the sense of estrangement habitually felt on land seems to fade, and the travelers find themselves at one with the cosmos. On the islands that rise out of the ocean water the traveler lives in harmony with universal transcendence: time stops, and the marvels anticipated by the community's belief system materialize. The traveler's experiences occur in the ocean; having entered the realm of water is a circumstance that invests his adventure with a certain degree of legitimacy. The more astonishing the experience, the easier it is to make it the conveyor of concepts that are difficult to substantiate on land.

A common characteristic of experiences in a massive space of water like the ocean is the abandonment of all anxieties. *Immrama* and *echtrai* adventurers spending hundreds of blissful years on island paradises are immersed in the peace and harmony of the universe, while on land conditions remain unchanged. Surrounded by water, they perceive realities that are unavailable elsewhere; it is there that the traveler engages in cosmic life and experiences the most exalted and true existence. Therein he can find materialized phrenic concepts that evade validation back home, and in some cases, he can even bring back items that are only available in aquatic spaces.

One of many fine examples of a voyage into this mythical watery realm is the *Adventures of Art son of Conn* (*Echtra Airt*), which is included in the *Book of Fermoy* (139-145), a fifteenth-century codex in the Royal Irish Academy. In this tale, Conn must enter the realm of water to obtain something that is unavailable on land.

The adventures in question are not, as the title of this *echtra* would have you believe, those of Art, but rather of his father Conn, who sets out into the Atlantic, not in a *peregrinatio pro amore Dei*, but in a pagan quest to find a boy whom to offer as a sacrifice. The *Book of Fermoy* copy is the only extant version of the tale, its language being Early Modern Irish (Gaeilge Chlasaiceach). The story begins as Conn decides to marry a girl (Becuma) that his son Art was set to marry,

> And they made a union, Conn and the maiden, and she bound him to do her will. And her judgment was that Art should not come to Tara until a year was past. Conn's mind was vexed because of the banishing of his son from Ireland without cause." (*Celtic Literature Collective*, s.v. "Art." n.p.)

But punishment for their iniquity would soon come. It is important to note that punishment here was brought upon Art's community (the text states that "there was neither corn nor milk in Ireland") because punishment was a contextual response to a moral transgression that created imbalance in the community. It follows that the community had to get involved in policing its members because the community ultimately paid for the individual's transgressions. Moreover, if Conn got away with his depravity it would send the message that there is lax enforcement for this type of transgression, giving community members a sort of *carte blanche* on questions of morality. These communal punishments worked to preserve social harmony and, additionally, they indicate that ancient Irish populations–in all probability–had a collective worldview to whose unwritten codes the individual was accountable. Therefore, punishment was required in order to restore stability and coherence in the community:

> Art left Tara that night, and Conn and Becuma were a year together in Tara, and there was neither corn nor milk in Ireland during that time. And the men of Ireland were in the greatest difficulty about that matter; and the druids of all Ireland were sent with the help of their science and their true wisdom to show what had brought that dreadful evil into Ireland. (*Celtic Literature Collective*, s.v. "Art.")

To expiate his sin and bring Ireland back to its previous wellbeing, Conn was told to sacrifice the boy of a sinless couple. This is a transcendental quest, so only a *watery* domain can provide a venue for Conn's efforts. Finding it a very difficult task, Conn takes a coracle and sails into the Atlantic in search of such a marvel; therein he has several adventures in the typical Celtic otherworld islands. Conn finds the child in one of the islands and after much haggling brings him back, but the boy is saved from the slaughter by a wise woman, and a cow is sacrificed in his stead. Not only do the Irish travel back and forth from their Atlantic otherworld, but they complete business deals and bring back commodities from it. Conn sails into a water world because he could not find the merchandise that he needed (a mystical boy) on dry land.

Conn's journey is not to be confused with the thoroughly Christian *peregrinatio* that is undertaken to expiate sins, where the actual journey into a water world is the penitence. Adamnán's (a.k.a. Adomnán) *Life of Columba* (c. 697) for example, contains the story of a humble man that undertakes the long journey to visit Columba in order to atone for his sins by pilgrimage, by the long and arduous journey "ad delenda in peregrinatione peccamina longo fatigatum itinere" (Adamnán 1894, 180). Conversely, Conn's journey is undertaken as a quest into the water world to bring back the sacrificial victim that he needs to expiate his sins.

Ancient Irish cosmology,[2] as reflected in the *immrama* and the *echtrai*, identifies the immense ocean to the west as a gateway to an otherworld whose

---

[2] I sometimes make reference to the "ancient Irish" rather than to "Celt" or "Celtic" due to the fact that extensive study of Irish DNA, done by Trinity College Dublin and funded by the National Millenium Committee, and the work of geneticist Stephen Oppenheimer of the University of Oxford, has shown that the population of Ireland, as well as those of England, Scotland, and Wales, originate in the Iberian Peninsula, that is to say, modern-day Spain and Portugal. Moreover, they originally spoke a language related that of the Basques of northern Spain. The designation "Celtic" retains legitimacy in the sense that peoples coming from the Iberian Peninsula might have been proto-Celtic to begin with, contributing the Celtic cultural traits that structure Irish/Gael identity. In this regard, see

basic composition is water, to what is essentially a different type of reality brought about by the agency of water, one where mythical wonders like Conn's boy proliferate. The watery realm's eventual metamorphosis into a sort of Heaven's outpost, where island-dwelling saints and holy people might give the traveler moral instruction, is an early-Christian afterthought. In fact, Columba, who was born into a pagan family as Crimthann (fox), reveals the intrusion of the Christian canon on early Irish ethea, as his new name Columba (dove) deflects the evocative power of pagan lore's most cunning animal towards the pietistic rectitude of one of Christianity's most symbolic creatures (Matt. 3:16, Mark 1:9-11, Luke 3:21-22, and John 1:32-34 all state that the Spirit descended in the form of a dove).

Otherworld-journey stories like the *Adventures of Art son of Conn* have their ideal venue in the Atlantic for many reasons, but the primordial one surely stems from the fact that this immense body of water is in a special geographical location in relation to the sun's path. The sun is perhaps the most bizarre, and consequently, the most unworldly object in the ancient world and, in an event that must have been counter-intuitive to premodern peoples, this provider of the light with which to comprehend the world was immersed–maybe even died–every night in *this* particular expanse of water. The Atlantic Ocean's role in all of this explains its ubiquitous underworld associations. Moreover, this uncanny characteristic of the ocean, a perplexing domain where the waters douse the sun, is a critical part of cosmologies according to which one travels into those waters primarily in spiritual and mystical voyages.

For many peoples and nations, water also provides a medium for myths of origins. As the Milesians made the initial landfall in their conquest of Ireland, their chief poet Amergin, sensing the birth of a new era, is said to have chanted strange verses that begin thus: "I am the wind that blows over the sea,/ I am the wave of the ocean…" (Rolleston 1911, 134). This may be the result of eastern influences: In Sumerian, Assyrian, Akkadian, and Babylonian religions there was a chaos monster named Tiamat, the primeval goddess of the ocean, who mated with Abzû, the god of fresh water, to bring into being the next generation of gods. In this account of the origins of the universe, we see that at the beginning all that existed was water: Tiamat (salt water), Abzû (freshwater), and Mummu (god of mists that rise from the waters). But when the children of Tiamat and Abzû came into being, the turmoil they caused made their parents

---

the articles by Jan Battles "The Irish are not Celts, Say Experts," 6, Laoise T. Moore, et al., "A Y-Chromosome Signature of Hegemony in Gaelic Ireland," 334-338 and Nicholas Wade "English, Irish, Scots," F-1.

decide to kill them. The subsequent string of misunderstandings and clashes among them gave rise to the universe as we experience it today (Cotterell 1997, 53).

The initial scenario of the Tiamat myth is a possible source of the Bible account (Gen. 1) where the abyss, called *Tehom* (תְּהוֹם), is the primeval ocean that existed *before* creation. This watery void is not part of creation because it is chaos, formlessness, whereas creation is form, arrangement, organization, and structure. It is also important to note that around and underneath the habitable land there lies that same primeval ocean from which God saved the poet, as described in Psalms: "He sent from on high, he took me; he drew me out of many waters." (Ps. 18:16, ESV). The depths are identified with Sheol, the grave, the abyss, the place of the dead, the shadows, the underworld of the Hebrew scriptures: "As the cloud fades and vanishes, so he who goes down to Sheol does not come up" (Job 7:9, ESV). Here, the dead lose every prospect of ever having a relationship with God or a connection with the world of the living (Sang Meyng Lee 2010, 44).

Given the ancient connection of the ocean with unstructured autonomy, Jonah seeks to escape his obligation to journey to Nineveh in order to pronounce a doom over the city by putting out to sea, the one place where the social contract could not reach him. In fact, by entering the belly of the sea creature he accesses a womb-like, pre-social, primordial environment and leaves the world of personal responsibilities behind. In Homeric epic the primeval ocean (Okeanos; ωκεανός) circles the earth and separates the mortals' world of social obligations from those joyful quarters of immortal retirement, the Isles of the Blest and the Plain of Elysium

In Greek and sundry other traditions, large bodies of water are decidedly benevolent. Okeanos is the place of origin of the gods (γένεση των θεών) as well as of all things (M. Bennett 1997, 13), the categorical sphere of origins. We might remember that the mythical Troy emerges from the waters, built over land that was exposed when the ocean receded and people began migrating down from higher ground (Chandler 1802, 3-4), and that Venice was built as a refuge *in* the sea by people fleeing Attila's hordes. Moreover, the Hindu Mother Goddess Lakshmi is born out of the froth of the ocean, the primeval milk that symbolizes reproduction, fertility, and immortality; Aphrodite, who comes forth out of the spume, has a similar origin: both bring to mind the Homeric concept of Ocean as originator of life, a timeless place where a poetics of eternity replaces chronoscopic consciousness.

Many of these ancient, mythical attributes attached to water were inferential constituents of the medieval imaginary, especially for those groups neighboring the vast, deep, mysterious western ocean. But even for people accustomed to seafaring in a closed sea like the Mediterranean, hugging coastlines while praying to the gods for good weather, the Atlantic Ocean has always been a realm of myth. Those living on the European shores of the Atlantic saw an endless expanse whose immensity allowed the imagination to populate with otherworldly beings and places; consequently, their stories would have been a source of entertainment and wonderment to Mediterranean visitors.

Ancient mariners from Mediterranean lands who dared to sail beyond the Straits of Gibraltar may well have returned with hazy stories about fantastic islands and implausible beings, fashioned, surely, not only from Celtic tales overheard while sharing a meal with their hosts but also from the fear and excitement of venturing outside their decipherable cosmos. The great ocean, with its limitless horizon, violent weather, and mystifying immensity, became the essential breeding ground for myth and legend.

The great expanse of water also had important spiritual attributes for medieval peoples: in feudal societies, where land was a resource defined in functional terms, where most of the land was someone's property, where land was the source of practically all wealth and power and this wealth was concentrated in the hands of the very few, the water world lent itself in a unique manner to flights of fancy. It was, after all, a world of free access, not commodified, not privatized, limitless, mysterious, bountiful, undivided, in short, a sphere of unrestrained activity for body and spirit. Moreover, as nobody actually lives *in* the Atlantic–there is no stable, sedentary settlement upon its waves–it is effectively marginalized from the "reality" of medieval life and its communal prescriptions. To add to its enigmatic alienation from "this" world of banal commitments, although water is the necessary ingredient for life, the ocean is made up of water that we cannot drink or use to irrigate the land, and furthermore, it absorbs the sun every evening, smothering the light that makes our perception of "reality" possible.

Being thus distanced and shielded from human jurisdictions, the ocean was culturally charted as an antipodal water world, an "other" space, a "different" space where mythical geographies gave expression to the mental landscapes of the medieval imagination. This "different" space, existing as a counterpart to familiar space, can be recognized as the "invisible country," Avalon, the place to which King Arthur sails from his sojourn in the *visible* world in the company of Nimue, the Lady of the Lake, his protector. In this sense, "the passing of Arthur seems mystically to represent the sunset over the Western Ocean: Arthur disappears beneath the horizon into the Lower World…" (Evans Wentz 1994, 321).

The earliest cultures arriving at the shores of the great ocean likely developed a binary cosmos much like the one to which Arthur would later belong, where the world of daily reality was mirrored by an "other" world where fairies, dwarfs, and magical beings held sway. In this cosmos there existed a number of passages that allowed for the individual to travel back and forth from one world to the other: Arthur sailed to that "other" place after his death in battle and is expected to return from it; Brendan and his monks undertook that passage into the "different" world by venturing into the Atlantic in search of a Christian wonderland, while Trezenzonio and Amaro set off on round-trip quests that also led them through those magical, enchanted geographies of what can appropriately be called the "Celtic" imagination.

This all begs the question: why couldn't Celtic heroes travel through spiritual realms by journeying by land to faraway, exotic places? The answer is that ancient Celtic storytellers assumed that certain fundamental human desires were so intense that they could not be satisfied on land, that is to say, within the boundaries of everyday existence. Satisfaction could only be sought by entering the world of water and thus escaping the land, that familiar stage where the battle for daily subsistence unfolds. This flight from the everyday doldrums is certainly present in some *echtrai* and in every *immrama*; these tales describe early navigators who venture into "other" spheres and register their experiences while traversing a world of water. This other sphere is a mental space as much as it is physical, a hypothetical cosmos through which the medieval psyche drifts as in a dream, roaming free, unconstrained by the limitations of a map.

In general terms, the passage into the other world -watery or landlocked- is often, if not always, tied to a search for an elusive, sometimes intangible object or place: Brendan searches the Atlantic for the Isle of the Blest; Ith sails to a land of milk and honey that his father, perched atop a colossal tower, has detected across the ocean; the knights of medieval narratives seek the Holy Grail, and even in the Renaissance Don Quixote is on a quest for eternal fame and glory. Evidently, these journeys are prompted by a basic spiritual need, so they are inward journeys as much as they are physical expeditions: a mythical voyage is a journey through the landscape of the mind.

Myth and its domains: the Atlantic's exceptional reality

Now the rhumb line in our portolan chart points towards infinity, taking us along the open ocean and into the themed environment of the medieval Great Mystery.

Judging by the number of myths, legends, and stories produced by pagan and early medieval peoples in western Europe, it is evident that the journey into the Atlantic has an ancient and very significant link to the otherworld journey and to fundamental, ultimate questions regarding existence. Such questions are part of the human condition: people in early medieval and pre-scientific societies were as curious as people in modern societies regarding extraordinary realms. Like us, they were interested in places that might exist beyond the mundane, physical spaces that they perceived through their senses, alternate regions where the human being might survive beyond this life and mesh with the universe's eternal, divinely arranged moral symmetry.

Europeans were by no means the only people who placed otherworld spaces on islands far into the ocean. The Chinese Daoist tradition puts the Immortal Isle, Penglai Shan (蓬萊仙島), in the farthest reaches of the Pacific, a place where the Eight Immortals, or Bāxiān (八仙), live in a sublime environment of eternal serenity (Renard 2002, 52). Japan has Horai (蓬莱), a very distant island of eternal youth in the Eastern Sea. Japanese legend tells us that the wise man Wasobiobe sailed alone into the ocean to meditate, fell asleep, and awakened to find himself in a paradisiacal land with a blissful population of youngsters. There the air was full of wonderful bird melodies, the sweet smell of flowers filled the nostrils, and the bounty of nature was astonishing. After a long day of feasting, hunting, and bathing in the warm waters, Wasobiobe went looking for his boat with the intention of returning home. He was warned, however, that in what had seemed a long day to him a hundred years had passed back home in Japan. Determined to go home, Wasobiobe had a magic crane fly him to Japan, where he promptly died of old age upon treading on one of its beaches (James 2005, 56).

In the myths of European seaside communities, this experience of time dilation is commonplace and reinforces the concept of the Atlantic as an exceptional space. Irish hero U sheen (Oisín), having journeyed to an island paradise in the Atlantic, lived happily for a hundred years in eternal youth without experiencing the ravages of time. He too pined for home and decided to return, dying as a decrepit old man the moment he touched Erin's soil. Spain's "Monk of the Little Birds" asked the Virgin Mary for just a glimpse of Paradise, and although that fleeting glimpse was granted, he found upon returning to his monastery that 300 years had passed.

In Europe, the otherworld was commonly described through myths that placed its fantastic geography within the endless, exceptional Atlantic. Thus, mythological forays into the preternatural space were inspired attempts to interpret life and to discover alternatives to *this* world of daily routine, toil, and uncertainty. And while travelers to discrete space frequently found utopias– marvelous domains of happiness and pleasure–no one should believe that such fantastic islands provided a practical guide on how to transcend or alter the status quo back home: these places reinforced the essential ethos of the pagan society whence the sailor came. In the Celtic Crescent, such *status quo* validations were amended subsequently to harmonize with Christian homiletic prescriptions.

So pagan and early Christian voyages westward were not associated with a search for alternative social, political, or economic arrangements: things of this world were too prosaic to be considered within exceptional realities. As such, these voyages did not offer any type of resistance to credenda or to social hierarchies but rather attempted to articulate a compelling image of the extramundane realms that were anticipated by their societies' fundamental ontology.

But because the Atlantic's exceptionality was to experience a fundamental revision following the establishment of Christianity, it became a contested space, a space where ancient, substratal thematic substance bubbled up to challenge the overlaying catechizing message. A case in point is the *Immram Máel Dúin*. It is the tale of the Irish hero Maelduin (Máel Dúin), who sails into the Atlantic with the intention of avenging his father's murder. God protects him in his perilous journey, which makes Maelduin reconsider his un-Christian temperament. As a result, he forgives the murderers and returns home a good Christian, having adhered to an essential Christian injunction (Rom. 12:17. Repay no one evil for evil. Have [a] regard for good things in the sight of all men. NKJV).

The Christianized version of the tale has the hero move through a thoroughly exceptional reality in the ocean, but it is entirely possible that an early oral version of this *immram*, conforming to pagan communal precepts, ended with the death of the murderers at the hands of the hero, as the fundamental complexion of the blood-feud plot and the pagan features of the events that led up to the hero's journey point squarely in that direction.

The extant *Immram Máel Dúin* story is one of Christian edification, so if my estimation of its pagan origin is correct, it is a good example of how an original ideation responsible for the structure and plot of the story was homogenized by the church and the Atlantic otherworld integrated into its message. The process of acculturation is more than evident, as the hero encounters numerous bizarre creatures and events from pagan lore in his travels; they speak volumes about the enduring cogency of the distinct ethos that, in the pagan mind, made the Atlantic an exceptional space. This means that the Christian proselytizers' efforts made the ocean's transcendentality a contested spiritual space, as can be observed in pagan anatomical features of otherworld stories that are extant–and dumbfounding–in theoretically Christian texts. The effort to make space and plot acquiescent to Christian proselytization, moreover, antagonizes the pre-Christian environment of the original story, distressing the message's coherence.

Another example of the contested nature of Atlantic exceptionality is offered by the enigmatic, 60-line Middle Welsh poem Preiddeu Annwfn, or "The Spoils of Annwn," preserved in the early fourteenth-century *Book of Taliesin* (the poem itself is probably from c. 900 A.D. [Lacy 1991, 428]). Its storyline has the legendary King Arthur actually invade the otherworld with three boatloads of men, seven of which survive and return with marvelous spoils taken from that realm. Most stanzas in the poem begin with the expression "Praise the Lord," which would seem extraneous to a story where the hero is invading the deity's abode, unless you interpret the incursion in the only reasonable manner, as that of a Christian marauder into a pagan paradise. This story allows us to perceive the resilience of Celtic substratal material: even as late as the tenth-century pagan otherworlds endured and even flourished around the British Isles, arbitrating the Christian message to the reader with their continuing social and cultural pertinence.

While not having the Atlantic as the environment where its events take place–although the hero sails through the North and Baltic seas, branches of the Atlantic–one truly remarkable text that can be brought forward as a prime example of the enduring importance of substratal material is *Beowulf* (c. 700–1000 CE). Immaterial for our purposes is the question of whether it was composed by an early pagan poet, with Christian material added later (this is my opinion), or composed later by a Christian poet who added pagan elements as a necessary expedient. What is significant is that the value system, attitudes, and expectations that inform the story are unapologetically pagan, and they integrate what is evidently a recognizable and compelling social, cultural, and spiritual landscape into the story. Consequently, it seems that it would be very difficult for contemporary consumers of the story to perceive the pagan elements as retrospective adornment. This means that several centuries after the introduction of Christianity, a pagan substratum was alive and well–even necessary–within the context of Christian cultural productions.

Marc Morris (2021, 47) explains that

> There is nothing [of Christian virtues] in *Beowulf*. Although the poem is ostensibly Christian – it speaks of a single God, to whom successful characters occasionally give thanks – almost all of the attitudes it celebrates are those of a pagan past. It exalts the loyalty of warriors to their lord, even to the extent of being willing to die for him, and its heroes are overwhelmingly concerned with their earthly renown. When Beowulf, for instance, is fighting against his second monster, it is not faith that sustains him, but belief in his own reputation, and a desire to win everlasting fame. When Hrothgar's hall is attacked, Beowulf says it is better to avenge the dead than indulge in mourning. When one brother kills another, their father is sad, but recognizes that it has been done "in accordance with the law of the blood feud."

This leads me to consider the reasons why the Christian message needed the exceptional, pagan Atlantic to succeed in reaching seaside populations. For one, the Atlantic where mythical navigators like Brendan, U sheen, Trezenzonio, Bran, Amaro, and Maelduin sailed was an age-old exceptional space for people around it, one that had supported foundational sacred concepts and otherworld myths for many centuries: it was more practical for Christianity to negotiate with this cultural colossus than to antagonize it. As part of the requisite concessions, Christian holy men like Brendan and Snédgus and Mac Ríagla would take leaves of absence from their landside duties and tour the pagan watery otherworld in an unconventional show of good will, bringing a Christian perspective to that environment, but also–and this is very important–becoming *immrama* heroes in the process.

When it comes to the Atlantic, the church's concessions to its pagan cultural ascendancy had an unanticipated result: they subverted the Roman Church's push towards a unified set of conventional beliefs. Yet these concessions, while creating a decidedly *Irish* faith that was recognized for its prodigiously syncretic character, also imbued Christian belief with features that were recognizable to the island's populations, allowing it to obtain island-wide devotion. At any rate, the ocean's topography was already in a "beyond," in an exceptional space outside the limits of commonplace experience that floats in a mist of abstract, symbolic time, disengaged from the linear, continuous strand of quotidian chronology. These characteristics meant that repurposing it as an ideogram for Christian values was feasible, but it required a compromise with the ocean's outwardly pagan functional features.

Beyond considerations that depend on Christianity's role in rearranging the ocean's exceptionality, this exceptional reality attached to the Atlantic was decidedly relevant to anyone living on its shores from time immemorial. In particular, it provided an essential backdrop for shared ideas regarding the attributes and whereabouts of the otherworld, a fact that accounts for the peculiar practice of ship burials among western Europeans.[3] It is for these reasons that the stories of pagan Ireland, when set in the Atlantic, assumed an allegorical dimension where places and events actually *required* symbolic interpretations. Among the early inhabitants of western Europe, exclusively realistic interpretations of sailors' incursions into the western ocean are rare. This is because the ocean was a framework of cultural expectations: the Atlantic's attributes were so bound to myth, that a realistic portrayal would have been unconventional.

---

[3] Excavations at Sutton Hoo, in East Anglia, unearthed an early seventh-century ship burial that contained the remains of an important individual, perhaps Rædwald, the ruler of the East Angles. The ship was intended to ferry his soul, symbolically, into the afterlife. Moreover, the Hjortspring boat grave (in Sønderjylland, Denmark) and the Nydam Mose ships (in Øster Sottrup, Denmark) give evidence of the fact that ship-burials were common in Scandinavia since the early Iron Age.

As mentioned above, once Christianity started making inroads into Ireland and other western European lands, because the ocean was a fundamental, time-honored and preferred venue for symbolic interpretations of existence, it would have been risky to exorcise it from Christian proselytizing agendas. Thus, to avoid the risk of alienating prospective converts, the Atlantic's exceptional reality was incorporated into the catechizing efforts of early Christian missionaries. Their agenda, then, included forging syncretic characters like Saint Brendan and Maelduin, champions now tasked with entering and colonizing ancient symbolic spaces.

Early Christian proselytizers, a literate and inquisitive group, must have been exposed not only to early Irish folktales but also to classical epics, geographies, and theories that gave a disquieting perspective on the Atlantic, texts that were found in many monastic libraries. It follows that they must have been anxious about the ancestral cultural and religious significance of the watery Great Mystery, a space that was considered exceptional in every folktale and every text. These accounts clearly show that medieval sailors from Mediterranean lands entered exceptional space when navigating Atlantic waters; moreover, the ocean's physical features tended to reinforce spiritual notions of its exceptionality.

To many seafarers, the ocean seemed to have volition. The farther out that they ventured into its waters, the stronger the currents and waves. Mariners that sailed too far west met the unexplainable "floating islands" of the Sargasso[4] and experienced more violent storms, higher seas, and stronger currents, at which point they'd have to allow their ship to be escorted in the direction that the ocean deities determined. They might try to fight them, but they would run the certain risk of being submerged in the raging waters. What is more, returning to land after such adventures was not always a welcome event: should they approach land at or near nightfall, chances of survival decreased, as unseen shallows, shoals and rocks menaced clandestinely in the darkness. At every turn, the Atlantic seemed to validate its status as an exceptional reality.

Another way in which the ocean could confirm its exceptional reality was by keeping travelers from ever reaching their destination. One of the reasons why sailors were never heard from again was the calm, when not the slightest breeze could be felt for many days and listless sails would hang uselessly from the rigging. On such occasions, the limited number of rations could start to run

---

[4] The idea of floating islands in the Sargasso, in the middle of the Atlantic, was still the subject of adventure stories well into the twentieth century. Frank Wall's "The Lost Empire," for example, a short novel serialized in *The Thrill Book* of July-August 1919, relates how explorer Godfrey Boone landed on one such island, populated by a lost race and heavily forested, and met with sundry entertaining adventures.

out, and rowing long distances was out of the question for a group whose food and water supplies would be severely diminished by the long days added to the voyage.

The Atlantic's ancient repute as an exceptional reality appealed strongly to the medieval imagination, attracting many individuals who pursued spiritual fulfillment in a relevant environment. Such individuals must have contributed imaginative material to the Atlantic's repute as a place where an alternative reality was operative. Who were these people? There is quite a bit of evidence suggesting that holy sailors ventured into open waters very early on, reaching far-off lands only attainable by undertaking long journeys that took them far from shore. The first of these holy sailors were the Papars, devoted travelers who very likely contributed much material to the mythical architecture of the Atlantic Ocean:

> Cognate to *papa* for father and linked to the modern usage of pope, *papars* was how these far-traveled men were known amongst the islands in the North Atlantic. Putting all their faith in God's mercy and providence, the papars were extraordinarily intrepid, as much explorers as seekers after solitude in the desert wastes of the ocean. Geography traces their progress northwards from Ireland's shores. (Moffat 2020, n.p.)

This progress takes them from the archipelago south of Barra, where one may find the placename Pabbay (Pabaidh); another Pabaidh and a Pabail on the Point Peninsula, on the eastern shore of the Isle of Lewis, Scotland; on Orkney Papa Stronsay and, northwards, Papa Westray. There is also a Papa Stour, off the mainland of Shetland. The Faroe Islands have Paparokur and Vestmanna, the place of the men who came from the west, Ireland (Moffat 2020, n.p.).

Early Icelandic historical sources state that, at the time the Norsemen arrived in Iceland in the ninth century, they found evidence (Irish books, bells, and crosiers) that Irish and/or Scottish monks (the Papars) had been settled there for some time. The Papars appear in early Icelandic sagas as Irish monks who lived as hermits in areas of what is now Iceland. They sailed to Iceland before the Norsemen, as substantiated in the sagas and by contemporary archaeological findings:

> Iceland was the last country in Europe to become inhabited, and we know more about the beginnings and early history of Icelandic society than we do of any other in the Old World. The *Book of Settlements* [*Landnámabók*] is our chief source [...]. As late as 860 AD, Iceland was still an empty land, except for a few Irish anchorites driven there by viking attacks and settlements on their homeland. These Irishmen [the Papars] are said to have been in Iceland as far back as 795, just after the beginning of the Viking Age, and for the next three-quarters of a century

they had the country to themselves. Then, around 860, the peace was shattered by Scandinavian seafarers who seem to have gone to Iceland unintentionally, having been blown off course; and soon afterwards, perhaps about 870, the first settlers established permanent homes there. (Palsson and Edwards 1972, 1)

These Irish monks were there, evidently, not just because their homeland was subject to the ravages of the Norsemen, but primarily because what they sought was unavailable within the familiar spaces of normal space and time, and yet was obtainable in the exceptional reality of the Atlantic.

Irish presence in Iceland in the eighth century was construed as a foray into the fabulous from the time that Irish monk Dicuil wrote about it, stating that three Irish monks made the voyage to the mythical "Thule." "Ultima Thule," for medieval cartographers, was a remote place beyond the perimeters of the known world, the *terra incognita* far into the Atlantic. Doubtlessly, Dicuil was referring to Iceland, truly a mystical *terra incognita* for early cartographers:

Letronne, *Récherches*, pp. 137, 138, shows that the details given so distinctly in Dicuil, can apply only to phenomena observable in the latitude of the southern part of Iceland, which leaves no doubt of the identity of Dicuil's Thule with that island. Iceland is said to have been discovered by the Northmen about 860. Dicuil gathered his information relating to it in 795. (Wright 1842, 375)

Looking at the years these holy men spent foraying into the ocean, it is entirely possible that they contributed to the Atlantic's repute as exceptional reality; they might also be responsible for much of the syncretism evident in *immrama* and *echtrai* sea-voyage stories. Having resided in the exceptional reality of the Atlantic for decades, these Irish anchorites, upon returning to Ireland and relating their adventures, would have relied upon the nation's pre-Christian mythical narratives to try and convey their stories in a way that made sense. As incipient storytellers, they must have assumed that the phenomena experienced in their travels and their sojourn in an island of fire mountains (volcanoes), rivers of fire and brimstone (lava flows), strange dancing lights in the sky (northern lights), and floating islands of ice (icebergs) had already been memorialized in the mythical cosmos of the pagan oral tradition; their acquaintance with that oral tradition may have been the catalyst that prompted their journey into the Atlantic in the first place. At any rate, for ninth-century religious individuals, these experiences were too complex to relate analytically: as storytellers, they needed to deploy their narrative within a mythical framework, one that was available in the oral tradition of pre-Christian narratives. To make their use of these narratives acceptable, however, they had to subject them to the adjustments required by Christian doctrine.

The reliance of written literature (essentially Christian in nature) upon the ancient oral tradition (pagan) has been widely substantiated, and no less a character than Saint Patrick may have been using those stories for his proselytizing activity:

> ... literacy came to be perceived as fundamentally Christian in nature. This perception flows naturally from Irish experiences of the widespread introduction of literacy in the wake of Christianisation. [...] In fact, [Saint Patrick] became something of a culture hero, a miracle-working man of letters. Later writers would portray Patrick, accompanied by a scribe, travelling the island, gathering tales of the past. Writing erased the discontinuities between the past and the Christian present: it provided a signpost to the future and ensured the survival of the Irish eschatological community. (Johnston 2013, 36)

As Patrick wrote down those "tales of the past," erasing "discontinuities between the past and the Christian present," he was almost certainly engaging that past in a process of syncretic alignment with Christian doctrine. Judging by the dates we have for the syncretic composition of most *immrama* and *echtrai*, the anchorites' contribution (direct or indirect) to Atlantic lore and to the Christianized form that these pagan stories would take is also well within the realm of possibility. It is also probable that at least some of the anchorites that ventured into that exceptional reality of the Atlantic as far as Iceland, contributing with otherworld vistas and sundry metaphoric renditions of their experiences to *immrama* narratives, were Céli Dé ascetics, a cast that was, curiously, ever on the move in their quest for *stabilitas*. Their astonishing stories, infused with pagan substance from *immrama* and *echtrai*, could even have contributed to the transformation of factual journeys, such as those of Columbanus (543–615) and Fursey (597–650), into metaphorical journeys to an exceptional reality.

> The *immrama* may have had a monastic background, but it was not a simple one. Hughes has argued that by the end of the eighth century the Irish pattern of *peregrinatio* had changed under the dual influence of the Vikings and the ideals of Céli Dé ascetics. The latter are probably the more directly significant, particularly in ideological and theological terms. The Céli Dé, who drew their inspiration from the strict Máel Ruain († 792), were influential right up to the end of the ninth century. [...] [Their] widely disseminated emphasis on *stabilitas* may have meant that the literal journey of the *peregrinus*, of a Columbanus or Fursa, shifted into a metaphorical quest for the otherworld. (Johnston 2013, 52)

From the outwardly syncretic aspect that pagan sea-stories exhibit, it is evident that Christian proselytes–anchorites or not–were responsible for updating the ancient image of the Atlantic as exceptional reality, a space where the supernatural was indigenous and the cosmos conjectured by myth seemed to materialize in the form of implausible islands like Iceland. The mythical navigation adventure story was certainly one aspect of the pagan belief system that was rehabilitated and brought up to date by the early Irish church without excessive elaboration. Arguably, the tone of facile improvisation that characterizes this reclamation has to do with common patterns of doxastic thought through which exceptionality is devised, established, and made relevant, patterns that are closely associated with basal religious notions that are shared by pagans and Christians.

Emile Durkheim, in his formal categorization of religion, stated that religion is a "unified system of beliefs and practices relative to sacred things, that is to say, things set apart and forbidden which unite into one single moral community" (2001, 46). Common to ancient populations on the Atlantic shore was the idea that the endless ocean contained those "sacred things" or places that were "set apart," within its exceptional reality. As a careful examination of the texts will show, this practice of venturing into the "exceptional" place that was originally "set apart" by pagan minds was co-opted by the church, with syncretic figures like Máel Dúin, Brendan, Malo of Aleth, and Columba sailing into a formerly pagan geography that, through their efforts, was efficiently invaded and colonized by the Christian value-system. Thus, its exceptionality endured.

Ostensibly, the refurbished accounts of pagan voyages, told to audiences that recognized their ancestral generic framework, would serve to unite assorted island polities (still in the process of being Christianized) into "one single moral community," one with new ideological lineaments to serve as a fresh adhesive. Therefore, the process of writing down the pagan oral tradition was also a process of Christianizing exceptional spaces such as the Atlantic.

This process was a sensible investment for the church. Unquestionably, the exceptional reality of the pagan Atlantic, once synchronized with doctrine, served the church well in its efforts to make inroads into those phrenic domains that had for so long hypostatized the cosmos to pagan communities. Pagan myth was thus put at the service of Christian religion at the fringes of the world of men, at the periphery of the οἰκουμένη.

But invading an alien doxastic system's exceptional space is a process that needs explaining in a wider context. While it can be argued very sensibly that pagan myth and religion do not synchronize with Christian dogma, it can also be maintained that, deep down, the ethea of both pagan spirituality and Christian doctrine are the result of a psychological mechanism that drives human beings to generate essential, constitutive meaning. As a result of this motivation, human beings *create* exceptional spaces like the Atlantic (pagans) and Heaven (Christians) and describe their place in the cosmos through a process that generates metaphysical order and explains chaos; this process is common to both pagans and Christians, and it is a collective affair.

We can regard the Atlantic Ocean as the largest and most important of these liminal spaces, a world where the physical laws of the universe were suspended and an alternate, sympathetic reality was operative.

The Atlantic was an almost tangible otherworld existing next door to the prescientific world of medieval folk. It validated the praxis of grasping observed reality through a lens of myth, which is one of the essential features of pagan and early medieval culture. Its exceptional reality was a definitive culture marker in the world of the druids, one that needed to be placed under a Christian jurisdiction. This made Atlantic exceptionality a contested space; for the proselytizers involved in morphing the ancient oral culture of seaside folk, this transformation needed to appear as the uncontrived evolution of an ancestral mythical space. Some of these narratives eventually came to be regarded as the products of Christian minds; to judge by the analyses of quite a few scholars of Irish antiquities, who confidently declare that early medieval Irish navigation narratives (*immrama* and *echtrai*) are exclusively Christian creations, it can be said that the proselytizers were eminently efficient in their efforts to convert the Atlantic's exceptionality.

The ease with which the fundamental cognitive orientation of Christianity sublimated the pagan voyage narratives (whose echoes still resonate clearly in the *immrama* and *echtrai*) is efficiently explained by looking at the ancient cultural environment in which these narratives were set, one that is primeval and whose source may be found in the earliest civilizations:

> Recent discoveries have proved how much the religions not only of the East but also of Europe were influenced by Babylon. The ancient world was deeply indebted to Babylon with reference to the arts of civilization and the same may be said with respect to many religious beliefs.
>
> The ancient Babylonians regarded the ocean with the greatest awe. They looked upon it as the personification of evil and of hell and in the roaring of its waves they seemed to hear the threatenings of the power of darkness. They regarded the sea as the home and under the domination of a mighty king, the representation of evil, whom they called Tiamat. [...] In the old Babylonian belief it was this dragon [7-headed serpent] of the sea that seduced the first the first human beings from their innocence and was the enemy of mankind. (Gath Whitley 1911, 152)

Awe habitually inspired a feeling of fascination with areas like the Atlantic, which could become objects of reverence and preferential stages for the location of alternate realities that sheltered the community's spiritual imaginary, regardless of creed.

For continental European folk, the Atlantic was also the setting for an exceptional reality, a place that elicited transcendental curiosity and amazement. It was an area beyond conventional time and space; it was the *beyond* through which one ventured at considerable peril; it was both an alternative, metaphysical reality present in people's *inner* world, and an immense part of the physical universe. It was a realm where Mediterranean merchants, sailing to the British Isles in search of Cornish tin from the Ding Dong Mines or Welsh copper from the Great Orme Mines, anxiously hugged the coastlines of the Iberian Peninsula and western France before crossing the narrow English Channel to reach their destination.

For the ancient Greeks, the Atlantic was a truly liminal space, part of a watery cosmos–*Okeanos*–encircling the whole of the earth and giving birth to the sun, the moon, and the stars on a daily basis; it was also the place where these went to die each day. In the *Iliad*, (21.194 ff) Homer has Okeanos (Ὠκεανός) as the mythical, world encircling source of all waters, whereas Hesiod (*Theogony* 337 ff) gives Okeanos a complex mythical biography featuring gods and goddesses. *Okeanos* also represented by Titan, was the godly personification of the ocean stream on which the habitable hemisphere or "globe of lands" (οἰκουμένη or *orbis terrarum*) floated.

The early Mediterranean cultures held that the great ocean was the uninhabitable place, the alien "other" place, and the peoples that inhabited its shores (Ireland, Scotland, Wales, Galicia, even far eastern Asia) were commonly identified by Greek and Roman authors as nations on the threshold of chaos, on the margins of the *orbis terrarum* and of civilization. Strabo, in book III of his *Geographica*, for example, holds that

> As I was saying, the first part of Europe is the western, namely, Iberia. Now of Iberia the larger part affords but poor means of livelihood; for most of the inhabited country consists of mountains, forests, and plains whose soil is thin—and even that not uniformly well-watered. And Northern Iberia, in addition to its ruggedness, not only is extremely cold, but lies next to the ocean, and thus has acquired its characteristic of inhospitality and aversion to intercourse with other countries; consequently, it is an exceedingly wretched place to live in. (Strabo 1923, 3)

These notions evidently helped enhance the idea, reinforced in Varro and Vitruvius, of Italy as the *medio orbe*, the natural center of the world (Zissos 2016, 228). Christianity, with its spiritual and intellectual center in Rome, squarely in the middle of the *medio orbe*, was no stranger to these prevalent assessments. As Lavezzo (2006, 7) puts it, "[…] in the symbolic geography of world cartography, the center is a charged site of social power." Thus, in a classical world that nurtured Christian thought, a comprehensive understanding of the Atlantic included the vague, yet commonplace notion of its remote, otherworldly heterogeneity.

> [In almost any medieval world map], Britain and Ireland tend to be placed at the edge of the world image, often somewhat distorted in shape, as if mapmakers had trouble accommodating them in a framework designed to hold the neat, circular form of the three continents" (Byrne 2016, 143).

Atlantic seaside communities had a different view of the neighboring immensity. Evident in their ancient narratives is the fact that from time immemorial the Irish understood their otherworld not as a dematerialized, abstract space but as an area accessible by sailing to the west. The materiality of this exceptional space meant that Irish saints *had* to be staged as seafarers venturing into the ocean in order to gain credibility for their claims to holiness: it was the necessary groundwork for the church to get a firm foothold on the Irish psyche. The Atlantic was eminently relevant in the spiritual cosmos of the ancient Irish, as it was a favored setting for their alternate reality. This importance is evidenced by the remarkable fact that the early Irish church felt the need to place critical proselytizing narratives there, far from Rome, the eastern "charged site of social power" whose world view the Irish, who had always looked west to their exceptional reality, could not fully understand.

The Irish Ordnance Survey puts the geographical center of Ireland in the townland of Carnagh East (An Charnach Thoir), in County Roscommon, where the 8° Meridian West meets the 53°30' North Latitude, a mere 52 miles from the Galway coastline and the open sea. So the awareness of living on an island in the Atlantic, separated from the "rest of the world," must have been a decisive element in the islanders' *Weltanschauung*. Consequently, if ancient people dwelling at the limits of the *orbis terrarum* were any different from their Mediterranean contemporaries, it may have been due to a certain disposition that is induced by the habitual perception of the marvelous, of the prodigy. Living next to the vastness may have led to a more intimate understanding of the contrast between the individual in his inconsequential smallness and an apparently infinite, liquid immensity that suggests transcendence. To look out on the ocean from the limits of medieval western Europe was to perceive a place that transcends the bounds of experience. Ancient and medieval individuals could not live in its waters, could not work there, could not survive there; the sun, the light went there to die, only to be born again from the opposite direction; it was extraordinary beyond the limits of their everyday experience; it was implausible, and yet, there it was. It is no wonder that many transcendental events related to pagan and early medieval myths have their ideal setting in and around the Atlantic: the most impossible and supernatural event of all–the Sun disappearing in its waters–was a commonly-witnessed daily occurrence.

Evocative of this mindset is a place called *Finis Terrae* (The End of the Earth) by the Romans, a rocky headland in extreme northwestern Spain that juts out into the exceptional reality of the Atlantic, a place thought to be the absolute last place in the *orbis terrarum*, and as such, a threshold to the afterlife. Celts, Goths, Romans, and early Christians saw this place as emblematic, a balcony looking out into the Great Mystery. "The Celts believed their god of the underworld, Dis, inhabited this place, so it was here that they held rites pertaining to death [...]. The Romans [...] would sit and watch the sunset and swear they could hear the hissing sound as the fiery sun sank into the ocean. [...] Christians saw it as the last stop of the journey in earthly life" (Mitchell-Lanham 2015, 42).

Not far from the *Finis Terrae*, Roman general Decimus Junius Brutus Gallaecus (c. 180 BCE–113 BCE), while on an expedition (138 BCE) in extreme northwestern Spain to subdue the locals, found that his legionnaires refused to cross the Limia River because, being in such close proximity to the Atlantic, they took it to be the River Lethe (λήθη), one of the five rivers of Hades, the realm of the dead. Its name means "oblivion" or "forgetfulness," for once souls crossed over its waters they lost all memory. It appears that none of the soldiers would budge until the general himself grasped a sword and a standard and went across, calling back to some of his officers by name to prove that he still had all his wits about him (García Cuartango, *ABC*, May 9, 2022).

Thus, for each culture in its own way, the Atlantic was a realm where the imagination could be set free, that is to say, it could populate the vast watery spaces with beings that existed and events that played out well beyond the boundaries of everyday experience. The ocean could not be tilled, a tax could not be imposed on its waves, cattle could not be counted on it, it could not be turned into property, a church could not be built on it to dictate doctrine nor a lord's castle to protect privileges; consequently, its most distinguishing attribute was that one essential, fundamental nourishment for the imagination: unconditionality.

Medieval imagination could move more freely the more disengaged it was from conventional objectifications and parochial proscription. Seemingly, the Atlantic presented opportunities for disengagement from social, economic, political, and religious constraints, being as it was an exceptional space, unbound and thoroughly oblivious to human requirements. Perhaps because of its impartial, unbridled autonomy, the ocean was the place where the community's collective conscience ventured forth, with its seafaring heroes, in order to test its beliefs and validate their substance at an ostensibly unprejudiced, independent forum. Finding Otherworld realms or the Isle of the Blest in the unconditioned impartiality of the alien vastness confirmed the truth and legitimacy of communal dogmata, showing that collective beliefs were not the product of compulsion, but were arrived at because they reflected universal truths.

Accordingly, the Atlantic was an unbiased geography that even Christianizing characters like Saint Brendan entered to bring back belief-validating news from the otherworld, boldly breaching the conventional boundaries between this life and the next. And while Dante, eight centuries later, will enter an otherworld that is to be found only in books and in the preaching of priests, Brendan enters a place that can be seen, touched, and feared as a *physical* presence.

Such places contest the overwhelming irrationality of the world by offering a window into the supernatural and by suggesting a measure of design and method to the universe. This allows the individual to function within a more purposeful, orderly communal environment, be it nurtured by the god Crom Cruach or by Patrick's God. Adjusting the pagan liminal spaces –in land or at sea– to align with the new religion of the Cross was, arguably, one of the church's greatest accomplishments in Ireland.

So it is that liminal spaces–thresholds between this and the "other" world–are essential to human fulfillment and peace of mind, be it that of a pagan or a Christian individual. Beyond the individual, communal ethea are supported by the collective acceptance of the mysterious power of these purposeful thresholds. This is important because prescientific minds *must* perceive the world through a "myth lens" and accept answers to "why" questions that cannot be empirically verified. But because the human intellect always demands answers, in the early Middle Ages questions regarding existence could only be answered tolerably when cryptic descriptions were proposed for something –life, the universe– that remained a mystery. These solutions, exemplified by liminal spaces, made it possible to have practical relations with the supernatural, so they were more functional than analytical: they were uncritical purposive constructs.

Myth and syncretism: *immrama, echtrai,* and visions

The study of the Atlantic Ocean's exceptionality and its role as mythical space in medieval seaside communities will be enriched by considering those Irish voyage and adventure tales called *immrama* and *echtrai*. An analysis of the extant, syncretic forms they eventually took will also focus our attention on the wider process of Christianization for which these stories provide a window. The myth substance that makes these tales unique–despite later homiletic accretions– is very different from that of the vision literature with which Christian holy men, Irish or continental European, depicted God's precincts. Herein I will analyze their characteristics and mark their differences.

Immrama (from the Irish: *iomramh* or "voyage") are a type of Old Irish tales that recount a hero's Atlantic Ocean journey to the otherworld. While they were set down after the Christianization of Ireland and have Christian features, they–beyond doubt–have their origins in the pagan imagination that produced early Irish mythology.

The emphasis in these stories is on the adventures of seafaring heroes as they search for the otherworld in Atlantic islands far to the west of Ireland. The hero sets out on his voyage on a quest to fulfill his destiny, making landfall on diverse fantastic islands inhabited by truly bizarre beings before reaching his destination. Some return to Ireland, while some do not.

> [The *immrama*] are all frame-tales. That is to say that the "rowing about," as one may literally interpret the term *immram*, provides the means by which all manner of incidents may be secured and joined within the story. In this kind of tale, episodes may be added or subtracted at will, as long as the frame itself is not damaged, Occasional internal inconsistencies sometimes reveal that such processes of addition and subtraction have indeed been at work. In the frame one must expect to find motivation for the events of the tale, a satisfactory conclusion, and some material which will link very clearly with specific episodes within the narration of the circumnavigation itself. (Dumville 1976, 75)

The *immrama* are not to be confused with the *echtrai* or "adventure." Both types of stories tell of a hero's journey to an "otherworld" that might be a Christian paradise, a dreamland, the land of the gods, or a utopia. The *echtrai* (pl. of *echtrae*) are from the seventh century, while the earliest *immram* is from the eighth century. Perhaps because of their earlier dates, *echtrai* contain less Christian and more pagan elements than the subsequent *immrama*, so where the *echtrai* improve comprehension of the pagan pantheon and the paradises they inhabit, the *immrama* have undergone a more thorough process of Christianization, their pagan features compelled to function in concert with the exigencies of the new faith. In the *echtrai*, the hero only travels to one location and can disembark in the otherworld without ever having given a reason for undertaking the voyage, whereas in an *immram* the protagonist always has reasons, as well as numerous adventures on many islands.

> There are four extant *immrama*, variously made up of prose and poetry or a mixture thereof: *Immram Brain Maic Febail* (Voyage of Bran son of Febal), *Immram curaig Maíle Dúin* (Voyage of Máel-dúin's curach), *Immram Snédgusa ocus Maic Riagla* (Voyage of Snédgus and Mac Ríagla), and *Immram curaig Úa Corra* (Voyage of the Sons of Uí Chorra). The

surviving versions of the tales range very widely in date. *Immram Brain maic Febail*, on linguistic grounds datable to the eighth century, stands very early in the development of narrative literature in the Irish language. *Immram curaig Úa Corra*, in its extant form, is dated near to the end of the middle ages, though there can be little doubt that a much earlier version of this story existed: the Uí Chorra are commemorated in the "Litany of Pilgrim Saints" (c. 800 C.E.) and the tale itself is referred to in medieval lists of titles of Irish tales. The older versions of *Immram curaig Maíle Dúin* (prose) and *Immram Snédgusa ocus Maic Riagla* (poetry) date from around the ninth and tenth centuries, respectively. The medieval tale lists also imply the past existence of at least one other *immram*, which is now lost, concerning Muirchertach Mac Erc – whose surviving "death tale" (*aided*) includes a dream voyage episode. (Duffy 2005, 363)

In addition, while the *echtrai* frequently contain a journey to an otherworld, the Atlantic is not, like in the *immrama*, the exclusive destination. They may involve sea voyages like in *Echtra Condla*, a journey underneath a lake as in *Echtrae Laegairi*, or into a fairy mound (Sidhe) as in *Echtrae Nerai*. Moreover, the *echtrai* might not incorporate a journey at all, but instead, involve contact with otherworldly creatures. In *Echtrae Nerai*, the hero Nera experiences prophetic visions while contemplating a hanged man, while in *Echtra Mac nEchach Muid-medóin* (The adventures of the sons of Eochaid Muigmedóin), the hero Níall (Níall Noígíallach of the Nine Hostages, d. 405 C.E., ancestor of the Uí Néill dynasties that dominated the northern half of Ireland from the sixth to the tenth century) becomes High King of Ireland by kissing a hag that was guarding a well (Koch 2006, 646).

Dumville (1976, 76) compiled a list of extant *echtrai* as follows:

Echtra Condla (or Echtrae Chonnlai, adventure of Conle)
Echtra Cormaic maic Airt i Tir Tairngiri
Echtrae Laegairi maic Crimthann
Echtrae Nerai (aka Táin Bó Aingen)
Ectra Airt maic Cuinn
Echtrae mac nEchach Mugmedoin

He added tales not titled *Echtrae*, but considered as such:

Baile in Scáil
The Five Lugaids
Tochmarc Emire (*The Wooing of Emer*)
Serglige Con Chulainn
Siaburcharpat Con Culaind
Imram Bran

In addition, he lists 17 other titles of *echtrai* that have been lost and three visits to the otherworld undertaken by the hero Cuchulainn that can be considered part of the *echtrae* milieu: *Forfess Fer Fálgae, Fled Bricrenn ocus Loinges mac nDuil Dermait,* and *Compert Con Culainn.*

In their search for their societies' otherworlds, the Irish heroes join a long list of voyagers on the same quest. Most non-Irish journeys exhibit patterns that are very different from those seen in the *imramma* and *echtrai.* This tells us not only that physical and conceptual encounters with the neighboring Atlantic contributed to essential processes of cultural development and learning, but also that Ireland's most ancient archetypes emerged in relative isolation from the classical world. In the subsequent periods of cultural accretion, classical models provided features that Irish storytellers and compilers unconsciously applied to their stories.

In those otherworld precincts in the Atlantic that are visited by *immrama* and *echtrai* heroes, we find archetypes that can be classified as 1- islands of delight, where we may include the islands of women, 2- islands of belligerence, 3- islands of Christian edification, many inhabited by hermits while others offer visions of heaven and hell, 4- islands inhabited by monsters and prodigies, and 5- islands inhabited by people who are all identical.

Regarding the first type, the islands of delight, Nutt offers the following description:

> [In the overseas otherworld] the magic land lies across the western main, it is marked by every form of natural beauty, it possesses every form of natural riches, abundance of animals, of fish, of birds, of fruit; its inhabitants are beauteous, joyful; a portion of the land is dwelt in by women alone; all earthly ills, both physical and moral, are absent; in especial, age brings neither decay, nor death, nor diminution of the joy of life; love brings neither strife, nor satiety, nor remorse. The lord of the land is Manannan (Bran) or Boadag (Connla); its inhabitants may or do summon mortals thither, alluring them by the magic music of the fairy branches of its trees, or by the magic properties of its inexhaustively satisfying fruit. Time passes there with supernatural rapidity (Bran), the mortal who has once penetrated there may not return unscathed to earth (Bran; the last trait is probably implied in Connla). (In Löffler 1983, 121)

The names of the Atlantic islands visited by the ancient Irish seafaring heroes offer a glimpse into the features of the Celtic otherworld: In *The Voyage of Bran (Immram Bran)*, for example, the hero visits many fantastic islands to the west as well as diverse spaces in Ireland itself (which for the Celts was their fantastic island home in the Atlantic), some of which can be recognized (=) as real places:

Aircthech, 'Bountiful Land'
Cíuin, 'Gentle Land'
Emain (Abhlach) = Emne, the island home of Manannán mac Lir; the Isle of Man
Ildathach, 'Many-Coloured Land'
Íle, = Islay, in Scotland
Imchíuin, 'Very Gentle Land'
Inis Subai, 'Island of Joy'
Line-mag = Líne = Mag Line, Moylinny, a plain extending from Lough Neagh to near Carrickfergus, Co. Antrim; probably co-extensive with the deanery of Moylinny; the townland Moylinny, Moylinny, in the parish of Antrim, Co. Antrim, preserves the name of this plain
Loch Ló, not identified, seems near Senlabor
(Loch Febail) = Lough Foyle, Lough Foyle, (named after Febal, father of Bran), between Co. Donegal and Co. Derry
Mag Arcatnél, 'Silver-Cloud Plain'
Mag Findarcat, 'White-Silver Plain'
Mag Meld, 'Pleasant, or Happy Plain'
Mag Mon, 'Plain of Sports'
Mag Réin, 'Plain of the Sea'
Senlabor, glossed as 'dún' (a stronghold) = seems near Loch Ló
Srub Brain, Stroove = a townland, and point, beside Lough Foyle (Loch Febail), south of Inishowen Head in the North-East of Co. Donegal
Tír na mBan = Tír na nÓg 'Land of Women,' see Emain (Abhlach)
Irish Sagas Online 2022, n.p.)

Several other stories also incorporate fantastic islands and realms that resemble those visited by Bran, and as in Bran's story, they are offered not as "other" worlds that exist only in the imagination, but as a part of *this* world, landscapes where the hero –at times a historical individual–enters physically:

A [...] problem in employing the modern term 'otherworld' in critical parlance arises, in many cases, from the underlying assumptions that the definition of the otherworld is predicated on the question of ontology: a literary world is 'other' because it is 'unreal' or non-existent outside the realm of the imagination. This is why scholars have readily dubbed such sites as the islands encountered by Saint Brendan and the Earthly Paradise as 'otherworlds' even though they were widely believed to lie within the earth's geography in the Middle Ages and, indeed, appear on numerous medieval maps. (Byrne 2016, 10)

It is important to keep this in mind when we begin comparing *immrama* and *echtrai* voyages to the "otherworld" with their classical counterparts, as the classic world's journeys rarely involve long sea voyages where the hero –very much alive and exercising all his faculties–encounters a myriad of strange islands with bizarre beings populating them.

An important characteristic of extant *immrama* and *echtrai* texts, one that will be on view throughout this work, is their syncretic nature. Their original world made up of a single, two-dimensional reality, a world in which the individual could sail into a supernatural dimension and find himself in an environment free from the constraints of time and mortality, one where he could freely interact with supernatural beings, was invaded by Christian dogma. This dogma interrupted archetypal signs and codes, and their original elements, valued for their links to ancestral practices, were reconditioned to promote the new religion. In the new Christianizing environment, pagan texts acquired a functional purpose: they contained critically significant and active cultural discourses to which Irish audiences still had favorable response patterns. Before Christians got their hands on it, that pagan reality was expressed in ways that showed how human beings, free from established dogmatic prescriptions, interacted with another dimension of reality, different from but not disconnected from their material dimension. The new masters of Ireland would change that.

The process of Christianization saw proselytizers redesign the journey to that diverse dimension in the Atlantic as an analog for a journey of spiritual improvement; those adventures became a pilgrimage to obtain deliverance of the soul from sin and its consequences. It is safe to say that, because of the continuing relevance of pagan mythical substance, it would have been problematic for proselytizers to ignore it in their efforts to articulate an understanding of Jesus among the pagan inhabitants of the ocean seaboard. Consequently, the church's lexicon and cultural frame of reference in Ireland were, to an unparalleled degree, unlike those of its earlier endeavors. Considering the unapologetic syncretism of their early texts, it seems that proselytizers were unperturbed by the fact that the foundation upon which they were building a Christian community, at the end of the world on the shores of the Atlantic, was made up of material vastly different from, and even discordant with their familiar Greek and Latin traditions. This seeming lack of concern is likely due to the fact that there was a general acceptance of the necessity to build upon a strong traditional myth foundation that was too well-established to uproot.

But moving between such disparate conventional attitudes regarding reality is not merely a matter of rendering images and intellections from one cultural cosmos to another in a different register, as a culture is not conceptually unbiased. Events and images portrayed in cultural products are the consequence of a definite, biased manner of conceptualizing reality, and appropriating those products by embedding dogma and rerouting images clearly complicates the meaning. This complication is the result of the persistence of pagan intellections in Christian syncretic works.

As an example of the syncretic nature of extant early Irish literature, we might speak of "The Buried Giant of Clonmacnoise," a story that dates from around the tenth century. In it, a giant woman dressed in green (a version of the pagan world's green woman, wood wife, wood maid, and skoggra) was spotted crying by a poet, and when asked the source of her distress she responded that her husband had just died and had been buried in the cemetery next to a monastery. A first inquiry found a body of a man no less than fifteen feet in length buried face down and surrounded by a great amount of green birch branches. He had all the marks of having died in battle. The next day, when curious people dug into the grave, they found that the body had disappeared. The intersection of the pagan supernatural (green woman, giant, type of burial, vanishing body) and the Christian environment (monastery, monks) was a sign of the persistent need for pagan material that allowed intelligible communication in this specific cultural environment.

Another example is the "*Tochmarc Becfola* (The Wooing of Becfola), a story of the Historical Cycle whose oldest extant version is in the *Yellow Book of Lecan*. It is the tale of the Irish king Diarmait mac Aeda Sláine's (d. 665) love for Becfola, an otherworldly woman who journeys in a chariot from the west (the Atlantic) to the royal court in Tara to marry the king:

> It was once upon a time when Aedh Sláine's son Dermot enjoyed Ireland's royal rule, his fosterling Crimthann mac Aedh being with him as a pledge from them of Leinster. He and Crimthann his alumnus, taking with them their various weapons and one single lad, went of a day to áth truim. They saw a lone woman in a chariot come out of the west and across the ford. Fairer she was than any one of the whole world's women. Dermot enquired: "whence art thou come, woman?" "Not from far," she answered. "What makes thee to be alone?" "I am in search of wheaten grain," said she. "Thou shalt find such with me," said Dermot. "We refuse it not," said the woman. Thereupon he conveyed her to Tara, and she shared his comfortable bed. (s.v. *The Wooing of Becfola*, n.d.)

In this story, the otherworld isle of Inis Fedaig and the island monastery of Devenish (modern Devenish Island, in Lower Lough Erne, County Fermanagh) are "revealed to be aspects of the same place" (Carey 2021, 26). This demonstrates that, in Ireland, it was impractical to extract the pagan otherworld from the message, so the pagan sacred place is repurposed and given Christian significance. Perhaps because of this imperative, there seems to have been little taste for an uncompromised harmony with Rome on the shores of the Atlantic, an upshot of which was the acclimatization, perhaps even subversion of the missionaries' intended message. Consequently, the developing Celtic Church began conceptualizing Christianity in step with local interpretations; these manifested in practices like the different systems for determining the dates for Easter, the distinctive methods of penance, and the "popularity of going into 'exile for Christ'" (Corning, 2006, 17) that would be expected of a culture steeped in pagan traditions of supernatural seafaring.

In contrast with the journeys of the Celtic imagination, otherworld vision literature, which was an important genre for the better part of the Middle Ages (sixth–thirteenth centuries), was also significant in ancient and classical culture. Rarely involving the physical journeys that were common in Atlantic seaboard tales, these stories were constructed using formulaic patterns that described the experiences of a person that traveled to the otherworld in a vision, dream, or near-death state. A guide was almost always present to explain everything that was experienced by the "traveler."

"Vision of the otherworld" stories were a popular subject in Jewish apocryphal literature. In the *Book of Enoch* (fourth century BCE), for example, the protagonist is taken by a strong wind up to Heaven, where the Archangel Michael takes him on a tour of Hell and Paradise. In the Bible, Elijah is spirited up to Heaven: "As they were walking along and talking together, suddenly a chariot of fire and horses of fire appeared and separated the two of them, and Elijah went up to heaven in a whirlwind" (2 Kings 2:11, NIV). Plato (428/427 or 424/423 BCE–348/347 BCE) has his *Republic*, for example, end (10.614–10.621) with the story of Er, a bad man who dies in battle but, when the bodies of the dead warriors are collected, it is found that his remains have not decomposed. As his body is being readied for the funeral pyre, Er revives and begins to tell a strange story about his journey to the afterlife. Perhaps the essential part of the tale is that in which judges sit in judgment of the souls that come their way: the good ones follow a path that leads upwards to a place of beauty and contentment, while the bad go down to a place of despair where they are condemned to pay for their wicked deeds. The message is that the soul is immortal, and the individual will be judged in the afterlife.

Cicero (106 BCE–43 BCE) gives us the *Somnium Scipionis*, or *Dream of Scipio* (*De re publica* VI 9 - 29), where he tells of a sort of out-of-body experience had by Roman general Scipio Aemilianus two years before his army destroyed Carthage in 146 BCE. In it, Scipio is visited by his dead grandfather Scipio Africanus, who tells him of his future deeds as he looks down on Carthage from a place full of stars and records the nine celestial spheres, of which the earth is the innermost and heaven the highest. Besides restating the basic items of the cosmological models developed by Plato, Eudoxos, Aristotle, Ptolemy, Copernicus, and the like, the story emphasizes the great rewards obtainable after death by the loyal Roman soldier who dies in the line of duty.

Plutarch (46 CE–c. 119 CE) concludes his *Moralia*, with the dialogue *De Sera Numinis Vindicta*, or *On the Late Vengeance of the Deity*, a conversation that takes place after an imaginary lecture by Epicurus. A protestation is raised regarding providence, specifically that the postponement of punishment incites the offender to keep pursuing his evil ways while at the same time it discourages the offended party. In response, it is argued that the god, in his delay, aims to let bitterness towards the criminal subside and, more importantly, give him time to repent his actions and save his soul. The composition closes with the long story of the wicked Aridaeus (later known as Thespesius), who had a fall and died but woke up three days later upon his funeral pyre to reveal the many portents witnessed by his soul on its out-of-body excursion through the other world. "He found himself in something like the midst of the sea but really among the stars where the souls of the dead were ascending like bubbles. Here he learned about divine justice" (Patch 1970, 81). The essential message is that the afterlife has a framework of authority designed to punish bad people. Back to life, his name is changed to Thespesius, and he improves his behavior.

The marvels witnessed by Thespesius in the afterlife have a spiritual, admonitory purpose and have scant structural analogies with the transcendental prodigies of the *immrama* and *echtrai*. The Greek otherworld sightseer sees "a great bottomless chasm, which was fringed within with 'pleasing verdure of various herbs and plants with all sorts of flowers and strong perfume.' Later he came upon a 'prodigious standing goblet, into which several rivers discharged themselves. [...] Also, he saw various lakes, one of boiling gold, one of cold lead, and one of iron 'very scaly and rugged'" (Patch 1970, 81). Plutarch owes much of this story to Plato's Myth of Er, which constitutes the epilogue of his *Republic*. But the difference is that, in Er's vision, evildoer Aridaeus is eternally tortured— scourged and tied up bent over spikes to discourage others from performing evil deeds–and there is no hope of salvation for him; Plutarch's Aridaeus (Thespesius) is effectively saved by his after-death vision.

Another example of classical otherworld excursions is in Plutarch's *De genio Socratis*, where Timarchus goes into the cave of Trophonius, son of Apollo and a mortal mother, who had inherited the gift of prophecy from his father and whose oracle was on a hillside near Lebadeia in Boeotia.

> As soon as he entered, a thick darkness surrounded him; then, after he had prayed, he lay a long while upon the ground, but was not certain whether awake or in a dream, only he imagined that a smart stroke fell upon his head, and that through the parted sutures of his skull his soul fled out... (Plutarch 1874, 407)

Timarchus does enter a sea of sorts, the favorite haunt of the Irish heroes, but with the difference that the Irish –it is important to reiterate– are portrayed as alive and in command of their senses when they enter the Atlantic otherworld, while Timarchus is in a cave, in a trance: "looking up he saw no earth, but certain islands shining with a gentle fire, which interchanged colors according to the different variation of the light, innumerable and very large, unequal, but all round" (Plutarch 1874, 408). Very different from the endless Atlantic of the Irish, the sea where Plutarch's islands are found has the characteristics of a landlocked body of water, with two rivers emptying into it from opposite directions:

> Into this sea were two entrances, by which it received two opposite fiery rivers, running in with so strong a current, that it spread a fiery white over a great part of the blue sea. This sight pleased him very much; but when he looked downward, there appeared a vast chasm, round, as if he had looked into a divided sphere, very deep and frightful, full of thick darkness, which was every now and then troubled and disturbed. Thence a thousand howlings and bellowings of beasts, cries of children, groans of men and women, and all sorts of terrible noises reached his ears; but faintly, as being far off and rising through the vast hollow; and this terrified him exceedingly. (Plutarch 1874, 408)

Timarchus has entered the cave seeking knowledge: "A little while after, an invisible thing spoke thus to him: Timarchus, what dost thou desire to understand? And he replied, Every thing; for what is there that is not wonderful and surprising?" (Plutarch 1874, 408). To this the "invisible thing" replies with a long list of contemporary assumptions about the world they inhabited. In the end, Timarchus finds himself at the entrance to the cave with a considerable headache:

> The voice continuing no longer, Timarchus (as he said) turned about to discover who it was that spoke; but a violent pain, as if his skull had been pressed together, seized his head, so that he lost all sense and understanding; but in a little while recovering, he found himself in the entrance of the cave, where he at first lay down. (Plutarch 1874, 412)

Many other well-known journeys of the classical world's heroes to the otherworld are not portrayed as physical journeys through *this* world, as they are in *immrama* and *echtrai*, but rather as visions or trance-induced experiences. The fourth century *Visio sancti Pauli* (The Apocalypse of Paul), considered part of the New Testament apocrypha, tells of Paul the Apostle's vision of Heaven and Hell. This conceptual voyage is a Christian morals pamphlet that has the Apostle observing the death and judgment of an evil man and the death and judgment of a righteous man, with the verdict befitting the moral makeup of each one.

It must be noted that distinctly Christian Irish voyages to the otherworld are also portrayed as visions, but some of them exhibit traits from Celtic mythology that cannot be concealed from the substantial Christianizing material. A case in point is *The Vision of Adamnán* (Fís Adamnáin), a work variously dated between the eighth and the eleventh centuries that is found in the *Book of the Dun Cow* (*Lebor na hUidre* [twelfth century]) and the *Speckled Book* (*An Leabhar Breac* [1408–11]); its authorship is unknown. On the Feast of Saint John the Baptist, Adamnán is taken to the otherworld, where his psychopomp (spirit who guides the souls of the dead to the otherworld) takes him on a guided tour of Heaven, of a midway space, and of Hell, the last of which is in a direction reminiscent of *immrama* and *echtrae* otherworlds: West (Gardiner 1993, 23). Heaven, described as a "bright land of fair weather," is a place whose description reminds the reader of Mag Mell (Magh Meall, the delightful plain), a Celtic pleasure paradise located on an island in the Atlantic far to the west of Ireland that was visited by several Irish heroes and monks, protagonists whose adventures form the thematic mainstay of Irish Atlantic otherworld voyages.

Adamnán describes the throne room as a place where God sits accompanied by three birds who sing and celebrate the eight [canonical] hours, praising and adoring the Lord (Gardiner 1993, 23). The birds in God's throne room are *immramic*, substratal remnants of ancient Celtic traditions.

In the Celtic otherworld context, birds frequently embody spiritual beings or function as heralds. In the *immram The Voyage of the Sons of Uí Chorra*, for example,

> The Lord is introduced, seated on the Throne, and bird-flocks of angels making music to Him, and the idea as there presented might stand for a development of the Dagda myth, where the god sits beside his magic apple-trees and vat of ale, and the birds of the Tír Tairngire sing to him. (Boswell 1908, 183)

A member of the supernatural race of beings in ancient Irish mythology called the Tuatha Dé Danann, the Dagda is a principal god in the pantheon of pagan Ireland. The *Tír Tairngire*, vaguely remembered in Adamnán's vision, is a Celtic paradise or Land of Promise; both Dagda and the *Tír Tairngire* supply elements upon which to describe the Christian God and His Paradise. The Christian Paradise and the *Tír Tairngire* of *echtrai* and *immrama* voyages are conflated in St. Brendan's grand excursion and in many other tales:

> St Brendan is seeking [the Tír Tairngire] in his *Navigatio*, and Cormac mac Airt visits the Fountain of Knowledge in *Echtra Cormaic*. Manannán takes his three-day-old son Mongán here to gain otherworldly knowledge; the latter stays for many years. The youthful Ciabhán is taken here but, according to some texts, elopes with the beautiful Clídna. After her adultery here with Gaidiar, Manannán's son, Bé Chuma is expelled. The

Tuatha Dé Danann bring the rowan tree from Tír Tairngire. In *Echtrae Airt meic Cuinn* [The Adventure of Art Son of Conn], the rulers of Tír Tairngire are Dáire and Rígru Rosclethan, called 'sinless' because they have intercourse only to produce their otherworldly son Ségda Sáerlabraid. (*Oxford Reference* s.v. Tír Tairngire, 2022)

Additional elements from ancient Irish mythology are evident: the *Vision of Adamnán*'s throne-space shows similarities with the immram *The Voyage of Snédgus and Mac Ríagla*: "A conception similar in kind, though different in form, is apparent in the dún with a hundred doors, and at each of them an altar, and a priest celebrating mass thereon, in the *Voyage of Snédgus and Mac Ríagla*" (Boswell 1908, 184n).

The Vision of Adamnán demonstrates how Irish otherworld vision texts can contain indigenous material and still deliver a convincing scriptural message. As the vision text encounters and absorbs social and cultural habits that flourished in pre-Christian Ireland, its absorbent complaisance casts its author's aesthetic choices in sharp relief: Faced with the prospect of offering an "imported" message to his community, he weaves filaments of familiar substance into the fabric of his vision, making it more congenial to the recently converted Irish (and very probably to himself as well).

While not denying that this text is thoroughly immersed in the mainstream of western European Christian culture, as can be perceived in the coherence of its biblical and apocryphal imagery, in *The Vision of Adamnán* the symbolic material from the earlier communal substratum is not ornamental but rather reveals implicit deep-seated practices, observable more clearly in the narrative habits of the island's older, pagan traditions. Incidentally, there is an awareness of these enduring cultural substrata that has survived to our times: In the film *The Field* (1990), for example, an Irish priest tells a visiting American businessman that Christianity is merely a thin veneer that has been painted over the Irish.

The *immrama* and *echtrai* texts, several of which will be analyzed in the following chapters, are more thematically bound to that earlier communal ethos than Irish vision literature. Having their origins in a more distant past, they resisted the impact of what was an alien, eastern Mediterranean religion's proselytizing efforts more effectively, so they provide more fertile ground for analyzing this Atlantic community's spiritual relationship with the watery *lusus naturae* that surrounds them. Predating the cosmopolitan exchange that brought Christianity to these ancient seaside communities, they–especially the *immrama*–are the ideational voyages of a collective consciousness that ventures into the unknown, symbolized by the Atlantic Ocean, to face its ontological fears and energize myths that support prescriptive communal perspectives on reality, life, and the afterlife. Despite subsequent Christianizing accretions, the researcher can see these adventures into the Atlantic otherworld as the result of the efforts of a community to frame its non-Christian, subjective reality and document its members' interactions with the physical world, a domain whose substance and phenomena they could only construe through collective myths such as those embodied in these stories.

I'd like to add here that when speaking about the communal perspectives of Atlantic seaside communities, I am not referring to psychological perspective; communal perspectives, communal mindsets, and collective myths have an essentially political character that allows the researcher to analyze shared social experience and subjective "truths" that are endemic to a particular group of people. They are tools that help us understand the energies that produce sets of subjectively formulated and negotiated definitions regarding reality. Understanding *immrama* and *echtrai* as repositories for *communal* mindsets, allows us to recognize how and why the community that produced them agrees on fundamental questions of existence.

In short, *immrama* and *echtrai* offer a glimpse into the way seaside communities fostered interpretive frameworks and promoted a structured, collective consciousness through which their members understood the world. Christian proselytizers transformed their signification system by altering the meaning of a context that, despite their efforts, remained structurally stable. On the other hand, subsequent vision literature is Christian in its inception, yet incorporates pagan elements to expedite a Scriptural message intended for a community still steeped in its previous ethea.

Myth and the identity politics of medieval travel

0.1. Circe turns Odysseus's companions into animals.

From Giovanni Boccaccio's book *De claris mulieribus*, 1360-1374.

The next harbors in our portolan chart are *immrama*, they will help us understand the importance of identity in the Middle Ages, how critical it was to belong to a group, and how meaning was attached to membership by composing myths of fantastic voyages into the Atlantic.

"An Irish knight named Maelduin [Máel Dúin], set forth early in the eighth century to seek round the seas for his father's murderers" (*Sacred Texts*, "Maelduin," n.d., 96). Thus begins *The Voyage of Máel Dúin* (original c. seventh century), whose hero, Maelduin, is the son of a lord named Ailill Edgebattle, who was killed by pillagers from over the sea who attacked his home and burned the church of Dubhcluain with lord Ailill inside. Maelduin's mother was able to escape and reach the King of Arran's abode, where she gave baby Maelduin as a foster child to the Queen. Eventually turning into a strapping young man, Maelduin learns of his true origin and decides to sail into the Atlantic in search of his father's murderers.

As far as the pillagers' actions, the question is: Why go to the trouble of transporting Ailill all the way to the church in order to burn him inside? Why not just run a sword through him as they plunder his home? The reason, I believe, is that the church is a symbol of identity, so that its burning by people who do not share in that identity, who come from the identity-less ocean, can be offered as a direct attack on the identitary community to which Ailill, Maelduin, and the story's compiler belonged. Because it is likely that the story has a pagan source, the church burning must be seen as a Christian accretion that redirected an existing tale of revenge and identity consolidation, as this was the story of a pagan community securing its coherence by demonizing groups that existed outside its perimeter. Evidently, groups are given consistency by the pressure exerted on their borders by the "other," by people who are "different," dangerous, and necessarily inadequate. When Circe turns Odysseus's men into animals, for example, she is essentially excluding them from their identitary sphere by virtue of their newly acquired "difference." It is significant that in so many myths and stories the "other" has its home in the Atlantic, an alien landscape where the most bizarre beings can exist.

Among the many exotic islands where Maelduin and his companions make landfall in their quest for the killers, one is of special interest in this regard, as it contains a warning against falling under the spell of a different identitary community (apostasy). This contrastive community is clearly alluded to in a particular island where every islander not only looks similar but also acts in the same manner. They all, in short, share identitary traits that identify them as "not us" and therefore undesirable:

> On another island they found many human beings, black in color and raiment, and always bewailing. Lots were cast, and another of Maelduin's

foster brothers was sent on shore. He at once joined the weeping crowd, and did as they did. Two others were sent to bring him back, and both shared his fate, falling under some strange spell. Then Maelduin sent four others, and bade them look neither at the land nor at the sky; to wrap their mouths and noses with their garments, and not breathe the island air; and not to take off their eyes from their comrades. In this way the two who followed the foster brother on shore were rescued, but he remained behind. (*Sacred Texts*, "Maelduin," n.d., 102)

The Voyage of the Hui Corra (*Immram curaig húa Corra*, or Voyage of the Sons of Uí Chorra) offers another example of the use of Atlantic myth narratives to provide stronger doctrinal reinforcements to identitary groups, in this case, the fledgling Irish Christian community. An obvious modification of a pagan text, it is one of three extant *immrama*, the ancient Irish voyage tales. This is the story of the three sons of Connall ua Corra, a landowner of Connacht, who before his sons' birth had made a bargain with the Devil. The three sons developed into the leaders of an infamous band of outlaws who robbed churches:

> Then those sons arose, and they took their weapons and went to Tuam. And they wrecked and burnt the place, and committed robbery and outrageous brigandage throughout the province of Connaught upon churches and clerics, so that the evil and horror of their robbery was heard of throughout the four quarters of Ireland altogether, till the end of a year they dealt in that wise, so that during that time they destroyed one more than half of the churches of Connaught. (*CELT: Corpus of Electronic Texts* 2009, 31)

But in time they were struck by a vision and were rehabilitated:

> Then came the Hui Corra to the place wherein the cleric dwelt, and they determined not to kill the cleric, nor to burn the stead, until the night should come, and the kine and cattle of the stead should come to their byres and their proper places. The cleric comes with them to the stead, and he perceived that they had this secret intention, and he put them into the fair-sided, shining silver, and food and ale were taken to them, so that they became exhilarated and mirthful. Afterwards, couches and lofty beds were spread for them.
> Then a deep slumber and sleep fell upon Lochan, and a marvelous vision has shown to him, to wit, he was taken to see Heaven and Hell. And then he awoke. The other two also awoke and said: 'Let us go,' say they, 'to wreck and destroy the stead.' 'Meseems,' quoth Lochan, 'that is not that is meetest for us to do. For evil is the lord whom we have served,

and good is the lord on whom we have hitherto wrought robbery and brigandage. (*CELT: Corpus of Electronic Texts* 2009, 33-34)

Through an otherworld vision, one that strongly encourages compliance within the Christian identitary community ("Heaven and Hell"), the contrite brothers now re-enter the identitary group that they heretofore had beset. They then traveled to the monastery of St. Finnian of Clonard (470–549), who commanded they restore all the churches they had destroyed. In a final act of penitence, they heeded the suggestion of St. Coman of Kinvara, keeper of the last church they restored, and set out on an Atlantic Ocean voyage on a currach (small boat) with five other travelers, a bishop, a priest, a deacon, a musician and the shipwright who built the currach. It is an ingress into the great mystery:

> One day, when they came forth over the edge of the haven, they were contemplating the sun as he went past them westwards, and they marveled much concerning his course. 'And in what direction goes the sun,' say they, 'when he goes under the sea?' (*CELT: Corpus of Electronic Texts*, 2009, 39)

As this story shows, identitary collectives are possessed of a collection of symbolic assets that can be manipulated as devices to reinforce the boundaries of a shared identity. The specific individuals that embark on this sea voyage are some of these assets; they have the critical mission of assuring that the borderlines that separate the "us" from the "them" remain constant, as they represent the community's shared authority patterns (the bishop), memories (the musician), knowledge (the deacon), skills (the shipwright) and beliefs (the priest). The Irish travelers' interactions with beings and places that they encounter along the way are meant to demonstrate to the reader that Christianity (the identitary collective at work in this allegory) is based upon universal and self-evident truths.

Their imaginative ocean journey was guided only by the direction of the wind, a route that they believe was charted by God. This divinely inspired itinerary takes them from a bizarre island to an even more bizarre island, places where they happen upon diverse peoples and meet with chimerical adventures. Every step of the way serves to concoct a vast allegory of Christian morality, with embedded warnings as to the dangers of flirting with apostasy:

> Then they went on board their boat and began to row, and they were thinking whither they should go. 'Whithersoever the wind shall take us,' says the bishop. Thereafter they shipped their oars and offered themselves to God.
>
> Well then, a mighty wind drove them due westward into the ocean of the great sea. And they were forty days and forty nights on the ocean, and many various marvels were shewn to them by God.

> First there was shewn to them an island full of men aggrieving and lamenting. One of the crew went to ask tidings of the island-folk, to know what they were about. He begins to wail and lament like every one. They leave him there and rowed forth into the sea. (*CELT: Corpus of Electronic Texts* 2009, 43)

The group finally reaches the Iberian Peninsula, where they decide to live and build a church. Finally, the myth has the bishop leaving the settlement and going to Rome, accompanied by one of the other travelers. From Rome, they return to Ireland and relate the story of their adventures, where it is eventually written down in the form of a poem.

The Voyage of Bran (*Immram Brain*) offers yet another example of communal identity agents going forth into the mythical landscapes of the Atlantic. Composed in the late seventh or early eighth century, it blends poetry with prose narrations known as "narrative envelopes." This *immram* has Bran fall under the spell of a strange woman who shows up at his royal house and tells of a wonderful otherworld land, Emain. He decides to sail there.

Along with the usual encounters with strange creatures and extraordinary islands, he reaches one where everyone is similar, all laughing uncontrollably. The sailor that Bran sends to reconnoiter the place becomes one of "them," to Bran's chagrin. Not knowing how to bring him back, they sail away and abandon him there:

> Thereupon Bran went from him. And he saw an island. He rows round about it, and a large host was gaping and laughing. They were all looking at Bran and his people, but would not stay to converse with them. They continued to give forth gusts of laughter at them. Bran sent one of his people on the island. He ranged himself with the others, and was gaping at them like the other men of the island. He kept rowing round about the island. Whenever his man came past Bran, his comrades would address him. But he would not converse with them, but would only look at them and gape at them. The name of this island is the Island of Joy. Thereupon they left him there. (*Sacred Texts*, "Bran," n.d., 30-31)

The unfortunate sailor has become one of "them."

Stories of magical voyages like these make the modern reader reflect upon the contrast between the modern idea of travel–the practice of tourism–as an edifying activity, and travel as edifying activity in the medieval sense. Moderns are not travelers, but passengers; we do not really travel, we do not experience the spaces *in between* home and destination, we merely *arrive*. The modern activity of traveling, at best, is intended to produce a more sensitive acquaintance with people whose ethos we do not share; at worst it is merely intended to provide a better suntanning experience. In the Middle Ages, however, travel was a vastly different pursuit, one driven by a distinctive set of animating principles. Travel accounts and geographies clearly disclose the medieval traveler's identity-bolstering mission, as these texts fundamentally grounded individuals in their own communities' constitutional ethos, nurtured communal expectations, and reinforced shared frames of mind. While this is especially true of the magical journeys described above, even accounts of real expeditions routinely focused on the more grotesque attributes of peoples and societies that the travelers encountered. The description of bizarre beings and places that were so different *from us* followed a calculated blueprint for describing the world according to the storyteller's communal ethos and, as a result, promoted cohesion and symmetry in the traveler's own identitary group.

Examples of this practice are Friar Odoric of Pordenone's account of travel to China (1330) and John Mandeville's *Travels* (c. 1357). Two centuries before them, Saxon canon and scholar Hugh of Saint Victor (1096–1141) wrote a *Descriptio Mappae Mundi* (1128–1129) that illustrates this point quite clearly. In his description of India, Saint Victor states that:

> In these regions are many marvelous monsters, if what is said is true. There are Pygmies, men a cubit tall, who live solely on the [sight of?] colors. There are enormous bulls. There are Centaurs, half-man, half-horse. There are also Icthyophages [fish eaters], who eat eels thirty feet long. There are elephants and unicorns. There are midgets. Between the Coaspim River and the Red Sea, there are Himantipodes, who walk with their feet upside down, and Manticores, ferocious quadrupeds who have the heads and faces of women. There are Cenophales, who have men's bodies and dog's heads. There are Blemii, who have [men's] bodies with no heads and eyes on their thoraxes, and Monopods, who have only one eye and only one foot apiece. (Tolan 2013, 24)

As we can surmise from this description by Hugh of Saint Victor, collective identities are contrived with the mythical descriptions of people, thought processes, and behaviors that are acceptable within their subjective perimeters, but they also depend on descriptions of bizarre *others,* as shown above, people that are not acceptable because of their discrepancies with the established norm. Such unacceptables have a critical function in the development and preservation of identitary assemblages, as they help to establish their boundaries by exerting external pressure and thereby consolidating them.

Myths based on descriptions of the identitary group as well as those of aliens and adversaries were dependent on a series of stereotypes and misconceptions that reflected the world according to meticulously calibrated frames of reference; critical constituents of those frames of reference were the travel narratives, which oftentimes depicted a bizarre *them* in explicit contrast to an idealized *us*. And while not all "others" were depicted physically as monsters, the descriptions of their practices show the marks of an ethnocentric blueprint according to which the world was conventionally described.

In the epic literature of Europe, the "going forth" of the epic heroes is a form of travel into the uncertainty of the "other's" world, and nowhere is this more evident than in the *Song of Roland*. The French heroes travel into an alien world of Muslims that needs to be brought into a particular frame of reference:

> In the great medieval French epic of the conflict between Christians and Saracens in Spain, the Chanson de Roland, the Christian poet endeavors to give his readers or, rather, listeners some idea of the Saracen religion. According to this vision, the Saracens worshipped a trinity consisting of three persons: Muhammad, the founder of their religion, and two others, both of them devils, Apollin and Tervagant. To us this seems comic, and we are amused by medieval man unable to conceive of religion or indeed of anything else except in his own image. Since Christendom worshipped its founder in association with two other entities, the Saracens also had to worship their founder, and he too had to be one of a trinity, with two demons co-opted to make up the number. (Lewis 1994, 133)

As an identity-building activity, medieval travel did not so much result in the understanding of other regions and cultures as it did in a reinforcement of the readers' identitary allegiance (*we* are not like *them*) and in the substantiation of their common spiritual convictions. In this sense, the myths generated by medieval travel narratives do not result in an expansion of the discerning glance, but in its opposite.

Critical texts show that there was a general feeling in the Middle Ages that western Europe was a besieged bastion of Christendom, that prodigious product of myth. "European Christendom might from hence [the rise of Islam] be considered as a fortified place, regularly besieged, and attacked by Mahometism. [...] Palestine had been invaded in 636, even Sicily had been ransacked in 653, and almost all of its inhabitants carried into captivity" (Otridge 1820, 177). In addition, most of Spain was lost to Christendom after 711. Partly as a consequence of these historical events, there is in the Christian Middle Ages a transvaluation of those people and places that are beyond the conventional experiential domain that turns them into a symbolic "not us," a transaction that is not meant to produce a more useful understanding of "the other" as much as a more purposive comprehension of the "us."

Medieval travel narratives and descriptions frequently reveal that travel, fantastic or otherwise, was buttressed by a genuine aspiration to know or understand the "world," but this was a world understood as "Creation." As a result, the travelers' experience was modulated by a collective ethos that caused them to observe physical reality through the thick lens of myth and communal belief. As a practical byproduct, travelers would consolidate their affiliation to their society by discerning, in the people they met, grotesque traits that were alien to the travelers' community; their gaze thus acted upon the observed geographies, animating "reality" with subjective meanings that promoted the community's ethos.

So, while fantastic travel in magical ships was often symbolic of spiritual contingencies and dilemmas (Guigemar, Galahad, Partonopeus, Trezenzonio), some of the most bizarre descriptions of the physical world (Saint-Victor, Mandeville) must be interpreted as connotative of the physical dangers that lurked out there, beyond the borders of the besieged bastion, Europe. While the bizarre creatures that are depicted may or may not actually exist, the dangers that they symbolize are real enough. Saint-Victor makes this point clearly: "In these regions are many marvelous monsters, *if what is said is true.*" Thus, when he embarks on a long description of these bizarre monsters, he is not overly worried about their actual existence (that's not the point); he is more interested in giving a formulaic depiction of that alien "beyond" inhabited by the "not us," whatever their shape may be.

Therefore, travel in both fantastic ships and wooden ships shared the characteristics of the imaginary voyage: Medieval societies needed to cast themselves as righteous protagonists in the drama of identitary conflict, as the normal, civilized cosmos in opposition to the bizarre, abnormal, deviant, alien "other" beating at the gates. Travel helped to foster social acknowledgement of collective archetypes, and it did so by modeling cross-cultural contact on Christian terms that imagined and symbolized "the other" as an aberrant version of the natural arrangement (as in the Muslim trinity in the *Song of Roland*). As such, the factual details of "the other's" aberrations were not terribly important.

Medieval sight and perception vs. modern practical judgment

As we've seen in the previous section dealing with identity, human beings do not just inertly observe the world of solid objects through the sense of sight, but also dynamically process the information obtained about those objects and their context, all the while deducing the type of interaction that might be had with them. That visual information is categorically arbitrated by systems of belief and representation, systems that make it just about impossible to see the world as it "really is." When we see a new object, incident, or creature in the world, we don't capture it in its essence, if there is such a thing, but rather interpret it using a processing system based on previous experience and mental structures of discernment. As such, human beings have a hand in creating the world that is observed; sight is not passive, but rather productive, so we see the world as a virtual image, a version of the world that has been processed through mental structures of discernment that are socially and culturally generated.

Evidently, the cultural chasm created by the passage of time serves to disconnect modern societies from pagan and early medieval ones, as we actively perceive and organize the world according to very different mental structures. Thus, I must concur here with Kant (2004, 51-57), who proposed that perception is an active organizing process, unlike the passive receptive process suggested by Locke.

Interestingly, these mental structures of discernment are created with language–written or spoken–, such that perception gained through our sense of sight is arbitrated through another sense, that of hearing, one that socializes what is perceived by sight with concoctions of the collective imagination like myth and religion. And language remains the most practical way to process what we *see* because it creates a symbolic syntax with which to arrange the objects and events of the world. Because it lends itself to arbitrary versions of reality, language, which ostensibly began as a practical tool for depicting the world we see and experience, was adapted early on to move within peremptory imaginary realms, projecting them to our ears as a concealed "reality." Visual authentication of the existence of worlds contrived by dogma is impossible, but language can negotiate the meaning of visual images and experiences so they comply with social, cultural, and homiletic prescripts. Language, because it can only make claims about truths regarding life, death, the world and our place in it, supports a parochial interpretation of the world around us. This is a defect, as we will see, acknowledged in Scripture.

Medieval minds experienced their life journey within a spiritual framework created by Scripture, that is to say, by language, for God, unlike His Creation, was quite invisible to everyone except Jesus: "No one has seen the Father except the one who is from God; only he has seen the Father" (John 6:46, NIV). Our exposure to God's truth is not through sight, but through the sense of hearing: "So then faith cometh by hearing, and hearing by the word of God" (Romans 10:19). Moreover, many incidents in human life were incompatible with any commonsensical portrayal of His handiwork (take Job, for instance). But as a glass of orange juice cannot understand calculus (even a well-educated one would give up trying after a few moments), so the human mind accepted its limitations when trying to understand the essence of God and when interacting with Creation.

Hence, mystery needed to be a significant part of the mind's *modus operandi*, as is suggested in the concept of *mysterium fidei*, the mystery of the faith, defined by the Catholic Church as mysteries or truths hidden *in* God. Human beings can only experience these truths as palpitations, barely noticeable under an otherwise unyielding shroud of faith. To only a chosen extraordinary few can the mysteries be revealed. St. Paul in *Colossians* 26-27 makes it clear:

> 26 τὸ μυστήριον τὸ ἀποκεκρυμμένον ἀπὸ τῶν αἰώνων καὶ ἀπὸ τῶν γενεῶν — νῦν δὲ ἐφανερώθη τοῖς ἁγίοις αὐτοῦ, 27 οἷς ἠθέλησεν ὁ θεὸς γνωρίσαι τί τὸ πλοῦτος τῆς δόξης τοῦ μυστηρίου τούτου ἐν τοῖς ἔθνεσιν, ὅ ἐστιν Χριστὸς ἐν ὑμῖν, ἡ ἐλπὶς τῆς δόξης:

> 26 the mystery hidden for ages and generations but now revealed to His saints. 27 To them God has chosen to make known among the Gentiles the great riches of this mystery, which is Christ in you, the hope of glory. (NIV)

Catholic theologian Nicholas of Cusa (1401–1464) writes in the sermon "Ego resuscitabo eum in novissimo die" that Christ, as the Son of God, *sees* a truth that human beings can only *hear about* in this life. Jesus's mission, then, was to have us *hear* all about it and be faithful, in other words, wait it out until we are resurrected and gain the ability to see the truth directly:

> Nos igitur id audimus in verbo Filii, quod Filius vidit. Et in hoc nota differentiam inter id, quod nos capere possumus per auditum, et inter id, quod videmus. Unde per auditum via fidei capio id, quod loqueris de civitate mihi ignota, tibi autem visu nota. Sic pergimus de auditu ad visum, de fide scilicet ad comprehensionem, et trahimur auditu ad aspirationem visus, quia alias quietamur. Et sic hic sumus audientes, ibi videntes et gustantes.

> Therefore we hear in the word of the Son that which the Son sees. And in this, note the difference between that which we can grasp through hearing, and that which we can see. Thus through hearing, by way of faith, I grasp that which you say about the city [of God], which is unknown to me, is however known to you through vision. So we progress from hearing to vision, from faith, namely, to comprehension, and through hearing we are carried to the aspiration of vision, because otherwise we may not rest. And so here we are listeners, there we are viewers and tasters. (Ziebart 2014, 239)

An understanding of the truth is only attainable in the afterlife, and then only through sight. Hearing, on which faith is based, is an edited form of experience, not as dependable as seeing, so we have to wait until we are in the afterlife to have direct exposure to the truth through sight.

But human beings are naturally curious, and they want to see the truth now. Pagan religions were mostly polytheistic, with individual gods tasked with very specific duties, so a personal relationship with a divinity that allowed the sight of all the truth in this world was problematic. To access the "truth" that was only forecast by religion, both pagans and Christians sought initiation into the mystery cults in the hope of getting a glimpse of it without giving up the ghost. Plato's philosopher who beholds "the vision of truth" (*Phaedrus*, 249c), for example, is portrayed as having been "initiated into the perfect mysteries."

But mystery cults promised a sight that was beyond their capability to deliver, and waiting to die was not good enough for many spiritual individuals. Impatient Spanish Carmelites like Teresa of Ávila (1515–1582), who complains that being alive prevents her from enjoying the sight of God and knowing His truth (hearing about it was not enough), undertake mystical journeys to achieve a sight that was forbidden to the living. These are Fray Luis de Granada (1504–1588), Fray Luis de León (1527–1591), Pedro Malón de Chaide (1530–1589), Juan de la Cruz (1542–1591), Pedro de Alcántara (1499–1562), Fray Juan de los Ángeles (1536–1609), Francisco de Borja (1510–1572), Cristóbal de Fonseca (1550–1621), and Beato Alonso de Orozco (1500–1591); they and many others would be undertaking such journeys in a Spain (sixteenth century) still mired in a medieval ethos. Evidently, *hearing* was not enough to satisfy the spiritual yearnings of the many.

The problem was that, as the medieval Christian turned his sight upon the physical world, God was not in sight: what a person would behold was a wonderful yet enigmatic landscape where the self would be exposed to the hazardous allurements of sin. Life beckoned with moral hazards that could compromise the happiness that consists in the enjoyment of God, Augustine's *Summum Bonum*, the supreme good. Within the shelters of cloistered life and celibacy, medieval ascetics attempted to decrease their field of vision and range of experiences in the world, as the Bible made it clear that sin has its greatest ally in the human eye. In Gen. 3:6 Eve *sees* that the tree is good for food and pleasant to the eye, so she partakes of its fruit; Prov. 21:31 states that *looking* on the wine when it is red causes excess of drinking; in Joshua 7:21 Joshua *sees* objects that make him sin: "When I saw in the plunder a beautiful robe from Babylonia, two hundred shekels of silver and a bar of gold weighing fifty shekels, I coveted them and took them. They are hidden in the ground inside my tent, with the silver underneath" (NIV);" in 2Sam. 11:2-5, as David walks upon the roof of his palace, the *sight* of a beautiful woman (Bathsheba) bathing herself inflames his passions, so he sends his messengers to fetch her and he takes her, defiling himself with her; even Job puts his sight-discipline at the top of his list of objections regarding his undeserved punishments: "I made a covenant with my eyes not to look lustfully at a girl" Job. 31:1 (NIV). Sight, when directed at the world, not only interfered with salvation, but also with the attainment of truth, as the story of Democritus (who is supposed to have blinded himself to achieve enlightenment) demonstrates.

Thus, the context in which the medieval person cultivates the sense of sight is 1- the wonderful work of deities (pagan) or of one Supreme Being (Christian), but also 2- a geography of wonders that undergird communal beliefs regarding otherworldly realms (pagan), or a mysterious morass of temptation to be traversed without falling in its traps (Christian).

Modern sight is entirely different from pre-modern sight; let us analyze why. The modern scientific mind sees an ocean of a certain depth made up of water with specific characteristics, currents, and islands that breach the ocean surface, pushed up by the earth's internal processes. Our environment is physical, measurable, and not morally relevant, whereas pagan and medieval minds contemplated their environment as a living, spiritually relevant context. Spiritual relevance is displayed in the way that voyagers of the *immrama*, *echtrai*, and related texts characterized their ocean journeys as navigations through beautiful plains where gods on chariots might cross their path; they reached paradises, kingdoms, abbeys, and palaces instead of uninhabited rocky islands in the midst of an insensate body of water.

Today, as our empirical "self" negotiates the external world using the body's sense organs, we are acutely aware of the separation of an "inner" world of experience from the external world of objects with which the self interacts. Our inner world senses and evaluates the context in which it operates *as* context, as the exterior, and there is an explicit distinction between them. For medieval folk, that distinction was not categorical, which is to say that inner and external experiences required each other. The reason for this is that the external world had close connections with the spiritual realm, as it was the intellectual construct of a supreme consciousness. As such, human interactions with it happened within a natural order that featured a spiritual dimension. The things of the world, then, allowed consequential dealings between God (Christians) or supernatural beings (pagans) and man.

Like the objects of the external world, medieval persons occupied their allotted space in a transcendental moral framework: burning down someone's house, for example, contravened divine directives and was a sin for which the individual was accountable to a supreme being; doing so today is an act that goes against the laws of a community of people. Today you might avoid detection and be on your merry way to down a couple of cold brews at the local alehouse, vindicating your pyromaniacal self by citing a semipopular psychological study that blames society for your tendencies; a pre-scientific, medieval mind could not extricate itself from divine punishments that easily.

For modern researchers, it is difficult to *see* the ocean–or any "truth," for that matter–from anything other than a modern perspective. We've fostered the growth of "objective" truth to a great extent, but we fail to see it in its human dimension because of the concomitant elimination of subjective truth. To enter the pagan and early medieval Atlantic successfully, to *see* it as it was perceived then, we'd have to sail with U sheen or Brendan. It is not an overstatement to say that medieval imaginative assumptions regarding the great ocean have not been properly considered by the scholarship. Contemporary researchers have had trouble truly grasping the intuitional aspects of the medieval ethos, evidently because they look at it through the prism of intervening centuries, and that prism has arbitrated the disposition of present standards of analysis.

Commenting on our misreading of medieval philosophy, Christopher F. J. Martin considers the conundrum: "tradition as a whole cannot be judged as not up to standard by the standards of that tradition. It could only be judged by outside standards: and it is not at all surprising that those with different standards should judge it badly" (1996, 29). He adds that we can "misunderstand medieval philosophy in much the same way that a visitor staying at hotels in a foreign country will misunderstand his hosts" (1996, 13).

Considering this centuries-wide chasm, one can readily see that part of the modern lack of understanding regarding the medieval imaginary has to do with the inadequacies of our analyzing gaze. We introduce into all our assessments a concern for practical value that is based, one might assume, on the self-absorbed concerns of modern society. When we respond to the Middle Ages solely in terms of intellectual analysis, following an exclusively functional program of investigation–contrived to serve prearranged objectives–we bottle it up in the urn of our own intellectual concepts, expectations, and interests.

But the focus and range of our analyzing gaze must hinge on an initial understanding that, beyond its well-documented wretchedness and calamities, the world of the Middle Ages is also one where people lived surrounded by the aforesaid mysteries and snares, a purposive context where people experienced the excitement and wonder that miraculous events often offered to the imagination. These events have been shown by modern science to have a simple explanation and today appear as the trivial outcome of physical forces at work. As a result, we are tempted to classify medievals as simply "uninformed" folk who knew little of their world, forgetting the aptitude for abstract, symbolic cognition that their experience generated. In a world replete with spiritual meaning, people got a peek at the reality of their spiritual cosmos in external phenomena.

Taking the natural phenomenon of lightning as an example, we see that Marduk, the principal god of the city of Babylon, commanded lightning and thunder to do his bidding; to the early Greeks lightning was a weapon of Zeus; in the Old Testament God was responsible for lightning: "See how he scatters his lightning about him, bathing the depths of the sea" (Job 36:30), "He fills his hands with lightning and commands it to strike its mark" (Job 36:32), "He unleashes his lightning beneath the whole heaven and sends it to the ends of the earth" (Job 37:3), "He loads the clouds with moisture; he scatters his lightning through them" (Job 37:11), "Do you know how God controls the clouds and makes his lightning flash?" (Job 37:15). Nath Í mac Fiachrach (a.k.a. Dathí, semi historical Irish king of the fifth century), was struck and killed by lightning while besieging a tower that housed Forménus, a hermit and erstwhile king of Thrace who forsook his great riches for a religious life. The story tells us that lightning struck as a result of Forménus's request that God bring punishment to Nath Í mac Fiachrach, although the *Lebor Gabála Érenn* adds that "scholars suppose" Forménus shot him with an arrow (O'Rahilly 1946, 212-213). In short, the sense of wonder with which someone in the year 450 C.E. perceived lightning and heard the ensuing thunderclap is not clearly understood and is mostly overlooked by modern analyses.

To this point, we might remember that even the methodical, level-headed Thomas Aquinas lived in a world not even remotely explainable through empirical investigation, a cosmos where the marvelous and prodigious often intruded into the "natural order": "'Those effects are rightly to be termed miracles which are wrought by Divine power apart from the order usually observed in nature' (*Contra Gentiles*, III, cii), and they are apart from the natural order because they are 'beyond the order or laws of the whole created nature' (*Summa Theologica* I, Q. cii, a. 4)" (*The Catholic Encyclopedia*, s.v. "Miracle.").

While it would be absurd to advocate for discontinuing the intellectual analysis of the Middle Ages, it seems logical to think that we can better understand the medieval mindset if we leave room to grasp, in its cultural artifacts, the way medievals perceived their universe, a universe that–in spite of religious dogma–was the subject of mystery and wonder. This would allow us to understand medieval creative processes in a much more intimate way. In short, to better comprehend their world, we should look at their world *with* them, and not just analyze them as they look at their world.

Let us further examine this experience of looking with them, of seeing how they see. For modern people, sight is essential because it is the primary sense that we employ to make our way around the world without falling into ditches. Sight allows us to understand our surroundings as well. Yet in ancient societies, an incapacity to see didn't just come with material dangers but was also connected with transcendent perils, as epitomized in the *Babylonian Talmud*, Tractate Sanhedrin, Folio 44a.: "One must not greet a stranger, with peace in the middle of the night, as perhaps he is a demon" (Rodkinson 1902, 133).

In Christianized medieval communities sight was just as important, and for reasons that were just as transcendental as they were practical. Sight is the sense that captures light, that primordial element in Creation;[5] it thus establishes a relationship between the Creator and the individual and is an essential step in the journey towards salvation. Accordingly, sight was also important because of its intimate relationship with the soul: sight allowed one to see God's Creation, to interact with it in morally meaningful ways, and the sun provided the light with which to do it. The concept of sight also provided a platform upon which to explain devotional intangibles, as in Augustine:

> For Augustine sight was [...] a literal activity of spirit, the issuing forth of spiritual light into physical light; and he understood Plato's extromission theory of vision not simply as the activity of the physical element of fire but as the activity of a higher light. This agency of sight was rooted in the attention of spatiotemporally unique individuals, and was also a kind of judgment. Augustine distinguished between natural light, the opposite of which is darkness, and spiritual light, the opposite of which is irrationality. [...] Although Augustine lists qualities for judgment by all five senses (alba et nigra, canora et rauca, suaveolentia et graveolentia, dulcia et amara, calida et frigida, et caetera huiusmodi), it is once again clear that vision provides the basic metaphor for his spiritual judgment. (Summers 1987, 116)

It follows that the verb "to see," to judge by Augustine's theological perspectives, has a broader, richer meaning when applied to the medieval world. Consequently, darkness was also experienced differently. The indispensable object in the sensory universe, the sun with its life-giving light, died in the Atlantic at nightfall. "Night was man's first necessary evil, our oldest and most haunting terror. Amid the gathering darkness and cold, our prehistoric forbears must have felt profound fear, not least over the prospect that one morning the sun might fail to return" (Ekrich 2005, 3). Nightfall placed medieval inhabitants of a cold, cloudy seaboard in a dilemma where vision was nullified, in a darkness that was intuited spiritually as an acherontic episode as much as it was experienced as a commonplace, closely linked to the quotidian wonder of God's Creation. In today's world, we experience darkness as the insignificant amount of time that it takes us to turn on a lamp. Artificial lighting has commodified light and made darkness an inconsequential part of our lives.

---

[5] In the beginning God created the heavens and the earth. Now the earth was formless and empty, darkness was over the surface of the deep, and the Spirit of God was hovering over the waters. And God said, "Let there be light," and there was light. God saw that the light was good, and he separated the light from the darkness. God called the light "day," and the darkness he called "night." And there was evening, and there was morning—the first day (Genesis 1:1-5, NIV).

The pagan and early medieval world also accepted that there were different types of sight, a circumstance that today we might equate with psychological disorders. Celtic culture, for example, assigned metaphysical value to vision, having a concept commonly called "Second Sight," which is an inaccurate translation of the Gaelic "an da shealladh" (pronounced an-da-hoo-lah), which means "the two sights."

> The vision of the world of sense, ordinarily possessed by all, is *one* sight, while that of the spirits, which is visible to certain persons only, is a *second sight* so that such persons are spoken of as having "the two sights." [Citing Andrew Lang], "[t]he chief peculiarity of Second Sight is that the visions often, though not always, are of a *symbolic* power." (Spence 1999, 173)

Today, vision is considered not much more than a physiological function that is common to many living organisms: anything beyond that is regarded with clinical concern. Nowadays we witness the sunset with indifference, while 1,500 years ago people must have assimilated it with private apprehension. The physical dangers to which they were exposed in the darkness were analogous to the spiritual hazards whose preferred metaphor was the absence of light. Gregory of Nyssa (335 CE–394 CE) elaborates the metaphor straightforwardly: "Scripture teaches […] that religious knowledge comes at first to those who receive it as light. Therefore, what is perceived to be contrary to religion is darkness, and the escape from darkness comes about when one participates in light" (Imperato 2002, 89). In the Bible (John 9:1-11:57, ESV), Jesus is identified with light, describing himself as antagonist to the spiritual wasteland that is darkness: "We must work the works of Him who sent me while it is day; night is coming, when no one can work. As long as I am in the world, I am the light of the world."

However, from the standpoint of a recently-Christianized villager on the western fringes of Europe, the daily period of nighttime darkness was very likely internalized not only as a time full of physical dangers (wild animals, highwaymen, harmful cold) but also as a spiritually perilous time, being that doctrine characterizes darkness as the opposite of religion. At night, when darkness prevails, it is better for many reasons to stay home and pray. Thus, the night was the enactment of a drama of timeless truths as postulated by doctrine and elucidated in Genesis, as it cloaked the world with the absence of righteousness and allowed evil to roam: "Take no part in the unfruitful works of darkness, but instead expose them" (Ephesians 5:11, ESV). Light is the necessary ingredient in the act of seeing, exposing, and sight confirms spiritual truth.

Consequently sight, as the perception of reality, was of extreme importance in the medieval world, but the reality perceived was arbitrated into the observer's mind by the cultural and religious baggage that made the individual a member of society. Thus, we will see in subsequent chapters how Columbus sailed past and saw what he was certain to be the Earthly Paradise in northern South America, how Ponce de León's expedition involved efforts to see the Fountain of Youth, how Brendan sailed in search of the Isle of the Blest, how Amaro was willing to sacrifice all for just a glimpse of Paradise, and how Florentine traveler Marignolli saw Adam's house on a mountain just outside the Garden of Eden. For all of them, it was important to *see* these places, but why? Was faith not enough? Was faith suspected by some to be concocted evidence of things not seen?

Since the dogmata that explained reality had non-objective underpinnings and yet emphasized the importance of sight as a corroborator of reality, they lay the foundations for a conundrum, as their criterion of discernment was rooted in sense perception. Although religion required that believers accept the truth of its doctrines on faith, it remained a captive of the senses, for to perceive the ultimate reality one had to see God, and only Jesus and a very small number of chosen ones had had that experience. As a consequence, the abovementioned travelers' endeavor to see the reality that was announced by religion was nothing less than an attempt at confirming, through sight, the truth of dogmatic pronouncements. Being that religion taught that light/sight substantiated the existence of its truths, they did not categorically exist until they were perceived. This proved to be a challenge to faith. As I have discussed in a previous section of this work, "seers" and saintly individuals like Teresa of Ávila and fray Luis de León had somehow managed to attain the sight of the deity, a privilege that was coveted by many; even the exploration of the physical world was enhanced by the desire to attain some evidence of the supernatural through the sense of sight.

Chapter 1

North

The Greeks live like frogs sitting around a pond.
Plato, Phaedo 109B

The Greeks' northern Atlantic

Before the fifth and sixth centuries CE and the advent of trade between southern Scandinavians and littoral populations in France and Germany, ancient Mediterranean societies had precious little information regarding the northern reaches of the Atlantic Ocean, especially of its part presently called the Norwegian Sea. Eastern European rivers offered access to the Baltic and the possibility of reaching Scandinavia's southernmost regions, but crossing the peninsula and reaching the Atlantic was an altogether different enterprise. In any case, trade and colonization along Mediterranean shores were profitable, and in contrast, the journey so far north was perilous and would offer a small return on investment. So it was that the Greeks were characterized by Plato as frogs sitting around a pond. Consequently, any information regarding the icy northern ocean would have gone through many lands and several languages before reaching the more sophisticated cultures of the ancient world.

The uncertainties surrounding northernmost Europe contributed to an intellectual neglect that lasted well into the Middle Ages. Well-respected historian and geographer Hecataeus (550–476 BCE) unriddled the world, creating an orderly diagram that included every region and listed all peoples that he assumed dwelled in it. Yet an area in his chart points to the shortcomings of his understanding: the Caspian Sea. Having the Caspian as a gulf of the Oceanus–that great body of water that surrounds the world–points to the fact that uncharted regions were the object of unsubstantiated assumptions by Hecataeus because they were not necessary to the understanding of the world. This is because Hecataeus was not charting the world empirically; his map captures a symbolic domain and is the product of theoretical thought, of his methodical reflection about what is important to know about the world, one based on what little is known about it. His map, then, is relatively independent of the material world that it is redirecting into a world of meaning. A conceptual composition, the notional character of Hecataeus's map is irrefutable, as he is evidently attempting to provide an idea of the world as a "meaningful whole," echoing thus the Greek ethos that all reality must be humanly meaningful:

1.1. Hecataeus's Map. c. 480 BCE.

The Caspian Sea as a gulf of Okeanos, top right.

But more analytical speculations began to circulate subsequently, as Herodotus (484-425 BCE) (*Histories* 1.203), Aristotle (384-322 BCE) (*Meteorology* 354A3-4), and later Ptolemy (100-170 CE) (*Geography* 7.5.4), held that the Caspian Sea was not a gulf of the Oceanus, that great oceanic river that circumscribed the Ecumene (the permanently inhabited portion of the earth), but that it was completely surrounded by land. The resulting conjecture was that there was a large expanse of land north and east of the Caspian that had never been referenced by conventional ecumenical reports.

1.2. The Herodotus Map. c. 450 BCE.

The World According to Herodotus, with the Caspian as a landlocked sea.

Yet the continuing absence of any real information about the northern Atlantic (neither Scandinavia nor the British Isles materialized in subsequent conceptions of the world) increased the levels of curiosity, motivating Pytheas to sail past the Straits of Gibraltar and north to the British Isles and the far northern waters (c. 325 BCE). To add to the enigma posed by the Caspian's landlocked nature, Pytheas's *Periplus* now gave an account of places out in the Oceanus, completely detached from the Ecumene, whose description seemed to add to the Atlantic's enigmatic nature. Strabo (*Geographica*, bk. II, 4, 1) asserts that

> Pytheas claimed that he visited the whole of Britain that was accessible to him, gave the circumference of the island as more than 40,000 stadia (c. 4,600 miles), and in addition gave a description of Thule and those regions in which there was no longer land or sea or air as separate entities but a compound of them all like a jellyfish. (Ireland 2008, 14)

The world, then, disintegrated far out in the Atlantic. The Ecumene remained physically confined.

By the time of Crates of Mallus (second century BCE), head librarian at the Library of Pergamum, a more rational mindset was beginning to prevail. His visual representation of the world as a sphere is closer to what a modern person would recognize; it received considerable attention from his peers and was even the subject of detailed analysis by Strabo (*Geographica*, bk. I, 2.24). He appears to have exhibited his 10-foot-diameter sphere in Pergamum circa 150 B.C.E. (Irby 2016, 829).

With Crates we have one of the first speculative descriptions of the Atlantic as having two shores, and as a reflection of the two continents on "this" side (Eurasia and Africa), two continents far to the west. On "this" side of the meridional plane drawn through the sphere he places the Ecumene in the north and the land of the Antoecians to the south, while on the "other" side of the Atlantic there lies the land of the Perioecians to the north (roughly corresponding to North America) and that of the Antipodes to the south (roughly corresponding to South America). Even on this sphere, whose original is lost (modern reconstructions have been made following descriptions of it), the north Atlantic is a blank, with the rough outline of Great Britain the only indication that he thought there must be *something* up there.

1.3. The Map of Crates. 180-150 BCE.

The world as a sphere divided into four sections.

Crates' deductions were not, however, based on observation, but owe their design to the Greek penchant for balance and proportion. Eratosthenes (c. 276 BC – c. 195/194 BC), in his famous and amazingly accurate calculation of the Earth's circumference, presented a problem for Crates, as the size of the Ecumene in his sphere was far too small (occupying only one-fourth of the sphere) relative to the size of the earth proposed by Eratosthenes. The solution was clear: achieve the necessary symmetry by adding two extra landmasses and an enlargement of Africa that would act as counterweights to the Ecumene. Problem solved. Thus were the Americas and the whole of Africa anticipated by Crates' elegant solution to what was, in effect, an aesthetic problem.

The *Norse* Atlantic: Niflheim

Sails a ship from the north / with shades from Hel. O'er the ocean stream / steers it Loki.

Patch 1970, 62

Those people who inhabited the Atlantic's northern reaches populated the ocean with the impressive array of places, monsters, giants, and gods that gives their mythology its most recognizable characteristics. Being intensely larger-than-life, they represent the colossal forces of nature. Where does this all begin?

The Scandinavian Eddic creation story begins with a void, Ginnungagap, a nothingness whose edges were occupied by two primeval realms: Niflheim and Muspellheim. Niflheim was a northern ice-world (north and south are inverted in the map below), a dark place where frozen mists hover in the atmosphere and it is too cold for habitation; Muspellheim is a southern, molten land of fire too hot to harbor life. Niflheim and Muspellheim are the two opposites whose antagonistic energies have formed Ginnungagap, the void between them. Midgard, a habitable place in the middle, was eventually formed as the northern ice mist became fertile when touched by the hot breeze from the south. As the ice melted, the water drops congealed to form a giant named Ymir. He represents the beginning of consciousness in the Norse creation story.

1.4. The Norse Worldview.

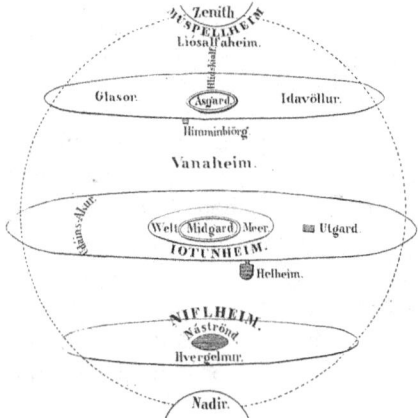

Norse mythical cosmos with North and South inverted.

Significantly, frozen Niflheim is preserved after the creation event as the dark place, Hell. As a true "underworld," Niflheim has far-reaching underground precincts, such that its environs extend below Midgard. Traditionally, the Norse Hell was considered a place for people who did not die honorably (the sick, the old, the evil), as opposed to Valhalla, paradise for the heroes. But there are questions as to the stability of Niflheim's symbolic significance, as Niflheim contained a well, Hvergelmir, from which many rivers flowed. Moreover, Baldr, son of the god Odin and the goddess Frigg and who by all accounts should not be consigned to Hell, ends up there. In some cases, it seems that "Hell wasn't a realm of punishment, reserved for those who didn't die an honorable death" (De Vries 2008, 27).

This ancient Norse underworld was located firmly in the northern Atlantic:

> The idea of a world of the dead across the sea, however, is implied in the custom of putting the dead in burning ships and sending them out over the waves, and perhaps implied also in that of burying boats in the mounds with the dead.
>
> Northward seems the characteristic direction of the soul's journey. The descent to *Hel* is not only underground but across water. (Patch 1970, 61-62)

Hel, daughter of the trickster god Loki and Angrboða, is the ruler of this northern realm, appointed to the position by the god Odin. It is noteworthy that the characteristics of this Norse realm at the northern reaches of the globe are very similar to the northern Atlantic description articulated by Greek navigator Pytheas. The unwelcoming features of the Atlantic's northern reaches were fertile ground for mythologies (Norse) and descriptions of landscapes, like Pytheas's, that seemed implausible to rational minds (Greeks).

Consequently, islands in the northern Atlantic acquire an otherworldly dimension; they are places where gods are fond of assembling in mid-ocean isolation:

> A rather late account (probably of the twelfth century) of a voyage to an island where a meeting of the gods is held appears in the *Vikar Saga* inserted in the *Gautreks Saga*, where we are told how Horsehair Grani wakened Starkad in the middle of the night and with him rowed in a small boat to an island. There, in a clearing next to a forest they found a meeting of the Allthing. Eleven men sat there in chairs; a twelfth chair was empty. This Horsehair Grani took for himself, and they all hailed him as Odin. With Thor he then debated the destiny of Starkad. (Patch 1970, 62)

Enchanted islands in the Atlantic are abundant in Celtic and early medieval voyages; these are places where godly characters reinforce and interpret communal moral codes, employing the thematic strands of otherworldly reward and punishment that buttress the community's social order and belief system. What is different in Norse mythology is its insistence on the contradictory character of the two sides of the void that, once in contact with each other, create a generative space in the middle where consciousness can emerge. A peculiar, *avant la lettre* form of Hegelian dialectics indeed. The assumption that there are diametrically opposite landscapes at either side of the void, antitheses whose point of contact creates a sort of compromise, can be thought of as a metaphor for the idea of the world as an organic process, coming into existence and developing in consonance with its internal regulating mechanisms and potentials. A product of this process is the emergence of consciousness in the form of the giant Ymir.

Ymir points to the fact that the Norse creation myth builds upon what they perceived as natural processes of nature in which a god is not involved, and consciousness, that storage room for all our thoughts, memories, reasoning, and judgment does not appear enveloped by a set of dogmatic guidelines that methodize its conventional operations. Intelligibility as well as reason and the coherent arrangement of reality emerge, unfettered, from Nature. Theirs is not a "creation" story in the strict sense, as there is no "Creator," but rather an ontological conceptualization of *the beginning*. As such, no anthropocentric manual containing "the truth" provides the Norse with a definition of life and the universe, as is the case with Abrahamic religions. There is no dogmatic certainty among the Norse: Their giants and monsters provide an analog to what is undefinable; they have their place in a symbology that gives expression to the great uncertainty that is life, as they exist beyond rational discourses. A monster, then, is a metaphor for the transcendence of perplexity.

On a side note, it is perhaps to be expected that the concept of hell of peoples in the eastern Mediterranean is diametrically opposed to that of the Norse. The searing summer heat of biblical lands would generate a concept of otherworld suffering that featured fire and brimstone, as heat was a familiar cause of misery to its inhabitants. For the Norse, the intense cold of the North Atlantic was that familiar source of anxiety, so the frozen mists of the north would prove to be a recognizable environment where torments for blameworthy individuals would be better understood.

The symbol

1.5. From Olaus Magnus's *Carta Marina*. 1539.

Northern Atlantic monsters that horrified sailors.

The didactic role that Christianity assigns to the symbol is the persistence of the pagan tradition of using monsters, effigies, and even household items like cups as metaphors for deeply felt anxieties. Pagan myths endure in Christian iconography in the sense that, as occurs in the Christian tradition, pagan symbols were more than metaphors, as they epitomized concepts, anxieties, and divinities that were critical to their interpretations of the world. The abhorrence of pagan idolatry common among medieval Christian scholars overlooked the fact that the Christian faithful kneeled in prayer to pieces of wood, carved according to sanctioned descriptions and engraved with the name of an individual saint or holy person; from their perspective, there was a transubstantiation of the wood into the saint. Thus, and without making metaphysical claims regarding sea monsters, I'd argue that a creature like the sea monster is a symbol of particular relevance, as it has a strong pragmatic meaning. While we might reject the notion that the depiction of a monster on a map becomes the substance of a transmundane being, that portrayal is nevertheless a psychologically powerful way to represent furtive misgivings regarding God's flawless Creation, not to be dismissed as a product of pre-scientific ignorance by offering an uncomplicated denial of the monster's existence.

Such mythical beasts proliferate in ancient and medieval folklore. Scandinavian mythology gives the Kraken as a giant sea monster, one mile long, that attacks people that venture into the Atlantic. The *Örvar-Odds*, an Icelandic saga from the mid-twelfth century, mentions two sea monsters, the Lyngbakr and the Hafgufa; in size and other physical features, this last one compares with the Kraken (Waggoner 2012, xxviii). Resembling the process that endowed the saint with a presence in the environment through wood, the monster was brought into the environment through the work of scholars well into the eighteenth century. The Kraken myth was so embedded in the belief systems of coastal peoples, that scientific texts such as Carolus Linnaeus's *Systema Naturae* (1735) included the Kraken as one of nature's creatures. Linnaeus subsequently mentioned the creature again in his *Fauna Suecica* of 1746 (Peattie 1992, 20-21), although he includes a caveat: "It is said that it lives in the Norwegian Sea; as for myself, I have never seen this animal" (Heuvelmans 2003, 116). An idea of the Kraken as zoetic creature invaded the world of science in the nineteenth century, as Danish biologist Johannes Japetus Smith Steenstrup (1813-1897) gave the world conclusive proof of the existence of giant cephalopods (Guerra and Segonzac 2014, 28).

The Kraken is part of a North Atlantic sea monster mythology that is a common feature of ancient European sea lore. It is worthy of note that ancient and medieval imagination populated the Atlantic with so many monsters that Pliny (*Natural History* bk. 6 ch. 38) stated that its islands "are greatly annoyed by the putrefying bodies of monsters, which are constantly thrown up by the sea" (Pliny 1855, 108). In fact, the Atlantic is viewed as the only body of water vast enough to house these prodigies, which, like Pliny's Arbas, are so large that they "could not enter [into the Mediterranean through] the Gibraltar Straits without grounding" (Bassett 1885, 204). In charting the ocean, as late as the sixteenth century Olaus Magnus was populating his famous *Carta marina* (1539), a sea map of the northern Atlantic, with various types of sea-monsters menacing ships:

1.6. Full View of Olaus Magnus's Carta Marina. 1539.

Image of the Atlantic as an enigmatic and threatening domain.

Subsequently, Danish bishop Erik Pontoppidan (1698-1764), in his *Versuch einer natürlichen Geschichte Norwegens* (The Natural History of Norway), published in 1752 and 1753, made a case for the existence of several Atlantic sea monsters, including the Kraken (Loxton and Prothero 2013, 207). In an interesting analog to St. Brendan's whale adventure, Erik Walkendorf (1465–1522), Archbishop of Nidaros (Trondheim, Norway), claimed that he found one of those gigantic mythical Norse monsters asleep and, believing it to be a rock, raised an altar and celebrated mass on its back, an activity the beast allowed without flinching. After the holy man finished and went back to shore, the beast disappeared under the waves (Nigg 2013, 147).

Such enduring monsters, for the Christianized medieval Norse, are symbols for an anxiety of metaphysical proportions, of the type that the proximity to the Atlantic can cause. This anxiety drew medieval folk out of their standardized ways of thinking and made them aware of a reality that was not explained in their domesticated universe; it also reveals the persistence of a long-concealed suspicion that, perhaps, the standard narrative that explained it all had missed some important things. And for many medieval Norsemen, unknowable things had their natural habitat in the vast unknown, the Atlantic. For them, a monster was the symbol of the unsettling subjective experience of doubt, of anguish, articulated symbolically in poetic and stylized visual depictions.

When we see past the uncomplicated, fear-based story of monsters trying to eat people and understand these phenomena as part of a subconscious world of foreboding, when we remember that this was a world of plagues, wars, entrenched inequalities, and meager life expectancies, we will be able to peer into the medieval mind's intuitive despair; we will recognize an anguish based on the unacceptable likelihood that the meaning assigned by dogma to the universe might not be absolutely accurate.

A monster like the Kraken and those that in Magnus's map attack ships at random–the sailors' deaths are not the consequence of some transgression– constitute a symbolic challenge to faith-based narratives regarding the inherent moral fabric of the universe. Such narratives attempt to rationalize the arbitrary horrors that are inherent to life with unconvincing apologia, affirming that the agonies and miseries of reality are not important, that what is important is not this world but the next. But if everything in heaven and earth was created by a caring, almighty God, those random disasters need explanations not offered convincingly in doctrine. As medieval minds venture into these dangerous considerations, they strike a parallel route to the ships on the map that dare sail into the Atlantic, flimsy wooden vessels that transport frail human subjectivities into an unresponsive and perilous objective reality.

Early medieval societies did not promote the type of intellectual inquiry that might have led to the development of a discussion, of philosophical or theological dimensions, regarding the anxieties produced by the unsympathetic character of the universe. The manifestation of such anxieties, then, was parabolic: Monsters rose from the depths of the North Atlantic to express apprehension, to articulate commonly submerged concerns about life, and to embody an angst that was not countenanced by doctrine in any commonsensical manner. As there were things in reality not accounted for in obdurate foundation stories, there were gaps in the hedge of dogma; a *lusus naturae* was a manifestation of those gaps, a symbol of reality in its naked, primordial, deregulated state.

North Atlantic monsters dramatically assail the unconvincing *decretum* that man is at the center of the universe and that the universe was created for the human being. Communal belief systems, especially powerful in the Middle Ages, strove to repress external, non-regulated reality, channeling attitudes in order to evade anxieties regarding the unbridled and unmanageable reality of the universe. These anxieties never disappear, however, but instead plunge below the mythologized surface of the medieval ethos, surfacing in the shape of monsters that emerge from the unknowable depths of the Atlantic. Medievals were so terrified of monsters in the ocean because tales of journeys into the Atlantic, since long before Brendan, Bran and Madoc, were thinly-veiled expressions of the human being's desire to overcome *this* existence, to live on, to not expire, to find the "Happy Other World" beyond the ocean, and sea-monsters were the symbolic expression of the suspected absurdity of such aspirations.

It is true that the predominant existential crisis in the Middle Ages was fueled by the perception of sin and the urgent desire to be forgiven. It was the predictable result of the individual's internalizing of credenda, of dogmas that sustained the communal belief system. But in recently or partially Christianized communities like the Norse such internalizing was anemic at best, and the remnants of previous mythologies as well as the evidence provided by sense-perception and reason conflated to subvert the assumptions generated by the new belief system. Because of the overwhelming prominence of faith in the Middle Ages, there has been a trend in modern critical studies to downplay the relevance of reason in the medieval ethos. But reason is always present, like an obstacle to faith, like a monster/guard blocking the entrance to Paradise.

North Atlantic monsters manifest themselves because reason was proscribed. Reason, in dogmatic logic, was the enemy of the Faith. That is precisely the manner in which Nicholas of Cusa (1401–1464) characterizes it in his symbol-laden *De Docta Ignorantia* (1440): Paradise is surrounded by a wall that conceals God, who dwells inside, from human sight. Furthermore, its gate is guarded by "the highest spirit of reason, who bars the way until he has been overcome" (J. Campbell 2008, 73). This highest spirit of reason that must be overcome to access truth is very likely Satan, who, aided by the human being's foolhardy curiosity regarding the physical world, is able to secrete, behind a wall of reason, the more substantial and relevant reality preached by Jesus.

Thomas Aquinas (1225–1274), in his *Summa Contra Gentiles*, book 1, tells us that "If the sole way of knowing God were through reason the human mind would remain in the deepest shadows of ignorance. [...] Because men are ordained by divine providence for a higher good than human frailty can express in the present life, the mind is summoned to something higher than our reason here and now can reach" (Bainton 1962, 143-144).

Earlier, Pseudo-Dionysius the Areopagite (writing before 532) had advised the faithful to ἀγνώστως ἀνατάθητι, that is to say, to strive upwards with incomprehension, leaving behind "both sensible perceptions and intellectual efforts, and all objects of sense and intelligence, and all things not being and being" (Stang 2012, 137). The Middle English *Cloud of Unknowing* (c. 1380) urges believers to forego considerations about particularities regarding God and His creation. In fact, the doctrine wherein we can inscribe these texts separates God from reality: God does not exist in the same way as His creation exists, so deliberation regarding the nature of reality is perilously disconnected from those mental activities that truly matter *en route* to Salvation. This only proves that reason was indeed quite relevant in the Middle Ages; it was a dangerous hazard against which the faithful needed to be in resolute and constant vigilance. It was the Norse's monster lurking in the depths of the ocean.

It follows that the analysis of "reality," that is to say, of the physical nature of the universe through the powers of reason, was an injudicious endeavor. Human beings needed to traverse reality, "the world," in the safety of a vessel–a symbol for faith–that could fend off anxieties arising from the inexplicable contingencies of the world–symbolized by the sea–, a vessel wherein one was shielded from the need to consider the nature of reality. A common allegory in the Middle Ages and early Modernity is that of the world as sea and the church as a ship plying its waters:

> In the highly selective corpus of proto-Orthodox and Orthodox writing that we call 'patristic,' representing only a fraction of Christian literature before AD 500, the sea, separating humanity from Paradise, assumed very rapidly an equally influential metaphorical role as the sea of the world (an image that would be spread through allegorical writings such as Guillaume de Deguileville's fourteenth-century *Pèlerinage de la vie humaine*). The sea was thought to be governed by the Devil who administered humankind's sins, which, according to Micah 7.19, will be hurled by God into the sea [...]. Origen (185–c. 254) is generally credited with having devised the influential image of the sea as the world, *in mari vitae*, which therefore reaches back almost to the beginnings of Christian preaching. Naturally, the sea of the world could only be braved by a ship that was built of the unsinkable wood taken from Christ's cross. The ship was the Church itself: *ecclesia*. (Sobecki 2008, 36)

This allegory has subsisted well into modernity. At the end of Calderón de la Barca's allegorical play *El divino Orfeo* (1663), Orpheus brings Human Nature to safety in the ship of the church.

Thus, in maps and lore, sea monsters are symbols of anxieties that emerge from medieval reason to subvert communal belief systems, acting as allegories for the onslaught of reason against faith. Such symbols routinely percolate into objective reality because, like the wooden image of a saint, the symbol needs a physical presence in the environment to be more effective. Medievals "see" and describe monsters; they even celebrate Mass on their backs as a sort of counter-offensive to the assault of reason upon the tenets of communal belief systems. Sea monsters appear out of the ocean depths, terrorize human beings sailing on flimsy ships or even at the shore, and return to the depths, evading any and all attempts to analyze or typecast them. Consequently, they refuse to take part in oracular, communal versions of nature. And the container of all these creatures was the ultimate symbol of "otherness," the Atlantic.

Living on land, if it is next to the ocean, did not exempt the individual from the ontological perils that lurked in the depths. As a consequence of the ocean's metaphysical features, any strange creature coming out of the sea would necessarily invalidate the habitual arrangements of normal reality. To illustrate the features of these land-invading sea monsters, I'll cite a text that collects longstanding oral traditions from Iceland. We start with the "hairy man":

> It happened a long time ago on one of the Meðalland beaches, the body of a man was found washed up on the shore, a man of very strange appearance. He was wearing no clothes, but was covered with hair, and had claws on his fingers and toes. [...] The body was moved to Skarði for burial. However, when the funeral was about to take place, and people were about to sing the funeral hymns, they found themselves in difficulties, because every letter in their hymnals had turned back to front, and twisted into forms of blasphemy and curses. [...] Whatever it was, it was not long after his funeral that people started noting ghostly activities in the vicinity of the Skarði church. These got so bad that it was considered impossible to travel around there after dark. People saw the "hairy man"–as the recently buried body was called–pounding the church with planks from his coffin. Various other strange things happened there... (Jennings, Reeploeg, and Watt 2017, 13)

Even on land, the sea could send agents of its disruptive forces to upset the familiar world of the living. The walking-dead "hairy man" is a superb representative of the doubts that overturn those comforting, faith-based descriptions of reality. Icelandic monsters coming out of the ocean go by the generic name of *fjörulalli*.

> *Fjörulalli*, they say, come up and out of the sea on islands, and around the coast in some places, usually around lambing time, and trouble the ewes, causing all sorts of mutations in the newly born lambs. There is one island in particular [on Breiðafjörður] near Geitey, called Mikilnefna, where ewes must never be kept at lambing time. Last year there were various ewes there, and they all had deformed lambs, for example with mouths in their throats, six to eight feet, a long tail like a dog, and so on... (Jennings, Reeploeg, and Watt 2017, 14)

These examples demonstrate how the depths that sea monsters inhabit are a symbol of the unfathomable place, one situated beyond the perimeter of the discursive circle wherein the community describes reality. Once the sea monster appears, the communal belief system's methodical, all-encompassing affirmations dissolve: the sea monster proves that the belief system is not all-embracing, that, in fact, it has boundaries outside of which monsters originate, in a place that has not been anticipated by credenda. By challenging taxonomies that promote human exceptionalism, a monster's very existence assails the belief system's portrayals of reality.

Moreover, as the Areopagite's abovementioned theology reveals, in the magical world of early-Christian communities, the prescribed supernatural view of the universe was unable to prevent subconscious, anxiety-producing doubt. Moreover, because these anxieties could be traced back to the intrusion of reason and reality upon the belief system, they made for a psyche that endowed symbols–particularly those that represented the menacing and intransigent phenomena of reality–with objective power. Symbols had this power not because they *exist* in concrete reality, but because symbols and the indomitable reality that was symbolized became analogous and concurrent because they conflated in direct synchronization. That is to say, symbolic reality invaded objective reality, and sailors were often on the lookout for the monsters portrayed on their maps as they sailed the Atlantic. With symbolic representations such as these, the medieval mind was able to articulate the person's innermost anxieties regarding existence, apprehensions that were otherwise indescribable. But sea monsters were not the only way to chronicle angst.

Another way to symbolize doubt about conventional descriptions of the universe was by endowing household utensils with magical powers. Painful illness, for example, seemed incompatible with religious narratives of a well-ordered universe made by a caring God. For people who suffered in spite of being righteous or innocent, Job's patience might have seemed a conventional foible: "Naked I came from my mother's womb, And naked shall I return there. The Lord gave, and the Lord has taken away; Blessed be the name of the Lord" (Job 1:21 KJV). Medicine was one way to "correct" the universe's shortcomings regarding mankind's preferential place in it, and medicinal concoctions were prepared and habitually delivered to the patient in cups. Such practical uses seem to have endowed cups with a great deal of symbolic power and magical properties, precisely because they hold liquids that, once ingested, can often reclaim for the healed the universe's anthropocentric design. The cups' properties were often memorialized in legend, like that of Hymir's cup, which defied the god Thor's attempt at breaking it (Adams Bellows 2004, 147).

There are fine examples of transcendental cups in British and Irish lore. The story of wise Irish king Cormac mac Airt has the monarch being deceived by a man who convinced him to exchange his wife and kids for a magical branch that made music, with melodies so sweet that it made those who listened fall asleep. In pursuit of the strange man, he was enveloped in a mist that transported him to a supernatural hall where Manannán, sea-god and ruler of the otherworld realm of Tír Tairngire, showed him a magical cup that broke into three pieces when three lies were told; it was only restored when three truths were spoken.

He awakened back in Tara with the cup and the branch. His grandfather Conn had a similar adventure: one early morning, as he went up to the royal rampart on Tara to watch for enemies, he stepped on a magical stone, Fáil, the stone of destiny. He was then surrounded by a mist and transported to a mysterious land, finding himself in the hall of the god Lugh. A girl wearing a golden crown brought a cup of gold and a silver vat with hoops of gold around it, full of red ale, the ale of kingship. There was a dipper of gold on its lip. Then Lugh explained that he would relate to Conn the length of his reign and those of his heirs. Conn returned to Tara with the vat and the cup after stepping into Lugh's shadow.

In the Scottish story of *Finn MacCoul and the Bent Grey Lad*, Finn is sent to recover the "quadrangular cup of the Fenians that the King of Lochlann had stolen from them. This cup had the property of providing any draft one might desire, just like the cup once given to Huon of Bordeaux by Oberon, king of the fairies.[1] Then there is the tale of Uistean, who slaughtered the Fuathan (malevolent spirits of the Scottish Highlands); therein the hero used a curative cup to restore the power of speech to the Earl of Antrim's daughter. The ornamented cup of Ballafletcher, in the Isle of Man, was dedicated to the peaceful spirit lhiannan-shee, a beautiful woman of the Aos Sí who takes human lovers (who live very brief, though blissful lives). This drinking glass would bring peace and prosperity to the family that owned it, but if it ever broke, the culprit would forever be haunted by lhiannan-shee (Spence 1999, 37).

Evidently inherited from pagandom, the cup is a very important symbol for Christianity. Just to give a couple of examples, *Ecclesia* (The Church) is portrayed as a woman who, having vanquished the Dragon –symbol of evil and sin– holds a Cross in one hand and the Cup of Salvation in the other. The Grail is the cup Jesus used in the Last Supper. The Lamb of God often holds a Cross in one hand and a cup in the other, and the Hand of God that holds man's fate is also portrayed as a cup, as Jesus demonstrates when in the Mount of Olives He speaks of the "cup of sufferings that awaits Him" (Becker 2000, s.v. "Cup").

Also common in North Atlantic pagandom was the use of effigies soaked in strange liquid; the process was intended to bend reality to the will of the person making use of the irrigated icon. Duff (930-966), King of Scotland, began to feel unwell for no apparent reason and, as the days went by, became so ill that his demise was imminent. Sorcery was obviously suspected. "It chanced that a soldier in the garrison of the castle had a mistress by whom he was made acquainted

---

[1] We might recall that Oberon is also a character in Shakespeare's play *A Midsummer Night's Dream*, where he is husband to Titania, Queen of the Fairies. In an earlier French version of the character, Oberon owned a magical cup that was always full for the virtuous.

with the practices and designs of her mother, who was one of the suspected witches, leagued with others for the destruction of Duff" (Boswell-Stone 1896, 22-23). The old witches were caught red-handed as they roasted a wax effigy of the king on an open fire, basting it with some strange liquid and reciting words of enchantment. Once the roasting was stopped and the witches executed, the king regained his health. Evidently, symbols had no distinct existence separate from their purpose, and their magical efficacy reflected the fact that they lacked their own specificity, their own individuality. There was no substantial disconnection between the symbol and the real: the effigy handled by the witches *was* King Duff.

Ninth-century Irish monk Dungal (who calls himself Hibernici exulis, or exile from Ireland), gives details of the several defensive features that safeguard body and soul within Charlemagne's Church of St. Denis.

> Ne David grabatum temptator callidus intret,
> Signetur Domini ista fenestra manu!
> Quadrus evangelii defendat numerus omne
> Corpus, et interius cunctipotens animam. (Dungal 2021, 401-402)

So as Dungal explains, the Universe's perils can intrude in the sacred space of a church, worshiper beware. To defend against them, symbols on the window–the Hand of God and the four evangelists–will, presumably, guard the edifice from such dangers and from the enemies of the faith, those "clever assailants." As in the case of King Duff, emblematized people or objects become physically present in the symbol.

This mindset owes its anatomy to the fact that medieval reality is synthesized by collective consciousness through a system of symbolic representations; these symbols are *transubstantiated* by the act of worship (or by witchcraft), so the symbol has no autonomous, purely aesthetic significance, and is devoid of inherent substance. A believer in that same Church of Saint-Denis, kneeling in front of a statue of the Virgin Mary, praying *to* it, is not interacting with a piece of carved wood. The medieval symbol often lacks inborn authenticity: it always gravitates towards something else, effectively becoming that something else.

Hence, the world conceived through perceptual experience in the Middle Ages is not simple, elementary, or self-evident. It exists insofar as it has been assimilated through ideological acts that make it understandable and assign value to it. Assimilative strategies are perhaps most apparent in people's reactions to events in reality. When medievals, for example, perceived the devastation caused by the Black Death outbreak (1348–1350), they were not simply experiencing unmediated data but were locating this data within a value system where they could establish relationships and determine agency. Within this system, the Jew was identified as the symbol of the pain and suffering brought by the pandemic; by destroying the symbol, it was thought, the plague would subside. It is relevant that "The persecution of the Jews waned with the Black Death itself; by 1351 all was over" (Ziegler 2009, n.p.). To the medieval mind, the demolition of the symbol had had the desired effect.

Much has been said regarding the ill-gotten economic benefits of destroying the Jewish communities. It has been affirmed that the many people who owed money to the Jewish moneylenders, as well as the authorities that stood to gain from acquiring newly-vacant Jewish properties, set the tragedy in motion. Jews were "easy targets of protest by the bourgeoisie and tradesmen, who believed that to eliminate the Jews was to eliminate their debts" (Rousmaniere 1991, 64). Yet the ferocity with which these communities were obliterated is not explained solely by drawing on such rationalizations. The fact is that a considerable number of events in medieval history have their origin in its myths and symbols. These are not fabricated or selected at will in order to eliminate debt; they are an essential manner in which people's experience of reality is structured and are the most relevant source of their identity.

Because of the symbol's transcendental capacity to transubstantiate, effigies, cups, monsters and different sorts of imagery gave *visual* evidence to the "truth" conveyed by myths. They helped to structure identitary patterns in an illiterate world and, in environments that were not particularly inclusive, helped identify those that were integrated into the identitary group as well as those left out of it, as were the Jews. In the case of groups based on religious identity, the individuals left out did not share in the sacred cosmology that underpinned the dominant group's myths, they didn't worship their effigies, and as such, were viewed with suspicion, negative expectations, and were described through unfavorable symbols. The image of Mohammed, for example, surrounded by devils and being tortured in hell in a fresco in Bologna's San Petronio Basilica (construction finished in 1390), is typical of a mindset that produced similar deleterious illustrations by William Blake in Dante's *Divine Comedy* (1824–1827) and by Gustave Doré in his *Divine Comedy* plates (1866–1867).

This mindset was dangerous: unsurprisingly, medieval Christians would situate the symbolic image of the Black Death in the Jew, and the Jew, an individual that had no franchise in their myths, was its living symbol. The obliteration of this effigy would be expected to result in the destruction of the symbolized object, the plague. Thoroughly examined, the Jews' tragedy proves that myth, just as much as economic, political, or social concerns, was an element of the medieval subject's transactions in the world of objects. In the analysis of medieval life, it is essential to access the composition of the subjective, mythical spheres that inspire and motivate activity.

Consequently, the medieval mind rarely sensed in a neutral, impartial manner. In the dualist world of medieval consciousness, people, objects, and ideas were judged as either benign or malignant, and this judgment was articulated through formulaic symbols. The semantics surrounding the Crusades are a case in point:

> It is significant that the term "Muslims" is absent from medieval sources. Instead, the crusaders' opponents are variously described by the chroniclers as "infidels," "Gentiles," "enemies of Christ/God" and above all, "pagans." William of Tyre (c. 1130–86) […], is interesting because he does not use the term "pagans," but he value-loads the descriptors, "infidels" and "enemies of God," by setting them in binary opposition to terms such as "the faithful" and "soldiers of Christ," which designate the crusaders themselves. These semantic oppositions are revealing of a clerical mindset that viewed the world in Manichean terms as a battleground on which the forces of Evil were engaged in an apocalyptic struggle with the forces of Good under the command of Christ. (Jubb 2005, 228)

This particular view of the universe consigns the people and objects in it to specific spots in what was essentially a *represented* reality, a reality of substances characterized by their symbolic qualities and anticipated trajectory. At its most fundamental level, medieval consciousness operated in an environment of presumed attributes; it was a world with subjective structure and critical attachment to integral symbols.

But change was in the offing, and the mid-fourteenth century would witness the near collapse of the medieval symbolic world. Up to the advent of the Black Death, symbols provided a tractable universe in which medievals were sheltered against perils that might threaten the life of their identitary community: Christianity. These symbols offered answers to most of their questions about good and evil, life and death, and so forth. Awareness of the essential indifference of the universe was kept at bay by invoking the mystery that underpinned belief and by the unspoken wisdom provided by these symbols, which seemed to be ubiquitous (frescoes and statuary in churches, illustrations in maps, bibles and prayer books, paintings, etc.).

But as the Black Death convinced people that the end–personal and communal–was at hand, pleading with their symbols–relics, statues, icons, images, and ceremonies–was deemed to have lost much of its effectiveness, as the epidemic was relentless. And while this did not represent a death blow to the symbol (the destruction of the Jewish community was considered effective), it began a process that weakened it: less than two centuries later Protestant multitudes would break into churches and destroy every symbol–

every effigy, statuary, relic, painting–they could lay their hands on, leaving a simple Cross to cover the scope of their beliefs. This represented a sea-change in religious consciousness:

> Besides targeting royal symbols, the Protestant movement was directed against Catholic material symbols–against stained-glass windows, statues of the Virgin and saints, holy medals, and tokens. One Calvinist lord sat happily on a desecrated church altar, feeding plundered Hosts to his parrot. This was the *Beeldenstorm*, the Storm of Images, and it marked a religious declaration of independence against ideas rooted in the oldest human cultures: it reflected a whole new religious consciousness. (Jenkins 2016, 218)

With the Black Death, the medieval person was provided with a frightful glimpse into the gloomy, terribly vacant universe, a place where symbols were inoperative. But the symbol survived, and even the Protestants, with their relentless burning of "witches," created a mythical reality where perceived threats to the survival of their identitary group were symbolized by individuals–witches–that had no franchise in their righteous enterprise. Symbols not only survived but eventually proliferated with increased intensity: we might recall that in the *Theatrum Diabolorum*, edited by Lutheran theologian Sigmund Feyerabend, the number of "angels of destruction" proposed by post-biblical rabbinical literature (90,000), was raised considerably. The *Theatrum's* title purports it to be a "useful and sensible book," and it contains essays by several prominent men of the times: Jodocus Hockerus Osnaburgensis, Hermannus Hamelmannus, Andreas Musculus, Andreas Fabricius Chemnicensis, and Ludovicus Milichius, among others. Hocker (Hockerus) explains all the trouble that can be caused by devils in 48 chapters, and in chapter 7 their number is meticulously calculated to be no less than 2,665,866,746,664, although Martin Borrhaus says that it is a "great temerity" for human beings to attempt such calculations, as this is knowledge that belongs only to God (Medway 2001, 394). That these devils are symbolic there can be no doubt, for there are special kinds of devils: that of blasphemy, the dance-devil, the wedlock devil, that of unchastity, of the miser, of tyranny, of laziness, pestilence, gambling, a pantaloon devil and a courtier's devil that the *Theatrum* represents "in a drama of five acts, the scene being at the court of Darius" (Holyoake 1895, 4931).

Inis Glora: truth, syncretism and collective subjectivity

Subjectivity is Truth.

Søren Kierkegaard

This section contains an analysis of competing truth and knowledge systems in the Middle Ages, using one illustrative Irish text. The analysis is nourished by ideas found in relativism, specifically by its foundational notion that beliefs and values are valid and reveal truth only relative to their particular social, cultural, and religious environment. This ancient and persistent idea was formulated by Protagoras (c. 485–415 BCE) over two and a half millennia ago in his now-lost book Ἀλήθεια (*Truth*). He began by stating that "Of all things the measure is man, of all the things that are, that they are, and of the things that are not, that they are not" (Kent Sprague 1972, 4). Evidently, Protagoras was curious about how two people can disagree while both being right; his ideas were subsequently glossed by Plato in his *Theaetetus* (1921, 41).

It follows that, if individuals' cognitive architecture is fashioned by their sociocultural environment, notions of truth must be communal, and different communities will have dissimilar conceptions of truth. Communities design a system of symbols that the individual will use as a lens through which phenomenal reality is contemplated, so it is entirely predictable that people from different communities will hold antagonistic opinions on the truth and both be "right." At the level of individuals, truth is dispersed like grapeshot fired from a cannon; only the community can conceive a comprehensive, stable notion of reality and truth. That notion is buttressed by a symbology that is particular to the community and represents communal subjectivity as objectivity; in this way symbol and reality are conflated.

This approach to truth is evidently endorsed by Søren Kierkegaard, who in his *Concluding Unscientific Postscript to Philosophical Fragments* argues that "subjectivity is truth" and "truth is subjectivity." This means that, at its core, truth is not just the detection of objective data; these are important but more important is how people filter and internalize them. Therefore, from a communal and moral standpoint, how we *relate* to factual data is more significant than the unmediated facts that we perceive, so the essence of truth originates in subjectivity rather than in objective facts (Kierkegaard 1992, 213).

Especially in the early medieval, largely pre-scientific world, truth is communal (and largely non-objective) because as such it synchronizes individual minds and maintains their concordance with the community's version of reality. General agreement on a version of "truth" and reality is necessary to establish and maintain a community's coherence; this is the reason why the punishments meted out to transgressors who dare to cast doubts upon synergistic truths have been among the harshest established in communal codes. I speak of "versions" of reality because the material world in which "reality" resides has no independent meaning, no autonomous truth; the medieval community replaces that inert world with an alternative world that is an extension of its beliefs and values, making it intelligible on the community's terms. In the case of Atlantic seaboard communities like the Irish, the ancient communal truth system of its pagan natives is encroached upon by a well-organized, newly arrived, competing system introduced by Christianity. Because of the subjective nature of truth, as Kierkegaard proposed, Christianity is able to hijack pagan stories and enlist them in its competing version of truth. But the products of this encroachment are syncretic artifacts that betray the intrusion, their ancient material engaging in a struggle to subvert the new subjective "truth" that interferes with its original ethos.

So we must always assume that pagan and medieval individuals associate *truth* more so with communal moral order than with sensory experience, as their essential engagement with truth takes place in a moral register. It is correct to suppose that communal moral principles are subjective, but as Kierkegaard (1992, 213) reminds us, they are also truths. Considered historically, "truth's" inescapable subjectivity has produced celebrated misunderstandings between people from different collectives. Perhaps the best known of these is preserved in the Bible (John 18:37-38), wherein Pilate questions the nature of truth:

> [37] Then Pilate said to him, "So you are a king?" Jesus answered, "You say that I am a king. For this purpose, I was born and for this purpose, I have come into the world—to bear witness to the truth. Everyone who is of the truth listens to my voice." [38] Pilate said to him, "What is truth?" (ESV)

Philosopher John Dewey (1859–1952) would likely explain that exchange by stating that truth is not merely a cogitative relation between intelligence and its object: "Truth is the sum of beliefs whose acceptance is necessary to salvation, rather than a logical distinction" (Dewey 1993, 12). For early Christian societies, then, truth was associated fundamentally with the correct knowledge of and accurate information about God and His Creation.

It would be helpful at this juncture to point out that Salvation is part of a truth system, the likes of which are referenced above, a communal covenant that serves to cohere the Christian community; in pre-Christian societies, analogous covenants were also common elements in the preservation of social and communal cohesion. This may not be well-defined in modern scholarship. Modern cultural regimens place a premium on innovation, objectivity, and the production of discourses that are syllogistic and analytical. From the modern standpoint, the production of truth claims is an exercise in objectivity and is generally the result of individual or small-group discrete effort. In comparison, truth in pre-modern, largely oral cultures is apt to be the result of a reticulated human environment where members acquire knowledge through integral participation in the communal ethos. As a result, in the Middle Ages, personal experience with truth is rendered within a matrix of communal assumptions.

Accordingly, when medieval individuals describe the truth, they engage in a re-description of experiential information, conveying it in a conceptual form that fits the pattern of communal categorizations. Alcuin (c.735–804) gives us a good example of this process, as he observes the butchered bodies of Lindisfarne's holy men in the aftermath of the legendary Viking raid of June, 793:

> In what is the confidence of the churches of Britain if St Cuthbert and so great a number of saints do not defend their people? Either this is the beginning of greater trouble or else the sins of those living there have brought it upon them. To be sure, it has not happened by chance but is the evidence of some great guilt. (Cavill 2001, 47)

Alcuin takes the fortuitous, incidental circumstances of existence on the planet and recomposes them to fit those categorizations: the Lindisfarne monks' guilt has brought this upon them, for the universe is arranged as per God's will, and nothing happens by chance.

Patrick also composes his abduction and enslavement in Ireland as per conceptual directives of his time:

> I, Patrick, a most unlearned sinner, least of all the faithful and most contemptible among many, had as my father Calpurnius, a deacon, son of the priest Potitus, of the village of [Bannavem Taburniae]. Nearby he had a villa where I was captured. I was about sixteen years old. I did not know the true God and was taken away to Ireland with many thousand men. We deserved it because we had fallen away from God and had not kept His commandments nor obeyed His priests. [...] And God sent His wrath upon us and dispersed us among the nations and to the ends of the earth. There God opened the sense of my unbelief. Late I deplored my sins and turned with a whole heart to the Lord my God. (Bainton 1962, 67)

Furthermore, it could be said that communal concepts and categorizations rewire the medieval mind in such a way that it not only interprets experience, as in Alcuin and Patrick, but produces it. Saint Godric of Finchale (1065–1170), for example, firmly believed that he happened upon the long-dead Saint Cuthbert (c. 634–687) while on a visit to Lindisfarne and that he also met the Virgin Mary along with Mary Magdalene on a day in which he was lying prostrate in front of an altar. During this experience, "The Virgin [...] sings to Godric, teaching him the song as if she were instructing a child and telling him that he must sing it at any time he is in need of help" (Fanous and Gillespie 2011, 61-62).

Godric was not a trailblazer: Pre-Christian inhabitants of the British Isles, like their Christian descendants, described experiences in conceptual forms that conformed to communal prescriptions and fit social patterns of discernment and decipherment. Druid poet Amergin speaks of having had shapeshifting experiences; the Welsh bard Taliesin metamorphosed into diverse animals when escaping the furious Ceridwen; Irish warrior Cú Chulainn experienced bizarre alterations to his head when engaging in battle.

While these transformations could function at a symbolic level, they were also much more than allegories. In the Middle Ages, there was a persistent belief that metamorphoses were real occurrences; this is revealed in the church's constant denial of their actuality. Tertullian (c. 155 CE–c. 220) specifically rejected the likelihood of any human being transforming into anything else, as happens in Ovid's *Metamorphoses* (8 CE); Ambrose (c. 339–c. 397) affirmed that "[t]hose made after the likeness and image of God cannot be changed into the forms of beasts;" Augustine (354–430) and Thomas Aquinas (1225–1274) also contributed to the relentless discrediting of the idea that humans can transform into animals (Salisbury 2011, 141-142). "The medieval church attempted to enforce this skeptical view of metamorphosis in penitential literature from Regino to Burchard, which forbade belief that a man 'can be transformed into a wolf, in German called Werewolf, or into some other form'" (Salisbury 2011, 142).

Spence (1999, 18-19) reports that many researchers, like the noted anthropologist Edwin Sydney Hartland, have regularly interpreted the ingrained belief in real metamorphoses, shape-shifting, and transformations among the early peoples of the British Isles as essential factors in their validation of collective truths. Belief in such supernatural incidents buttressed stable patterns of human action and helped to shape people's moral and political lives. The fact that this belief was common and widespread undoubtedly supported the production of allegorical tales that substantiated communal truth.

The remote Irish island of Inis Glora (Inishglora), in the North Atlantic off the coast of the Mullet Peninsula (Leithinis an Mhuirthead), is one of the places where our exemplar, the "Children of Lir" legend, unfolds; it is part of the Irish Mythological Cycle of stories and reveals communal truth designs through the whimsical adventures of children mutating into swans. The tale of the youngsters' metamorphosis provides a set of symbolic events that serve to illustrate and reinforce collective truths; considering the pre-modern ethos, worlds such as this one, evidently created to underscore communal cognitive blueprints, can be said to be more socially relevant than the realm of tangible, observable reality.

King Lir (Lir is the genitive form of the word "sea" in Old Irish) sports a very revealing name: the Welsh Llŷr is a common noun used to designate the sea, but it also designates sea deities and warriors among pagan Brittonic-speaking peoples, as illustrated by the name of mythical hero Manawydan fab Llŷr (Manannán mac Lir), Irish warrior and king of the otherworld (mac Lir, by itself, means "son of the sea"). So the sea, which in the Christianized version is a menacing and alien space, was likely not so in the original version, as it symbolizes the children's affectionate father:

> Southward by broad Lough Derg his palace stood:
> Northward, beside Emania's lonely mere,
> In FinnahA, embowered 'mid lawn and wood,
> King Lir abode, a warn or, not a seer;
> Well loved was he, plain man with great, true heart,
> Who loathed, despite his race, the sorcerer's art.
> Five centuries lived he ere that better light
> Shone forth o'er earth from Bethlehem:-ne'ertheless
> He judged his land with justice and with might,
> Tempering the same at times with gentleness;
> And gave the poor their due; and made proclaim,
> "Let no man smite the old; the virgin shame."
> His prime was spent in wars: in middle life
> He bade a youthful princess share his throne. (Vere 1881, 187)

The story begins as Bodb Derg (King Bove) is elected king of the Tuatha Dé Danann, a position that was coveted by Lir. To make peace with his defeated rival, Derg gives Lir his daughter Aoibh in marriage. Aoibh has four children by Lir: Fionnuala, a girl, and three boys, Aodh and the twins Fiachra and Conn. The couple lives happily with their wonderful children at their side:

> Thus happy lived the pair, and happier far
> Since four fair children graced the royal house,
> Fairer than flowers, more bright than moon or star
> Shining through vista long of forest boughs.
> Finola was the eldest-six years old:
> The yearling, Conn, best loved of all that fold.
> These beauteous creatures with their mother shared
> Alike her blissful nature and sweet looks,
> Like her benign, like her blue-eyed, bright-haired,
> With voices musical as birds or brooks:
> Beings they seemed reserved for some great fate,
> Mysterious, high, elect, and separate. (Vere 1881, 188)

But Aoibh dies:

> Ah lot of man! Ah world whose life is change!
> Ah sheer descent from topmost height of good
> To deepest gulf of anguish sudden and strange!
> A nation round their monarch's gateway stood:
> All day there stood they, whispering in great dread
> The Herald came at last- "The Queen is dead!" (Vere 1881, 189)

Bodb Derg offers another daughter to Lir: "'... take [t]o wife my daughter, for thy children's sake.' Sadly he mused: but answered: 'Let it be!'" (Vere 1881, 189).

Lir marries his wife's sister Aoife, but his new bride, jealous of Lir's love for his children, orders a servant to kill them; when the servant refuses–and unable to do the deed herself–she turns the children into swans who must dwell for 900 years in diverse bodies of water: Lough Derravaragh (in County Westmeath, north of Mullingar) for 300; the Sea of Moyle, between Ireland and Scotland, for 300, and lastly in Sruth Fada Conn (Irrus Domnannthe, modern Sruwaddacon Bay, in County Mayo) for the final 300 years. King Bodb Derg learns of his daughter's treatment of his four grandchildren and turns Aoife into an air-demon.

Postliminary Christian editing of the legend is evident throughout, but is most clearly seen in the ending: to return to their human form, the children must be blessed by a monk, so they fly to the Atlantic island of Inis Glora, where a priest blesses them. Being 900 years old, they die and go live happily ever after with their parents in heaven. Inevitably, during the time they spent as swans around the coasts and isles of the Atlantic, Saint Patrick succeeded in converting Ireland to the Christian faith. As Mallory states, "later Christian redactors substituted a stilted Christian ending" that circumvents the pagan ending [...] "A glimpse of the [*Children of Lir*'s] original ending may be preserved in the 'Dream of Oengus,'" where a divine youth (Oengus) falls in love with a girl that he later finds in a lake turned into a swan; to rescue her, "Oengus changes into a similar shape and flies with her back to his mansion at Brú na Bóinne," where they live happily (Mallory 1997, 162).

As medieval minds are adapted for collective, consensual perception, they habitually record "truths" in a figurative manner: Aiofe's peculiar capacity to effect real transformations in her stepchildren is likely to have been conventional within pagan belief systems, but in the narrative logic of the Christianized text it functions as a communal metaphor for evil's subversive potential. Thus, as the children enter the watery world, it is made clear that they have departed a place that is being Christianized and have trespassed into an "other," alienating, pagan notional cosmos: "Farewell, Lough Davra, with thine isles of bloom! / Farewell, familiar tribes that grace her shore! [...] / Farewell! the voice of man we hear no more..." (Vere 1881, 195).

In keeping with the conceptual, metaphorical nature of the new, Christianizing message, this chaotic, watery, pagan "other" world to which they are sent will only dissipate (as has the story's original pre-Christian ethos) at the arrival of Christian symmetry and consistency in the person of the blessing monk and of Ireland's greatest saint, Tailkenn (St. Patrick). In another version, the spell is broken not by the priest but by Patrick's presence, as foretold in the acclimated story: "Till he, the Tailkenn, comes to sound the knell / Of darkness, and we hear his Christian bell ("Children" 1881, 364).

> Then one morning, after nine hundred long years, they heard the sound of a Christian bell, and the children of Lir at last became human again. Then a monk (who some scholars say represents St. Patrick) sprinkled holy water on the children. Fionnula put her arms around her brothers and then, consumed by their own mortalities, died. The monk buried the four children in one grave, and in a dream that night, he saw four swans flying up through the clouds to join their mother and father to take their place in Irish legend. (Wenzell 2009, 67)

This story, in all its extant versions, is an example of Irish syncretism at its best. It is also an example of the proselytizing drive to reinforce a communal ethos now based on Christian values. The medieval mind, and for that matter, much of the world before the emergence of Protestant individualism, equated the communal ethos with what was "good" or with "the truth," while individualistic frames of mind were viewed with suspicion. As Nietzsche portrays it: "The delight in the herd is more ancient than the delight in the ego; and as long as the good conscience is identified with the herd, only the bad conscience says 'I'" (Seung 2005, 42).

Conceptually, and with the Christian editing of the legend, the North Atlantic watery world, erstwhile home to the pagan "happy otherworld," is here remodeled into a spiritual wasteland, a sepulcher of darkness and peril for the soul. This is depicted quite aptly: "There anguish fell upon them: they heard the booming / Of league-long breakers white, and gazed on waves / Wreck strewn, themselves entombed, and all entombing" ("Children" 1881, 365). So while in the original version of the legend the children's anguish might have been the result of their metamorphosis and of their removal from hearth and home, in the extant text, contextualized in Christian terms, it results from dwelling in a shadowy realm existing beyond the design, symmetry, and stability of *the* faith.

In the pagan original, the children's incapacity to connect with the community of swans in their new environment or, for that matter, with any other bird, was a function of their essential alienation, as they will always remain children in the guise of swans; in the Christian format, their anguish is understood not as social but as spiritual: their alienation, originally intended to incite emotion, is in the extant text a formalistic necessity, as forming communal relations in the watery world would have effectively codified and given social symmetry to an environment that is an ideogram for the spiritual void of pre-Christian life.

Additionally, the fact that the watery world was originally a spiritually beneficial concept and not anathema is evidenced by the children's loving father, a pagan ruler whose name, Lir, means "sea." The children, hence, are literally the children of the sea, of a loving father whom they cherish; after the Christianizing deviation of the legend, perspectives change, as it is now inferred that they have been sent into a watery pagan darkness for those 900 years. The story then is turned into a message to the catechumen: the children will suffer the torments of alienation until they experience and are fully integrated into Christian spiritual arrangements. So in this particular legend, the Atlantic backdrop changes its symbolic function as it passes into the hands of Christian editors. An evidently pagan story of metamorphosis and the wages of evil is turned into a vehicle that will deliver a new paradigm for a communal "truth."

If the children's metamorphosis seems incongruous with what is generally perceived as a Christian text, that is because the tale is pagan and the Christian enhancements disturb the original premise. We must remember that while syncretic activity masks and redirects the dynamic forces of a subjugated, original text, its residual energy never dissipates completely. This energy is clearly felt in characters and events that seem to be at odds with the dominating spirit of the narrative. But for the proselytizers, such incongruities and seemingly irreconcilable dissonance were necessary evils, and they'd likely be perceived, in tales like "The Children of Lir," as minor defects in a practical vehicle for an urgent "truth." That "truth" is the one espoused and promulgated by the church, and it was indispensable to deliver it using vehicles such as this legend, which were considered practical and available.

In addition, for its Christian editors, this story's utility hinged on the fact that its original version already pointed to an adaptable, coherent organization with unambiguous supporting relations among its parts. This organization hinged on the intelligibility of the moral message: worldly evil and jealousy cause the children's misery and probable death; victimized innocents, they embark on a journey that is comparable to the dead's souls crossing into the otherworld, and that crossing takes them into Atlantic waters, a realm that had been the site of Celtic ontological considerations. Moreover, the original pagan portrayal of the dead's souls transforming into swans as they cross into the otherworld is evident in the story's fundamental image:

> "[T]he souls of the dead [were] represented as birds as far back as the Egyptian papyri of the various Books of the Dead and as the Epic of Gilgamesh. Bird souls also abound in Celtic legends of the Isle of Maidens across the waters where the dead are transformed into beautiful swans" (Lansing Smith 1997, 133).

In the course of time and after the punishment of the wrongdoer, the children experience a sort of Christian rebirth: the return home. Subsequent to the editing work of proselytizing hands, the journey to the Celtic otherworld realm becomes a voyage into the darkness of the previous, and perhaps still competing, worldview, while the return is a reawakening in Christ, an event that takes place only after the haze of evil and ignorance has been lifted by the arrival of the faith: "'Brothers! The Tailkenn [the "tonsured one," Saint Patrick] treads our Erin's earth!' / And as the lifted mist gave view more large / They saw a blue bay with a fair green marge" ("Children" 1881, 375).

The characters' binary existence in both the confused pagan cosmos (pre-Christian Ireland) and the new, systematized world of the faith is acknowledged in some respects at the end of the tale when the siblings ask the priest to "Make fair our grave where Land and Ocean meet" ("Children" 1881, 375), that is to say, at the boundary between the tangible, quantifiable, newly Christianized land and the unyielding, incalculable, pagan Atlantic.

When we read the extant text of "The Children of Lir," we can still, to this day, feel the tension produced by contending ontological contexts. Pagan and Christian substances compete to create, in their own particular manner, a frame of reference for the reader to observe reality and discern a "truth" based on moral codes. The pagan society that produced "The Children of Lir" needed to conceptualize that reality in compliance with social and religious expediency just as much as subsequent Christian communities.

Consequently, "The Children of Lir" illustrates how "truth," absorbed by credenda, occupies contested space in syncretic texts. In its extant form, this traditional Irish story displays a tension between the original (pagan) strategy for revealing "truth," based on the unadorned notion that evil is the unregimented absence of good, and the new one, with its schematized dogma, in which evil is un-Christian and can only be curbed through the acceptance of the Word of God. Strategies for moral understanding have always been managed by the community to avoid confusion, but as "The Children of Lir" shows, narrative dissonance can result from the oscillation between competing value systems; the Irish medieval community is undergoing profound transformations that are clearly revealed in syncretic productions like this.

But why employ pagan symbols to convey Christian truth? I believe that the swans are there to create not only the semblance of uninterrupted rhythm between pagan and Christian cognitive cadency but also to evoke the liminal atmosphere that swans–ancient symbols of departing dead souls–can create. Unlike what happens in modern awareness and perception modes, people in medieval Europe rarely experienced existential dislocation as an abstract concept; their anxieties about the features of the universe that were not convincingly explained by their priests needed to be symbolized, and this happened in the form of non-human creatures (swans, sea-monsters...). Existential angst as experienced today was, at most, very rare. This is because medieval persons were in some measure created as observers of reality through their means of identification with prevailing religious and social ideologies and by the correct interpretation of their symbols.

Therefore, in the intimate act of conceptualizing the world that is perceived through experience, medieval people would operate within the closed set of interpretive schemes that was operative within a social matrix whose credenda depended on symbols. Accordingly, the medieval person's "truth" was built upon a *socialized* perception of reality whose discernible marks were not objective (science has a long way to go before it succeeds in explaining reality) but metaphorical; Christian medievals consequently perceived a *created* world in which the person was a constituent member of a divine project.

A popular myth such as "The Children of Lir" is, then, politically reconstructed. No reference to modern politics is intended: it is *political* because it is designed to coalesce social energies, which, in medieval Europe, are thoroughly intertwined with religion. In the broad geography offered by the objective, tangible world, a mythical story like this helps to *situate* the consumer of the myth in a desirable subject position *vis-à-vis* commonly observed social behaviors while, at the same time, affording that person a moral design with which to interpret such observations.

So it was expedient for the proselytizing early Irish church to invade ancient, popular myths like that of the swan children and redirect representational energies already present in it. But, as observed above, that invasion by Christian exigencies turns "The Children of Lir" into a contested ideological space.

Accordingly, in the Middle Ages "truth" emerges from that which is verbalized and articulated in communal symbols that buttress the community's shared beliefs. A medieval individual does not just experience reality in the raw: that experience has a certain systematized structure that is constantly reinforced by the symbol. Popular literature tends to aestheticize and make accessible the subjective assumptions of belief by energizing them with captivating and enjoyable popular substance, so tales like this become indispensable tools to convey truth.

In almost all early syncretic texts there are competing versions of truth. Pagan Irish legends like "The Children of Lir" were symbolic creations that were buttressed by the acceptance of metamorphosis as–for all one knows–a real thing. From time immemorial, they had reinforced communal subjective frames of reference and were essential in the organization of pagan acts of intellection; their Christian assimilation is a disturbing process of acculturation and adaptation in which the original pagan material, I reiterate, resists, and pushes back, exposing Christian accretions as artificial anomalies. The result is that these texts emerge as aggressed environments and contested spaces.

"The Children of Lir" has proven to be a very popular and enduring myth. The critical social relevance of mythical tales such as this suggests that the medieval *subject* is inherently predisposed towards the mythical. This is so in the sense that the medieval, pre-scientific mind observes through a myth-lens that establishes frame-of-reference alignments for its observations of external objects and phenomena; these are edited as *representable* events like mutating children that explain a universe that, at this stage of western European cultural development, cannot be described through other methods.

Myth's mission, then, is to *socialize* real-world experience through the establishment of apposite symbolic spaces and events such as those created in "The Children of Lir," thus furnishing a systematized "reality" for the medieval subject. Once the medieval mind socializes external stimuli, "objectivity" becomes synchronous with social covenant. In "The Children of Lir" a newfangled Christian system for generating "objectivity" and identifying truth has been brought into play; it is a system based on a strategy to re-synchronize pagan data by embedding new codes that will alter its purpose. As such, it modifies the story to change the meaning it conveys while not modifying how it conveys it. This has allowed for the original pagan symbolic space to be re-constituted as epitome for understanding the preeminent, superlative truth that is conveyed by Christian faith, a truth that is now socially inscribed and compulsory.

One of the essential aspects of this myth, one that must have attracted the attention of the early church, is its efficient construction of symbolic space. In this story, a relatively stable environment of home life and parental caring has been disrupted by the death of the mother and the arrival of the evil stepmother. As a result, the ergonomic arrangement that formed the family's perspectives on the universe has been dismantled. The watery realms where the children are sent to dwell epitomize their new perspective: where in the original the children were likely kept alive by the compassionate sea and other bodies of water, the Christian environment confronts them with a sea that is an alienating, purposeless universe that is unresponsive to human needs; in it, they must now fend for themselves.

But it is important to note that the space constructed around the children in the extant text is symbolic, which means that it is promotional, tractable, and will eventually yield to human concerns. Human concerns can be of a subjective, emotional nature, as I suspect the original pagan story presented them, or of a more spiritual, religious nature, which is the way they were eventually framed by Christian editors. The myth, then, presents us with a general environment of alienation whose ontological energies were seen as malleable by Christian proselytizers, who redirected them to accommodate new spiritual requirements.

Symbolic space–as formulated in "The Children of Lir"– is constituted as a countermeasure to the objective universe's oblivion and its detachment from human concerns. In symbolic space the medieval mind de-structures the universe's insensible framework and restructures it in human terms, mending the visceral dislocations that purely material influx provokes in medieval ethea. As in so many revised stories of pagan origin, once "The Children of Lir" has been sublimated into the new religion, that symbolic space becomes the stage for the "performance" of a Christian truth that is indispensable to convey to Atlantic seaside communities. Moreover, situating part of the story on an island in the Atlantic places it in a traditional, time-honored region where symbolic space has always proliferated. Moreover, it shrouds the story in that misty haze that attends the great ocean, a place where prosaic cognitive strategies break down and an "other" cosmos becomes contextual. In short, the once pagan Atlantic, with its islands, bays, and venerable indigenous cultural affiliations, is the space where, employing primitive myths and legends, a remote Irish clerical community would begin to contrive a symbolic genealogy for its flock's place in the Christian commonwealth.

Yet, and notwithstanding the proselytizers' great efforts to transfigure the story, a counterpointing subtext emanating from a dense, consolidated cosmos of sea-gods and metamorphosed children clearly breaks through the surface. The existence of that other cosmos is still a critical part of the narrative logic of the story, although it has been diverted and exploited to create a distinction between the "darkness" of that cosmos and the light of the Christian faith. Moreover, because of competing, ambiguous claims to its symbolic space, in "The Children of Lir" we can hear the strong echoes of a society, recently Christianized, that is still striving to assemble its *social* reality in terms of newly-sanctioned collective values. In consequence, the inventory of human behaviors and social interactions articulated in the narrative has been hastily re-codified into the sphere of Christian belief: because of that celerity, the spiritual syntax of that belief can be observed to falter in its thrust to introduce a measure of doctrinal intelligibility into an intransigent world of metamorphoses and demigods.

Accordingly, with the adapted story the priestly editors attempted to re-standardize people's awareness of their surroundings through the revised version of an ancient and conventional mode of perception, providing a recalibrated lens for their consciousness. The point must be stressed: medieval people would certainly not conceive of truth in the manner in which empiricists the likes of Locke, Berkeley, and Hume taught generations of thinkers to do. Rather, truth tended to abide within communal ideological environments. Consequently, if we are to understand the church's efforts to claim a story like this, we must regard the general criterion for truth in medieval societies as a social arrangement of knowledge that uses representations as symbols that directly relate to normative systems of belief. Thus, a skilled rearrangement of these traditional representations to integrate them into the new dogma was critically important.

The church can be regarded as successful in its endeavors. If one were to ask a medieval Irishman the purpose of life, he very likely would have responded that it was "the attainment of salvation." There is nothing particularly unusual about this statement, as most western Europeans would have responded in the same manner. Yet this constitutes a sea-change in the island's culture, as there was nothing even resembling salvation in Celtic cosmology. If we continued chatting with this person, it would become apparent that this concept of purpose had imposed a compulsory pattern of perception on him. In the inflections and wording of his speech, we would recognize that pattern by the canonical overtones and apocalyptic nuances. Furthermore, his figures of speech and choice of metaphors would have revealed an idiosyncratic mode of self-understanding that was anchored on collective Christian archetypes.

The affinity between the systemization of this man's remarks and communal spiritual arrangements would become evident as this individual expanded on his view of reality. We'd quickly realize that even when the symbolic articulation of his environment resembled that of his pagan ancestors, it nevertheless had been restructured to promote an allegorical construction of self and community in consonance with the church's credenda. In essence, symbolic discourses such as that of "The Children of Lir" would have been assimilated by this individual in an organized, conventional manner that reflected the successes of the proselytizers.

In view of this, it can be said that phenomenal reality was absorbed and interpreted by the medieval Irishman through a myth imaginary that, while having roots in the pagan past, now promoted the Christian message. With the introduction of Christian belief, reality was now seen as created by an almighty being, one who cares for humanity; in this new scenario, a pagan reality that did not include a concept of universal *purpose* needed to be articulated in a different, apposite register and the universe's impermeable, unreceptive nature needed to be challenged. Pagan myth was a convenient and accessible tool with which to accomplish this: at a subconscious level, the early Irish were already able to perceive a reality that had been symbolically constructed according to recognizable social blueprints. Evidently, these blueprints were then subjected to doctrinal patterns dictated by the church, an institution that considers the soul as the enduring part of the human being, and reality the territory where the soul proves its worth.

Additionally, if we were to access the psyche of, let's say, a tenth-century Breton, Welsh, or Irish Christian whose livelihood depended on or was somehow tied to the ocean, we would most certainly find a mythology, that is to say, a mythical dramatization of reality, but that dramatization would very likely exhibit more syncretic characteristics than that of inland populations. Inland, people might assemble a concept of reality that coordinates more closely with the designs of social blueprints: all around you, there is water to drink, soil to provide sustenance, solid ground on which to walk, materials with which to build shelter, and people with which to interact. Doctrine prescribed to people a way in which to *know* the world that, on *terra firma*, was not terribly problematic.

On the other hand, the Atlantic presented an ontological problem. Doctrinal prescriptions necessarily tasked the individual with a role to perform; they were a set of instructions which, if followed, would help him save his soul. And material "reality" was the exclusive site on which to perform it. But such a performance could not take place unhindered next to the Atlantic, a place that resisted ontological arrangements. Inexplicably, the sun sank into it; it rained but its water level was constant; rivers poured massive contents of water into it without altering its immutable tides. Was it infinite? If not, whatever was on the other side was not accounted for in the itemized catalog of God's Creation. The church, then, could more readily succeed in Atlantic coastal territory if it could somehow repurpose an ancient symbolic system by infusing it with its standardized prescriptions. It found a way to accomplish the task through its transubstantiation of pagan texts like "The Children of Lir."

We see in early Irish literature that pagan myth had already begun to construct a symbolic system to describe the vast, unruly presence of the Atlantic Ocean, specifically by placing otherworld and magical realms within its expanse. In an already Christianized Atlantic seaboard, the enduring intractability of "other," "unconventional" pagan spaces always threatened to undermine the coherence of the Christian narrative that was superimposed on it. Christian truth is grounded upon the boundless, infallible wisdom available in sacred writ, and yet pagan underlying material has the enduring subversive capacity to contravene credenda and formulate a competing "truth." Christian forays into the pagan Atlantic on the backs of pagan texts were an incursion into symbolic domains that were not countenanced by doctrine nor Scripture. Challenges to the validity of scriptural explanations surfaced everywhere in *immrama* and *echtrai*, buttressed by a contrasting tradition of symbolic creatures and events, cryptograms signaling truths that were firmly imbedded in the pagan mind.

Merlin: society and the self

1.7. From Robert de Boron's *Merlin en prose*. c. 1200.

Merlin Dictates Prophesies to a Scribe.

Merlin (Myrddin Wyllt) is a character that appears in medieval Welsh stories and legends. In Middle Welsh poetry he is depicted as a leading bard and is the narrative voice in several poems in both the *Black Book of Camarthen* and the *Red Book of Hergest*. A version of the legend tells of Merlin having gone mad after a battle, then wandering the forests where he acquires his magical powers.

While there is evidence that Merlin's legend reflects historical events (q.v.), there is some indication that there was a Celtic tradition of "mad man" tales from which the Merlin legend may have derived some of its features. There is, for example, an Irish story called *Buile Shuibhne* (The Madness of Shuibhne) that recounts the adventures of King Shuibhne mac Colmáin of the Dál nAraidi (his name appears as early as the ninth century) (Shaw 1998, 115). Having been cursed by St. Rónán Finn after he expels and then attacks the saint and kills one of his psalmists, Shuibhne sets off for the Battle of Mag Rath (near modern Moira, 637 A.D.), where he is driven insane by all the carnage and savagery. For seven years he roams the forest of Ros Bearaigh, swinging from tree to tree like a primate, after which he wanders around Ireland, Scotland, and western England. In the end, Shuibhne is killed by the jealous husband of a woman entrusted with feeding him. The jealous man used the spear that Shuibhne had used to kill Saint Ronan's psalmist, thus the saint's curse ("you shall die by the same spear") comes true.

Brought into the Arthurian legend by Geoffrey of Monmouth (c. 1100–c. 1155) as a wise wizard, son of an incubus and a mortal woman, Merlin sinks his roots very deep into Britain's ancient traditions. He may be the alternate manifestation of a Celtic Zeus-like god associated with the sun: some of the legends tell of his disappearance in a glass house into the sea, where he receives constant visits from the Lady of the Lake (the Dawn). "The Lady of the Lake being represented coming every day to solace Merlin in his loneliness, is in thorough harmony with the mythological notion that made the dawn-goddess ally herself with the sun-god" (Rhys 1892, 158).

Stonehenge, which according to Geoffrey of Monmouth was transported from Ireland by Merlin using his vast intelligence ("It is not by sinew but by knowledge that these stones shall be moved") (Geoffrey 2008, 152), may also have been a place of worship for a Merlin/Zeus-like sun god, which would explain the legendary connection with the wizard echoed in Geoffrey's account. The Brittonic (now Welsh) speaking folks that populated Britain before the coming of the Saxons called him Myrddin Wyllt, place him in Cumbria, northwestern England (a word derived from Cymru, the Welsh name for Wales), and surround him with a host of diverse tales and anecdotes. These narratives are preserved in numerous poems written in Wales (in medieval Welsh, or Cymraeg) and later on in southern Scotland.[2]

Much of the research on this important character puts forward the hypothesis that Myrddin Wyllt (Merlin the Wild Man) was almost certainly an actual person whose story begins as a soldier at the Battle of Arfderydd, which the B-text of the *Annales Cambriae* lists as "Bellum arterid" and places in the entry for the year 573 (Goodrich 2003, 106). Specific data for an actual Merlin is circumstantial, as there aren't precise historical records in Britain for the early post-Roman period and, what is more, information of all sorts passed from generation to generation largely through oral means. The battle itself is mentioned not only in Geoffrey of Monmouth's *Vita Merlini*, but frequently in several medieval Welsh texts such as *Trioedd Ynys Prydein* (Triads of the Island of Britain) and the *Llyfr Coch Hergest* (The Red Book of Hergest). Reference to the battle is also made in a hagiography, the *Life of St. Kentigern*, written by Jocelyn of Furness, while fourteenth-century Scottish historian John of Fordun says that it was fought "in the field between Liddel and Carwanolow," by a place called

---

[2] For an insightful account of the Merlin legends, see Stephen Knight, *Merlin: Knowledge and Power Through the Ages* (Ithaca, NY: Cornell University Press, 2009).

Arthuret. Historian W. F. Skene identifies the location as two small hills known as the Arthuret Knowes, one mile from Longtown, in the Carlisle district of Cumbria in northwestern England (Ardrey 2008, 173).

The extant material is not clear as to the nature of the conflict, but it is apparent that the adversaries were two rival British factions, seemingly without the involvement of the English. The combatants were the warlord Gwenddoleu ap Ceidio on one side, and possibly his cousins Peredur and Gwrgi on the other. The power base for these last two is not evident: they were either princes of Ebrauc (Modern York), or of Gwynedd, a kingdom in northwestern Wales. The princely titles may have been embellishments for effect: most likely this was a "clan skirmish among the *Coelings*, the descendants of *Coel Hen Godebog*" (Bromwich 2006, 220). During the battle not only is Gwenddoleu slain, but Merlin, fighting for Gwenddoleu, kills the son of his twin sister Gwenddydd, the young man being a warrior on the side of Peredur and Gwrgi. This last event, together with the loss of the warlord and the sight of the hundreds of slain warriors that littered the field, sent Merlin over the edge. He goes mad and spends the rest of his life wandering through the "Caledonian Forest, once haunted by Merlin, and which stretched from sea to sea" (Stuart-Glennie 84) north of the Clyde River, in Scotland. There he acquires great powers of prophecy and magic.

Therefore, while there may have been a man who provided the starting point for the diverse Merlin narratives, the fact is that they reflect a series of popular elements and literary tropes that probably account for the development and popularity of the legend. Dominic Alexander (2008, 126) has suggested that the essential motif of the Merlin legend, that of the encounter of the brutish holy man with a king, is very ancient, first appearing in Gilgamesh's meeting with Enkidu (*Gilgamesh*, 2nd millennium BCE). He also points out that in the early Hindu *Vedas* (1700–1100 BCE), saint and wild man are evidently one and the same. Clearly, the *homo sylvester* topos is one that is widely spread throughout ancient folklore.

An additional indication of the Merlin legend's connection with antiquity is the fact that Geoffrey makes Merlin the offspring of an incubus who slept with his mother (whose name is given as Adhan in the oldest version of the thirteenth-century *Prose Brut*).[3] This has biblical parallels with Genesis,

---

[3] Originally written in Anglo-Norman, the *Prose Brut* is a collection of medieval chronicles that recount the history of Britain. It describes the founding of Britain by Brutus of Troy, great-grandson of Aeneas, and gives an account of the reign of Welsh king Cadwaladr, who reigned in Gwynedd c. 655 - 682 AD. It also includes legendary kings such as King Arthur, and some parts of it are based on Geoffrey of Monmouth's text.

chapter 6, which states that the "sons of God" desired the "daughters of men," at a time when giants walked the earth; the progeny resulting from these unions were said to be "mighty men" (verse 4). In this light, Merlin's heredity could be considered a rhetorical device that provides an explanation for his preternatural powers.

Yet what is of most interest to us here is the fact that several versions of the Merlin story have him being born out of the sea, subsequently disappearing "across the sea, whence he came" (Higginson 1899, 60). The above-mentioned *Trioedd Ynys Prydein* (Triads of the Island of Britain) has a description of "The Three Generous Heroes of the Island of Britain" where one of these, called Nud or Nodens (subsequently called Merlin), emerges from the sea bringing 21,000 head of cattle and eventually becoming king, warrior, magician, and prophet. He hails, then, from a kingdom under the waves; to it he will return after all of his trials in this world are finished.

Merlin's [a.k.a. Nud, Nodens] associations with the divine (he is conflated with Zeus in Celtic legend) and with the Atlantic otherworld are solid: "For me, however, the other stories which leave Merlin in an isle off the Welsh or the Armoric coast have more interest […], as they help more than anything to explain, how the Zeus of the Celts could become so intimately associated with the sea as we found him [Zeus] under the names Llud, Nud, Nodens" (Rhys 1892, 159). Further associations of Merlin/Nud/Nodens with the Atlantic appear in the remains of a Celtic sanctuary in western Great Britain. A visit to the Nodens temple complex at Lydney Park, overlooking the Severn Estuary, reveals a mosaic floor whose surviving fragments show sea monsters, dolphins, and bronze reliefs portraying a sea god, tritons, and fishermen. A bronze object recovered from the site depicts a sea god on a chariot surrounded by tritons (Geoff Adams 2005, 71).

It is more than likely that in the earliest oral versions of the Merlin tale, composed shortly after the Battle of Arfderydd in the sixth century (Byghan 2018, 85), the main event in Merlin's experience of "this" world was the loss of his mind amid the carnage. It is in the aftermath of the bloody event that he flees the world of men in order to live out his existence as a wild man in the forests. The sources clearly point to the cause of his madness: the bloodbath, or in other words, the irrational social and political structures that surround him. By stressing Merlin's slaughter of his own nephew in the battle, the story puts the spotlight on the disparity between the individual's personal, intimate volition and the social and political structures in accordance with which he must conduct his actions. In the poem *Yr Afallennau* (The Apple Trees) from *The Red Book of Hergest* one encounters Merlin's lament regarding his twin sister Gwenddydd:

> Now Gwenddydd loves me not and does not greet me
> I am hated by Gwasawg, the supporter of Rhydderch–
> I have killed her son and daughter.
> Death has taken everyone, why does it not call me? (Byghan 2018, 85)

Collective structures activate and guide individual behavior, and as a member of society, Merlin has little choice but to contribute to their permanence. On an individual level, Merlin would never think of harming his sister's boy, let alone her daughter, but his commitment to the socio-political arrangement supersedes individual will; in the insanity of a group conflict that has pitted him against his nephew, he kills him. Madness in Merlin has a societal, not a personal origin. Merlin fully realizes this fact, and that is the reason why he decides to leave society and become Myrddin Wyllt, Merlin the Wild. Undoubtedly, the adjective speaks of Merlin's desire to stop perpetuating a collective mindset that produces outcomes such as this battle: he is no longer a player on this insane stage, and having retreated from society, he is given the title of "Wild."

The many Merlin tales, be they as disparate and unrelated as Briton folk tales and Geoffrey of Monmouth's account, still reveal the strong bond that connects people's individual self with the social forces in which this self is implicated. They reveal that the relationship between our individual selves and society is dialectical: we cooperate in order to perpetuate it, and it, in turn, controls our actions in very significant ways. Merlin kills his nephew at the Battle of Arfderydd; King Arthur kills his son Mordred at the Battle of Camlann: murder is portrayed with both personal and social features. In the Merlin tales it is never an individual incident, but a relational affair, it occurs precisely as a consequence of the deformation of the individual will by its social burdens. Society is so much more powerful than the individual, that the individual seems a feeble atom, hostage to absurd social forces beyond his control.

The Merlin saga makes it evident that issues that have proven so problematic for modern societies are issues that also disconcerted the medieval world. In Merlin's story, we witness the drama inherent to the relationship between the self and the social realm; it is a spectacle that articulates the uneasy relationship between agency and volition. Effectively, the legend deals with a problem that has been endemic in the human experience ever since people began to form societies.

Merlin, the person, has emerged from the independence and immunity of the Atlantic wilderness onto the social obligations of dry land. The implications of this change of neighborhood are clear: on dry land, the individual does not have the power to construct an authentic self. His horrible act on the battlefield makes it obvious that society is out of touch with the individual, that our actions are dictated by social designs that obstruct our volition and over which we have no agency. To be a member of society, Merlin has to abandon his individuality and become an implement that helps that society function. In rebelling against that role, Merlin forsakes the social realm and becomes a wild man in remote forests, striving to round out his true self unopposed by social constraints.

Merlin may have been *socially* determined to commit murder, but the freedom he lost as a member of society he subsequently regained in the forest. He has refused to keep cooperating, and the broad magical powers that he gains among the trees are an allegory for his newly expanded consciousness and awareness of the world and our place in it. When at last he returns to the great western ocean whence he emerged, he will have left behind all traces of "social" behavior and regained a mental geography where human society is not operational and the will may ramble in unrestricted freedom.

Chapter 2

South

The Canary Islands: fantasy and the imagination

2.1. Hieronymus Bosch's "Garden of Earthly Delights." c. 1500.

The "Drago" tree, endemic to the Canary Islands, appears on the extreme left.

Sometime between 1490 and 1510, Dutch artist Hieronymus Bosch (c. 1450–1516) painted what many art historians consider his best work, the triptych whose modern title is "The Garden of Earthly Delights," housed in Madrid's Prado Museum since 1939. It appears that Bosch intended the three scenes of the inner triptych to be read in chronological order from left to right. In the left panel, we see the Earthly Paradise, with God holding Eve's wrist and presenting her to Adam, who is sitting down with his toes touching God's robe. Next, the central panel is a scenic view of a bountiful creation, where human beings–many engaging in questionable behaviors–strange animals, large fruits, and fantastical dwellings crowd the space. Last comes the darkest of the three panels. It portrays human beings as if they were being punished for their neglectful stewardship of God's creation, agonizing in a nightmare of misery and the torments of damnation.

What is of interest to us in "The Garden of Earthly Delights," is a detail that has been generally overlooked by art historians: Bosch's setting for the Earthly Paradise, in the left panel, is the Canary Islands. It is not difficult to come to this conclusion when one spots, at the panel's far left, a *Dracaena draco*, a tree commonly called "drago" in the Canaries that is autochthonous to the islands. It is such a unique tree that it is impossible to mistake it for anything else, and Bosch has depicted it masterfully. "One conspicuous, indeed legendary, endemic species of the Canaries is the so-called dragon tree (*Dracaena draco*), which was the source of the 'dragon's blood' much prized by early European seafarers as a source of varnish, medicine, incense, and dye" (Blondel 2010, 55).

In opting for the Canaries as the location for the Earthly Paradise, Bosch may have been tapping into a familiar tradition, conventional in the Middle Ages, that identified this Atlantic archipelago with Eden; tracing this tradition to its sources takes us very far back in time, to a place where historical fact inevitably fades into speculation. Likewise, its attendant mythology conceivably goes back as far as the time when the Canaries were first spotted by seafarers. King Juba II of Mauritania (r. 25 BCE–25 CE) wrote to the emperor in Rome about an expedition that he dispatched to investigate the islands. "His explorers sighted several of the 'Fortunate Isles,' and their description left no doubt that the islands were the Canaries. They related seeing no humans but encountering ferocious dogs" (Din 1988, 4). By the time of Ptolemy (90 CE–168 CE), the tradition of the Canaries as Earthly Paradise was entrenched in the cultural mainstream: "Evoking the motif of 'the earthly paradise,' the phrase 'happy islands' also suggests Ptolemy's 'Fortunate Isles,' a place of endless bliss at the western edge of the world, which he identified with what we now call the Canary Islands" (Morris 2002, 73). What's more, the term "Fortunate Isles" seems to have been of common usage among the Romans when referring to the Canaries (Javierre 2004, 396).

Speculation about the islands' transcendental features was encouraged by Pliny the Elder (23 CE–79 CE), who, basing his account on King Juba's descriptions, wrote that they were uninhabited, although he claimed that there were imposing buildings there, so ancient that they were in ruins. Plutarch (45 CE–120 CE) adds that the islands were inhabited, that the soil was so rich that it produced spontaneous vegetation, and that "it is firmly believed, even by the barbarous natives themselves, that this is the seat of the Blessed" (Abreu y Galindo 1764, 166).

Writing in the early Middle Ages, Isidore of Seville (570–636) tells us that he can understand why earlier writers thought that the Canary Islands were the Earthly Paradise. In his *Etymologies* (XIV, 6, 8) he states:

> Fortunatarum insulae vocabulo suo significant omnia ferre bona, quasi felices et beatae fructuum ubertate. Sua enim aptae natura pretiosarum poma silvarum parturiunt; fortuitis vitibus iuga collium vestiuntur; ad herbarum vicem messis et holus vulgo est. Vnde gentilium error et

saecularium carmina poetarum propter soli fecunditatem easdem esse Paradisum putaverunt. (Isidore vi)

The name Fortunate Islands suggests that these isles are rich in all types of resources; their delightful abundance seems to have compelled writers to consider them the seat of all joy and bliss. The most precious trees produce fruit spontaneously; the hilltops are covered with vines that grow where no one has planted them, and instead of grass you will find cereals and vegetables. That is why the gentiles and the pagan poets, swayed by the fertility of the soil, considered those islands to be Paradise. (My translation)

In addition, Geoffrey of Monmouth may have been referencing the Canary Islands when in the *Vita Merlini* he has King Arthur traveling there to be healed:

Insula pomorum que Fortunata vocatur
ex re nomen habet quia per se singula profert.
Non opus est illis sulcantibus arva colonis,
omnis abest cultus nisi quem natura ministrat.
Ultro fecundas segetes producit et uvas
nataque poma suis pretonso gramine silvis.
Omnia gignit humus vice graminis ultro redudans,
annis centenis aut ultra vivitur illic.

The island of apples, which is called the Fortunate
island has its name because it produces all things
for itself. There is no work for the farmers in
plowing the fields, all cultivation is absent except
for what nature manages by herself. On its own the
island produces fertile crops and grapes and native
apples by means of its own trees in the cropped
pastures. On its own the overflowing soil puts forth
all things in addition to the grass, and in that place
one lives for one hundred years or more. (Huber 2007, n.p.)

As Patch (1970, 284) shows, Geoffrey may have been echoing Isidore of Seville in the Spaniard's description of the Canaries, the Fortunate Isles of the classical world. Accordingly, the identification of Avalon (Celtic word for "island of apples") with the Canaries ("Fortunate Island") in the *Vita Merlini* is quite clear.

As medieval seafarers picked up where the ancients left off and ventured farther into the Atlantic, some of the myths associated with its islands may well have been reinforced by observed reality: the Canary Islands, perhaps the first archipelago to be visited outside the Mediterranean, offered explorers a vision of immensity and majesty that was beyond the scope of their experience:

massive mountains that could be seen towering above the clouds long before the coastlines were spotted, soil that was hot to the touch, volcanoes, people who lived in a utopian stone age and had dogs that did not bark, pyramids, mummies.

Moreover, encounters between Canary Islanders and early medieval sailors may have presented Christendom with an epistemological conundrum. For the nascent religion, whose dogmatic concepts of geography were formed by an admixture of Old Testament notions and Greek and Roman models, the only three continents (Europe, Asia, and Africa) were surrounded by a body of water and were inhabited by the descendants of Noah's sons, Ham, Shem, and Japheth. Furthermore, every individual in those populations could trace their origins to Adam and Eve. The existence of an archipelago outside of the prearranged cosmos disturbed such postulations: here were seven islands and nearby islets beyond the Straits of Gibraltar whose populations did not sail and, more importantly, did not show any evidence of ever having had the ability to do so. This meant that they had no traceable link to either Adam or Noah, nor had they the remotest idea about the teachings of Christ. Yet, and possibly unbeknownst to medieval mariners, the islanders had been visited before by ancient sailors and explorers (Mauritanians, Numidians, Phoenicians Carthaginians, and Romans) that must have been flabbergasted by them and consequently began a fruitful exchange of wares and worldviews (Abreu y Galindo 1764, 173). Additionally, the discovery of Roman amphoras in and around the island of Lanzarote (Cobo 1996, 75) proves that trade with the islanders was taking place long before the Spanish conquest of the Canaries.

It is almost certain that what the Canary islanders were exchanging with the visitors went well beyond commodities and baubles. What makes this apparent is the fact that there seem to be parallels between ancient Canary Islander cosmology and European mythology, correspondences explained neither by subsequent medieval encounters nor by cultural tampering on the part of Spanish authorities. Such analogies are, more likely, products of that early exchange between two sets of people astounded by their mutual discovery.

Indigenous populations in the Canaries had a well-developed mythological cosmos. That mythology was devastated when the Spaniards arrived in the fifteenth century, bringing with them a rigorous enforcement of Christian dogma. Yet some of the myths, legends, and fantastic characters that sustained the Canarian ethos (the maxios, spirits of dead guanches that travel over water; Tibicenas the hell-hound; the transparentes, a type of leprechaun that roams the forests) were preserved in folk stories and by some of the more open-minded priests and administrators that Spanish church and crown assigned to the islands.

These Guanche myths and legends are conserved in works by many writers. To reference just a few, I would mention churchmen Pedro Bontier and Juan le Verrier's *Historia del primer descubrimiento y Conquista de las Canarias, principiada en el año de 1402, por el Sr. Juan de Bethencourt...* (History of the First Discovery and Conquest of the Canaries, Begun in the Year 1402 by Juan de Bethencourt... [first quarter of the fifteenth century]); explorer Aloisio de Cadamosto's (Alvise Ca' da Mosto [1432–1488]) (Of the Seven Canary Islands, and of Their Customs [printed in 1533]); chronicler Gomes Eannes de Zurara's (1410–c. 1473) *Crónica de Guinea* (Chronicle of Guinea [1450]); and Andrés Bernáldez's (d. 1513) *Memorias* (Memories [c. 1493]). Other writers who contribute to the information on the Canary Islanders' culture are historian Juan de Barros (1496–1570), historian Francisco López de Gómara (1511–1566), and father Alonso de Espinosa (1543–1502), who interviewed surviving Guanches several decades after the conquest of Tenerife (1496).

Among these ancient tales is one that explains how in a very remote past there was only one vast island that, after a massive earthquake, shattered and formed the seven islands in the Canary Archipelago. Even Bartolomé de las Casas, the heroic defender of Indians during the Spanish conquest of the Americas, took this Canary Islander myth for a fact (Uriarte 2006, 165). The astonishing elevation of its islands' landmass, and its uncanny verticality, could easily lead reasonable observers like de las Casas to such a conclusion, and even the islanders' myths of origin reflect their own sense of wonder at such geographic grandiosity: once Achamán, the creator god, literally "the sustainer of heaven and earth" (Abercrombie 1916, 106), had finished creating the Canary Islands, he stood atop the Teide Volcano, their highest point, for a bit of thoughtful reflection. Witnessing the majesty of his creation, he decided to create human beings in order to have its beauty and perfection recognized (Moreno Martínez 2007, 50). It is also telling that in Gran Canaria the name for this god is "Acorán": contact with Arabs sailing to the island from a recently Islamized northern Africa (seventh century) could very well account for this appellation, homonym with Islam's Holy Book.

Another interesting facet of ancient Canarian myths is the concept of Wen-tāqqa, the "axis mundi" or pillar that holds up the heavens, which Canary islanders placed at the Teide Volcano. There is an analogous concept in Herodotus, where he speaks of the great Mount Atlas which natives of northwestern Africa believe to be the Pillar of Heaven (Larcher 1844, 84). It may also be found in Hesiod: "By harsh necessity, Atlas supports the broad sky / on his head and unwearying arms, / at the earth's limits, near the clear-voiced Hesperides" (Hesiod 2004, 24).

Other exchanges between Canary Islanders and people as far afield as India are less probable, but that has not stopped researchers from speculating and reaching conclusions that seem gratuitous at first sight, but nevertheless offer some fanciful, albeit tantalizing possibilities. Let us consider some of them.

There is the ancient Hindu text *Vishnu Purana*, which mentions the White Island of Atala and locates it in the "seventh zone of heat," which, according to Colonel Wilford, translator of the text, the writers placed at 24 to 28 degrees of latitude, a location that might signal "the starting point of the fabled Atlantis" (Gardiner 1993, 215). The fact that this latitude is exactly where the Canary Islands are situated (Purdy 1816, 9) makes it feasible to speak of early contacts between Indians and European or North African travelers in India that brought mythical tales about the archipelago with them. That the *Vishnu-Purana* refers to the Canaries almost seems feasible: "White Island" is an indigenous Guanche name for the largest of the Canaries, Tenerife, with its immense volcano that is often capped by snow. Hindu myth also talks of Atala being one of the seven regions of Patala, that is to say, one of the seven lower regions of the universe (*Vishnu-Purana* 1894, 128). Seven is the exact number of islands in the Canary archipelago.

There is also the implication that the Canary Islands, once part of a larger landmass, were a transit point for populations that were dispersing across the Atlantic from east to west: there is the happenstance that in North America the Aztec word for water is *Atl* (Starr 1920, 5), which links up with the Greek words *Atl*as and *Atl*antic, and more remarkably, the coincidence that the Cherokee word for mountain, transcribed as "odalv," is pronounced "oatala" (Feeling 1975, n.p.), evoking the Canarian mountain of the *Vishnu-Purana*.

There is another peculiar detail that some see as proof of a link between the Canary Islands and India and to some degree may explain a distribution of analogous myth material from the Atlantic to the Indian Ocean: linguist Edo Nyland (1941–2009) maintains that the Guanche language of native Canarians is related to the Dravidian languages of southern India (2001, 342). He goes on to theorize that both Guanche and Dravidian are remnants of the original language spoken in the neolithic Sahara before catastrophic desertification dispersed its populations. In this scenario, ancient Saharan myths and information regarding the Canary Archipelago were carried in various directions as a consequence of said dispersion; this also explains the possible references to the Canaries in the *Vishnu Purana*.

Texts like those of Frank Joseph (1998, 5-38; 2011, 50-53) collect several interesting assertions regarding the origin of the Atlantis myth as well as sundry other ancient myths, reviewing several possible links with the Canaries (and with Wisconsin, of all places). A quick analysis of the general claims regarding Canarian connections is relevant at this point, as many will be found to be sophistic and counterintuitive, while others may contain a small grain of truth.

The Museo Provincial of Las Palmas, in Gran Canaria, holds the model of what a typical indigenous town looked like before the arrival of the Spaniards. The town consisted of several concentric rings, much like what Plato described for Atlantis, and this is claimed to be proof of Atlantean connections (Joseph 2011, 50-53). On my recent (2017) visit to the Provincial Museum of Las Palmas, I saw the model in question. While it is indeed a village surrounded by concentric circles, the small dimensions of the portrayed village make it unlikely that it has any connection to Atlantis or to the genesis of the Atlantis myth.

The Atlas myth, that of a giant holding up the world, is said to be very much in line with the Guanche deity Achamán, or Ater, represented in Canarian petroglyphs as a man with upraised arms holding up the sky. A Canarian origin for this myth is improbable: I'd suggest a more plausible origin: this symbol is dispersed throughout the ancient Mediterranean and may have been brought to the islands by its original Guanche settlers, who shared myths and symbols with their ancient neighbors on the Mediterranean coast of northern Africa. It is there that native tradition held that Mount Atlas was the pillar that held up the sky, as Herodotus explains

> Once more at the distance of ten days' journey there is a salt-hill, a spring, and an inhabited tract. Near the salt is a mountain called Atlas, very taper and round; so lofty, moreover, that the top (it is said) cannot be seen, the clouds never quitting it either in summer or winter. The natives call this mountain "the Pillar of Heaven;" and they themselves take their name from it, being called Atlantes. They are reported not to eat any living thing, and never to have any dreams. (Rawlinson 2022, 134)

So this Greek myth of a bearer or a support for the heavens may very well have a North African origin, carried by the Guanches to the islands and by the Greeks to the eastern Mediterranean, where they developed and enhanced it.

Adding to the fables that surround the islands, Pliny the Elder comments in his *Natural History* (bk. 6, ch. 32, "Of the Fortunate Islands") that the islands are infested with great animals, which are often cast out in a putrid condition, and Proclus of Lycia, a Greek Neoplatonist philosopher, reported (c. 410 C.E.) that

> … [the native Canary Islanders] say that there were even in their own time seven islands in that sea sacred to Persephone, and three other huge ones, that of Pluto, that of Ammon, and in the middle of these another belonging to Poseidon, two hundred kilometers in length. Those living on it have kept alive the memory from their ancestors of the Atlantis that actually came into being, the hugest island there, which over many cycles of time was the overlord of all the islands in the Atlantic

Ocean, and was itself Poseidon's sacred island. This is what Marcellus has written in his *Aethiopica*. (Proclus 2011, 178)

Although there may have been a Marcellus, he is unknown. More likely, Proclus is referring to Marcianus of Heraclea, who wrote a *Periplous of the External Sea* circa 390 C.E. Regarding this account, however, signs of the overt Hellenization of Guanche descriptions are evident, as the Canarian natives were unlikely to have such insightful acquaintance with the Greek pantheon.

With Proclus, as with "Marcellus" before him, we can see the process whereby, when speaking of faraway, unknown lands, writers allow their imagination to run riot, the same process satirized by Lucian in his *A True Story*. It may have come as a shock to ancient peoples living around the Mediterranean, fantasizing about what lay beyond the Straits of Gibraltar, to learn from sailors and travelers that there actually were islands and people–very strange people with stories to tell–in that vast unknown.

Canary Islander stories, told to ancient and medieval European sailors in the Guanche language, could not have been translated with any level of accuracy and must have lent themselves to very creative interpretation and editing. And such editing would reflect the excitement, curiosity, and sense of wonder generated by discoveries that may be comparable to finding life forms on one of the moons of Jupiter nowadays. What seems at least possible, when reading these ancient authors in detail, is the likelihood that early Canarian sagas and myths slowly made their way back to the eastern Mediterranean in Greek merchant vessels and, swelled with imaginative accretions, generated and/or modified myths and legends concerning the great sea to the west, the greatest of which is that of Atlantis.

It is important to note that medieval myths regarding the Atlantic, and specifically the Canary Islands, are resilient. Tales of the Guanches having very light skin and blond hair are likely the result of dashed expectations: early sailors expecting to find people with dark features in islands off the coast of Africa may have been surprised to find people with lighter skin and reddish hair, features common in some Berber groups like the Kabyles, who inhabit the hills between Algiers and Bougie, and the Shawia of the Aures Mountains. "They are distinctly white-skinned, even when sunburned. [...] some have yellow hair and blue eyes" (Cort Haddon 1924, 36).

So while one need not look any further than the islanders' northern African ancestry to account for their features, their geographical location in the Atlantic made them the object of thoughtful–but also unbridled–speculation that transcended the Middle Ages and reached modern times. Herman Wirth (1885–1981), put in charge of the Ahnenerbe by Himmler in 1935, was a firm believer in the Guanches' Nordic ancestry; he bought into the story of Atlantis, believing that it was inhabited by a superior race and that the Canaries were that lost continent's last vestiges.

His disciple, the folklorist, theologian, ethnologist, and archeologist Otto Huth (1906–1998), professor at the University of Tübingen, was inspired by ancient and medieval accounts of the Guanches' fair skin, blond hair, and blue eyes, to the point that he even planned an archaeological expedition to the Canary Islands to look for potsherds and stone tools that would confirm the presence of ancient Nordic peoples in the archipelago. In September of 1939, Heinrich Himmler intended to send Huth to the Canary Islands with a small research team to do just that, but the start of the Second World War frustrated the project. General Franco, however, tasked Spanish archeologist Julio Martínez Santa Olalla with searching for the Nordic footprint in the Canaries, and Santa Olalla is known to have sent many documents detailing his findings to Berlin (Forino 2012, 197).

One of the events that had prompted Huth's interest in the islands was the "discovery" of Guanche mummies, many of which had, indeed, reddish and yellow hair. The aboriginal islanders, he concluded, must have been archetypes of the unadulterated line of the Nordic race. However, besides ignoring the northern African explanation for the particular color of the mummies' hair, Huth also failed to consider that the mummification process could have had a bleaching effect on it. But the German scholar was undeterred, as he proclaimed that "Separated from the disturbances of European world history, the ancient Nordic civilization blossomed undisturbed on the happy islands until it was destroyed" (Pringle 2006, 187).

Besides the archeological pursuits of the mid-twentieth century, there have been philological endeavors aimed at "proving" the hypothetical Nordic or Celtic ancestry of the aboriginal Canary Islanders. As Jaime Rubio Rosales explains (51-52), these are centered on the use of certain morphemic coincidences to create outlandish etymologies. To cite some examples: Tamarán or Tamara is thought by some to be the aboriginal word for the island of Gran Canaria, although this is highly questionable. For the ancient Britons, Tamara was the goddess of rivers and streams, for whom the river Tamar, on the border of Cornwall and Devon, is named. But this seems to be a haphazard coincidence: we might point out that tamara (tomer) is also a Hebrew word meaning "palm tree," and that támra is Arabic for date. So why not a Semitic link for the Guanches? Tara, a neighborhood of Telde, in Gran Canaria, is an ancient population center for the aboriginal islanders. The word echoes of Celtic culture, as the Hill of Tara was the ancient seat of Irish high kings. But Tara is also the goddess of fertility in Tibetan Buddhism. Bentayga, a mountain in Gran Canaria that was of religious importance to aboriginal groups, has the distinction of beginning with the syllable "ben," which in Irish means peak or summit. But in Hebrew, ben (ibn in Arabic) means "son of," a coincidence that, if we were to apply the faulty logic of the proponents of Nordic/Celtic connections, would lead us in the direction of the Levant (Guanche sons performing rites of manhood on the summit?!) in seeking Guanche kinships.

But not all theories reach the same degree of absurdity. The Guanche word for water, "ahemon" (Chil y Naranjo 1879, 140), is truly intriguing. In Plato's *Critias*, Euaemon is mentioned as one of the kings of Atlantis, who "for many generations reigned as princes of numerous islands of the [Atlantic] ocean besides their own..." (Plato 2013, 117). King Euaemon married Rhea after her first husband, the Titan Kronos, was exiled by the Olympians (Kronos is also identified with water and is associated with the Atlantic Ocean, the "Chronos maris" of the Romans).

Across the ocean, it may be more than a coincidence that the Arawak indigenous people of the Atlantic coast of northern South America have a god called Aimon Kondi. Besides the affinity of the name Aimon with "ahemon" and "Euaemon," he is the protagonist of a story that reminds one not only of Plato and Atlantis, but also of the Bible's Book of Genesis. Closely identified with water, Aimon created the world and human beings, but disgusted by their debauchery, he willed an immense fire that engulfed the world, and to top it all, caused the Atlantic to invade the land in a great flood. Interestingly, in his second try at creation things did not go much better, but this time he decided to save a righteous couple, Marerewana and his wife, in order to kick-start his new world (Skyes and Kendall 2002, 5). The aboriginal Guanche, classical Greek, and pre-Columbian Arawak concurrence in this regard (ahemon; Euaemon; Aimon) may have an origin that cannot be explained by contending that it is mere coincidence.

So ancient myths concerning the Atlantic and its islands are still influential in the endeavors of people who are intent on exploring mythical origins and searching for fabulous worlds in the pre-historical past. For people with more sinister intentions, they've provided a mythical geography with which to justify their attempts to dominate other groups and monopolize culture and the economy. The Canaries have been an essential source in this regard, from ancient times to our days.

The Spanish discovery of Ireland, or the polarization of reality

2.2. *Lebor Gabála Érenn.* Fol. 53. Twelfth Century.

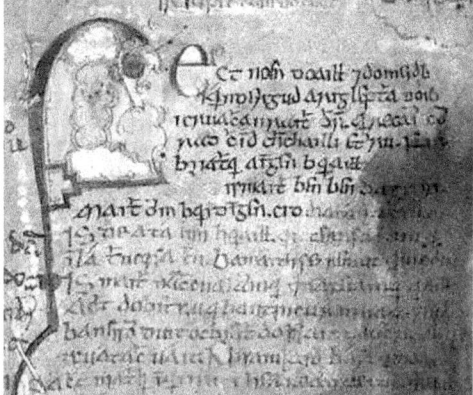

The Book of the Taking of Ireland

The *Lebor Gabála Érenn* (The Book of Invasions or of the Taking of Ireland) is a compilation of prose and poetry that claims to tell the true history of Ireland, from the earliest times to the Middle Ages. It is a medieval text with several versions, the first of which seems to be that of an anonymous writer of the eleventh century. More a collection of myths than a history, it appears to incorporate a hodgepodge of pre-Christian mythology and medieval Christian lore.

In one of its stories Breogán, a mighty king in Spain, wants to expand his power and influence. Seeing the courage of his soldiers, the scarcity of corn in his realm, and considering the great number of sons that he has fathered, he resolves to send one of them forth to conquer a foreign land. Moreover, bad weather and his constant battles with invading Goths have made him weary and disillusioned in his lands. He, therefore, calls a council of the principal persons in his family, where it is decided that Breogán's son Ith should be dispatched across the great ocean to discover a western island. One version states that Breogán decided on the general direction of his son's expedition after he discovered a beautiful island, on a starry winter night, from the top of the Tower of Brigantia (today's Torre de Hércules, in Galicia). Using a contraption that today we'd call a telescope, he peered across the endless expanses of the enigmatic Atlantic to discover a promised land to the north.

Ith, who was a very intelligent and enterprising prince, fitted out a ship with all the provisions needed for the trip on the great western sea and set sail with his son Lughaidh and 150 of his best soldiers. Landing on the northern coast of Ireland, he made a sacrifice to Neptune, but the omens were not encouraging. Some locals approached the landing party and asked, in the Irish language, what they were doing there, to which Ith answered in the same language that he was a descendant of the great Magog, just like them, and that is the reason why he spoke the same language. Learning that the island was governed by three warring brothers, he set out to Oileach Neid, the place where the dispute was taking place, and successfully brought their dispute to an end using sound reasoning. He told them that they were blessed with a beautiful island full of milk, honey, fish and corn, whose weather was neither hot nor cold, but perfect for the upkeep and improvement of human bodies. Ith left to return to his ship and was thanked by all present for his arbitration.

But the brothers, remembering the encomiums that Ith heaved upon their island, immediately began to fear that, upon his return to Spain, Ith would inform his father of the wonders of Ireland, provoking an invasion. So they sent their armies after Ith and his men and wounded the prince after a ferocious battle; he died of his wounds on the voyage back to Spain. Enraged, Breogán assembled a fighting force of Milesians (the Miles Espánie, from the Latin "Miles Hispaniae," or Soldiers of Spain) and set sail for Ireland, which he subdued after many natural and supernatural events. The conquering Milesians now became the inhabitants of Ireland's "World Above," while the previous inhabitants, the conquered Tuath Dé, took to the "World Below" and became the Aos Sí, a supernatural race that lives underground in fairy mounds along the western European seaboard and in the British Isles.

The story leaves us with a "World Above," inhabited by good, strong, valiant, victorious individuals, and a "World Below," populated by the treacherous, vanquished group, a typically Manichean perspective over good and evil. There is, besides the narrative association with Spain, a particular link between this Irish myth and a Spanish one: certain mythical creatures from northwestern Spain, the "mouros" or "mourinhos," were believed to be primeval inhabitants of the area that were forced to retreat to underground realms by newcomers; there, they have accumulated fabulous treasures that are guarded by dragons called "cuélebres."

In medieval societies, knowledge of the physical properties of the world, accumulated since antiquity, had been subordinated to collective assumptions taken from religion. In the general absence of scientific inquiry, religion could endow the confusion that is existence with accessible patterns for ease of interpretation. It is religion, through its holy texts, that informs us that at the beginning the world was inchoate and amorphous, and that God initiated orderly distribution by separating light from darkness, earth from water, and so forth. The Bible, a work put together from fragments of much earlier beliefs, demonstrates that dualist thinking exists since the beginnings of culture and society.

Pythagorean philosophy also provided a similar pattern for classification, the Table of Opposites (male/female; right/left; odd/even, etc.) to which Aristotle makes reference (*Metaphysics* 986a 22-25). Therefore, in making sense of the cosmos, medieval people tend to give structure to their worldview by separating all things into opposites. Reality is polarized. This dichotomizing extends to narratives that describe past events that have communal importance, events as the Milesian invasion of Ireland.

As the medieval intellect is not socially prepared to assimilate gradation, people and things tend to be understood as beautiful or ugly, good or bad, useful or useless, with rarely anything ever populating that elusive in-between. This is how myth reflects mental structures in the medieval world: people are either magnanimous and compassionate (Ith), or greedy and malevolent (the three warring brothers). Thus, the characters in the story of Breogán, conqueror of Ireland, are fundamentally one-dimensional, enabling the consumers of this myth to understand their actions and reactions effortlessly through uncomplicated and categorical figures; as a practical tool, they also help to sort out and simplify the mosaic of contradictory events that is the essence of existence.

In this myth's design, we also see a diagram for the creation of order out of the chaos that is the world and our perception of it. As the principles that underpin this design do not tolerate compromise or even the consideration of diverse alternatives or possibilities, a dichotomic world of antithetical, mutually exclusive pairs is developed. As such, myth moves forward not only by detaching and segregating the discordant and perplexing aspects of the person's experience into opposites but also by projecting these onto different characters (Ith/the three brothers), groups (Milesians/Tuatha Dé) and places (World Above/World Below).

The dichotomy "this side/that side" of the Atlantic is also evident in some versions of the story, where the Aos Sí (formerly known as Tuatha Dé) are said to live in mounds on mysterious lands on the far side of the great ocean. Having turned into mischievous, anti-social beings, the Aos Sí must be constantly appeased with gifts and offerings from us in the World Above, disclosing an ancillary disjuncture: our instinctual, primitive, animal nature (Aos Sí, World Below) lives in tense, antithetical standoff with communal coherence (World

Above), and compliance must be secured constantly (surrendering the primitive part of our nature in the form of gifts) to ensure the equilibrium, restraint, and moderation that are necessary for communal life.

The rigorous nature of this dual arrangement gives medieval individuals an expedient range of potential behaviors that they can expect from others, precisely because of the common assumption, reinforced by stories such as this, that everyone around them is aware of and observes the same unambiguous moral guidelines. The person would have every reason to believe that, in the event of someone's social transgression, as is the three brothers' crime against Ith, the transgressor would be in conflict with the whole of society (the "World Above"), and the community would utilize all required measures in order to restore social balance and stability and consign the perpetrator to a very real "World Below." This Manichean mental landscape has the consequence of equating social transgression with sin, a formula that, if we bear in mind the Ten Commandments, has a venerable tradition in the Judeo-Christian West.

This essentially means that what modern individuals would see as a socially defined offense could, and usually would be interpreted in the Middle Ages as the perpetrator's subjective transgression against God: "For the classical and medieval mind, crime was more the sin than the infraction [...] an affront to nature, to communal goods, and the moral ordering inherent in the human person. [...] Cicero [...] saw crime as a confrontation with nature itself" (Nemeth 2012, 36).

Thus, this epic story of Breogán's conquest of Ireland speaks eloquently about the configuration of socialized selves in the Middle Ages. This tale of conquest and liberation, then, is an enacted metaphor for the Manichean mental landscape that was inherent to the medieval person, the image of a fundamental design for cognition that was an imperative postulate in medieval societies.

Isla Encubierta: the function of mystery

Al Bakri, Andalusian Moor who lived in the eleventh century, never traveled outside his native Andalusia. In spite of it, his many books on geography were very influential in the Middle Ages, to the point where many expeditions were launched in order to find Atlantic islands that showed up on his maps and appeared to have vanished.

Several of these fact-finding missions were dispatched from the westernmost Canary Island of El Hierro, and Portuguese interest climaxed when an unidentified island said to be west of the Canaries was "spotted" by a sailor who shortly thereafter turned up at the court of the Portuguese king Henry the Navigator (r. 1394–1460). As his story unfolds, when he attempted to approach said island, violent storms drove his vessel away; upon returning, the island had vanished. Later, another sea captain asked Portuguese king John II (r. 1481–1495) for a ship with which to sail to a mysterious island that at times could be spotted far off in the Atlantic.

In 1556 there was even a joint Spanish-Portuguese expedition headed by Hernán Pérez de Grado to find the island, to no avail despite considerable expenditure. Several other expeditions would follow, most of which are documented in B. Bonnett Reverón's excellent article "La Isla de San Borondón"[1] The Spanish began to refer to the island as the "Isla Encubierta," or "Concealed Island," one that many had seen, but few had ever been able to make landfall there or explore its physical characteristics. It seemed to offer an experience seldom encountered in other places: somehow, it was always able to preserve that wonderful sense of mystery that tends to fade with discovery and scrutiny. The island was then "built" through a series of mythical anecdotes.

To buttress the distinctive outlook of medieval folk, one that is heavily dependent on the enigmatic "truths" of religion, there need to be places in Creation that somehow substantiate those truths' basic principles, places that, like the ultimate truth heralded by the faith, are not readily accessible through mundane experience. Catching a glimpse of the Concealed Island is an incident that infringes upon everyday experience as if sent from a different dimension to prove a point, from a transcendental cosmos that was, before that glimpse, generated solely by language. The island is an apparition from that inexplicable, ethereal world beyond nature proclaimed from the pulpit; its untouched land is sacred geography that gives a foretaste of that ultimate truth, of that revelation that mankind has been forever seeking.

Ancient communities endowed islands with a hallowed dimension, so one that appears and disappears at will must have been especially important. This primeval sacrality of islands is well-documented in the names of many isles around Britain:

> The names of many of Britain's islands speak strongly of a spiritual significance, and some of them incorporate names of very powerful deities. […] The most famous Scottish holy island is Iona, from where St Columba launched his mission to convert the Picts in the sixth century. Iona then became the chosen burial place of Scottish kings for several centuries, thereby continuing the association of the west with the dead, but this time under Christianity. […] One deity with a large following throughout Iron Age Britain was the Celtic sea god Manannan Maclir. The origins of his name possibly lie in the Sanskrit word *men*, meaning "to tower." Certainly, the Isle of Man–named for Manannan Maclir–

---

[1] B. Bonnett Reverón, "La Isla de San Borondón," *Revista de Historia* 2, no. 4, (1927): 227-235.

> looks like a towering island when viewed from the sea. The ancient name for Anglesey–Ynys Mon–might also have been chosen in honor of this deity, and the same could be true of Manan Gododdin, the ancient name for the lower reaches of the Firth of Forth, north of Edinburgh. [...] When Christianity gained a foothold in Britain in the last century or so of the Roman era, the celebration of sacred islands assumed a new character. Many of them were named after saints or were simply called "Holy Island." There are three of the latter in Britain to this day–one in northern England [Lindisfarne], one in Scotland and one in Wales–while scores of islands are named after saints. [...] The vast majority of the saints' islands lie off the coasts of Wales, Scotland and Ireland, revealing the fusion of Celtic Christianity with the much older tradition of the mysteries of the west. (Palmer 2012, n.p.)

Medieval exploration, as voyagers like Columbus, Ponce de León, Marignolli, and Brendan have shown, is a seeking of knowledge, but pre-modern knowledge, even that which is gained through sensory perception, is the product of discernment strategies designed to make sense of the world in a particular way. Exploration entails the anticipation of beholding places and witnessing events that confirm communal truths: Columbus sailed past what he was certain was Earthly Paradise, Ponce's quest involved the Fountain of Youth, Brendan sought the Isle of the Blest, Marignolli saw Adam's house on a mountain just outside the Garden of Eden. In many ways, the reality they beheld was adjusted to fit the conceptual macrocosm that they brought with them on their journey. For them, there was an eternal truth that predated all things in the world and from which all the objects in the world were made; as such, all places and objects that were subjected to the medieval gaze were invested with features that exceeded their superficial, physical attributes. St. Augustine illustrated this discernment strategy eloquently:

> Therefore in that eternal truth, from which all temporal things are made, we perceive by the vision of the mind the form according to which we are and according to which we perform anything with true or right reason, whether in ourselves or in bodies, and thence we have the true knowledge of things conceived as if a word within us. [...] It is of more sublime reason to judge concerning these corporeal things according to incorporeal and eternal reasons. (McKeon 1930, 313-314).

For the medieval explorer venturing into the Atlantic, to "know" something was to proceed from the superficial experience of sensory perception to the envisioned and arbitrated *essence* of the object. The individual "knows" the object by gradually building it through myth, by articulating it with a complex set of "incorporeal and eternal reasons." If he gazes at the object without engaging those "eternal reasons," the object will not have any relevant meaning, and the explorer will be staring into an ontological void. At this point in the life of humanity, science had not co-opted all attempts at understanding the world, so interpretation according to socially sanctioned discernment strategies was the available instrument to arrive at the real "essence" or "truth" that flows out of the object perceived in nature.

Evidently, these strategies have abundant textual foundations. Neoplatonic philosopher Plotinus (c. 204–270 C.E.) gives us a glimpse at them:

> And all things that exist, so long as they continue to exist, necessarily, in virtue of their present power, produce from their own essence a dependent reality around them at their exterior, a sort of image of the archetypes from which it was generated. Fire produces the heat that comes from it. And snow does not only hold its coldness inside itself. Perfumes especially witness to this, for so long as they exist, something flows from them around them, the reality of which a bystander enjoys. (Dillon and Gerson 2004, 75)

His disciple Porphyry (c. 234–c. 305 AD) adds that

> The soul contains the reason-principles of all things, but it acts on them [only] either by being provoked to actualize them by some external stimulus or through directing itself towards them inwardly. (Dillon and Gerson 2004, 79)

This points to a supraintellectual intuition with which the pre-modern mind would "actualize" external objects and *produce* a reality around them. Unempirical quests are heavily dependent on neoplatonic standards of analysis, a form of inquiry that is not necessarily contingent on evidential certainty regarding the material world. This allowed the explorer to supply what was missing in the knowledge of the physical world by using conventional discernment strategies to *produce* it; as a result, the observer's participation in the production of "reality" is fundamental. Consequently, medieval voyagers had an enhanced power to enact meaning when they did not know the truth through empirical means, so it was the mystery, the unidentified places that most attracted them, that made them begin not just a journey, but a quest. Accordingly, the reality that they observed was penetrated and given form by their heavily laden gaze.

The quest to find the Concealed Island endured for centuries, and it is still a part of Canary Islands lore. In its September 1, 1953 edition, the Madrid newspaper *ABC* reported that the island, known in the Canaries as San Borondón and Isla Sirena, had been spotted recently off the northwest coast of the island of El Hierro. Five days later the same newspaper reported that not only had it been seen, but it lingered long enough to have its picture taken. The two-page spread included the photograph. In 2011 several people claim to have spotted it on a flight from the island of La Palma to Tenerife (Merino 2011, n.p.).

Isla Encubierta is a chimera, an incomplete story waiting for closure. In a way, it is a story that required this essential incompleteness, this lack of closure as its crucial component. In the end, it gave a measure of legitimacy to undemonstrated doctrinal claims regarding the existence of otherworlds.

The *Periplus* of Amaro and the Celtic cultural orbit

Who was Amaro and is his story based on a real navigator that dared to sail deep into Atlantic waters? Is there any part of his portentous story that is true? As I have attempted to make clear throughout this work, in the Middle Ages the concept of truth was not inherent in the story itself, that is to say, the reader or listener was not interested in distinguishing between fact and fiction when exposed to the story: the truth of a text was found in the ability of its characters to perform communal beliefs and values in compelling ways. The medieval mind did not need to retrieve a perfect paradigm of phenomenal reality from its texts; it only needed them to revitalize the certainties of its beliefs and break the power of bewilderment produced by a categorically unsympathetic universe. Amaro is one of those characters that perform their community's ethea quite convincingly:

> St Amaro had a fixed idea that wouldn't leave him in peace: at least once in his life he wanted to look upon the Garden of Eden in which Adam and Eve had lived at the beginning of time. In his books he had read that the paradise from which Adam was driven was a splendid garden, a garden which, even if it was now uninhabited, could still be found somewhere on earth. According to these books, the earthly paradise was in the first region of Asia. Finally, one day he took to sea, spreading the sails to the winds and letting them carry him. At long last, he landed on the shores of a delightful island and came within sight of a marvelous palace, studded and resplendent with precious stones. Everything shone with an incomparable light. At the gate stood a youth with radiant features, a sword in his hand. With his heart in his mouth, Saint Amaro approached the magnificent portal, asking the gatekeeper permission to enter. After man's original sin, however, no mortal was granted the right to enter Eden, and for this reason the angel denied the holy traveler the permission to proceed. Amaro had to be satisfied with gazing at the garden from the threshold. From there, however, he was still able to discern splendid meadows covered with flowers and watered by limpid, luminous streams. (Scafi 2013, 36)

Created as a communal expedient, it is highly unlikely that the character Amaro, a Spanish navigator who ventured into the Celtic Otherworld, is based on a historical figure. A French pilgrim to Santiago de Compostela named Amaro founded a hospital for lepers in Burgos in the thirteenth century, but nothing in his biography could provide a practical model for the *Periplus* and the types and variety of phenomena that it contains. There is also Saint Maurus (512–c. 584), who was the first disciple of Saint Benedict of Nursia (480–c. 547). A long *Life of Saint Maurus*, purportedly the work of one of Saint Maurus's sixth-century contemporaries, recounts Maurus's journey from Italy to France.[2] While this hagiography, like the *Periplus*, is full of adventures and miracles intended to amuse and edify the reader, they are not the sort of exploits that one can confidently associate with the Spanish text.

Saint Amaro's voyage into the Atlantic is told in Portuguese (fourteenth century, Codex Alcobacensis 266, fols. 124r-137r) and in fragmentary Spanish (fifteenth century, U. Salamanca, BUSal., ms. 1.958, fols. 105r-110v) sources; it has been described as "una metáfora de la búsqueda de todo cristiano por su verdadera patria espiritual," that is to say, "a metaphor for every Christian's search for his true spiritual homeland" (Vega 1987, 13; my translation). Ribera Llopis (1993, 35-36) explains that while it is apparent that the Portuguese version is explicit in its objective to describe the earthly paradise, the Spanish version leans toward identity formation, in other words, it pays special attention to the voyage as critical formative element in the character's life. In both versions, a voice (God) advises Mauro and company to set forth in a boat without a specific destination, but in the Spanish version, he is instructed to make his own boat, into which Mauro loads all sorts of provisions.

The *Periplus* holds that Amaro was a Catholic noble from Asia whose goal in life was to visit the Earthly Paradise. Desperately seeking information and not finding it, and being close to despair, one day God appeared to him and instructed him on the way he could make the journey. Like the hero of an *immram*, Amaro was to board a boat and follow the path of the sun across the endless Atlantic, a space that we can instantly recognize as a "Celtic" cultural marker, site of the otherworld, a cosmos that is the product of age-old, recurring cultural practices that predate the coming of Christianity.

---

[2] The extant text of the *Life of Saint Maurus* (*Vita S. Mauri*) is the transcription (or fabrication) of Odo, Abbot of Fossé. Odo relates that he acquired the "very old manuscript" at considerable expense from a cleric returning from a pilgrimage to Rome. According to Odo, he did not alter the substance of the adventures and miracles in the original manuscript, but he did change the style, which he characterizes as *incultus sermo*. See Lechner 1900, 263-264.

One critical point makes the supposedly Christian origin of the story quite suspect. Medieval people understood their surroundings at a different level than that allowed by objective awareness. This means that their perception and assessment of the environment were permeated by non-objective knowledge. Sundry medieval geographical texts and maps show an organizing intellect that takes the physical attributes of the environment to be the thin surface of a more profound sacred geography. As has been discussed in previous chapters dealing with pagan and medieval concepts regarding the Atlantic–and will be considered in the section regarding the Bible–the sacred has a pertinent and regulating place in the mapping of a world created by God. Accordingly, Western European Christians conventionally envisioned geographical paradise as being in the East, in Mesopotamia: "The most popular idea from the early Medieval period was that paradise lay somewhere to the east" (Livingstone and Withers 1999, 70); "The imaginative power and rich thematic interest the Earthly Paradise would have held for a medieval Christian audience is obvious. Paradise was widely believed to still exist within the boundaries of the earth and was often depicted as the most easterly land on medieval *mappae mundi*" (Byrne 2016, 130).

Furthermore, western European Christians sought sources of inspiration and looked for ways to tap into sacred energies by again turning east, towards Rome and Jerusalem. One would think that only a dysfunctional Christian would head in the opposite direction, west into the Atlantic, where it was the pagan Celts that journeyed on such quests. The Bible is clear as to the location of the Earthly Paradise:

> [10]A river watering the garden flowed from Eden; from there it was separated into four headwaters. [11]The name of the first is the Pishon; it winds through the entire land of Havilah, where there is gold. [12](The gold of that land is good; aromatic resin and onyx are also there.) [13]The name of the second river is the Gihon; it winds through the entire land of Cush.[3] [14]The name of the third river is the Tigris; it runs along the east side of Ashur. And the fourth river is the Euphrates. (Genesis 2:10-14, *NIV*)

But saintly, Catholic Amaro, who is said to be a noble from Asia (and therefore from the East), apparently never read the Bible, so he set sail "the wrong way," westwards looking for paradise. His chosen direction becomes understandable once we see this legend in the tradition of the *immrama* and Amaro as a Celtic traveler to the otherworld who has been modified to spread a Christian message. Once on water, he entered a world familiar to anyone who has read

---

[3] Most likely southeastern Mesopotamia: "As to Havilah and Cush, we know that there was a Cush in Mesopotamia during the days of Nimrod, the ruler of Babylon, Erech and other important cities in that region 10:8-12" Ronald Youngblood, *The Book of Genesis*, 38.

immrama and *echtrai*: after six days and seven nights, Amaro and his cohorts reached an amazingly fertile island with five great cities.

As in many ancient Irish sea voyage tales, where one of the foremost rewards for the traveler was the availability of women, in this island the men were coarse, while the women were exceptionally beautiful, so competition from the locals for their favors would have been weak. Bran, the Irish hero of the echtra *Voyage of Bran*, spends what he believes is a year on the Island of Women; and in the immram *The Voyage of Máel Dúin*, hero Máel Dúin (Maelduin) and crew also land on an island where women treat them to sundry delights. Amaro and friends spend six months on this island of beautiful women, after which the hero hears a voice telling him that he should depart this island, which is cursed by God. Plainly, this is part of subsequent editing by Christian hands.

Here it becomes evident that the Christian proselytizers' aversion to sexual delights has brought about this codicil. There can be little doubt that this imperative to leave the island is part of subsequent Christianizing rectification: if the island was cursed by God, why was the Amaro retinue allowed to spend a six-month, delightfully pagan sojourn there? Was the disembodied voice taking a long vacation? In any case, Amaro leaves, sailing through a "Red Sea" until he reaches another island where there is a beautiful fountain (Fuente Clara) and beautiful people that live to the ripe old age of 300. The fountain motif and the 300 years–ubiquitous in Irish tales–are yet another case of the pagan Celtic subtext showing through the Christian overlays.

For the Celts, fountains were very important. In the *Echtra Cormaic i Tir Tairngiri* (Cormac's Adventure in the Land of Promise), Irish high-king Cormac mac Airt journeys to the Land of Promise, the abode of the sea-god Manannán mac Lir. Once inside Manannán's castle courtyard, he gets a glimpse of "a shining fountain with five streams flowing from it. The inhabitants of that world took turns drinking the water from the fountain." The sea-deity Manannán mac Lir "tells Cormac that the fountain which he saw, with the five streams flowing from it was the Fountain of Knowledge, and the streams were the five senses through which knowledge is obtained" (Paice MacLeod 2012, 37).

For Celtic peoples, water freely flowing from the soil was proof of the existence of supernatural forces that were responsible for the mysteries inherent in life, and being near a fountain, drinking from or immersing in its water was a way to get close to the otherworld, gain knowledge and purify and heal the spirit. Christian appropriations of pagan beliefs dealing with fountains, from the baptismal rite to the Lourdes sanctuary, are well documented; the significance of the fountain on the *Periplus* island can only be revealed by considering this story in its original *immramic* context.

The Atlantic of the Celtic otherworld has several places where heroes like Amaro experience timelessness and meet superannuated individuals. Irish hero U sheen (Oisín) lives 100 years with the beautiful Niam on an island where no one grows old, and in the Irish legend, *The Children of Lir* (Oidheadh Chlainne Lir) the four children are turned into swans and must spend 300 years in each of three places in watery areas near the coasts of Ireland. Back in Spain King Alfonso X, in his *Cantigas de Santa María* (Cantiga # 103 in the Escorial codex), reproduces the ancient Galician legend of the "Monk of the Little Birds" (Monxe de Paxariñas), who asked the Virgin Mary for a glimpse of paradise. His wish was granted when he entered a garden he was fond of visiting, fell asleep next to a fountain to the song of a little bird and made what he thought was a quick visit to paradise. But the monk woke up 300 years later. Returning to his abbey, he was surprised to learn that none of the friars knew who he was. This legend exists in Aragón as well, where a certain abbot named Virila visits paradise for what he thinks is a short time and wakes up 300 years later. As for Amaro, after three weeks on this island, an old woman advises him and his associates to leave, lest they get accustomed to the wonderful life to be had on the island.

Amaro and friends spend a long time sailing on this unmistakably Celtic, *immramic* Atlantic, encountering three ships with monsters inside, monsters that take the bodies of the dead to the "Mar Cuajada," also known as "Mar Tapada" or "Covered Sea," very likely referring to the Sargasso Sea, a massive patch of free-floating seaweed in the mid north Atlantic. This reference is evidently from a pagan Galician (e.g. Celtic) legend that identifies the "Mar Cuajada" as the place where the bodies of the "cuélebres," mythical part-dragon part-snake beings, are taken after death. On the way, Amaro and crew receive advice from apparitions in the form of women and find a hermit on an island where savage beasts destroy each other on St. John's Day, which coincides with the summer solstice.

In this segment of the story, it is obvious that the original, pagan framers of the tale selected this day because of the Celtic fascination with the sun, or better yet suns, a day when the two opposing rulers of the year, the waxing sun (Oak King) and the waning sun (Holly King) vied for dominance (Franklin 2002, 5). The belligerent beasts, incongruous in a Christian setting, make perfect sense in the pagan cosmos, as they were metaphors for an event that was deeply embedded in an ancient belief system. Accordingly, the change of name to "St. Johns's Day" is part of the unmistakable Christian patina overlaying the pagan Celtic content. Moreover, the choice of name for the now Christian traveler, Amaro, may also have its origin in the Celtic word for mariner, which in Welsh is "morwr" and in Irish and Scottish Gaelic is "maraiche."

Eventually, the story's ending is beaten into shape by the dominating religious concerns, and the Amaro expedition makes landfall at a place where they find a monastery called Valdeflores; there, the monk Leonites provides directions on how to reach the Earthly Paradise and informs them that he will accompany them on the journey.

On the road to the Earthly Paradise, Amaro and company find a mountaintop nunnery called "Flor de Dueñas," where a holy woman named Baralides gives them more specific directions on how to reach their destination. In the original pagan version, it is likely that this holy woman was a Celtic "Veleda," a seeress endowed with the gift of prophecy. To add to the story's already heavy load of *immramic* features, Baralides gives Leonites a branch from one of the pair of magical trees that grow in the Earthly Paradise. In *Immram Brain maic Febail* the earliest extant immram, Bran mac Febail hears music, falls asleep, and wakes to find a branch of silver with white blossoms, a symbol of the wonderful island where Brain can live forever in bliss without growing old.

Following Baralides's directions, Amaro arrives at a huge castle made from gems and precious metals, where the gatekeeper informs him that he has reached the Earthly Paradise. Here we again see an analog to the many spaces of wonder to be found in Celtic narratives, specifically where the hero arrives at the otherworld abode of a god or a high king. In the Middle English Breton lai *Sir Orfeo* (late thirteenth or early fourteenth centuries), for example, an otherworldly king brings the hero "to his palace gay;/More beautiful I never spied./He showed me castles, rivers wide,/Towers, and vast forests, mead and plain./Again to horse, again we ride,/And so he brought me home again" (*Sir Orfeo* 1909, 9). Evidently, not all medieval places of wonder can claim a Celtic derivation: By way of contrast, *Pearl*, a late fourteenth-century Middle English poem, has a grieving dreamer being "granted a vision of the New Jerusalem that is modeled closely on the vision of John in the *Book of Revelation*" (A. Meyer 2002, 10). More than a Celtic otherworld paradise, this New Jerusalem "is a stunning and sophisticated literary example of the architectural approach to divine revelation in the medieval west" (A. Meyer 2002, 10).

Because Amaro is still alive, he is not allowed to enter the huge, bejeweled castle, but can only peek through a keyhole to see what is inside. This affords him a glimpse of the Tree of Life, birds whose songs leave the listener awestruck, musicians, flowers, the Virgin Mary, beautiful ladies, and other wonders too numerous to describe. Amaro pleads with the gatekeeper to be let in, but is informed that while he was looking at the wonders of Paradise, 300 years have passed; this uniquely *immramic* time-dilation event makes it seem as if Amaro's voyage made him, like the astronaut of the celebrated "twin paradox," age less than those he left behind. Thus, he is experiencing time dilation while gawking at Paradise.⁴ As such, he will shortly learn that his companions are long-gone, and that he has had a city named after him on the coast of that exotic land. Amaro spends his last years in that city, in a house built next to the Valdeflores Monastery, and when he dies he's buried next to Baralides and her niece Brígida (Brigid).

This story is deeply ingrained in the popular imagination of people in northwestern Spain. In 1925 it was still extant in the oral traditions of Galicia (Ribera-Llopis 1993, 35-36), and it is evident that, like the *immrama* and *echtrai*, the primordial seed of the story very likely belongs to a pre-Christian, Celtic otherworld story that was found ductile by medieval Christian storytellers and proselytizers. Too many elements (the fountains, the 300-year intervals, the sea journey to Paradise, the exotic islands…) are common and point to a strong undercurrent of primordial Celtic culture and oral traditions that span the Northern European Atlantic shore.

In a process not unlike that undergone by the ancient Irish texts, the *Periplus* would have endured a "Christianizing," "transforming" deep editing that allowed the story to be served back to people during the mandatory Sunday sermons. These people would recognize the familiar story, but with its hero and his motives transformed to fit into a new vision of the otherworld. This may have saved the original, orally transmitted pagan story from oblivion and, consequently, may account for the evangelizing formulas that underpin it. It is significant that the great Spanish historian of literature Marcelino Menéndez Pelayo places Amaro's adventures firmly within the sphere of Celtic culture, identifying it as part of that tradition of "leyendas, también de origen céltico, relativas a los viajes de San Brandán, de las cuales queda un reflejo en nuestra *Vida de San Amaro*," that is to say, "legends, also of Celtic origin, relative to the travels of St. Brendan, of which we have an example in our *Life of Saint Amaro*" (Menéndez Pelayo 2017, 200-201; my translation). While Menéndez Pelayo points to the many translations of the *Navigatio* circulating in Europe as models for the *Periplus*, it should be added that many elements in the *Periplus of San Amaro* that are of evident Celtic origin do not appear in the St. Brendan story, a story that, by itself, cannot account for all those Celtic features.

---

⁴ A truly fascinating trait of *immramic* literature is its insistence on time-dilation. "A [...] phenomenon predicted by special relativity is the so-called twin paradox. Suppose one of two twins carrying a clock departs on a rocket ship from the other twin, an inertial observer, at a certain time, and they rejoin at a later time. In accordance with the time-dilation effect, the elapsed time on the clock of the twin on the rocket ship will be smaller than that of the inertial observer twin—i.e., the non-inertial twin will have aged less than the inertial observer twin when they rejoin" (*Encyclopaedia Britannica Online*, s.v. "Time Dilation," accessed April 23, 2022, www.britannica.com/science/time-dilation).

But how did a Spanish monk become what is essentially an *immrama* voyager? To understand how the practices that transformed pagan Irish culture have analogies in Spain and Portugal, it will be useful to recognize the Iberian Peninsula as a region well within the cultural orbit of the Celtic world. We can then begin to understand how a Celtic cultural substratum with distinctive elements, robustly embedded in the intellect of the peoples of Europe's Atlantic seaboard, subsisted until the arrival of Christianity and even survived, albeit amended to fit the new religion's requirements.

Several classical geographers attest to the fact that Spain was heavily populated by what they called "Celts." Herodotus (1920, 353) gives the first known reference to the existence of Celtic populations in the Iberian Peninsula; Ephorus c. 405–330 BCE, assumed that the "Keltiké" inhabited most of Iberia as far as Gades (Cádiz) in the southwest (Strabo *Geographica* 4, 4, 6); Eratosthenes c. 280–195 BCE, observes that the Celts inhabited the Peninsula as far as the southwest, calling these people the Galatae, an evident synonym for the Celts (Strabo *Geographica* 2, 4, 4); other mentions to Celts in central Spain are given in a passage in Pseudo-Scymnus ascribed to Ephorus, wherein one reads that the source of the river Tartessos (the Guadalquivir), was in the land of the Celts, and Diodorus writes of the various Celtic populations in the south of Iberia. Pliny the Elder assumed that an early home of the Celts in the Iberian Peninsula was the territory of the Celtic tribe in the south-west (today's Extremadura and south-central Portugal), basing his opinion on the abundance of Celtic sacred rites, the Celtic language spoken by the natives, and the preponderance of towns in the area exhibiting Celtic names. Strabo (3, 1, 6) reiterates Posidonius's assertion that the Celts were the largest group inhabiting the area between the rivers Tajo and Guadiana. The references are too numerous to include them all here, and there is much written about the even more obvious presence of the Celts in the north and northwest of Spain, especially Galicia and Asturias.[5]

To better understand the processes that led to a text like the *Periplus of Amaro*, let us focus our attention on ancient northwestern Spain. This culturally Celtic area experienced Christianity in three very distinct ways: first, as a strange new (and outlawed) cult brought back home by Spanish legionnaires that had served in the Roman military, in units such as the well-traveled Legio IX Hispana which was instrumental in the conquest of Britain, the Gallic Wars, and had such notable commanders as Julius Caesar and Gnaeus Julius Agricola. Then, after Constantine's famous Edict of Milan (313), as a popular religion that was tolerated by the Roman state and, subsequently,

---

[5] I owe most of the information in this paragraph to Lorrio and Ruiz Zapatero's very incisive and comprehensive study of the Iberian Peninsula's Celtic populations.

as the state religion of medieval kingdoms such as Asturias, León, Navarra, Aragón, and Castile.

As Christianity became increasingly entrenched in the power structures of these polities, it came to occupy a critical space in the organization, design, and establishment of values; these values' concomitant ideals and principles were championed by the monarchs and were a decisive factor in the validation of regal autarchic authority. Its ever-growing power allowed the early medieval church to systematize social relations, authenticate political power and align pre-Christian culture with Christian tenets. A fine exemplar of this alignment is the *Periplus*.

Moreover, church leaders understood early on that culture, a privileged instrument for human interaction, is also a contested space for rival groups and ideas competing for power. As a symbolic system, it structures people's view of reality and helps sustain institutionalized political and social hierarchies. In short, culture has a strong reciprocal relationship with power. Thus, the normative organization of power in these primitive kingdoms had a corresponding impact on the configuration of culture because, in line with its sundry political aspirations, the church viewed the articulation of a clear ideological message through cultural artifacts like the *Periplus* as a strategic priority.

In this regard, the church's alloyed outlook on pre-existing pagan rituals should be noted, if one is to understand its attitude towards pagan oral literature such as the *Periplus of Amaro*. There is ample evidence to suggest that Christianity's Pilgrimage Road to Santiago, which traverses all of northern Spain from the Pyrenees to the shrine of Saint James in Compostela, has its origin in a Celtic pilgrimage associated with the god Lug (Alcaraz 2014, 56). Moreover, the church of the Virgen da Barca in Muxía, a village on the western edge of Galicia overlooking the Atlantic, stands upon a pagan shrine where sacred curative and magical rocks like the "pedra de abalar" and "pedra dos cadrís" were visited by the Celts. As late as 1105 several monks were sent there by church authorities to suppress the pagan Celtic sun worship that was still practiced in the area. Interestingly, to this day people visit the stones in search of cures for sundry ailments. The "pedra dos cadrís," is very popular with people with rheumatism and like conditions; it is believed that if you pass under it nine times the stone will deliver a cure. The "pedra de abalar" can be used to predict the future. Other stones specialize in determining the virginity of a bride-to-be and yet another makes barren women fertile (Hodum 2012, 161).

This repurposing of pagan sites is an apt parallel for the repurposing of pagan stories and myths practiced by the church throughout Christendom. Outside the Iberian Peninsula, there are many documented instances when a pagan shrine or ritual, such as the Roman Pantheon or the Lupercalia, was repurposed as a Christian church or festival (Ristuccia 2018, 91 ff). This attitude towards the shrines is evidenced by the letter (Epistola ad Mellitum) from Pope Gregory I to Mellitus (d. 24 April 624), first Bishop of London in the Saxon period and third Archbishop of Canterbury, who as a member of the Gregorian mission was sent to England to convert the Anglo-Saxons from their native paganism to Christianity. As Mellitus readied to join Augustine of Kent amid the pagan Anglo-Saxons, Gregory wrote:

> When, therefore, Almighty God shall have led you to the most reverend man our brother Bishop Augustine, tell him that which I have resolved upon, thinking long with myself, about the Angles: that the temples of the idols in that nation ought not by any means to be destroyed; but let the idols in them be destroyed. Let water be blessed, and be sprinkled in the said temples; let altars be constructed; let relics be set up: because, if the temples are well built, they ought to be changed from the worship of devils to the service of the true God, in order that, whilst the nation sees that its said temples are not destroyed, they may put away error from their hearts, and acknowledging and adoring the true God, may more easily flock to the places which they have been accustomed to frequent. And as they have been accustomed to slay many oxen in sacrifice to devils, some festivity must be substituted for this likewise; [...] let them keep the festival with religious banquets, and no longer sacrifice animals to the devil, but, in their own eating, kill animals to the praise of God, and let them give thanks to the Giver of all things for their fulness; so that, whilst some joys are reserved to them externally, they may more easily give their minds to interior joys. For there is no doubt that it is impossible to cut off all things at once from hardened minds, since even he who strives to ascend to the highest place rises by steps or paces, and not by leaps. (Flanagan 1857, 31)

This letter seems to point to a change in Gregory's strategies, revealing the moment at which he accepted that pagan culture was too strong to simply eradicate without any negative consequences:

> The instructions in the Epistola ad Mellitum also signaled a significant departure from Gregory's earlier letter to Aethelbert of Kent, written in June of 601 and predating his letter to Mellitus by less than a month, in which he ordered the English king to destroy all of the pagan shrines in his territory. (Spiegel 2007, 11)

The conversion of pagan shrines into Christian churches is analogous to the adjustment and reorientation of preexisting legends and myths that had been transmitted orally and were firmly rooted in the pagan culture of the Celtic Crescent. Comparable to the refitting of physical pagan cult sites, a repurposing process would tame pagan oral narratives like the *Periplus of Amaro* and affiliate them to archetypes that rationalized and promoted the Christian canon. Such a repurposing could have been the result of concerted efforts by communities of missionaries, or the work of lone proselytizing monks attempting to reach their medieval flock with a Christian message, having inserted it in a recognized, familiar pagan story.

This notion of a Celtic cultural substratum warrants further analysis. In considering the decidedly pagan, pre-Christian features that characterize narratives such as the *Periplus of Amaro*, the Trezenzonio voyage, the *immrama*, the *echtrai* and even such outwardly proselytizing tales as the *Navigatio Sancti Brendani*, it is helpful to construe their unashamedly pagan elements as part of an original ideological design that still guides the imaginative and formalistic flow of the narrative (the characters' motivation for traveling; the ocean voyage; the strange islands; the bizarre beings that populate them; the outlandish events; the time-dilation; the regulatory presence of women, etc.) whereas the evangelizing calibrations (the characters' religious affiliation; the pious motivation for the voyage; the finales' predictable epiphanies, etc.) are part of the attempt to provide normative direction to this oral literature's insubordinate material.

Finally, in my own voyages through Celtic literary landscapes I have come to visualize the literary end-product of this proselytizing effort, that is to say, the *immrama*, the *echtrai* and analogous Spanish texts, as druids on whose neck crucifixes have been hung and who've been made to attend Mass against their will.

Chapter 3
East

Greek underpinnings of medieval mythology regarding the Atlantic

The epic is the most socially relevant genre in any society, the result of an effort to conceive a nation, build substantial links of affection between individual and community, and provide the archetypal *essentiae* that describe folks in the communal assemblage. In the effort to conceive a separate community, distinct from others that may have influenced or dominated a nation's culture, epic literature struggles to create a sense of uniqueness that includes transcending its models, if any.

Ireland is a place where the imaginative transformation of tangible reality has been traditionally conditioned by a preponderant sense of isolated *distinctiveness*. Its geographical location at the ends of the known world, devoid of land routes that would connect it to the continent, gave its culture a sense of self-reliant "otherness" as regards its place in Europe's early medieval cultural hierarchy. This sense almost certainly supplied its bards with dynamic and extensive inventive powers, as is demonstrated in the *Book of Leinster* (Lebor na Nuachongbála, c. 1160), where a catalog of ancient Irish epic forms confirms not only the characteristic "otherness" of the Irish but the remarkable variety of Ireland's epic literature. Among the different manifestations of this epic cosmos, we find the *catha* (battles), the *longasa* (voyages of exile), the *tógbala* (conquests), the *airgne* (slaughters), the *tochmarca* (wooing), the *uatha* (adventures inside caves), and the *immrama* (sea voyages).

Despite its relative isolation, Greek legends and myths made their way to Ireland at an early stage in the island's cultural development. The Irish Tethra, god of darkness and king of the dead, stands out as a particularly pertinent character in connection with Greek myth. A chieftain of the Fomorians, defeated in the Second Battle of Mag-Tuired (Maige Tuired, or Plain of Pillars), he becomes king of the dead in Mag Mell, an otherworld paradise said to be in the ocean. This Irish tale traces a distinct parallel to the Greek story of Kronos, a god who, after his defeat at the battle that pits Zeus against the Titans, becomes the ruler of the Isles of the Blest, also in the Atlantic:

> Father Zeus the son of Kronos gave (to the surviving demi-gods or *dἠμῐ Θεοι*) a living and an abode apart from men, and made them dwell at the ends of earth. And they live untouched by sorrow in the Islands of the Blessed along the shore of deep swirling Ocean, happy heroes for

whom the grain-giving earth bears honey-sweet fruit flourishing thrice a year, far from the deathless gods, and Kronos rules over them; for the father of men and gods released him from his bonds. (Hesiod 2004, 15)

This Greek mythological abode in the Atlantic has analogs in the island sought by Brendan on his round-trip and, as the terminus of a one-way expedition, to the Fair Green Isles of the Ocean sought by the legendary Welsh voyager Gavran ab Aeddan and other storied navigators of the British Isles. In the *Trioedd Ynys Prydein* (The Triads of the Island of Britain) there is a mention of Gavran and other mythical travelers (these three were lost in the western wonderlands):

> The three Vanished Losses of the Isle of Britain: First, Gavran son of Aeddan and his men, who went to the sea in search of the Green Isles of Floods [*Gwerdonau Llion*, the "Green Islands of the Current"], and were never heard of more. Second, Merddin, the Bard of Aurelius Ambrosius, and his nine Scientific Bards, who went to the sea in a House of Glass, and there has been no account whither they went. Third, Madoc son of Owen Gwynedd, who went to the sea with three hundred men in ten ships, and it is not known to what place they went. (Stephens 1893, 21)

There is clearly a kernel of historical truth in these stories, and Greek mythical material appears to have been used to enhance events. As is the case with so many epic and mythical characters, Gavran seems to be loosely modeled after a historical individual that was not actually called Gavran: "The name Gavran ab Aeddan is a mistake, for Aeddan was king of the Scots, who died in ca. A.D. 607, and Gavran was his father; but Aeddan had a son named Conan, who was drowned in the sea in the year 622, and that fact is the basis of this legend" (Stephens 1893, 21).

The language of the *Triads*, as we can see in the citation above, leaves much room to roam for the imagination. The mystery of the heroes' ultimate whereabouts allows one to believe that they did not necessarily perish (never heard of more; no account of whither they went; it is not known to what place they went), which would nurture the possibility that they reached a paradisiacal land, following the Greek model, whence they did not care to return. They were, after all, sailing the Atlantic, home to mythical islands such as the ones described to the Greeks by the Theban poet Pindar:

> But they whose spirit thrice refined
> Each arduous contest could endure,
> And keep firm the perfect mind
> From all contagion pure;
> Along the stated path of Jove

> To Saturn's[1] royal court above
> Have trod their heavenly way,
> Where round the island of the blest
> The ocean breezes play;
> There golden flowerets ever blow,
> Some springing from earth's verdant breast,
> These on the lonely branches glow,
> While those are nurtured by the waves below.
> From them the inmates of these seats divine
> Around their hands and hair the woven garlands twine. (Wheelwright 1830, 15-16)

Or they might have come ashore at Homer's mythical Elysian Fields, also located in the Atlantic ("at the ends of the earth"), after which many a Celtic paradise was modeled:

> The first mention of the Elysion Field (Greek *Elysion pedion*), or Elysion Plain, occurs in Homer's *Odyssey* (4.561-569). In the course of his return home from Troy, Menelaos learned that he was not fated to die in his native Argos, rather, the gods would send him to the Elysion Field at the ends of the earth because he was married to Helen and so was the son-in-law of Zeus. There also Rhadamanthys dwells, and the living is very pleasant, for it neither snows nor rains, and the River Okeanos sends the refreshing breezes of Zephyros upon the people there. (Hansen 2005, 161)

An Irish eighth-century immram, *Immram Brain maic Febail* (The Voyage of Bran mac Febail), serves as another excellent example of possible Greek influences on Irish mythological narratives. It is a text that, when considered in the light of Pindar and Homer, calls attention to the heterogeneous nature of medieval Irish culture. *Immram Brain* is the earliest extant immram, or voyage tale, and is composed of two parts in verse that are enhanced by "enveloping" explanatory prose sections. In the first part, Bran mac Febail is walking alone in the vicinity of his stronghold when he hears music, falls asleep, and wakes to find a branch of silver with white blossoms. He takes it back to his royal house, where he sees a strange woman that sings fifty quatrains to him, advising him that

> Fil inis i n-eterchéin
> immataitnet gabra réin,
> rith find fris' tóibgel tondat
> cethóir cossa foslongat.

---

[1] Saturn is the Roman equivalent of the Greek Kronos.

> There is a distant isle,
> Around which sea-horses glisten:
> A fair course against the white-swelling surge,
> Four feet uphold it. (K. Meyer 1895, 4-5)

The island is a paradise of joy, lovely blossoms, and singing birds where everything exists in harmony and splendor, just like the Greeks envisioned it:

> Ní gnáth écóinuid na mrath
> hi mruig dénta etargnath,
> ní bíi nach gargg fri crúais,
> acht mad céul m-bind frismben clúais.
>
> Cen brón, cen duba, cen bás,
> cen nach n-galar cen indgás...
>
> Unknown is wailing or treachery
> In the familiar cultivated land,
> There is nothing rough or harsh,
> But sweet music striking on the ear.
>
> Without grief, without sorrow, without death,
> Without any sickness, without debility... (K. Meyer 1895, 6-7)

The woman, adding an Irish frame of reference to her report, informs Brain that:

> Fil trí cóictea inse cían
> isind oceon frinn aníar;
> is mó Érinn co fa dí
> cach ái díib nó fa thrí.
>
> There are thrice fifty distant isles
> In the ocean to the west of us;
> Larger than Erin twice
> Is each of them, or thrice. (K. Meyer 1895, 12-13)

This woman that appeared at the royal house had come from the Island of Women; inspired by the description of its wonders, Brain sails there the next day. On the voyage he meets the sea-god Manannán mac Lir, who is driving his chariot across the ocean as if it were land; the god explains that what Brain sees as an expanse of water, he sees as a beautiful plain, and that his (the god's) island is a place of wonder and delight. The tale then shows signs of subsequent Christian input, as Manannán declares the island to be a place where original sin has not arrived; more Christian proselytizing is evident in the incongruous statements added to the sea god's account, such as his foretelling of the coming of Christ. Manannán also predicts the birth of his own son, Mongán.[2]

During his voyage, and in lax harmony with Homer's *Odyssey*, Brain first comes within sight of the Island of Joy, where the sailor that he sends to reconnoiter ends up laughing and staring like all the islanders and is left behind. He then reaches the Island of Women, where the queen, seeing Brain's hesitant demeanor, flings a thread of yarn at him that adheres to his hand; as it becomes impossible for Brain to free himself from it, she pulls him in much against his will. These women, of course, remind one of the sirens, Greek mythological creatures who lured men to perdition, captivating them with their song.

Remarkably, in *Immram Brain maic Febail* one may detect echoes of very early versions of the siren myth, as the incident where Brain is bound with a thread of yarn suggests an acquaintance with the original meaning of the Greek word siren. Likely origins of the word are the noun seirá (σειρά), meaning string or rope, and the verb eírō (εἴρω), which means to tie, connect, or fasten. So a Seirḗn (Σειρήν) is one who binds, entangles, and ties someone, not one who sings someone to perilous slumber. Incidentally, this episode seems like an ancient euphemistic version of a mid-twentieth-century integrative psychology statement: "Woman possesses the superior love power, the irresistible erotic attraction of the magnet" (Marston 1931, 427). In any case, Brain and his mates do get to enjoy the women and stay for many decades, but to them, it seems that only one year has elapsed.

In time, one of Brain's homesick crewmates, Nechtan mac Collbran, convinces the others to return to Ireland, but the queen of the Island of Women warns them that if they touch the soil of Erin they will instantly turn to ashes, which is what happens to Nechtan. The people who have gathered on the Irish shore to speak with Brain tell him that they don't know who he is, but that they've heard his name in their ancient legends; he tells them the story of his adventures and sails into the sunset, that is to say, into the Atlantic.

This *immram* discloses its Greek influences–mostly from the *Odyssey*– throughout: the otherworldly women occur in both the Odyssey (Circe, sirens) and *Immram Brain* (Queen of the Island of Women), and the ocean voyage

---

[2] There is a historical Mongán mac Fiachnai, prince of the Cruthin and son of Fiachnae mac Báetáin, who died c. 625 CE. The Cruthin or Cruithnig were a people of early medieval Ireland, very likely Picts of British origin who controlled sections of present-day Antrim, Laois, Galway, Derry, and Down (see John T. Koch and Antone Minard 2012, h 231). The historical character's relation to the *Immram Brain* (Voyage of Bran mac Febail) is not entirely clear.

where gods interact with men is present in both (Zeus in the *Odyssey*, Manannán mac Lir in *Immram Brain maic Febail* [Voyage of Bran mac Febail]). The island of women is also a shared environment: (Ogygia [Ὠγυγία, in Book V of the *Odyssey*], where Odysseus spent seven years of sexual bliss with Calypso and Strabo (1920, 95) places in the Atlantic Ocean, and the Isle of the Sirens [*Odyssey*, Books XII-XIV], which Homer places to the west between Aeaea and the rocks of Scylla in the *Odyssey*, have an analog in the *immram's* Island of Women). Moreover, the *immram* shares with the *Odyssey* the fact that space and time are not absolute concepts, but relative to a frame of reference (Manannán sees land where Brain sees ocean waves; Brain spends one year on the island while many decades pass back in Ireland; with Calypso on Ogygia, Odysseus experiences no pattern to the passage of time, as he lives with a divinity). The decisive role of women in determining and regulating the path of seekers is also common to both texts.

Intruding in the Irish narrative is the cursory proselytizing material that Christian transcribers added in the seventh or early eighth century: these are catechizing elements that stand out as impertinent and unessential in the story of a voyage to an Atlantic otherworld of sea-gods and acquiescent females. Both voyage and otherworld are evidently pagan in origin, pagan in ambiance, and pagan in spirit. Moreover, they show primary Greek elements (as mentioned above) that don't match up well with the proselytizing efforts of the Christian transcribers. While some cursory Greek cultural elements may originate in these later transcriptions of the original Irish text, the core thematic features of the story are conceivably the result of earlier contacts between the Greeks and people who eventually came to settle in Ireland.

Greek influence is palpable in many other early Irish texts. Despite Greece's considerable distance from the great ocean, the Atlantic has been an important and enduring component of the Greek imaginative world since at least the time of Homer. The "River" Okeanos, identified by Homer in the eighth century BCE as the location for the Isle of the Blessed, acquired additional mythical importance when Colaeus (Κωλαῖος) of Samos (circa 639 BCE) was blown off course through the Straits of Gibraltar and into the Atlantic, discovering an immense body of water where a "river" was thought to be. Consequently, Greek conceptions of the universe and their attendant ethos began to transform as more and more Greeks crossed through the Straits of Gibraltar and beheld the ocean.

A theoretically infinite body of water precisely where the sun went to die each day would become the natural stage for the proliferation of mythological accounts regarding the "other" world. Islands and beings within it, as reflected in Hesiod (2004, 270-286), would acquire that particular quality attached to extraordinary things:

And again, Ceto bore to Phorcys the fair-cheeked Graiae, sisters grey from their birth: and both deathless gods and men who walk on earth call them Graiae, Pemphredo well-clad, and saffron-robed Enyo, and the Gorgons who dwell beyond glorious Ocean in the frontier land towards Night where are the clear-voiced Hesperides, Sthenno, and Euryale, and Medusa who suffered a woeful fate: she was mortal, but the two were undying and grew not old. With her lay the Dark-haired One in a soft meadow amid spring flowers. And when Perseus cut off her head, there sprang forth great Chrysaor and the horse Pegasus who is so called because he was born near the springs of Ocean; and that other, because he held a golden blade in his hands. Now Pegasus flew away and left the earth, the mother of flocks, and came to the deathless gods: and he dwells in the house of Zeus and brings to wise Zeus the thunder and lightning. (Hesiod 2004, 99)

Islands where time does not pass, flying horses, soft meadows full of spring flowers, sexual bliss. All these elements are clearly present in the *immrama*. There is ample scholarship identifying Greek sources for ancient Irish texts. French scholar H. d'Arbois de Jubainville documents some of those sources, and two that he considers essential are: 1- the character of the Irish demigod Tethra, referenced above, who is identical to the Greek Kronos in every essential respect and 2- the events surrounding the two instances where the ocean has overwhelmed the land with floods in Irish mythology, both occurring after the mythical migrations (*tochomlada*). The first, *Tomaidm locha Echdach*, left behind the lake that is at present named Lough Neagh; the second, *Tomaidm locha Eirne*, produced the present Lough Erne.

These Irish flood stories have their counterpart in three Greek mythical deluges, occurring during the reigns of Deucalion (Δευκαλίων), Dardanus (Δάρδανος), and Ogyges (Ὠγύγης). Deucalion's deluge, mentioned by Apollodorus in his *Library* (A.7.1), was caused by Zeus to punish the Pelasgians for their vanity. Before the catastrophe, the Titan Prometheus had warned his son Deucalion to build a large chest (larnax); in it, he and his wife Pyrrha were able to float and survive, landing after nine days on Mount Parnassus. Dardanus's deluge, mentioned by Dionysius of Halicarnassus (Book 1.61-62), inundated the plains and forced survivors to move to the mountains, where very little land could be cultivated. Ogyges's flood, to which Plato may have referred (*Timaeus* [22], *Critias* [111-112], and *The Laws* Book III) is assigned the date of 9500 BCE by the Greek philosopher, which roughly coincides with the end of the last ice age and explains the surge of water (d'Arbois de Jubainville 1996, 23).

It might also be argued that the Irish mythical battles of Mag Tured (*Cath Maige Tured*) and Mag Itha (*Cath Maige Itha*), the battles between Nemedians and Fomorians, the slaughter of Conan's Tower, and other such encounters pitting good against evil have a precedent in the Greek struggles of Zeus against his father Kronos and the Titans. In any case, such correspondences cannot be fortuitous, and it is perfectly feasible that Celtic and other peoples coming to Ireland from sundry parts of Europe brought mythical archetypes with them, models to which native Irish mythology adapted stories from the island's remote past. On the other hand, twelfth-century Christian scribes like Máel Muire mac Céilechair and his two collaborators who compiled the *Lebor na hUidre* (*Book of the Dun Cow*) might also have adjusted ancient Irish mythical narratives to fit Greek patterns; such stories already (and independently) may have contained elements that reminded them of the Greek archetypes with which they were familiar. Their labors and those of scholars like them were critical in saving many age-old Irish myths.

It should be added that their work, with all its Greek material, was subsequently used to throw some light on the past of a nation that had been subjugated, colonized, and its language, culture, and history suppressed. Consequently, "salvaged" Irish myth seems to hold an exceptional place in the nation's ethos: while myths like that of El Cid in Spain or Roland in France resulted from historical characters and events, the Irish had to swim against the current, as myths that were totally independent of any historical past–many of Hellenic design–were deployed to produce an idea of national identity: this, in turn, had a significant impact on the idea of a national historical past.[3] In this sense, it becomes difficult to exaggerate the assumed importance of the *Lebor Gabála Érenn*, or *Book of Invasions*) or the *Lebor na hUidre* (*The Book of the Dun Cow*) as repositories of material upon which to substantiate a sense of identity. One might add Welsh monk Nennius's imaginative *Historia Brittonum* (ninth century) or Giraldus Cambrensis's (Gerard of Wales's) *Topographia Hibernica* (1188) to the list of such influential works.

There are other factors at work in this distinct identitary process. When one considers that in ancient Ireland the druids were the custodians and archivists of all history, myth, law, science, and religion, and that they were always reluctant to write any of this knowledge down lest intruders or outlanders

---

[3] Even today myths are agents of identity formation and promotion in Ireland. The observance (July 12) by Irish Protestants of the anniversary of the Battle of the Boyne (1690) and the festivities surrounding it commemorate a battle between Catholic James II of England and his Protestant nephew William III (William of Orange), who had deposed James the previous year. William's victory is hailed in Protestant identitary groups as a victory for their religious rights, but this ignores the fact that Pope Alexander VIII was, as part of the "Grand Alliance," an ally to Protestant William and an enemy to Catholic James, and that significant groups of Protestants fought on James's side (Hachey & McCaffrey 2015, 12).

tamper with it (or their own people challenge their interpretations), the implications of the *Lebor na hUidre* and similar medieval manuscripts as privileged–if unconventional–portals of access to "knowledge" of the past becomes apparent. The use of imported Greek material for such endeavors only highlights the synthesized nature of national identity schemes.

As I have mentioned above, and aside from any adjustments made to ancient Irish myth by medieval scribes, an earlier influx may be at work in the Hellenization of the island's mythology. The suggested early interactions between Irish populations and Mediterranean voyagers in and around the seventh and sixth centuries BCE, as infrequent as it must have been, ought to have had a considerable impact on people living at the edge of the world and next to the privileged font of mythical material, the Atlantic. Moreover, the Celts, who even if they do not figure in the Irish DNA profile are said to have reached Ireland in the seventh century BCE, could have brought a considerable cultural baggage with them, much of it in the form of myth.[4] The continental Celts' interaction with Mediterranean cultures was robust and is historical; moreover, lexemic footprints suggest an archaic appearance of Greek cultural material in Ireland, although some lexicologists with patriotic agendas, like Charles Villancey (*A Vindication of the Ancient History of Ireland*, 1786), tend to embellish the results of their efforts and exaggerate those footprints.

To give just a few possible lexemic footprints, the Thracian phrase "Bosphorus" (Βόσπορος) that designates the narrow strait that separates Europe from Asia, translates as "passage of the cow." One of the most primitive words in Irish is "*Bo*," meaning "cow." The English word "howling," from the Greek "ὀλολύζω" (*ololuzó*), to cry aloud, and in Latin "*ululatus*," has a counterpart in the Irish "*ulluloo*." The cry of Irish women at a funeral, a sound likened to the howling of a dog, is a *caoin*, a word analogous to the ancient Greek word for dog, *kýōn* (Wilde 2006, 146-147). There are also publications, especially from the nineteenth century, that consider –with remarkable detail– the not so far-fetched notion of

---

[4] Recent and definitive DNA results on large segments of the population of Ireland have come as a shock to many, who took it for granted that Ireland's ethnicity was overwhelmingly Celtic. The fact that Celtic culture and language are evident in Europe's Atlantic islands and shores may have a simple explanation. It is the same explanation one readily gives for the fact that populations like Guatemala's, Bolivia's, or other Latin American countries have scant traces of Spanish DNA, but their language and religion are decidedly Spanish. As happened in the Americas, often an indigenous population changes language, adopting the language of a dominant, relatively small group of newcomers. Language (and its attendant culture) can travel while population groups remain relatively stationary.

Phoenicians from Tyre coming to settle and trade in Ireland, having sailed up from their settlements in the Iberian Peninsula (Villanueva 1833, 48-52).

So Irish myths regarding the Atlantic, as suggested above, show signs that a distinct Mediterranean tradition provides at least some underpinning patterns and prototypes to the Irish narratives; it is more than probable that the Hellenic archetypal material, readily detectable by Christian scholars/scribes engaged in transcribing Irish narratives, was amplified in their proselytizing transcriptions. In a sense, it might be argued that James Joyce, in his assimilation of Homeric epic, is inserting his *Ulysses* into a time-honored Irish tradition.

Myth as agent in exploration and in the interpretation of reality

3.1. Prester John's Kingdom.

Spanish sixteenth century portolan chart of East Africa. "Preste Iuan de las Indias" is seen enthroned on the left.

In the west, at a time when several Irish voyage tales (from the eighth and ninth centuries, if not earlier) were being "rescued" in miscellanies like the *Book of the Dun Cow* (Lebor na hUidhre, c. 1100), and the *Yellow Book of Lecan* (Leabhar Buidhe Leacáin, c. 1390-1401), geographic uncertainty was driving much speculative literature and opening wide spaces to the imagination regarding unexplored regions. Unopposed by factual information and impelled by myth, the medieval imagination invaded a manifold array of narrative formats.

One of these was the folktale, an example of which is that of Prester John, a Christian monarch that was thought to rule in a distant land to the east, among Muslims and pagans. His myth was reinforced by means of diverse formats: several maps from the thirteenth to the sixteenth centuries included his kingdom (Carlson 2012, 121); there is a forged letter from Prester John to Byzantine Emperor Manuel I Comnenus (1143–1180) that circulated widely in Christendom, eliciting a reply from Pope Alexander III (1159–1181) (Dathome 1994, 57); in Otto of Freising's *Chronicon* of 1145, the author informs us that while in Rome he heard that a Nestorian Christian king in the East had had many victories against pagans and that his march on Jerusalem had been prevented by the overflowing Tigris River (Claster 2009, 254); and the *Roteiro da viagem* detailing explorer Vasco da Gama's (1469–1524) journeys informs the reader that da Gama just missed bumping into Prester John's envoys while in Mozambique (Kleinschmidt 2003, 173).

These textual underpinnings allow a myth like this to remain within the scope of the plausible, which is important not only because they increase its entertainment value in a "world lit only by fire," but also because myth has been a practical tool for those in power, as it can be a means to control and manipulate political and social circumstances. In this regard, the influence the Prester John myth had on the organizers of and participants in the Crusades has been broadly substantiated, as in Harry W. Hazard's informative *A History of the Crusades* (1975, 517 ff.).

After the Spanish first crossed the Atlantic and made landfall on the eastern seaboard of the American continent, encountering Prester John's realm by sailing west across the western ocean was contemplated as a possibility. When Vasco Núñez de Balboa (1475–1519) initially beheld the Pacific, after his crossing of the Darien Mountains in the Isthmus of Panama (1513), he may well have thought that, unlike the other Spanish explorers that were then sailing in and around the Caribbean, he had actually arrived at the China Sea. Asia, he probably surmised, must have been relatively nearby. One can assume that Balboa envisioned his achievement in this manner because the closeness of Asia to the American mainland was taken for granted by many geographers at the time. Sebastian Münster's 1561 map of the Americas, created almost five decades after Balboa's famous crossing, still records the popular belief regarding the proximity of Asia to the Americas, as demonstrated by Japan's (Zipangri), India's, and China's (Cathay) position.

Waldseemüller's 1516 *Carta Marina*, created at approximately the same time Balboa is reaching the Pacific coast, is a case in point. A revision of his 1507 map *Universalis Cosmographia* (which marks Prester John's kingdom with a red cross), the 1516 version shows the Pacific (on the extreme right-hand side) correctly on the western side of the American continent, but as a miniature sea beyond which is Asia.

3.2. Sebastian Münster's Map of the Americas. 1561.

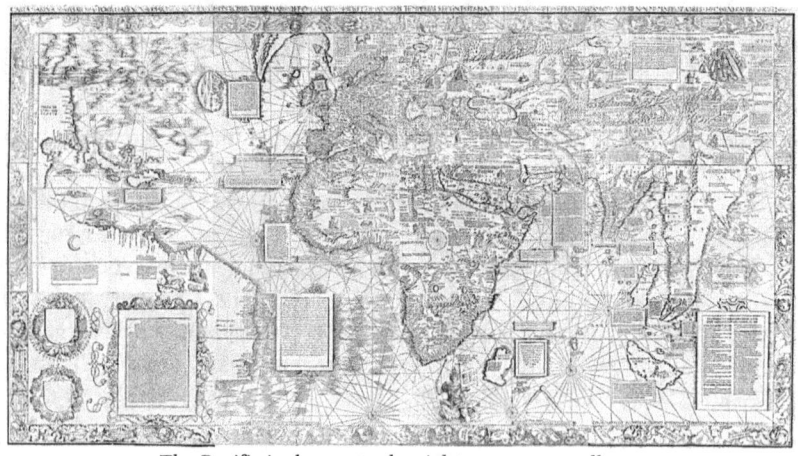

Japan is placed very close to Mexico, and India and China close to North America.

3.3. Martin Waldseemüller's "Carta Marina." 1516.

The Pacific is shown on the right as a very small sea.

Moreover, Balboa could have assumed that what he had reached was the edge of Ptolemy's *Magnus Sinus* (Μέγας Κόλπος), the gulf that opened between Thailand and India, an area that may have been conflated by some interpreters with the South China Sea. In that case, the Spanish explorer may have believed that by trekking north along the coast he might reach the city of Cattigara, a port in mainland southeast Asia (Indochina) reportedly reached by the first-century Greek sailor Alexander, who describes it in his periplus (Hourani 1995, 35). Turning towards the sunset after reaching the northern part of the gulf, Balboa might have assumed that he'd be on the western (Indian) side of the gulf and even in Prester John's kingdom, as Waldseemüller's explanation of his 1507 map states: "A red cross symbolizes Prester John (who rules both eastern and southern India and who resides in Biberith)" (Thacher 1896, 149).

3.4. The 11th Asian regional map from Ptolemy's *Geographia*. 150 CE.

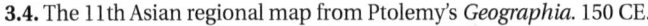

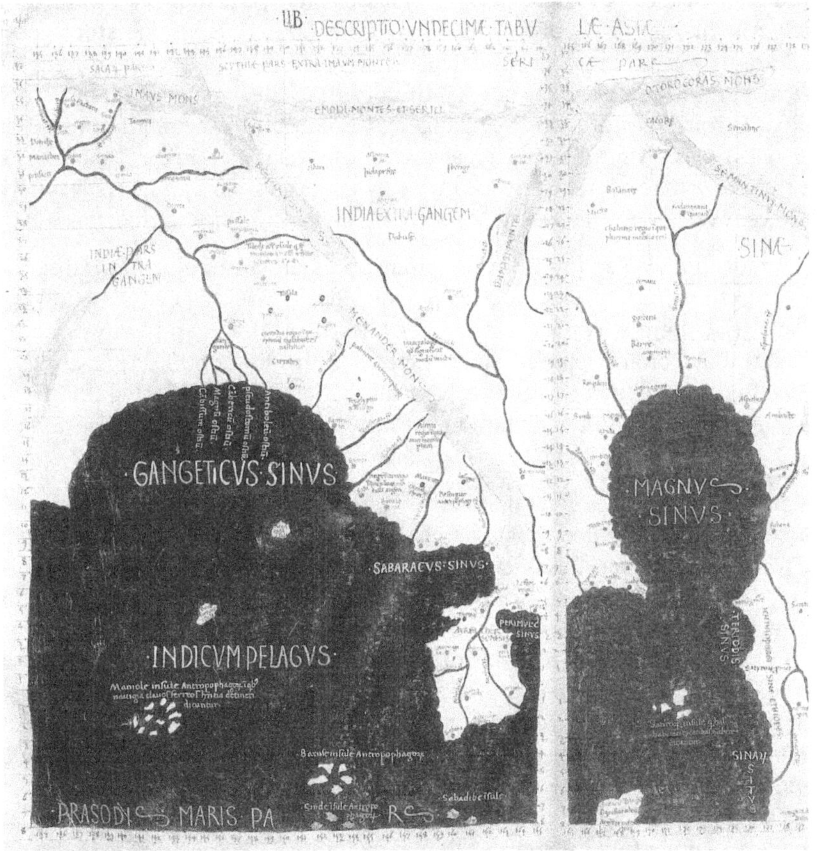

The Magnus Sinus (right), on whose western shore Balboa likely believed he had arrived.

Such conjectures on Balboa's part would have been supported by Ptolemy, but it should be noted that subsequent world maps, like that of Orontius Finaeus (1531), gave similar information: "Finaeus believed that America and the Orient were partitioned only by a gulf, in effect showing North America as Asia "Extrum Cathay" (Suárez 1992, 75). Florentine explorer Amerigo Vespucci, exploring the coast of South America at the service of Spain, describes it in these terms: "We were thirteen months on this voyage, encountering great dangers and discovering endless Asian land and a great many islands, most of which are inhabited: for, to judge by the many times I calculated with a compass, we sailed some five thousand leagues" (Vespucci 1992, 15).

One may assume that both Columbus and Vespucci believed that they had reached an outlying region of Asia. There is little doubt that Columbus crossed the Atlantic carrying the Prester John legend in the back of his mind, following his dream of reaching the East by traveling west. Andrés Bernáldez, a.k.a. "El cura de los Palacios," relates a story that was later picked up by Washington Irving in his *Life and Voyages of Christopher Columbus*. As the story goes, Columbus was trying to communicate with some natives in Cuba through a Lucayan translator who was not very proficient in the language of that part of Cuba. Through gestures and sign language, Columbus came to interpret what the native was saying: there is a great king whose kingdom is in those mountains over there, a man of great power who wears white garments and has his orders followed even though he does not speak to his underlings; they call him the saint.

> In all this we see the busy imagination of the admiral interpreting everything into unison with his preconceived ideas. Las Casas assures us that there was no cacique ever known on the island who wore garments, or answered in other respects to this description. This king, with a saintly title, was probably nothing more than a reflected image haunting the mind of Columbus of that mysterious potentate Prester John... (Irving 1892, 359)

The Prester John phenomenon makes it apparent, therefore, that the drive to discover and control new lands can be energized by myth: that of the Fountain of Youth, for example, has been instrumental in nurturing such ventures. This myth has a very long history, appearing in writings by Herodotus in the fifth century B.C.E., the *Alexander* romance (third century C.E.), and several Prester John stories. Crossing the Atlantic, Spanish explorers Ponce de León and Hernando de Soto searched for it throughout North America between 1512 and 1539, and while their exploits may not have been driven exclusively by the Fountain (Ponce de León wanted to take slaves from the native populations; de Soto searched for gold) it was almost certainly on their minds. Gonzalo Fernández de Oviedo, in his *Historia General y Natural de las Indias* of 1535, insists that Ponce de León's futile search for the Fountain, based on nonsense he heard from the Indians, weakened his brain and led to his death (Pastor Bodmer 1992, 106). Yet, partly as a consequence of his search for a mythical fountain, he discovered Florida and advanced Spain's interests throughout the Caribbean. Myth, then, is able to stimulate action, chart the course of history, and launch armies and curraghs while ever-regenerating in new and unexpected ways:

Since the Fountain of Youth had always been a characteristic of the European image of Eden, one suspects that the Spanish actually put the idea in the minds of the Indians. The explorers asked for it so often, that the Indians may have cooked up the myth for Spanish consumption. (O'Sullivan and Lane 1991, 22)

It should be noted that Ponce de León and de Soto do not mention the Fountain, but writers like Fernández de Oviedo, who knew of their exploits, assure their readers that the idea of finding it was firmly implanted in their minds. It must be remembered that these legendary explorers were not acting according to subsequent *zeitgeister* based on rational, scientific *logos*: those *zeitgeister* were products of the Enlightenment, of its veneration for reason and its methodical efforts to do away with mythology. At the time that these men sailed and explored, not only was Spain still well-entrenched in its medieval *ethea*, but humanity had not yet risen above its need for mythological patterns of speculation.

The Bible and geographical uncertainty

3.5. Ptolemaic World, by Hartmann Schedel. 1493.

Noah's sons Japheth, Shem and Ham hold up the map. The Atlantic does not show, evidencing a complete lack of knowledge regarding the western ocean. Left panel displays a series of chimeras believed to inhabit far-off lands.

In a mysterious world where maps were crude instruments that–more often than not–contained some factual information intertwined with lavish mythical material, it was not unreasonable for people to turn to the Bible, the Word of God, for information about their world. And their familiar world was a small cosmos indeed, just a bubble floating in a vast ocean of uncertainty. As historian Arthur Percival Newton (1873–1942) puts it:

> As one surveys the world of the earlier middle ages, one cannot fail to note the comparatively narrow area that was clear and familiar to Latin Christendom and how it was hemmed in on all sides by the mists of the unknown. Its western shores were bounded on all sides by the dangers of the unnavigable ocean, the north was closed in with ice and the regions of perpetual darkness, to the east there lay the vast spaces of the steppes, dreaded as the lands whence again and again for 1,000 years there had surged forth devastating hordes of Scyths and Alans, Huns and Tartars to sweep down upon the peoples of Christendom with fire and sword. Only southward could men look out upon dangers that they understood from the land of the infidels, but even there only the fringe of the Muslim lands was seen clearly, and beyond them again the haze closed down once more upon the torrid sands of the unknown desert. Civilized men seemed to live in the one bright spot in a shrouded world and, lacking knowledge, they imagined around them wonders of all kinds. (Newton 1950, 159)

Much of what medieval people understood about their world depended upon mythical and biblical material that originated in belief and not in observed fact. And, by definition, such understanding was scopic because holy texts have political connotations and tend to be the resources of the wider community rather than of local, autonomous wards.

Because observations of the world and the objects in it were interpreted in the peremptory light of the sacred texts, geographical knowledge was subordinate and incidental to the *meaning* of that knowledge relative to the revelations contained in the Bible. As so many medieval travelers show us, the world was an element of subjective signification, in the sense that the world was the stage where the Christian experienced God's creation and worked towards salvation. Travel, exploration, and discovery were as much a quest to confirm and substantiate biblical truths as they were expeditions to obtain material profit. As such, medieval travelers always journeyed in a historicized cosmos, and they described the raw world that they observed by choosing from a repertoire of myths, beliefs, symbols, and biblical stories that were not part of the geographical area they were visiting.

An example of their mindset comes from the Salamanca conclave of 1487, where in the Dominican convent of San Esteban there gathered some of the brightest minds of Catholic Spain to discuss Columbus's model of the world. "The clerical council included professors of mathematics, astronomy, and geography, as well as other learned friars and dignitaries of the Church" (Wilson 1892, 73). Despite the explorer's scientific descriptions, the whole idea of the world being a sphere and of people living on some "other side" of the Atlantic was deemed preposterous. In fact, "[p]hilosophical deductions were parried by a quotation from St. Jerome or St. Augustine; and mathematical demonstrations by a figurative text of Scripture. [...] [T]o assert that there were inhabited lands on the opposite side of the globe would be to maintain that there were nations not descended from Adam, it being impossible for them to have passed the intervening ocean" (Wilson 1892, 73).

Seen in that light, the resulting narrative of the travelers' voyages is often a patchwork of factual information and symbolic material where the distant geography is socialized into the travelers' faith and collective mythologies. Therefore, considering the predisposition with which the travelers report their observations of the world, the *truth* of their experiences is not as much dependent on the external qualities of the observed physical world as it is on the nature of their subjective perception, a type of perception that owes its intuitive attributes to communal mythoi such as those ingrained in the Bible and in the flamboyant excursions of the Christian imagination (as is the Prester John legend).

In epistemological terms, the supremacy of subjectively rarefied experience over objective reason critically defines the medieval traveler's understanding and awareness of remote places. As such, his awareness is not regulated by external, detached reality, but is conditioned by the dictates of his inner life, a life permeated by religion. So when an explorer like Columbus declares that he may have come very close to the Garden of Eden (while cruising the coast of northern South America) and within sight of Prester John's realm in Cuba, he articulates the communal subjectivity that is at work in his perception of the world, one that distinctly contextualizes his more objective analyses. As Paul Zumthor writes, "Columbus's *Cartas de Relación* are at once a travel/quest narrative and a chronicle of utopia. They combine the religious and the political, prophetic strategy and monarchic propaganda" (1994, 811).

This speaks to the constitutive power of collective subjectivities with respect to the intelligibility of observed reality, that is to say, medieval *meaning* is relative to the individual's communal ethos. The medieval person cannot observe without *belonging*, so travelers like Columbus, Marignolli, or Mandeville cannot perceive as individuals who are detached from dogma or from the broad cultural frame of reference that is shared by the vast majority of people who belong to their cultural, social and religious collective. Thus, a "canopy of belief" provides a sacred shade of intelligibility to their world, making it a precinct where providential order can thrive unhampered by the impertinent light of objective reason.

As the crucial element in that numinous canopy, the Bible provides a complete package of beliefs, values and guidelines on how to *see* the manifestations of physical reality. The subjectivity of those beliefs, values, and guidelines, needless to say, is not impartially discerned by the medieval mind, which considers the collective preferences and convictions of its religious community as the authoritative criteria for perceiving reality and assigning value to what is perceived. Christian dogma, as I have discussed in the section dedicated to sight, promotes a reality based on faith, on what is unseen, and yet it is dependent on the senses for validation of its credenda. Thus, the way newly colonized populations *saw* reality had to be corrected with the cultural and religious lenses that made its image acceptable to the conquerors. The importance of this closed system of perception explains in some measure the unambiguous urgency and obsession with which the Spanish conquerors of the Americas and their attendant clergy "corrected" the observation strategies of the cultures they found there, turning their populations from *spectators* (of the material world) to *witnesses* (of God's Creation). Unlike the infidels, indigenous Americans had never been exposed to the "true" structure and symmetry of the cosmos; they needed to be inducted into the providential order with all due haste; they had to be made to see, to perceive "reality" accurately.

The Bible, then, contributed to the context within which Christian travelers and explorers assigned meaning to the lands and peoples they encountered. Evidently, the farther and more unusual the territory, the more perplexing and complex became the task of assigning meaning, especially in places that were never foreseen in the Bible. In such places, medieval imagination ran riot and, as a result, set in motion the creative freedom to mix fantasy with reality. This made for enthralling stories, giving them an appeal that explains the popularity of travel narratives like *The Travels of Sir John Mandeville*, a remarkably thought-provoking and intriguing adventure precisely because "[i]t was impossible for the medieval reader to distinguish the true from the false in tales such as these" (Newton 1950, 161).

The Bible is virtually silent on the watery realm due west of the Mediterranean. An ambit such as this, not considered in the Holy Book, was perilously unfastened from interpretive restrictions and thus susceptible to anomalous perception, as no divine analysis of it was available. As with the indigenous American cultures that the Spanish endeavored to "correct," pagan Atlantic myths (especially Irish ones) dealing with themes that were completely alien to the Bible needed to be "Christianized" to conform to the requisite optics. Yet, and very likely due to their ancient isolation from the biblical domain, their themes and especially their characters show a resiliency that betrays their pagan origin, in spite of the painstaking and deliberate work of adapting them to Christian dogma:

> A principal consideration of developing Irish mythology is that the principal characters *evolve* away from their pagan sources: the gods become demi-gods, who become heroes, who become exceptional men. The later Christianizing of the tales is achieved through resurrection and baptism: St. Patrick raises Cú Chulainn from the dead despite the latter's pagan background in order that he might bear witness to the truth of Christianity. The *immrama* tales provide similar important parallels with the *Navigatio* [*Navigatio Sancti Brendani*] through using both pagan and secular material to convey the Christian message. (Mackley 2008, 59-60)

One obstacle faced by later Christian revisers of early pagan texts is that geographical information contained in the Bible is very limited. Because the Holy Book does not give much information on areas that are far removed from the events that it reports, pagan literary characters that inhabited such remote spaces had very resilient non-Christian characteristics, developed in geographical contexts that were beyond the Bible's parochial range. This means that early Atlantic seafarer narratives like the Irish, which portrayed their heroes' journeys to the pagan Atlantic otherworld in magical *currachs*, could only be "Christianized" in relatively unconvincing ways, whatever the skill and talent of the reviser.

To more accurately chart the extent of the geographical information contained in the Bible, it should be remembered that, in many ways, the Christian Holy Book was dependent on outdated, ancient Greek geographical knowledge. Exhaustive catalogs of biblical places, like George H. Whitney's *Hand-Book of Bible Geography* (1871), attest to the fact that the Bible's writers understood that the spaces that really mattered were those where the religion's constitutive events took place. The rest of the world was just a backcloth, and the old Greek geographical data was a more than adequate description of it:

> Thus, by the end of the sixth century BC the circuit of Greek geographical knowledge included the Atlantic coast of Europe as far as the British Isles and perhaps Ireland (although these were little more than toponyms of uncertain location). The rivers of western Europe were known, but the Alps and anything that lay to the north of them were still vague, except perhaps for the amber route to the Baltic. (Roller 2015, 48)

That circuit had not widened much by the early Middle Ages. Medieval Christians saw the Pillars of Hercules, at the Straits of Gibraltar, as a signpost of sorts: "This is the End of the World." Ignore the warning and sail westwards into the unknown expanse at your peril. What was there? What would happen if you journeyed into the mystery? Would you sail forever without ever again spotting land? Would you arrive at an unyielding barrier that marked the periphery of Creation? If so, what might lurk behind it? And what of the supernatural creatures that populate travel narratives? Could they live in islands shrouded by mist in the far reaches of what medieval people called the "*Mare Tenebrosum,*" or "dark sea"? Perhaps the dead found their final abode in its foggy vastness. The Bible did not contain any information about what lies beyond the western horizon, and hence did not offer answers to these questions. Even when logic announced that the earth must be round, medieval perspectives on the world were channeled through sacred texts, and these were mostly silent on that great beyond that extended to the west.

The reasons for the lack of geographical certainty regarding the Atlantic are many. Analyzing the period of great cultural surge at the apex of the Roman Empire, we find that even the limited knowledge of the world bequeathed by antiquity and Greek learning waned. In many ways, Rome represented a gravitational center that attracted the attention of its citizens: people in Hispania looked east just as those in Anatolia looked west toward the resplendent hub of culture and innovation. Comfort, security, and economic prosperity depended on a good relationship with the core of their world, the great city on the Tiber. With the advent of Christianity, the acquisition of knowledge through the discovery of distant lands was initially regarded by the church as a senseless waste of time, since all viable knowledge was contained in the Bible.

A good example of medieval attitudes concerning geography is contained in the *Topographia Christiana,* or Christian Topography, a work by the Christian monk Cosmas Indicopleustes written circa 550 C.E. Cosmas, an Egyptian, was very interested in geography, having traveled to India, Sri Lanka and Ethiopia, places about which he gave detailed descriptions and cultural information. An otherwise savvy observer, Cosmas consistently argues that the earth is flat and censures those dimwits who, like Ptolemy (and many of Cosmas's own contemporaries) proposed that people lived on a ball that floated in space.

So it was with remarkable creativity that Cosmas put together an extensive selection of absolutely disparate texts culled from scripture and gave the world this Golem that he called *Topographia Christiana.* To put some adhesive on its incongruent components, he inserted notes (παράγραφοι) into the body of his text, hoping thus to give a more lucid account of the world as he saw it. It is significant that he refers to persons who adhered to old (pre-Christian) conceptions of the world as Greek (Ἕλληνες), not necessarily because they were actually Greek, but because, like Ptolemy, they refused to see the light of the ideas brought forth by Christianity and still believed the world to be a sphere. This is critical: those proposing more scientific approaches to reality might be considered to be, in the words of Cosmas, beyond the realm of the church, that is to say, pagans (ειδωλολάτρες).

The world as a sphere presented the medieval mind with a counterintuitive notion, that of the Antipodes, places in the earth's surface that are diametrically opposed to where "we" stand. That notion was championed by Macrobius (370–430 CE) and Isidore of Seville (c. 560–636 CE), but had many irate detractors, like Lactantius (240–320 CE), advisor to Emperor Constantine I, who asked in his *De Falsa Sapientia*, iii, 24:

> Is there anyone so foolish as to believe that there are men whose feet are higher than their heads? Or that things that lie flat with us hang suspended there; that crops and trees grow downwards; that rain and snow and hail fall upwards upon the earth? (McCready 1996, 108)

Cosmas was emphatic about those clueless fools who

> ...do not blush to affirm that there are people who live on the under surface of the earth [...] But should one wish to examine more elaborately the question of the Antipodes, he would easily find them to be old wives' fables. For if two men on opposite sides placed the soles of their feet each against each, whether they chose to stand on earth or water, on air or fire, or any other kind of body, how could both be found standing upright? The one would assuredly be found in the natural upright position, and the other, contrary to nature, head downward. Such notions are opposed to reason and alien to our nature and condition. (Cosmas, bk. 1, n.d, n.p.)

With his mindset, Cosmas exemplifies the decline of geographical knowledge immediately after the fall of Rome. Nevertheless, before dismissing Cosmas's work as fantasy, we should remember that he included useful and accurate information that could not be found in any other text of the time; these pertain, for example, to trade expeditions into the interior of Africa, to the ancient Ethiopian kingdom of Aksum and to Indian Ocean trade routes; he even considers the practicality of sailing eastward from the Persian Gulf to China (White 2009, 11).

Cosmas's work represents the conventionally approved perceptions of a period that lasts for much of the Middle Ages, a period marked by the disregard for common sense and its substitution by dogmatic concepts centered on Scripture. Nothing beyond the Bible was worthy of consideration; furthermore, *Mappae mundi*, mostly didactic and symbolic in nature, were produced as visual homilies of sorts, as graphs that confirmed the truths established by doctrine and the Bible. It was not until the fifteenth century that Ptolemaic cartography eventually prevailed in Europe, very likely for strictly practical reasons (Biddick 1998, 269).

Hence, myths and narratives concerning the vastness west of the Straits of Gibraltar seem to have been, for the church, useless flights of fancy bordering on disobedience and, moreover, may well have demonstrated a conspiratorial disregard for the "truths" contained in the Holy Book. Were one to judge by precepts in Christian doctrine, then, pagan myths concerning Atlantic realms would by necessity contain heterodox matter: they narrate experiences that take place beyond the pale of sponsored speculative scenarios, and they tell of the accidental discovery of evidence that the universe may have countless dimensions of wonder beyond the cosmos described in the Bible, beyond the tilled, populated medieval οἰκουμένη, dimensions for which perception strategies did not prepare the explorer.

Eventually, Bible knowledge would be put to the test not only by the new discoveries that began taking place in earnest in the fifteenth century, beyond the biblical Pale, but also by the enduring pre-Christian perception strategies. By showing that the universe is not a simple, closed set of possibilities, the pagan myths that Christian proselytizers encountered in Europe's Atlantic seaboard had the power to unsettle, perturb and deconstruct the tedious, codified present. They had an enduring power of contingency and astonishment that made it difficult to concede that all attainable knowledge is contained in the Bible. Accordingly, a salient characteristic of Atlantic myths, legends, and travel narratives like *immrama* and *echtrai* is that they speak in the language of immeasurable transcendence; by their very nature, they complicate and resist Christian biblical systematization.

Brân: of heads and the composite ethos

3.6. Jephthah's sacrifice - Maciejowski Bible. c. 1250.

Jephthah decapitates his daughter as a sacrifice to Yahweh.

Aeschylus's lost play *Bassarides*, as we know from a synopsis in Pseudo Eratosthenes, states that Orpheus was dismembered by Thracian followers of Dionysus because he was now worshipping Apollo. Orpheus's head, having been severed from its body, kept itself busy by singing mournful ballads while it floated down the river Hebrus and then eastwards to the Isle of Lesbos (Burges Watson, 2013, n.p.). In *The Syrian Goddess* (Περὶ τῆς Συρίης Θεοῦ; De Dea Syria [second century C.E.]), the waggish Lucian tells us that a head floating down to Byblos is a yearly occurrence:

> A human head comes every year from Egypt to Byblos, floating on its seven days' journey thence: the winds, by some divine instinct, waft it on its way: it never varies from its course but goes straight to Byblos. The whole occurrence is miraculous. It occurs every year, and it came to pass while I was myself in Byblos, and I saw the head in that city." (Lucian 1913, 47)

Ever since the aesthetic power of decapitation reared its ugly head in antiquity, bards have been employing it to enhance their productions' entertainment value. Dante used it to great advantage in the eighth circle of the *Inferno* when meeting with troubadour Bertrand de Born's specter, while many Christian saints, such as Denis of Paris, Justus of Beauvais, and Nicasius of Rheims were popular for their loquacious, decapitated heads.

Lands adjacent to the Atlantic are no exception: there is the famous talking head in *Sir Gawain and the Green Knight*, and we can say that the legend of the youth Donn-bó, an unrivaled poet from Ulster whose head kept on singing after it was severed from its body, speaks to the time-honored Irish fascination with the subject, a fascination widely studied by Patricia Palmer in her *The Severed Head and the Grafted Tongue: Literature, Translation and Violence in Early Modern Ireland* (2014).

This allure is likely the result of the way knowledge and data were stored in pre-literate societies. Endowed with extraordinary mnemonic abilities, bards, filid (elite poets) and druids memorized a great amount of data and transmitted it directly to their community; books were not available to store and deliver knowledge, so in ancient societies no storage devices mediated between the transmitter of knowledge and the receiver. Consequently, the head, library of the pre-literate world, was the repository of a society's culture, history, myths, and identity: a head that outlives the death of the rest of the body may serve to represent the continuity of communal myths, ideas, concepts and beliefs after the death of the individual that conveyed them. One of the most talkative severed heads in early Welsh mythology is that of Brân.

Brân (literally "Raven" or "Crow") is a giant and King of Britain who owns the "Cauldron of Renovation," a very special cauldron that can bring the dead back to life.[5] His name appears in numerous Welsh Triads, but his most important role is in the Second Branch of the *Mabinogi*, a.k.a. the "Mabinogi of Brânwen," Brânwen being the daughter of Llyr (Llyr is the Welsh word for sea) and Brân's sister. It is here where Brân's epithet of "blessed" first appears. Although the protagonist is an ancient mythical Celtic king, the general contours of this tale probably date to the tenth century, and the extant text is from the fourteenth century (Nutt 1888, 219). Brân is married to Penarddun and is also the brother of Manawydan and Nisien and half-brother to the troublesome Evnissyen. For our purposes here, I will conflate and summarize the different versions of the story.

One day Matholwch, King of Ireland, came to ask for Brân's sister Brânwen's hand in marriage. Believing that this would be beneficial to his kingdom and his people, Brân consents to the marriage without consulting with Evnissyen, who feels insulted and mutilates King Matholwch's horses.

Because Evnissyen's actions had dishonored the Irish, Brân sends the extraordinary cauldron along with his sister as a gesture of conciliation and wedding gift all in one. But things begin to sour when the Irish king, still feeling his reputation sullied, not only sends his new wife Brânwen to the kitchen to do menial tasks and cook for the court, but also orders the butcher to visit Brânwen every day, after he's cut the meat, and strike the unfortunate woman in the ear.[6]

Three years go by, with the Irish drawing up all boats on shore to prevent Brânwen from escaping. But she outwits them by training a starling, after which she commands it to take a note to her brother, a mission the bird promptly accomplishes. Upon reading the note, Brân prepares his fleet and his army and

---

[5] Cauldrons are endowed with mystical properties in the Atlantic shores' cultures of ancient Europe. "A Middle Welsh tract, 'The Thirteen Treasures of the Island of Britain,' includes Dyrnwch the Giant's cauldron, which is probably equivalent to the cauldron of Diwrnach the Irishman, gaining possession of which is one of the heroic tasks demanded by the giant Culhwch ac Olwen. For Cú Chulainn, magic cauldrons were important enough to be brought back from Alba twice. The numerous literary references highlight the cauldron's importance in Celtic culture, especially as a symbol of inexhaustible plenty [...]. Mighty rulers of the Otherworld, as in the Welsh Arthurian poem "Preiddiau Annwfn," and the "Dagda," senior deity of the Tuath Dé, owned marvellous cauldrons. The cauldron welded by the Irish smith-god Goibniu provided all the food at Otherworld feasts. A connected symbolism is that of resurrection of the dead..." (Koch, *Celtic* 358).

[6] The butchering trade and those who practiced it were considered particularly filthy and lowly in the Middle Ages. "On the eve of Edward I's ceremonial entry into London in 1274, concern about the dirty and congested conditions along Cheapside prompted the mayor to order the removal of the butchers' and fishmongers' stalls, 'lest any filth should remain in Cheap against the coming of the king" (Archer 1988, 4).

heads to Ireland (he wades through the water, as there is no ship large enough to contain him). In the ensuing battles, because he sees that the Irish are bringing their dead soldiers back to life, Brân (in another version Evnissyen) breaks the cauldron and is subsequently wounded in the foot by a poisoned arrow. Realizing that he will soon die, he instructs his seven remaining warriors to decapitate him and carry his head off with them, as it will prove pleasant company in their travels. He then commands the seven to embark on a peculiar mission: they are to go on the road for a long time, feasting in Harlech for seven years while the birds of the goddess Rhiannon sing to them all that time.

All this singing links the story of Brân to other texts studied herein in that it draws attention to the fact that music is not just a background prop, but is constitutive of the context in which the heroes act and, what is more, arbitrates their experiences. The allusion to music, in fact, manifests the underlying algorithm that conducts the interpretation of the heroes' emotional state; in short, music is a wordless language with which an affective context is articulated. We perceive this throughout *The Atlantic as Mythical Space*: in Orpheus's crooning head singing mournful ballads; in the Virgin's comforting songs to Godric in Lindisfarne; in the strange woman who sings to Bran mac Febail in his royal house; in the haunting songs of Niam and the islanders that charm the hero U sheen; in Madoc's desire to establish a kingdom "of love and music" across the ocean; in the beautiful *sianan*, or traditional ballad to which Snédgus and Mac Ríagla are treated in the island where the men of Ross have been exiled; in the music of the fairy branches that summons mortals to Manannan's overseas kingdom; in the serenade that bird-flocks of angels deliver to the Lord in *The Voyage of the Sons of Uí Chorra*, in a voyage where the heroes are accompanied by, among others, a musician; in the magical musical branch for which a man convinces Irish king Cormac Mac Airt to exchange his wife and children; and in the beginning of *The Children of Lir*, where Lir's wife and children have voices that are "as musical as birds or brooks." The medieval reader/consumer of these texts is informed that music is playing in the background because music is a method of encoding data that is socioculturally relevant: it brings back memories of emotional states entered into during events such as communal celebrations or less cheerful occasions. In short, the mention of music adds an emotive dimension to the narrative and gives it a communal context, keeping in mind that the medieval person almost always experienced music communally.

So Brân's head and its followers depart for the island of Gwales while serenaded by otherworldly birds. There they will dwell for fourscore years until they open the door that looks onto mainland Wales, after which they will have to leave for London, where they will bury the head in the White Mount looking towards France. The years they lived in Harlech and Gwales they passed in joyful bliss, not remembering the terrible past events; it is only when they open the door that looks to the mainland that all memories come rushing back. In the end, the head lived on for 87 years.

Physical geography is a backdrop for the Brân story: the island of Gwales, modern Grassholm (Welsh: Gwales or Ynys Gwales) is a little desolate island that lies 13 kilometers (8 miles) off the southwestern coast of Wales. It is situated "about six leagues to the North-West of Milford Haven, and is the first land seen in coming towards Milford, from the Westward, being a high round Island, and steep: This was a far more dangerous Coast formerly for vessels" (Carlisle 1811, Aa2). But there is also a mythical geography that attends the story and has seeped deep into the imagination of people in the area. Higginson (1899, 38-39) states that Welsh sailors talk of islands to the west which they call the Green Meadows of Enchantment, where one can at times land, but that can vanish right in front of your eyes. Fairies that live in them (the seven survivors from Brân's expedition) come and go to the mainland from these islands and even do their shopping at the markets of Milford and Langhorne.

The salient episode in the Brân the Blessed story is that of the decapitation of Brân by his followers, a type of death that he himself has requested. This incident, I believe, holds the key to correct interpretations of the tale. First, we should point out that this medieval story shows vestiges of pagan assessments of bloodletting as a cleansing rite, buttressed by the Christian adoration of blood as an emblem of redemption. Recurring mention of decapitation in pagan and early Christian literature suggests not only that there was a pervasive fascination with the gruesome subject matter, but also that there is a cultural tradition at work in which blood, shed in particular ways, has not only spiritual but also medicinal properties. It has been documented that in Germany the blood of decapitated convicts was collected by the "headsman in a bowl and then given to the sick to drink" (Owens 2005, 124).

Brân's kingdom–centered on Harlech, on the Welsh coast–overlooks the Irish Sea (a branch of the Atlantic), a condition clearly intended to enhance the mythical attributes of the tale. Evidently, his ownership of the cauldron places him in that mythical geography between life and death so often associated with the Atlantic. He is portrayed as a giant whose redemptive spiritual characteristics are reflected in his physical strength and size. By giving the cauldron to the Irish, he effectively gives the gift of everlasting life to mortals: these make ill use of it, and Brân must pay for it through his own blood sacrifice. Thanks to this particular form of sacrifice, his spirit, symbolized by his decapitated head, continues to live on through his followers. The parallels to the Christ narrative are evident.

The story of Brân shows the dynamic way in which old pagan forms of allegorical inspiration can function within a new aesthetic and be relevant to a new ethos. The fact that Brân's story, in its extant versions, retains much of its gruesome elements and unmistakably pagan compositional features speaks to a particular quality that made it palatable to proselytizing editors: the pagan Brân already had Christ-like characteristics that obviated the need for intense adjustment.

Thus, the tale has a remarkable syncretic character: it was a pagan tale that appealed to the church, which saw the story of Christ told in a way that was recognizable to pagans or even to recently Christianized folk. Hence, if any mythical tale from the period portrays the features of a composite culture as it negotiates its ethea, it is this one. It reminds one of Rollo, conqueror and first Duke of Normandy, who, according to Adémar de Chabannes, offered human sacrifices circa 932 and at the same time made important gifts to several churches in Normandy (Neveux 2008, 42).

In the Brân story, we detect how the Christian acculturation of indigenous cultures on the European Atlantic seaboard was a process of accepting and redirecting resilient ancient legends; consequently, cultural artifacts kept flourishing well into the High Middle Ages in a syncretistic manner. Concern for the "impurities" that might seep into religion by the acceptance of pagan elements was not especially strong, as this story illustrates.

The form in which narratives such as that of Brân have reached us reveals the complex cultural and social transactions at work in a syncretic society as it manages its composite ethos. Such a society is not just the result of the meeting of different religions, but also of different cultures, ideologies, and perspectives on reality. A composite ethos is constructed by the restructuring of meaning through a process of negotiation between traditional and new criteria for interpreting reality. The process of rearranging meaning is not one where previous meaning is exorcised, that is why a composite ethos often evidences a basal incompatibility between two disparate conceptual domains. Allegorizing the continuing authority of Christ's message using a pagan talking head is a case in point.

Moreover, it is a process where Christian proselytes are not engaged in producing creative works but are rather placing ideological overlays on a community's collective imagination and redirecting its allegories. Consequently, in pagan literature that is appropriated by Christian proselytes, meaning is articulated within a labyrinth of ambivalences where it is difficult to sidestep the hazards of absurdity: Obviously pagan heroes enter obviously pagan spaces like the Atlantic while praying to the Christian God and, even more incongruously, encountering Christian saints in sundry wondrous islands of the pre-Christian imagination.

Thus, these external alterations in the pagan culture's symbolic inventory can show how tales such as Brân's, the *immrama,* and the *echtrai* might be useful in answering deeper questions regarding the process of Christianization on both shores of the Irish Sea. The case of Ireland is of particular interest, as on that island there existed a mass of people who were essentially excluded, culturally and linguistically, from the Roman world that had thrived in Britain and western mainland Europe. The Irish were therefore immersed in a pre-existing, non-Latin local tradition, and as Christianity did not arrive there on the heels of any Roman legion, no government authority could impose or compel the islanders to strict adherence or standardized interpretation. So the composite culture whose characteristics are divulged in early medieval Irish texts must have developed within a space of cultural indulgence where synthesis thrived, evidently propitiated by the early church in Ireland.

Students of Irish cultural practices can only access written medieval texts. It is important to note that these written texts have been set down in a cultural environment that has–in varying degrees–amended original cultural traits that had previously been transmitted orally. Many show signs of the merger of ancient pagan traditions with the requirements and narratives of the new, Christian religion. So while extant texts provide practical clues, the challenges intrinsic to the task of scrutinizing synthesis in the Irish cultural context stem from the fact that there can be no access to unadulterated exemplars of ancient oral traditions from the *file* and *ovates*. Although their original forms may be glimpsed behind the Christ-like features of characters like Brân, it still leaves us to speculate as to the prototypal, pristine forms his story might have taken before the transition from spoken to the written word.

I speak of forms, in the plural, because an important issue to consider in this regard is that oral literature is alive, not made up of words that are fixed and petrified in the unchanging pages of a book. Oral literature transforms and modifies its content as required by changing circumstances, audiences, and bards. This would account for the relative ease with which Christian modifications were incorporated into the corpus of ancient pagan literature, accustomed as it was to incorporating change. Yet another reason why such modifications encountered few obstacles is that, because of the abovementioned historical circumstances in which Ireland became Christianized, the merger took place within a more tolerant cultural environment, in such a way that the spiritual insights of Celtic paganism and Christianity coalesced without much dogmatic resistance. Thus, Brân came to symbolize Christ, the Christian Brendan became an *immrama* adventurer, and the pagans U-sheen and Máel Dúin exemplars of Christian piety with surprising conformity: In spite of the unavoidable incongruities, nowhere in the literature does one find mention of this syncretism as an illegitimate compromise between conflicting theological views.

There may be an additional explanation for this phenomenon. On the one hand, from the pagan perspective one might imagine a type of unconscious syncretism, that is to say, syncretistic practices would have been relatively common in religions without the constraints of a holy book or well-structured canons. But on the other hand, the deliberate syncretism of the early Irish church is more difficult to define. Soteriological religions like Christianity mark out an inflexible program of thought and action that leads to salvation, so syncretism should have been anathema for the early proselytizers. But what medieval Irish texts confirm is that the early church saw itself as a system with an overriding function: to bring salvation to a people long alienated from conventional cultural practices, even if the price to pay was adaptability.

In Ireland, the Christian system did not come into conflict with another soteriological religion, so one might speak here of a sort of asymmetrical syncretism where one participant (pagan belief) provides its ancient narratives–just as it provided holy wells, gathering places, festivals, and other culturally significant spaces–as vessels to be repurposed and filled with spiritual content by the other (Christianity). So even though the church did not have the broad-spectrum official status that it enjoyed in the Roman Empire, neither did it have the concerted opposition of competing interpretations of Christ and His message that it had within the Empire. Consequently, pagan traditions, when in contact with the early Irish church, did not threaten its functioning in large measure; as a result, the boundaries between the church's agendum and ancient pagan traditions were blurred and a composite society flourished.

Chapter 4

West

Atlantis: a panoptic reflection

4.1. Athanasius Kircher: *Mundus Subterraneus*. 1678.

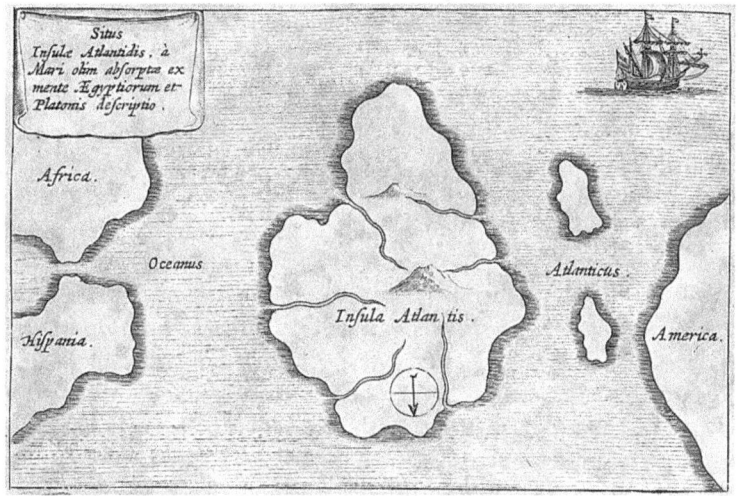

Atlantis ("as per Egyptian and Platonic descriptions"). It is placed in the middle of the Atlantic, with north and south inverted.

Throughout history, what I'd call the horizon of the fabulous has periodically migrated farther afield, being pushed along by discoveries and breakthroughs that revealed barren realities where human imagination had had room to fly. Beginning with that fateful voyage of 1492, a system of economic and social interactions commenced that would eventually lead to our present "global village." The Spanish Empire, the first truly worldwide corporation, began sustained efforts to bring distant subjects, literally scattered across the globe, into a relatively synchronized collective.

The 1492 breach of the mystifying Atlantic set humanity off on a long march towards a concurrent present, initiating the dissolution of ancient ways of conceiving a world whose predominant attributes had been dispersion, mystery, and arcane distances. On a larger scale, the empire continued what older regional empires had begun, which is the forced merger of previously scattered peoples, compressed into a new, consolidated amalgamation.

One can only try to imagine the emotional distress felt by a Tzotzil or an Otomi in Mexico, a Chamacoco, Guaycuru or Aymara in South America, an Ati or Bajau in the Philippines, a Taotao Tano Pacific islander or a Fang or Bubi in equatorial Africa when forced to change their languages to Spanish, change their native names to Spanish names, change their religions to Christianity and transform their ancient economic systems to one that served the Spanish Empire's economic interests. All these peoples, including the provincial Spaniards sent to establish this compulsory amalgamation, must have sensed, in one way or another, the erosion of the mystery and imaginative freedom that previously endless distances had bestowed upon their understanding of the cosmos. And they all must have, in time, viewed themselves as dismayed constituents of an integrated worldwide conglomerate that provided them with compatible kinsmen in all the corners of the earth.

Nevertheless, for people whose principal forms of transportation included the sail and the horse, the erosion of mystery was a slow process. At the dawn of the twentieth century the planet still held unknown, mysterious areas that allowed fantasy to prosper: Jules Verne and his *Voyages Extraordinaires* enjoyed great popularity, with tales like *Journey to the Center of the Earth*, *Twenty Thousand Leagues Under the Sea*, *Around the World in Eighty Days* and *Mysterious Island*, set in exotic and even uncharted parts of the globe. Today, a time when the earth has gradually become the "global village" so many politicians talk about and Google Earth can put virtually every corner of the planet on our computer screens, the horizon of the fabulous has shifted to space, with sagas such as those of *Star Trek* and *Star Wars* captivating the viewing public's imagination. But even space has been brought within humanity's domains of rational perception.

To give as example: The last original *Star Trek* episode was broadcast on 3 June 1969, "Then, just six weeks after the airing of that final *Trek* episode, on 20 July, Neil Armstrong and Buzz Aldrin completed John F. Kennedy's vision for the 'New Frontier' and landed on the moon." And while 500 million people watched the moon landings, viewership for the *Trek* episode was "dismal" (Kapell 2010, 4). Although several offshoots of the series have been successful, such viewership numbers may signal the start of another shift in the horizon of the fabulous: discoveries and breakthroughs show that the universe is an eminently hostile place where life may well be improbable at best, where lethal radiation is prevalent everywhere and the unimaginable distances make it impossible to even think about reaching other solar systems, let alone other galaxies. Furthermore, Curiosity and its sister rovers on Mars have revealed a lifeless world that until recently had been the habitat of our most comprehensive fantasies.

Perhaps Mars illustrates this most recent displacement of the horizon of the fabulous. The Martian invasion that Orson Wells described in the 1938 radio drama *War of the Worlds* truly terrified audiences, causing panic in a significant number of listeners who took it as a real emergency broadcast. Such an audience reaction would be unlikely in the twenty-first century: using the gigantic Arecibo Radio Telescope for many years, listening for the slightest little "ping" that would point to some extra-terrestrial intelligence, many scientists now suspect–though few acknowledge such suspicions–that there is nothing out there.

So more in tune with modern consciousness is the 1996 extreme slapstick film *Mars Attacks!*, where small Martians with a distended brain, green jumpsuits, and a nasty disposition chase humans around and take over the government. Earth is saved when a teenager discovers that Slim Whitman's song "Indian Love Call" makes their brains explode. The British series *Red Dwarf* and Douglas Adams's *Hitchhiker's Guide to the Galaxy* trilogy also offer interesting slapstick comedy that targets space travel. Although it is the "last frontier," space has become the realm of low comedy: human fantasy is at a crossroads.

By way of contrast, in the Middle Ages, the horizon of the fabulous extended in every direction of the compass. As the Roman Empire crumbled, what lay beyond Rome's ecumene became clouded in an even thicker haze of mystery, a fog that allowed fabulous beings to roam freely in undiscovered and strange lands. Interestingly, one reason for the proliferation of the fabulous is linked to religion. There was a glitch attending the Bible, which supposedly contained all the necessary knowledge a Christian would ever need: as stated in a previous chapter, it had a limited geographical range. Outside that range lay the Atlantic Ocean which, unlike the far East, sub-Saharan Africa, or the icy north, was adjacent to the civilized communities of western Europe.

So in an era when people were growing increasingly curious about their macro-environment, the most enigmatic ambit was whatever lay beyond the western ocean. A person standing on the Atlantic shores of Spain or Ireland was actually staring out into the fabulous, the unknown, the mysterious, the font of myth, the sanctuary of wonders yet to be discovered. There was still a marvelous abundance of undetected places in the world where one could "get there first" and experience a deep sense of accomplishment and fulfillment. As Simon Parkin puts it in an article in *The New Yorker*:

> While we benefit from the invention of penicillin, of airplanes, of the internet, we also suffer antibiotic resistance, looming climate disaster, online comments. And one pleasure enjoyed by our forebears, now largely denied to us, is the thrill of cartographic discovery. Our world is mostly mapped, its common species mostly named. For a while, video

games filled the gap, presenting new, uncharted virtual lands to satisfy players' wanderlust. Soon enough, though, commercial guides to these places followed, denying even virtual explorers the chance to get there first. (2016, n.p.)

Consequently, as we grapple with the loss of spaces that once sparked our sense of wonder, we look at medieval western Europeans with a tinge of jealousy. They had no such problems: their conceptual cosmos was endowed with an abundance of fabulous spaces, such as the Atlantic, where extraordinary beings existed and astonishing events could take place. And as they stared in wonder to the west, the principal myth, the fountainhead saga regarding many of the mysteries and myths that resided in that great ocean, was that of Atlantis.

Plato gives us the most comprehensive account of Atlantis in his dialogues *Timaeus* and *Critias*. The first one takes place one day after Socrates explains what a model state should look like. Critias tells Socrates the story of a journey that the Athenian statesman Solon took to Egypt, where priests of Sais told him stories concerning ancient events that had hitherto been unknown to the Greeks.[1] Sonchis, one of the oldest priests, begins by informing Solon that, culturally, Greeks are mere children whose knowledge cannot compare to that of ancient Egypt, and he prefaces his stories by telling him that the destructions of mankind have been many, and that there will be many more. Greeks, for example, remember only one catastrophic flood, but there have been many, and more can be anticipated. Atlantis, for example, perished in one such forgotten episode.

It is likely that whatever historical truth the tale of the catastrophe may have contained was not of great concern to Plato, as he used the tale as a platform upon which to deliver his didactic message. As a morality tale, whatever historical legitimacy the Atlantis story may have had would have to take second place to its edifying function. This is made evident by the fact that Plato presents his Atlantis as a type of earthly paradise, obliterated by the gods after its leaders lost their way and put their own interests above those of their people, an educational outcome that is, in many ways, analogous to the biblical Adam and Eve story. Atlantis, much like Eden, was the object of purifying, divine wrath.

But the deluge that according to Plato destroyed the Atlantean paradise was not confined to it: the Greek army that, as described in his dialogue *Critias*, had been sent just before the flood to stop and push back an invading force from Atlantis, perished in that same catastrophe. Such a fanciful clash between

---

[1] Solon's journey to Egypt is corroborated by Plutarch in his *Life of Solon* (ch. 26) and his *De Iside et Osiride* (ch. 10).

Greeks and Atlanteans may be an enhanced rendering of reports by Greek traders, doing business in the extreme western edges of the known world, of clashes with locals after transactions soured and the parties resorted to weapons. Presumably, besides making use of such reports, Plato was also influenced by older traditions of world-ending floods and earthquakes that were common in the ancient world. Such a one is reflected in the account given by Utnapishtim in the *Epic of Gilgamesh*, c. 2100 BCE.

The Atlantis flood story seems to be encoded in the mythology of most ancient cultures. This leads one to believe that it is based on a worldwide event and, consequently, may have a simple explanation. The most recent glacial period ended 12,000 years ago, when mile-high sheets of ice, covering millions of square miles, introduced their content of water into the oceans. Plato estimated relatively well when he placed the Atlantean cataclysm at 9,000 years before his time. When the meltdown began, sea levels were a staggering 500 feet lower than what they are today (Stein 2008, 37). The subsequent rise in sea levels was sizable and extensive, and it must have been imprinted in the psyche of pre-literate peoples that surely experienced this global catastrophe as a world-ending event.

Oral traditions everywhere must have kept the record of a terrifying time when water kept advancing upward, inexorably, year after year, covering ever more land. The catastrophe lasted long enough to make an indelible and ubiquitous impression, one that migrated to the written word once early societies became literate. For pre-scientific cultures, the only way to explain this nightmare scenario was to consider it a supranatural affair, attaching to it a contributory chain of circumstances–foremost of which was human transgression–that triggered it. Ultimately, humanity survived to tell the tale, the world was regenerated and one of the greatest shared stories in human history was born.

It would seem, then, that Plato galvanized speculative interest in Atlantis and in Atlantic Ocean tales and legends that had been a cultural substratum, for many centuries, in the popular domain. But he was neither the first nor, obviously, the last to write on the subject of a magical land far off in the western ocean. Hellanicus (Ἑλλάνικος) of Lesbos (490-410 B.C.) is known to have written a work named "Atlantis" where mention is made of Poseidon (founder of Atlantis), of his son Atlas (the first king of Atlantis), and of Atlas's twelve daughters and one son (Caerols Pérez 1991, 83). Herodotus calls the body of water beyond the Pillars of Hercules the "Sea of Atlantis" (Strassler 2007, 202), and Hesiod, in his didactic poem *Works and Days*, gives the geographic location of the Isles of the Blessed (μακάρων νῆσοι) as the "Western Ocean" (Westmoreland 2007, 70). The Theban poet Pindar places them there as well, although he speaks of only one island (Sacks 1997, 8-9). Strabo (*Geography* 2.3.6) remarks that the philosopher Posidonius wrote much about the vanished continent of Atlantis and informs us that Aristotle also made observations on the topic; both works are lost. Pliny the Elder (*Natural History* 6.199) places an island called Atlantis in the vicinity of the Canary Islands, Seneca augurs the existence of a new world to the west, Pliny the Younger refers to a great number of sandbanks just beyond the Pillars, and Philo, when speaking of great catastrophes, mentions three cities in the Peloponnesus (Aegira, Bura and Helica), and Atlantis, now "beneath the sea in consequence of an extraordinary earthquake and inundation" (Yonge 1855, 208). Saint Jerome, Saint Augustine, and Saint Anselm also make reference to the cataclysm. Owing to the lost world's unrelenting celebrity, father Las Casas, quoting Proclus's commentary on Plato, dedicates a whole chapter of his *History of the Indies* (bk. I, ch. 8) to Atlantis.

Modern contributors to the preservation of the legend are varied and form a mottled fabric of interests and objectives. One of the best known, Lewis Spence (1874–1955), wrote *The History of Atlantis* in 1926, a work that was reprinted in New York by Cosimo Classics in 2007 and included chapters such as "The Sources of Atlantean History," "The Geography of Atlantis," "The Races of Atlantis," "The Stone Age in Atlantis," "The Kings of Atlantis" and "Life in Atlantis." Modern efforts like this helped to perpetuate the legend by elaborating an imaginary history and geography that have the look and feel of a report based on objective evidence.

Ireland, the "other" Atlantis

Ireland is similar to Atlantis in that it is a large island in the Atlantic Ocean. The difference is that Ireland is a physical island, but that difference did not matter much in the myth-bound mindsets of the ancients. Because of its geographical location, it was very early endowed with a mythical history that outmatched that of Atlantis, a history not only set down by peoples from the eastern Mediterranean, but also by the Irish themselves. The Irish imaginary established Ireland as a fabled land, a place where uncommon spaces, beings, and events proliferated.

In the tales of the Mythological Cycle and in the *Book of Invasions* one gets a clear idea of Ireland as a most relevant place for gods to do battle, ancestors to roam the caves and hillsides, bizarre beings to engage in activities that change the course of daily life and supernatural women to lure heroes to magical islands in the western ocean. In many ways, Ireland is more *mythical* than Atlantis.

For a start, the earliest inhabitants of Ireland, the Tuatha Dé Danann, were gods who, having been expelled from heaven due to their great knowledge, descended on Ireland in a cloud of mist. In the *Lebor Gabála Érenn*, a medieval

Irish Christian pseudo-history, the Milesians (*Míl Espáine*, or "Soldiers of Spain") defeat the Tuatha Dé Danann and drive them underground. Many other mythical races come to settle in Ireland, people who originate in several places, the eastern Mediterranean being a favored origin point. This geographical preference may indicate a historical truth, but it is more likely that once Christianization began on the island, a biblical ancestry was cooked up in which the Irish were at once racial and cultural members of a clan whose lineage stretched back to Abraham and beyond.

The links between the nation's present and its concocted past are manifold. Geoffrey Keating, compiling a string of archaic texts for his General *History of Ireland*, which he first published in 1634, states that his text contains "A full and impartial account of the first inhabitants of that kingdom, with the lives and reigns of a hundred and seventy-four succeeding monarchs of the Milesian race" (1723, 7). He then goes on to establish "The Pedigree of the Right Honourable, the Precept William Obryen, Earl of Inchiquin, to King Milesius of Spain," Keating's protector (1723, 12). Furthermore, he states that Partholanus "discover'd the coasts of Ireland three hundred years after Noah's flood, and it was a thousand and eighty years after the Flood when the sons of Milesius set foot upon the Irish shore (1723, 32).

Keating is only one of the most recent writers striving to join this "other Atlantis" to the absolute beginnings of the biblical story; an earlier endeavor is the *Lebor Gabála Érenn*. Accepted as conventional history up to the nineteenth century, the *Lebor Gabála* (Book of Invasions) contains the account of six times that the island was subjugated by six different groups: the people of Cessair, the people of Partholón, the people of Nemed, the Fir Bolg, the Tuatha Dé Danann, and the Milesians. For diverse reasons, the first four groups were either annihilated or forced to leave the island; the fifth group hypostatize Ireland's pagan deities, while the last group represent the Irish people, the Gaels (Koch 2006, 1693-1695).

This first invasion establishes a connection to the Bible story, joining this remote island to the transcendental events by telling us that Cessair, daughter of Noah's wayward son Bith and his wife Birren, orders her people to create an idol that will advise them on how to escape the flood, as old man Noah is punishing Bith by not letting him and his family on the ark. This idol informs the group that they can escape the coming catastrophe by sailing to Ireland. After the long journey, their three ships reach the west of Ireland, but two of the craft sink in the attempt to land the voyagers. Cessair, forty-nine other women, and three men survive: Fintan mac Bóchra, Bith, and Ladra.

According to the *Annals of the Four Masters* (Annála na gCeithre Máistrí [compiled between 1632 and 1636]) they landed in Ireland at Dún na mBarc (on

Bantry Bay, County Cork) a mere forty days before the flood in "The Age of the World, to this Year of the Deluge, 2242" (1626, 3).

The men then share the women equally, although, according to my calculation, they would each get 16.6666. J. P. Mallory (2013, 16) has a more divisible number of women, 150, which would give each of the three men 50. As is to be expected, Bith and Ladra shortly die, presumably of exhaustion, and Fintan is left with all the women. In a move that reminds one of Aesop's observation "Be careful what you wish for, you just might get it," the emaciated Fintan marshals what little energy is left him and makes a run for it, hiding in a cave in the hill of Tounthinna [Tulach Tuindi, Tul Tuinne] over the River Shannon, near modern Portroe, Co. Tipperary. He will be the only survivor when the Flood finally comes. Subsequently, and in truly pagan style, he shapeshifts into a one-eyed salmon, then an eagle, and then finally a hawk. The superannuated Fintan lives for 5500 years after the flood, changes back into a man, and relates the history of Ireland to the High King Diarmait mac Cerbaill.

More invaders would subsequently reach the island, each contributing to the mythical legends and biblical accessories that inform its earliest history. Being a physical island with a real population, the myths regarding Irish origins are more elaborate than those of Atlantis, as they must reflect known power structures and beliefs that are all too real and directly impact the lives of human beings.

This is how Ireland began its association with the biblical story. One may presume that a pagan story underlies this and other, analogous origin narratives. Important is the fact that in this story Ireland becomes a land of women, not unlike the many Atlantic otherworld islands where heroes make landfall in pagan voyage narratives. Moreover, there is an evident similarity to *immrama* stories in the inordinate number of women for every man, eliminating the competition that caused distress in other Irish legends. The western landfall and other geographical details are further clues to a probable archaic, pagan origin that the thick biblical canopy works to conceal.

These myths of origin are privileged platforms upon which to view the process of Christianization in Ireland. They are symbolic expressions of identity, power, and belief that often serve to validate prevailing identity patterns and power structures. As such, they are concocted heritage narratives that strengthen and legitimize religious, social, and political order. The pagan origin stories talk of old gods retreating to underground realms at the arrival of human beings that conquer the island after a bitter war. The gods fight humans; humans win. At the center of the idea of *belonging*, then, was the sense of a common past where the people of Ireland did away with the gods in order to populate, establish peace, and govern the land. With the advent of Christianity, this origin needed a facelift, as doing away with a deity was not palatable to the proselytizers.

What we perceive in Irish biblical origin stories is precisely that facelift; we recognize a concerted effort to plunge the island's communities into the baptismal font of common–albeit fabricated–sacred memories. We also see the tension between an earlier deep-rooted ethos (the shape-shifting, superannuated Fintan is its pertinent graphic symbol), and a novel belief configuration, a stress triggered by the ethical demands of the new belief system as it subsumes archaic ethea. Origin stories are, in effect, snapshots of this process, a symbolic affirmation of the social transformation of Ireland into a Christian nation. Myths about Atlantis, a theoretical land in the ocean that no one had ever seen, were not subject to the same processes or ethical antagonisms.

The early navigations into the Atlantic

Out of the murderous innocence of the sea.
W.B. Yeats

4.2. Black-figure Cup Painting of a Greek Vessel. c. 520.

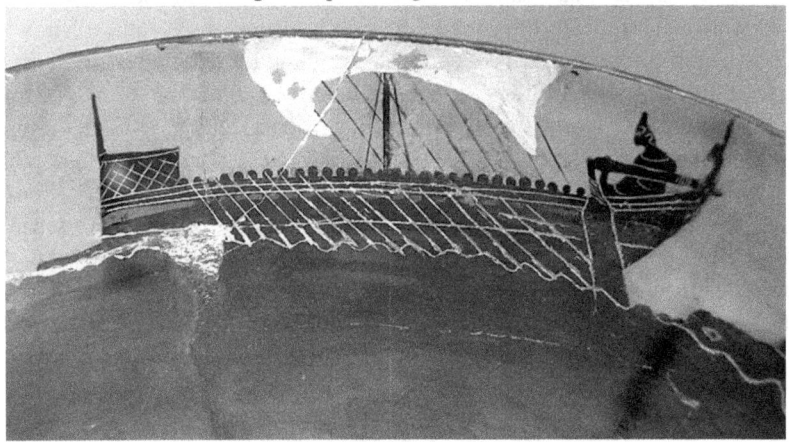

Fast and maneuverable, but impractical for long Atlantic voyages.

The earliest accounts of navigation into the Atlantic tell of treacherous conditions and perilous adventure. Herodotus informs us that the first sailor to venture out into the Atlantic was Colaeus (Κωλαῖος) of Samos, who circa 639 BCE was blown off course through the Straits of Gibraltar (Strassler 2007, 343). Crossing into the Atlantic became the stuff of legends from the start, as the result of this first recorded passage was that "by some divine guidance [Colaeus and his crew] came to Tartessos. This trading post had not yet been exploited at this time, and so these men returned with a greater profit from their cargo than any other Hellenes of whom we have an accurate account" (Strassler 2007, 343). Interest grew in whatever lay beyond the Pillars of Hercules, and by 500 BCE Euthymenes (Εὐθυμένης) of Massalia had reached equatorial Africa, returning with, one would presume, tales of marvels that would equal any material treasure he may have procured (Roller 2015, 45).

Atlantic sailing seems to have been predominantly motivated by the trade in amber and metals. In the Bronze Age, Ireland exported gold to Britain and continental Europe and imported amber, and Mediterranean economies may have been importing tin from Cornwall as early as 2000 BCE (Cary and Warmington 1929, 29). The first named sailor that may have made the voyage to Great Britain is Midacritus (c. 600 BCE): "There is an odd notice of one Midacritus, who 'first brought tin from the tin island': long presumed a Phoenician, he is now thought a Greek, who merely picked up tin at Tartessus or perhaps made an isolated dash to Cornwall" (Thomson 1948, 55). The British Isles were rich in raw materials that were coveted by advanced societies in and around the Mediterranean, materials whose transport required excellent seamanship.

In the fifth century BCE, at the height of their people's power in the Mediterranean, Carthaginian navigators Himilco and Hanno sailed out of the Mediterranean and into the Atlantic in search of new trade routes. Himilco's account of his adventures has been lost, but Pliny the Elder (*Natural History* 2.169a) and Postumius Rufius Festus Avienus, (*Ora Maritima*, fourth century CE) mention and quote from his account (Bogucki 2007, 437). Of Hanno's voyage the single source is a Greek periplus, said to be a translation of a tablet Hanno supposedly hung up in the temple of Ba'al Hammon (the Greek Kronos) when he returned to Carthage. While Hanno, sailing south, may have reached the coast of present-day Gabon, Himilco sailed north hugging the coast of the Iberian Peninsula, and veered west, passed Madeira, and swung around to the Canaries; of the great Teide volcano, Pliny quotes Himilco as stating that "The wonderful high crown of the mountain reached above the clouds to the neighborhood of the moon, and appeared at night to be all in flames, resounding far and wide with the noise of pipes, trumpets, and cymbals" (Elton 1890, 22-23).

It is worthy of note that Himilco's discovery of the immense volcano in the Canaries is not transcribed in scientific terms (trumpets, pipes, cymbals, neighborhood of the moon, flames) but is rather a metaphysically-saturated statement laden with normative ideas about the oceanic otherworld. In this regard, the sound-laden environment reminds us of Ovid's *Metamorphoses*, where Triton makes sundry sounds to make waters recede and the land rise from beneath the waves:

> [Jupiter] calls upon the azure Triton standing above the deep, and having his shoulders covered with the native purple shells; and he bids him blow his resounding trumpet, and, the signal being given, to call back the waves and the streams. The hollow-wreathed trumpet is taken up by

him, which grows to a great width from its lowest twist; the trumpet, which, soon as it receives the air in the middle of the sea, fills with its notes the shores lying under the sun. (Ovid 1899, 32)

Likewise, and shortly after 25 BCE, King Juba II of Mauritania commissioned an expedition with the express objective of finding the Isles of the Blessed. Juba believed himself to be a direct descendant of Hercules, "and this led him to curiosity about the Garden of the Hesperides, site of the hero's last labor, and by association the Islands of the Blessed" (Roller 2013, 48). Himilco's and Juba's expeditions show that when navigators ventured into Atlantic waters, they were journeying into the classical world's otherworld. The narratives that describe their voyages are in fact structured, to a significant extent, as symbolic quests that reflect formulaic ideas and assumptions regarding the Atlantic. In the accounts of their travels, these navigators may have been engaged in the materialistic pursuit of searching for new trade routes, but what is truly consequential is that they were doing it within the confines of mythical space.

By c. 325 BCE Pytheas (Πυθέας) of Massalia sailed to the northernmost point of Great Britain in midwinter and made interesting observations about his discoveries. He determined with accuracy the latitude at which he found himself, and that this far from the οἰκουμένη (habitable world) the sun rose only four peches (πῆχυς, a measure equal to the Latin cubitus, each peche being 18.2 inches) on top of the horizon. Furthermore, Pytheas indicated that the sea turned to ice at these latitudes, an observation that Strabo, who is an important source for Pytheas, expressly rejects as one of the fabrications of this colossal "liar" (Roseman 2005, 24).

Although Pytheas was navigating through the classical world's mythical space, the account of the *real* wonders that unfolded before his eyes in the northern Atlantic was judged as a fictional exaggeration by the commonsensical Strabo. Moreover, although the journey, presumably, took place on the whole as Pytheas tells it, Strabo is justified in reading the navigator's account with a measure of suspicion, as it seems that in it he not only included his own observations but "added all the reports that reached him respecting distant countries, without always drawing a distinction between what he saw himself and what was told him by others" (Smith 1876, 627-628).

Strabo's objections to Pytheas's inclusion of others' accounts, valid as they are, in no way nullify the explorer's commitment to conveying the "truth" of what he saw. They do bring us back to the previous consideration of sight not just as passive awareness, but as an active agent that in many ways produces that which is "seen." In the Greek sailor's descriptions we perceive the merging of conceptual and material landscapes into a synergistic whole: *how* he sees animates *what* he sees and brings it into the world of meaning. Pytheas does not glance blankly at the world: remembering that he was a "Greek" sailor places him within a cultural context, and this is important if we are to analyze his account accurately. Culture, Greek or not, is an organized version of the world that has been designed by/for a community, so *how* Pytheas sees is culturally determined; his account has contextualized the material world through which he travels into a cultural frame of reference that, despite Strabo's protestations, explains his inclusion of "what was told him by others." Presumably, those "others" were also contributing to the cultural context into which the material world was habitually inserted, so if Pytheas included "others' accounts," it is merely because the knowledge provided by sight was harmonized with communal ethea in a participatory manner, which is to say that the physical world was discerned and articulated within a *collaborative* cultural framework.

Another Greek who weighed in on Atlantic lore is the Stoic philosopher and geographer Posidonius (Ποσειδώνιος) of Apameia (c. 135 BCE–c. 51 BCE), who is mentioned by Strabo and who, in his treatise *About the Ocean and the Adjacent Areas*, seems to have been interested in Plato's story of the demise of Atlantis. Herein we find the story of Eudoxos (Εὔδοξος) of Kyzikus, a Greek sailor in the service of Ptolemy VIII, who was inspired to sail to India by a shipwrecked Indian sailor (aptly named Bogus) that had been rescued in the Red Sea and taken to Ptolemy. On his return voyage from India, Eudoxos was blown off course and forced south along the east coast of Africa, where he found the remains of a ship that, after listening to stories told by the natives, he concluded was from Cádiz, in southern Spain. Finding this ship on *this* side of Africa could only mean that one could sail around that continent; the mythical Atlantic was somehow connected, in the far south, to the *real* world of material fact and tangibility.

Armed with this new data, Eudoxos undertook the voyage twice in order to find the place where the Atlantic and the Indian Ocean connect in southern Africa. He started at Cádiz and sailed west and south into the nameless immensity of the Atlantic. His first attempt seems to have ended in failure, and although Pliny claims that he was successful in his second, there is no additional, extant information regarding an achievement that would have been extensively memorialized. "The most probable conclusion is that like the Vivaldi brothers who attempted to repeat his voyage in 1291 A.D., he perished on the journey" (Tozer 1935, additional notes xxiii). Telling the story of Eudoxos, Posidonius could hardly avoid mentioning what must have been on his readers' minds, Atlantis, of which he states, probably after much reflection, that "it is possible that the story about the island of Atlantis is not a fiction" (Vasunia 2001, 232).

Posidonius is an example of the implication of myth in the telling of real events that have unfolded in the Atlantic. Modern readers might consider it remarkable that the author felt compelled to speak of Atlantis in a story of discovery and exploration, in a chronicle of a mariner's rational, scientific attempt to identify and map an important sea route. But readers of the time may have found nothing remarkable in the Atlantis speculation, and it is reasonable to suppose that Posidonius was anxious about deficiencies in his account, that in the telling of his countryman's explorations of the physical environment he might only focus on the tangible in detriment of the transcendental, resulting in an incomplete description.

Such an assumption is based on the way ancient and medieval minds endow physical space with subjective substance, much more so than modern minds. Space (the environment/the cosmos) is where gods, spirits, and human beings interact; as a result, it cannot be analyzed in an exclusively empirical manner. As such, the world is an arena for human subjectivities: individuals from ancient cultures can only engage in the affairs of sentience in spaces that support myth-based inferences. Space is not just the irrelevant distance from point A to point B because God, the gods, created space expressly as a sphere where human awareness of the cosmos' created, divine nature would transpire as people travel from point A to point B.

Although space and the objects in it have constant physical interaction with human beings, that space is essentially a projection of people's unbounded subjective cosmos. This explains why Columbus got a glimpse of Paradise on the coast of South America and came within shouting distance of Prester John's realm, why maps and travelers' accounts are full of bizarre creatures, why fourteenth-century Florentine traveler Giovanni de' Marignolli saw Adam's house on a mountain and Ponce de León scoured Florida in search of the Fountain of Youth. That is also the reason why Posidonius included speculation about Atlantis while analyzing the account of Eudoxos's voyage of exploration. He was only a man of his time.

In essence, then, the Atlantis myth that Posidonius felt obliged to mention reveals that Eudoxos was traveling in subjective space, in a world that, because of its inherent metaphysical attributes, concerns readers profoundly as human beings. As a result, narratives regarding the exploration of the world often have homiletic features: Atlantis, having been destroyed because of its population's misbehavior, speaks to the consequences of immoral action; it clarifies the rules according to which mankind became organized in societies, and justifies conventions that allow people to deal with each other and with the supernatural in a productive manner. Moreover, it reminds people that the world that Eudoxos is surveying is susceptible to the consequences of deviating from these organizing principles. Lastly, as the Atlantis myth has been endowed with a distinct geographical space to the west of the known world, it follows that, for the reader, the story of Eudoxos's voyages into the Atlantic summoned up the myth associated with the great ocean with each word on the text; that is another reason why Posidonius could not ignore it.

So it is that land emerging out of Atlantic waters was inevitably transcendental and was endowed by the ancient imagination with fantastic attributes. Early Greek, Phoenician and Carthaginian voyages beyond the Straits of Gibraltar, be it north to the British Isles or south to the African tropics, seem to have been mostly coast-hugging affairs. After breaching the Straits, they sailed either to the north or to the south, but never westward in any consistent manner, so archipelagos like the Canaries were not well-documented. As such, they existed in a fog of myth and mystery, as it was assumed that it was impossible to cross the ocean: "From Gadira (Cádiz) gloomward thou shalt not pass; turn back again the gear of the ship to the broad continent" (Pindar 1890, 77).

Euripides shows that any land mass emerging from the western ocean and completely surrounded by it was endowed by the pre-modern imagination with the aforementioned mythical characteristics:

> To the strands of the Daughters of the Sunset,
> The Apple-tree, the singing and the gold;
> Where the mariner must stay him from his onset,
> And the red wave is tranquil as of old;
> Yea, beyond that Pillar of the end
> That Atlas guardeth, would I wend;
> Where a voice of living waters never ceaseth
> In God's quiet garden by the sea,
> And Earth, the ancient life-giver, increaseth
> Joy among the meadows, like a tree. (E. Segal 2003, 246)

Likewise, island populations can reflect their habitat's fabulous nature. Plutarch, for example, speaks of a traveler named Demetrius who voyaged to the farthest parts of Scotland; there he came across islands off its coasts that were isolated, its few inhabitants being "holy men who were all held inviolate by the Britons. [...] Moreover, [...] in this part of the world there is one island where Cronus is confined, guarded while he sleeps by Briareus" (Melrose 2016, 103).

Those who for some reason may have been blown off course out into this open ocean of mythical renown would have encountered vast expanses on which you sail for many days without any land in sight, an alien experience especially for mariners from a small sea nestled between southern Europe and northern Africa. There they would have encountered storms the likes of which are rare in the enclosed Mediterranean and may even, unexpectedly, have come across some of its magnificent islands which, in situations such as these, could have appeared as ethereal manifestations.

Mediterranean sailors were not the only ones sailing Atlantic waters. People on the Atlantic shores are known to have been accomplished mariners, a fact reflected in Julius Caesar's *Commentarii de Bello Gallico* (3. 8 & 13), where the Roman conqueror expresses admiration for the seafaring skills of the Veneti of Brittany. The Veneti ships were very good for sailing the great ocean and braving Atlantic storms, but they had one weakness that Caesar exploited when battling them: "… since their ships had no rowers, they were totally dependent on the wind in their sails to move" (Freeman 2008, 168). This characteristic of the Celtic Veneti's ships may be reflected in the many stories of Celtic heroes allowing the deities to guide their vessels, as human muscle was not involved in powering them forward. The fact is that losing superiority in shipbuilding was a constant worry for Mediterranean merchants and military men, so much so that the *Codex Theodosianus* explains how "The Romans [in 438 C.E.] tried unsuccessfully to prevent the barbarians from acquiring plans from Roman shipbuilders" (Leighton 1972, 140).

It should be mentioned at this point that even the Irish monks that sailed to Iceland in their coracles during the eighth century C.E. very likely did not risk taking a straight route: they must have reached that isolated island by sailing north to the nearby Outer Hebrides, from there to the Faroe Islands (149 miles), and from there to Iceland (280 miles), not impossible distances for the sturdy hide-bound coracles.

But why did the Irish anchorites risk life and limb to reach faraway islands in the Atlantic? Clearly, it was not just because of their need for isolation, as they could have found remote solitude in many parts of Ireland. It may be that islands have always been particularly alluring, especially islands in the mythical Atlantic. There is something special about land coming out of the great ocean: it is a safe harbor amid the endless emptiness, the security of a permanent foothold after days or weeks of undulating anxiety; it is the fruitful emerging from the barren; it is creation materializing out of the void.

As discussed in a previous section, sight was culturally-mediated in the Middle Ages, so it would play a decisive role in the imagery associated with Atlantic islands. Depending on weather conditions and currents, islands can seem to appear and disappear from sight, change shape in the mist and grow out of the distant haze. A distressed sailor's imagination might make him see a beautiful city on a desolate island or a magnificent rainforest on a sandy, rock-strewn atoll, features that inexplicably vanish at the next sighting. And if the mariner happened to be sailing on the Atlantic, that "Sea of Darkness" described by Ovid, the islands perceived in this manner would inevitably transmit an even stronger charge of mystery. For the arbitrated gaze of a medieval sailor, these phenomena were not explained by science.

For the classical world, the Atlantic was a space where a dramatized version of existence could play out; a space from which the mysteries of the universe would emanate to indulge that instinctive appetite for astonishment that is indispensable to the human spirit.

Magical ships and the esoteric substance of travel

4.3. The first known representation of a sailor consulting a compass on board a ship. 1403.

In a manuscript copy of John Mandeville, *Le livre des merveilles* (1403, originally published c.1355-57). 1403 manuscript is held by the Bibliotheque National de France, Paris, B MS fr 2810, fol.188v.

Medieval travel to the western ocean, whether portrayed as fantastic or factual, contains a strong element of imaginative symbolism. As truly exceptional forms of transportation, all ships were, in some measure, magical; a ship was a miniature κόσμος, a self-contained microcosm that offered the necessary elements for survival, incorporating the essentials of life on an alien wasteland of insensate majesty. The ocean, where no human habitation could possibly endure, home to the otherworld for many cultures, could be visited in relative safety on a ship, a vessel that floated magically over the void.

Since antiquity, ships have been portrayed as magical. Some of the better-known magical vessels are the ones that the Phaeacians (Φαίακες) employed in the *Odyssey*. According to Homer, those ships darted across the water, were steered by thought, and did not need pilots or rudders; furthermore, they knew the route to every city and country in the world and neither storm nor mist nor calm inconvenienced them (*Odyssey* 8.57-63). Their ships were so efficient, that even Poseidon was infuriated because the Phaeacians had been ferrying so many men in safety; in his fury, he turned one of their ships to stone (*Odyssey* 13.84-88).

Odysseus entered the Okeanos, or the underworld, when he decided to consult the seer Tiresias regarding his journey home. But Tiresias was dead, so to reach him in Hades he had to sail west into the Atlantic, which, as Circe had warned him, entailed the procurement of an exceptional sort of ship. Once procured, Circe recommended that the hero not bother with a pilot or a rudder because the vessel, impelled by the North Wind, would find its way there on its own (*Odyssey* book 11). This may give us an idea of Odysseus's likely trajectory to the otherworld: Geography tells us that once a ship enters the Atlantic from the Mediterranean and is blown south by the North Wind, the only possible landfall beyond the medieval pale is in the Canary Islands, a standard location for otherworld speculation.

Norse myth gives us the ships Skíðblaðnir and Ringhorn, property of the gods Freyr and Balder respectively. Skíðblaðnir could sail on water and through the skies, and always enjoyed favorable winds:

> Skíðblaðnir rightly belonged to Frey, because as the god of sun and rain, he was also considered a fertility god. Ships were identified with fertility and the life cycle in many ancient myths, and Skíðblaðnir, as the manifestation of the summer cloud, brought new life to northern lands. Ringhorn, another ship in Norse mythology, had a contrasting function and symbolized the opposite phase of the life cycle. As the light god Balder's burial ship, Ringhorn symbolized death and winter. (Andrews 1998, 182)

Ancient druid tales also seem to have made use of magical ships to propel mythical travelers west across the Atlantic to otherworld realms. Eighteenth-century Scottish historian James Macpherson, in his *Introduction to the History of Great Britain and Ireland*, claims to have accessed the following, otherwise unknown tale:

> Sgeir, an ancient druid, though his command extended over the elements, was dissatisfied with the narrow limits of his knowledge, and panted for a sight of the Green Island of the West. One day, as he sat meditating on a rock, a storm arose, and a cloud, under whose skirts the waters were

troubled, rushed towards him. From its womb issued forth a boat, with her sails bent to the wind, and hung round with a thousand oars; but it was unfurnished with mariners, itself seeming to live and move. An unusual terror seized upon the druid. He heard a voice, though he saw no human being: 'Arise, behold the boat of the heroes! Arise, and see the green isle of those who have passed away.'

Under the influence of a secret but irresistible force, he embarked in the miraculous boat, and sailed, during seven days, in the bosom of the cloud. His ears (says the tale) were stunned with shrill voices; the dull murmur of winds passed him on either side. He slept not, yet were not his eyes heavy. He ate not, yet was he not hungry. On the eighth day, the waves swelled into mountains; the boat was rocked violently from side to side: The darkness thickened around him; when a thousand voices at once exclaimed, 'The isle! The isle!' The billows opened wide before him: The calm land of the departed rushed in light upon his eyes. (1773, 238-240)

Even though Macpherson's depiction of the "miraculous boat" sailing to the Atlantic "happy place" sounds like a work of thoughtful reconstruction, it does contain the type of basal material that allows modern scholars to trace the tradition of British and Irish ocean travel literature back to its pagan origins. Critically, Sgeir's story includes many of the items, types of characters, topography, and climate that subsequent stories locate in islands visited by Christian sailors like Saint Brendan. Interestingly, Christian holy men like Brendan sailed on magical ships in the Atlantic, vessels that did not exist in the Christian tradition.

Another tale from Ireland, the immram *The Voyage of Snédgus and Mac Ríagla*, has a magical ship on which righteous individuals travel the Atlantic. As the story goes, the men of Ross were being ruthlessly oppressed by Fiacha. They complied with his every demand, but he still wanted more. At the end of his first year in power, Fiacha (a word that means "debts" in Irish) summoned the men of Ross to a meeting in Boynemouth (in Meath, north of Dublin) to demand even more of them. When they assured him that they could not do more, he had them spit in his palm, observing that only half of the spittle was blood. Fiacha then told them that until all the spittle was blood, they needed to work harder, casting the hills into the hollows and planting trees in the plains to make new forests. When a deer interrupts the gathering and Fiacha's men pursue it, the men of Ross seize the opportunity and kill Fiacha. As punishment for their crime, Fiacha's brother Donnchad puts the men of Ross in a large house to be burned alive, but after consultation with Saint Columbcille's[2]

---

[2] Columbcille (521–597) was an Irish saint and seer who is said to have had amazing prophetic powers. He is credited with having predicted the great Irish famines and the advent of railroads. See O'Kearney, 83-84.

representatives, he decides to have 60 pairs of them cast into the Atlantic at the mercy of God.

Snédgus and Mac Ríagla, the two messengers that had been sent by Columbcille to deliver the men of Ross's redemption, were on their way back to Ionia when they decided to sail out into the Atlantic on a pilgrimage. So off they went in their coracle, braving currents, wind, and waves until after three days their thirst became unbearable. At that point, Christ took pity on them and had the currents bring them to a place with a stream of fresh water, where they drank to their satisfaction. Seeing the power of Providence, they decided to leave their voyage in the hands of God, put their oars inside the boat, and let the ocean take them where it chose.

And it chose to deliver them, in their ship without oars or sails, to the magical islands of pagan lore that one anticipates in the *immrama*. There they saw salmon bigger than a bull-calf, warriors with the heads of cats, a loquacious bird with a golden head and silver wings that told them stories from the Bible, and other wonders so markedly alien to Christian reasoning that the story becomes a truly astonishing example of religious syncretism. There are men with the heads of hounds and manes of cattle, others with the heads of pigs. Eventually, on one of these isles they discovered the men of Ross that had been exiled into the great ocean; in this pleasant replica of Ireland the women sang them a beautiful *sianan*.[3] Here they were also told of two lakes, one of fire and one of water, which would have devastated Ireland were it not for the intervention of Martin and Patrick, who had spent much time praying for the Irish. This island was also the home of biblical Enoch and Elijah, living there in secret until the Day of Judgment.

They departed the island, and after many days God–through the magical ship without oars–brought them to another one, a lofty place where a great king presided over a righteous populace. Scrutinizing his palace, they noticed that every door had an altar, a sign of the king's unassailable virtue. In what seems like a druid's sanitized prophecy, they were advised here that a great punishment awaited the people of Ireland, that people from over the sea[4]

---

[3] It is not clear whether a "siannan" (or "sian") referred to a species of music or to a particular song in ancient Ireland. The word also refers to the whistling of a spear or dart as it flies towards its target, a meaning it has in the tale of the second battle of Magh Tuireadh. See Eugene O'Curry, *On the Manners and Customs*, 385.

[4] This is very likely an allusion the Cambro-Norman invasion of Ireland in 1169 and dates the story (at least this edited version) to a period not much later than that year. Thus, it reflects the deep-rooted practice of explaining disasters as divine retribution; in this case, the Cambro-Norman attack is the result of a notorious disregard for "God's teachings" among the Irish.

would lay waste to the land because of their neglect of God's Testament and of His teachings: "Then wine is dealt out to them, and the king saith to the clerics: 'Tell the men of Ireland,' he said, 'that a great vengeance is about to fall on you. Foreigners will come over sea and inhabit half the island; and they will lay siege to you. And this is what brings that vengeance upon them (the Irish), the great neglect they shew to God's Testament and to His teaching. A month and a year you shall be at sea, and you shall arrive safely; and [then] tell all your tidings to the men of Ireland'" (Stokes 1888, 25). This story depends on the means of transportation offered by a magical ship which, guided by the Hand of God, takes the travelers to their destination.

Evidently, a pagan cruise in a magical ship into the netherworld has been co-opted here to convey specific dogmatic prescriptions. This magical currach sailing around the Atlantic allows the righteous Snédgus and Mac Ríagla to travel to the otherworld and return with messages intended to enhance compliance with religious dogma and secure social stability. The message is that if Martin and Patrick had not spent so much time and effort praying for the Irish, they would have been eliminated from God's Creation, so they had better start behaving like the righteous inhabitants of the lofty island, the ones whose king has an altar in every door of his palace.

Furthermore, the story incorporates the Judeo-Christian precept of divine retribution. To enhance social stability, divine retribution allows punishments to be dispensed to everyone for the crimes of a few, assigning a type of collective responsibility that can transform every person within an identitary group (the Irish in this case) into a dogmatic enforcement officer. Communal welfare is therefore dependent upon individual compliance, and everyone becomes responsible for his or her neighbors. Considering that righteous, God-fearing people often suffer senselessly, the origins of much adversity can be rationalized through divine retribution and collective liability, as suffering becomes traceable to the sins of one's neighbors and countrymen.

In this sense the ship, a vessel in which all aboard share route and destination, is an apt metaphor for collective liability. As a crew member, your personal destiny (destination) is shared with a group. The guiding winds and currents that govern Snédgus and Mac Ríagla's currach are a conventional metaphor for divine will: collective destiny is intimately connected to Salvation, so obeying God's commands (the guiding currents) is critical.

In addition, collective liability can be articulated in the socio-political arena: in this same *immram*, the men of Ross that killed Fiacha expressed, in doing so, a will that violated the principles of group membership. As righteous as their actions may have been, they essentially rebelled against the prescribed communal itinerary and struck out in a direction that was at odds with the collective. It might seem a bit odd that their punishment was to be put on a ship (60 pairs of them) by Donnchad, Fiacha's vengeful brother, and forced to share a journey into the Atlantic. But this is a lesson of sorts: now crossing the ocean, they must adhere to standardized principles of behavior and perforce sail in the same direction. If the ship sinks due to one person's negligence or individual rebellion, all on board drown. If there is disagreement as to the destination, it is likely that the ship will never arrive anywhere. Donnchad's decision to put the men of Ross on a ship might seem sophistic if not viewed as a protracted experiential learning session, as a lesson in collective discipline.

Magical ships became popular in medieval courtly narratives. Knightly seekers and lovers have sailed in them into the Atlantic in voyages that enlightened them, expedited their quest, or lured them into bewitching traps. In the long poem *Partonopeus de Blois* (c. 1175), the knight Partonopeus, whose exploits are said to take place in the time of king Clovis (c. 466–c. 511), is hunting in the forest. He kills a boar, but gets lost and despairs of ever finding his way back to civilization.[5] He then sees a mysterious ship, and as the crew is invisible, he identifies it as an enchanted ship of fairies:

> And now the stripling gain'd Loire's flowery side,
> And saw the fairy ship at anchor ride;
> Breathless, he climbs the deck; a favouring breeze
> Springs, and the shallop darts across the seas. (*Partonopex* 1807, 14)

Hoping that it will carry him away from the wilderness, he comes on board. The vessel takes him to an enchanted castle which he views as the work of necromancers and where he is given an opulent welcome. Partonopeus then discovers that this is Empress Melior's kingdom, and she informs him that she has dispatched the magical ship to bring him to her kingdom so that she can make him her lover.

Adhering to its courtly love framework, the story has the hunter become the hunted and, more importantly, has the boy become a man in two distinct ways: he is successful in the hunt, and he finds love. Before coming to Melior's kingdom, Partonopeus had met only one of the conditions of attaining manhood, killing the boar, a solitary physical activity that takes courage and strength, but the other condition, the one that requires finesse, subtlety, and sophistication (this is, after all, the age of courtly love), needed magical

---

[5] This is the magical hunt topos so common in courtly love lais, such as *Guigemar, Guingamor, Graelent, Desiré* and *Melion*. Also, boars are associated with ancient Indo-European rites of initiation into manhood: "Ce sanglier n'est autre que le monstre triple des mythes d'initiation héroïque indo-européens" (Philippe. Walter, *Tristan et Iseut*, 94). [This boar is none other than the triple monster of Indo-European myths of heroic initiation]; my translation. The killing of this monster inevitably brings a curse to the slayer.

intervention and the concurrence of a woman. This is the part that did not go so well for Partonopeus, as during the lovemaking the knight, lacking courtly sophistication and in a fit of uncontrolled lust, comes close to committing rape. Consequently, Melior bans him for two years (*Partonopex* 1807, 16-17).

Evidently, the magical ship facilitates the hero's progress and evolution in a very significant and socially relevant manner, making his voyage an extended metaphor for his development as a man, a lover, and a human being. Finally, an indispensable characteristic of *Partonopeus's* ship that reminds one of the Phaeacians' vessels in the *Odyssey* is its remarkable speed: "La nés sigle dusque a la nuit/ Plus tost que cers levriers ne fuit (The ship sails until nightfall more swiftly than a stag fleeing a greyhound)" (Eley 2011, 31-32).

Marie de France (c. 1160–1215) included, in her Breton lai *Guigemar*, a superb instance of a magical ship. As in *Partonopeus de Blois*, the young Guigemar is out hunting, carefree and impervious to the demands of love, when he wounds a white stag. By some bizarre glitch in the laws of physics, the projectile bounces back and wounds Guigemar. To the young man's chagrin, the fatally wounded animal begins to speak to him, informing him that, to cure himself of his own wound, he must fall in love with a woman that will love him back. He then enters a ship without sail, crew or rudder where he falls asleep, only to awaken dockside next to a beautiful tower. There, a beautiful (and married) lady falls in love with him, and he with her; this is the beginning of an affair that lasts until the jealous husband finds out and sends Guigemar back home in the magical ship.

The pair will eventually meet up again in the "real" world and, after sundry adventures, live happily ever after. Here again, we see another boy completing his initiation into the ranks of courtly lovers: he is successful in the hunt but requires the intervention of a magical ship, an enchanted vessel that is guided not by the hand of man, but by the invisible currents of literary conventions. The passage through mythical waters lets him finally obtain the therapeutic love of a woman. *Now* he is a man in a very relevant, courtly love construal of the term.

Another magical ship plying mythical waters is the one that was boarded by Galahad, of Arthurian legend, when a maiden led him to the shore to meet up with the knights Perceval and Bors. There they spotted Solomon's Ship which, as was probably expected by many readers of the period, did not have a crew. The maiden, once on board, confessed to being Perceval's sister and presented Galahad with a girdle, one that she had made for him with her own hair. It is then revealed that King Solomon, who had foreseen that Galahad would be his last descendant, had prepared the ship as well as King David's sword (The Sword of the Strange Hangings) for Galahad's use. Inside, the onboard bed is one that Solomon framed with three spindles of the Tree of Life and whose genealogy could be traced to the branch that Eve took from the Garden of Eden. Moreover, the ship might have seemed abandoned, but it announced its magical constitution immediately: on its side, Galahad could read an inscription stating that only a man with an unwavering belief in God and in Jesus could board the vessel. This was, unmistakably, the Ship of Solomon. The sword stowed on board had prophetic inscriptions and only Galahad was able to handle it.

Once underway, they swiftly crossed the sea to Corbenic, the Grail Castle, where Galahad cured the Maimed King with blood from the Bleeding Lance. He was then tasked with taking the Grail in a rudderless boat to the land of Sarras, where pagan King Escorant imprisoned the knights for a year. Galahad and Perceval died in Sarras, and Bors survived to tell the tale at Arthur's court.[6]

There is another interesting account of magical voyages into the Atlantic in early medieval Galicia, on the northwestern shores of Spain. The account of this voyage, known as *The Voyage of Trezenzonio to the Great Isle of the Solstice*, is in the late eleventh, early twelfth century Latin manuscript *Trezenzonii de Solistitionis Insula Magna*. As the story goes, after one of the many devastating Muslim raids suffered by Galicia during the eighth century, a certain Trezenzonio, after wandering through the devastated land, climbs to the top of the Tower of Hercules (Breogán's Tower), in Brigantium (today's A Coruña), from where, aided by the light of dawn and a huge mirror, he spots the reflection of an island where no island should be. Recognizing it as "The Great Isle of the Solstice," he immediately decides to sail there. He then builds a boat that prodigiously, without the benefits of a compass or maps, takes him forthwith to the mythical island. Once on the island, he wanders for several days around a utopian world, unsullied by the hand of man, with mild temperatures and benign weather, abundant food, and no adversity of any kind. After some time, he spots a massive basilica adorned with jewels and dedicated to Saint Tecla. He decides to stay on the island, and after a seven-year sojourn, an angel appears to Trezenzonio and orders him to return to Galicia.

Apparently, Trezenzonio was not aware of the compulsory nature of the angel's demand and decided to ignore it. But the divine messenger did not find

---

[6] This essentially follows the French *Vulgate Cycle* and Malory's version of events in *Le Morte d'Arthur* (see Barbara Tepa Lupack, *Illustrating Camelot*, 2008, 171). In Wordsworth's poetical version, Galahad survives and marries The Egyptian Maid, a very beautiful woman whose ship, the "Water Lily," was blasted out of the sky by a jealous Merlin. The Egyptian Maid had been sent to Arthur's court to marry one of the knights of the Round Table. Having perished as a result of Merlin's rage, only Galahad's touch was able to bring The Egyptian Maid back from the otherworld (see Christopher Bruce, *Arthurian Name Dictionary*, 160). In Tennyson, the Grail is never found, as finding it would eliminate a critical element of wonder and mystery in the story.

the traveler's disregard very humorous so, for his refusal to obey, Trezenzonio was struck with leprosy and, on the return trip, all the goods that he had collected on the island and placed in his ship rotted away. Moreover, upon arriving back home he noticed that the Tower of Hercules was on the verge of collapse and Galicia had been repopulated. Evidently, Trezenzonio experienced one of those time-dilation events that so many *immrama* heroes also experience.

It is difficult to explain the reason for the time-dilation that takes place on Trezenzonio's journey in his extraordinary boat. Einstein argued that time moves more slowly for a moving clock than for a stationary one. As magical ships ferrying heroes to mythical realms move them speedily through a transcendental dimension, time slows down and is essentially neutralized. There is the implication that time in the stationary, "real" world has continued to run at its accustomed speed, while for the wayfaring hero it has come to a virtual standstill. So, where the immramic traveler feels that a small amount of time has elapsed (like Einstein's conceptual astronaut traveling close to the speed of light), back home (the inert domain of the ordinary) many years have passed. In immramic literature, once the hero travels through liminal spaces, the passage of time becomes so superfluous that it almost ceases to exist as a defining factor in his adventure. In such spaces, the hero moves with astounding velocity, unwittingly anticipating Einstein's time-dilation concept.

Because of his self-interested insurrection, Trezenzonio returned to Galicia on his magical ship without any proof of his extraordinary vacation in the Great Isle of the Solstice. He told Bishop Adelfio of Tuy of his journey, but he was unable to return to the island because the Tower of Hercules was on the verge of collapse, so he would no longer be able to see the island from its top.[7]

Some similarities may be found between Trezenzonio's story, and "visions of the otherworld" stories also from Spain. Valerio del Bierzo (c. 630–c. 695) describes visions experienced by the monks Máximo, Bonelo and Baldario: Máximo has what today we might call a near-death experience, one where he is transported by an angel across a river to a luxurious paradise; he also catches a glimpse of Hell from afar, which gives the angel an opportunity to give moral instruction to Máximo on how to behave in order to avoid being consigned to the flames. Bonelo experiences a rapture and is taken by an angel on an excursion that is quite similar to Máximo's in its moralizing contours, but includes more details regarding the Devil's domestic arrangements. The hermit Baldario has a vision as a result of an illness that causes his soul to leave his body. He encounters Jesus on a mountain accompanied by a throng of elderly persons all dressed in white and is invited to spend some time there before returning to his body

---

[7] Full story in James D'Emilio, "The Paradox of Galicia," 60 ff.

(Amador de los Ríos 1864, 415-416). But Trezenzonio's story, as we have seen, has the peculiarity of sharing most of its characteristics with *immrama*, while those other monks' adventures in Paradise are formulated as visions, untethered to the vagaries of real ocean voyages that are essential to the *immrama* and some *echtrai*. Moreover, the parallels between Trezenzonio's voyage and those of Irish *immrama* and *echtrai* characters are quite remarkable, evincing common cultural models and cognitive structures among the "Celtic" peoples of Europe's western rim. Pertinently, we might remember that in chapter XIII of the *Lebor Gabála Érenn* (The Book of Invasions or of the Taking of Ireland, compiled in the eleventh century), Ith discovers Ireland while perched atop the same tower in Spain where Trezenzonio discovers "The Great Isle of the Solstice."

As we can see, there was a significant proliferation of magical ships and voyages in the Middle Ages. There is, for example, the French tale of Eustache the Monk (c. 1300), who had the power to make his ship invisible, a ship that only became visible after the monk was beheaded:

> Là il coupa la tête à Eustache et alors tout le monde vit clairement le navire, qui, pendant la vie de ce Moine apostat, étoit tout invisible. (Michel 1834, xix)

> There he beheaded Eustache, and then everyone clearly saw the ship, which, during the life of this apostate monk, had been completely invisible. (My translation)

There is also Tristan and Iseult's ship, which, while not magical in itself, is the place where the magical potion that makes the two protagonists fall in love is consumed.

While present-day readers may take these outings as products of uncontrolled fantasizing, it is important to note that these magical excursions were not necessarily taken as imaginative fiction by a general population brought up on a steady dose of miracles and portents. In the ninth century, Agobard, a Spanish-Visigoth priest and archbishop of Lyon (c. 779-840), commented with indignation (c. 820) that Christians in his region firmly believed that four people in his parish had been sailing on magical ships and stealing fruits from trees. "Agobard concluded sadly that in his day folly had taken the upper hand, and Christians believed things which in better days even pagans would reject" (Kieckhefer 2014, 46).

U sheen in the Island of Youth, or the trappings of identity

The *an Fhiannaíocht* (Fenian Cycle of Irish mythology, a.k.a. Ossianic or Fionn Cycle) relates myths that seem to be based on historical events of the third century C.E. These tales focus on the exploits of the renowned Fionn mac

Cumhaill and his warriors, the Fianna Éireann, who thrived during the age of Cormac mac Airt, a High King of Ireland whose reign is variously dated between the second and fourth centuries C.E. The cycle enjoyed great popularity during the early thirteenth century, propelled by one of its most exceptional stories, *The Interrogation of the Old Men* (Agallamh Na Seanórach). Many of its tales are recorded in *The Book of the Dun Cow* (c. 1100) and *The Book of Leinster* (c. 1160) (*Britannica*, s.v. "Fenian Cycle").

U sheen (a.k.a. Osian, Ossian, Osheen, and Oisín), son of Fionn mac Cumhaill and Ireland's most famous poet, is the subject of one of the cycle's most popular tales. U sheen, which means "young deer," received this name because his mother, Sadbh, is said to have been turned into a deer by the druid Fer Doirich. Fionn mac Cumhaill finds her in a wood but does not kill her. Sadbh returns to human form, settles down with Fionn, and gets pregnant. But the malicious druid turns her back into a deer and she returns to the forest, where she gives birth to U sheen. There are three disparate versions of how his father eventually finds him: naked on the heights of Binn Ghulbain, in the form of a fawn, or being challenged by him over the possession of a roasting pig.

The tale of U sheen, who was whisked away across the Atlantic on a white charger by Niam Chinn Óir, a spirit maiden, was molded into a ballad ("The Wanderings of Oisin" [1889]) by William Butler Yeats (1865-1939), who saw in the fable a suitable medium to express his Neo-Platonic interest in theosophy, folklore, and spiritualism. In his ballad, Yeats has an extremely old Oisín (U sheen) tell his story to St. Patrick, who with predictable rigor characterizes the maiden as a "demon thing": "Oisin, tell me the famous story / Why thou outlivest, blind and hoary, / The bad old days. Thou wert, men sing, / Trapped of an amorous demon thing" (Yeats 1892, 1).

The maiden (Niam Chinn Óir) character is analogous to the Old French, Celtic fairy mistresses that appear in Marie de France's Lanval, Renaut de Bâgé's Le Bel Inconnu, and the anonymous Partonopeus de Blois, all written in the twelfth century. The fairy mistress motif probably arrived in France shortly after the Norman conquest of England, an event that produced stronger cultural exchanges between the British Isles and the continent. As in the Irish tale, the French stories include the otherworldly woman who selects a mortal man as her lover because of his exceptional personal qualities. She can bestow eternal life on her chosen lover, but she always includes a *geis* or prohibition of some kind. The man eventually disregards the prohibition and is consequently punished for it.

The conventional story is told by the elderly U sheen, who has outlived all his contemporaries, every member of his tribe, and anyone else who might remember him. It is a story that has its roots in historical people and events: U sheen is the son of Fionn mac Cumhaill, leader of the Clanna Baiscne (Fianna

Éireann or Finnian Militia). Having sided with Munster in its war against Leinster, his race, the Feni nation, is annihilated at the battle of Gavra (or Gabhra, 284 C.E.), a clash of such proportions that its memory has been "preserved for more than fifteen hundred years" (Haverty 1872, 40). The bards pick up the tale in the aftermath of the battle, when U sheen, his father, and some of the few surviving members of the Feni tribe go hunting in a forest. There, to their surprise, they spot an enigmatic maiden with golden hair drawn in by a silver ribbon, dressed in a flowing white robe and riding a white stallion with golden hooves and a gold crescent upon its head. To add to the mystery, the maiden's robe has strange markings the likes of which the men have never seen.

Seeing their wretchedness and the gloom in their faces, she takes an interest in them, asking them why, unlike other hunters, they plod along apathetically. They reply that they are the last of their kind, that their kin have been annihilated and their world has perished. They in turn ask her to identify herself; she answers that she is Niam Chinn Óir (Niamh of the Golden Hair), one of the daughters of Manannán mac Lir, god of the sea. She is a virgin whose home is an island across the great ocean, Tír na nÓg ("the land of the eternal youth," also known as Tir Tairngire, "the land of promise"). Moreover, she has traversed the Atlantic's waters upon this extraordinary horse, Enbarr[8] of the Flowing Mane (also spelled Aonbárr), because of her great love for the famous poet/hero U sheen, with whom she has fallen in love even though she has never seen him.

U sheen is instantly struck by her beauty and falls in love with her, but learns that he cannot marry her unless he accompanies her across the great ocean to her home. There he would have one hundred young men to command, one hundred horses, and the same number of sheep, swords, silk robes and bows, and she would have one hundred maidens to serve her.[9]

---

[8] Aonbarr Mhanannáin was the name of Lugh Lámfada's horse in the Irish Mythological Cycle, an extraordinary animal that could gallop over land and sea. Importantly, Embarr also means "imagination" in old Celtic.

[9] Interestingly, in the Bible 100 is the number that represents fullness, a full reward. NIV Gen. 26:12-13: "¹²Isaac planted crops in that land and the same year reaped a hundredfold, because the Lord blessed him. ¹³The man became rich, and his wealth continued to grow until he became very wealthy." Mark 10:29-30: "²⁹Truly I tell you," Jesus replied, "no one who has left home or brothers or sisters or mother or father or children or fields for me and the gospel ³⁰will fail to receive a hundred times as much in this present age: homes, brothers, sisters, mothers, children and fields—along with persecutions—and in the age to come eternal life." Matthew 13:23: "²³But the seed falling on good soil refers to someone who hears the word and understands it. This is the one who produces a crop,

Tantalized by such allure, U sheen wants to know how they are to get across the great ocean, as it seems an impossible task. She tells him that the magical horse on which she rides can get them to the other side, as the water does not yield to its tread. Convinced by Niam, U sheen mounts the horse with her and they dash onto the waves, hurtling ever westward in a timeless daze, with Niam's song putting U sheen in a sort of trance that disrupts the passage of time. Spatial discernment is also disturbed and heteroclite, as they come across an uncanny deer hunt, maidens holding up golden apples, and lovely youths hovering casually above the surf.

Before arriving at their destination, they stop over at an island where a beautiful princess is kept under a spell by a brutal giant that wants to marry her. She will be held under that spell until she acquiesces or a hero comes to her rescue and slays the brute. U sheen immediately volunteers for the task, for he is not afraid (he *is*, after all, Irish). After waiting three days and three nights, the battle is joined, and following a vicious contest the much-wounded U sheen comes away with the victory and cuts off the giant's head. He is healed with a balm provided by the beautiful princess and buries the giant in a deep grave, placing on it a headstone that he engraves in the Ogham alphabet.

Back on the uncanny steed, Niam and U sheen advance ever westward over the waves until the girl's singing begins blending with soft melodies that can be heard in the distance, as if coming from the setting sun. As they near the shores of a remote landmass, a panorama of beautiful trees filled with colorful birds shows ever clearer; once on land and at the prompting of Niam, a group of young people run towards them and embrace them. For a hundred years U sheen lives happily among this race of people, in eternal youth and with Niam as his wife. But one day he finds a bloodied spear floating in the sea and is reminded of his nation. He returns to Ireland on Niam's steed and finds a race of dwarfs who tell him that all the Feni have vanished from the earth; he eventually falls from the horse and, upon touching Erin's soil again, turns into a decrepit old man.

The character U sheen, the last of his clan, traveling to a fantastic world across the Atlantic where he will not grow old, acts as signifier for a vanishing identity. As he no longer has any attachment to a land that once belonged to his clan– his clan has disappeared–he flies off into the emptiness of the Atlantic to a safe place, one of eternal youth where the cosmos of communal memories and narratives that configured his clan's identity can survive with him. However, the

---

yielding a hundred, sixty or thirty times what was sown." Furthermore, the number 100 corresponds to the Hebraic letter "Qoph," "...and its energy intelligence is that of growth and holiness" (Robert Haralick, *Inner Meaning*, 269).

bloodied spear reminds him that communal identity cannot survive the demise of the community, so in a final fit of desperation, he travels back to Ireland and, as a splendid allegory for his loss of identity, wilts as he touches her soil.

To understand this story as an allegory, one must recall the conceptual distinction between allegory (which addresses preponderant issues of communal relevance) and the self's narrative identity (the construction of one's life story by articulating life experiences into a developing version of the self, one that supports a sense of purpose and meaning and allows the individual to assign value to interactions and events). In essence, the distinction between the two was not especially significant in the Middle Ages. Contemporary Western thought has contributed much to the fundamental rift that has opened between them, as the poetic–inherently communal in the Middle Ages–has been thoroughly subjectivized and the self, bolstered by the ascendancy of existential anxieties, has in many ways eclipsed the communal.

In the modern scenario, our accumulated experiences are subjected to privately challenged and conflicting sources of authority, only one of which is the community. Unlike the stable, unquestioned collective truths that shaped the identity of U sheen and his contemporaries, the modern self and identity are commonly constructed privately, not collectively. This means that it is difficult for us, today, to understand that U sheen structured his self's narrative identity within a sheltering infrastructure of clan and tradition, and it is difficult to understand because we have replaced clan and tradition with indifferent bureaucracies and abstract institutions that have ostensibly dissociated our psyche from communal tutelage.

Unlike modern individuals with detached, self-sufficient, and resilient identities, U sheen would have felt destitute and alone in a world that lacked the communal solidarity and psychological support offered by his identitary group. So the fantastic journey into the Atlantic represents the individual's coping with anxieties not previously experienced and is an expression of a never-before-experienced reflexivity of the self, abruptly removed from the identitary community that had such a critical role in its formation. Additionally, this journey that so expressly and deliberately transcends temporal constraints is the self's symbolic retreat from Ireland, the time-bound island that no longer serves as a repository for his identity.

This story has its roots in the catastrophic separation of individuals from ancestral lands and from clans to which they belonged and that, in great measure, provided them with a sense of identity. It speaks to a fate shared by many early medieval tribal groups in Western Europe, people such as the Luigni and Gailenga in Ireland, who were dispossessed and dispersed in the year 847 for "plundering the territories in the manner of heathens" (Tomlinson 2007, 216).

If, as William O. Frazer has suggested, identity is the result of social action and is contingent upon social relations, making features of one's own "group identity [...] seem to be inherent, innate, 'natural,' while their absence or difference seems correspondingly unnatural" (2000, 3-4), the cause of U sheen's plight can be perceived as cognitive perplexity. Frazer adds that social life in the Middle Ages is "storied," that is to say, people form identities by placing themselves within a string of "emplotted stories" (myths, legends, epic poems, religious narratives) that are shared by a community and try to understand the events surrounding their lives by assimilating them into available narrative patterns. Hence, the U sheen story can also be understood in terms of its applicability in the analysis of the design and evolution of medieval identitary blueprints. Indeed, from the moment that his tribal group, the Feni, was obliterated at Gavra, the familiar cosmos in which the few survivors held full membership and to which they were attached with instinctual bonds was dissolved. Capitulating to the new circumstances might in effect constitute collaboration in the ruin of that familiar "storied" cosmos that was responsible for their sense of belonging and self-worth. Defeated and wandering, early medieval survivors like the Luigni and Gailenga–or in this case the Feni–could only sketch an image of their plight through a purposeful story like that of U sheen.

As happened so many times to so many tribal groups in the early Middle Ages, the Feni's world has ended in a catastrophic event not contemplated in the "emplotted stories" with which they assembled their social identity. This story preserves historical traces of that identity (individual names, familial relations, clan affiliations, and conflicts) but as the clan has essentially "died," its continuation, in the form of U sheen, cannot occur in "this" world, as this is the material world where the clan no longer exists; the action must be displaced to the otherworld, where existence endures. This idea is dramatized in the final section of the tale, when U sheen touches the soil of Ireland and instantly turns into a decrepit old man.

The key concept is that of displacement: the "lost world" drama of their substratal melancholy must be played out as dislodgment, it must be scripted in the alternate reality of the shadowy ocean with a protagonist whose mental state is altered by that same sense of social displacement. Obviously, the blissful place where the strange story unfolds cannot be Ireland if removal and dispossession are at the core of the tale. Because of their vital function in the story, the sense of displacement and loss, along with the nostalgia that fuels the ill-conceived return, must be shown as overwhelming the protagonist. Even the prospect of living forever in the paradise offered by Niam must seem empty and purposeless away from the identitary solace of "home." In this Atlantic otherworld, where U sheen's every whim is instantly indulged and he can live in meaningless bliss, his sense of purpose is shattered. The community whose "emplotted stories" defined his social life and his sense of purpose was in Ireland, and he longs to return though he knows it is impossible to do so.

Placing the story across the Atlantic was also a scheme that helped the U sheen story-makers save their tale from the contamination to which an Irish setting, with its material reality, would inevitably contribute. The hero's environment needed to be liminal, one where U sheen's passage from his identity's real-world context to an immaterial, identity-less environment is manifest. This is demonstrated by the sundry spectral features in the story, the most important of which are the haunting songs of Niam and the islanders. Here music functions as a symbol for an altered mental state caused by U sheen's passage, one that leads him to the unconventional reality of a self removed from its identity-generating collective.

But before we declare that medievals interpret this story as pure allegory, we should remember that during this period many people still observed and documented prodigies. In cultured Rome, Ammianus Marcellinus (c. 325 CE–c. 391 CE) spoke of portents and omens that went unheeded by great men to their ruin (1911, 327), while at around the same time Julius Obsequens was compiling his *Liber Prodigiorum*, recording numerous prodigies such as unidentified flying objects. In Visigothic Spain, Isidore of Seville (c. 560–636 C.E.) includes a section entitled *De Portentis* in Book 11 of his *Libri Etymologiarum*, describing therein many portents, transformations of bodies, and even fabulous races of men, and even Pliny (23–79 C.E.) was fond of cataloging prodigious events (e.g. *Natural History*, bk. XXXVI, ch. 70). The seventh-century *Liber monstrorum de diversis generibus*, deserves special mention here, as it is an Anglo-Latin catalog of about 120 fabulous creatures,

> ... gathered together, as the opening words tell us, from the deserts, islands, mountains and other 'hidden parts of the world.' The time and place of composition are unclear: scholars have suggested dates as wide-ranging as the sixth and ten centuries CE, and a provenance that might be Irish but is more likely Anglo-Latin. Directly and indirectly, the *Liber Monstrorum* draws on a great number of earlier sources, both classical and Christian, including the work of Virgil (70–19 BCE) and Pliny (23–79 CE), Augustine of Hippo (354–430 CE) and Isidore of Seville (560–636), and many others. It survives today in just five manuscripts, all dating from the ninth and tenth centuries. (Weinstock 2014, 171)

In 1185 Giraldus Cambrensis (Gerard of Wales, c. 1146–c. 1223), accompanied one of English king Henry II's sons, John, on his expedition to Ireland. The result of this tour is his extraordinary *Topographia Hibernica* (*Topography of Ireland*), a work that is part history, part geography, part catalog of prodigies and marvels, and part miracle story, full of sweating statues, phantom islands, women with beards, passionate goats, speaking crosses, perpetually burning hedges, genital combustion, and fish with golden teeth, all of it abundantly illustrated. Even the *De secretis mulierum* (*On the Secrets of Women*, c. 1300), by the Pseudo-Albertus Magnus, has a section entitled "Concerning Monsters in Nature." For medieval people, prodigies were evidently an agreeable epistemological alternative to the uninspiring material reality of the times, especially in islands like Ireland and Britain, located off the far western edge of the known world.

Beyond alternative realities, prodigies, and altered mental states, there is in this story a down-to-earth discourse on the nature of the human being as social creature. U sheen speaks to a medieval conception of identity based on a matrix of allegiances that generated concentric circles of collective loyalty. This matrix had a precise configuration of value: at a time when most towns and villages were islands of light surrounded by dark forests and many dangers lurked for the traveler, the level of value increased as these circles became smaller, that is to say, that the kingdom occupied the largest (and least important) circle, and one's immediate locality, clan or familial kinship group the smallest and ultimately most significant circle. Medieval allegiances, then, were likely to gain in value and consequence the more specific and restricted they became.

This tendency bolstered the power of the clan to apply greater pressure than any other foci of allegiance over the process of identity development. The historical Feni changed their allegiance from the kingdom of Leinster to the kingdom of Munster without a knock on their identity, for they are first and foremost the Feni: it is this smaller and most restricted circle of allegiance that is significant, whose dissolution after the Battle of Gavra is of utmost consequence for U sheen. It is so substantial, in fact, that U sheen abandons a life of bliss and eternal youth to return to Ireland to look for its remnants. Significantly, what the hero does find in Ireland is a race of "little people" who look and act very differently from the Feni, an experience that highlights the hero's sense of dispossession and identitary disarticulation.

So as U sheen's prodigious voyage on an enchanted horse unfolds over the Atlantic Ocean, we can observe how the medieval mind frames questions of identity, belonging, and dispossession in terms of remarkable events, extraordinary beings, and portents that stand as paradigmatic images of its efforts to understand the world. U sheen's courage and virtue are represented by his battle with a giant, while his loyalty is represented by his forsaking eternal bliss to return to his clan's locality. Moreover, his total allegiance to his kin cannot be challenged, for even after evidence of their demise is given to him, he'd rather speculate that they've become wolf hunters that only come out at night.

Accordingly, the seemingly outlandish story of a voyage on a magical horse to an island of bliss in the Atlantic is rooted in the way in which medieval mindsets construct icons to describe abstract social concepts. The great ocean, with its imposing, mysterious immensity provides the foundation upon which the myth is structured: The link between medieval perceptions of the material world (Ireland) and that of worlds offered by myth (the Atlantic) lies in the fact that they exist in a close, symbiotic relationship. The mythical world can be seen and touched by just walking along the shores of the ocean. This familiarity that binds the two realms generates a compelling method of meaning-production through which people shape their interactions and compose a communal, consensual reality. Thus, as the story of U sheen demonstrates, medieval receptiveness to the concept–and plausible reality–of mythical or prodigious worlds far out to the west shaped the perception of the material world, as much as the material world provided elements with which to compose a mythical cosmos in its most daunting venue, the Atlantic. This interaction constituted a fundamental dynamic in the seaside communities' understanding of the universe.

St. Brendan: verisimilitude as social covenant

4.4. St. Brendan and the Whale. c. 1460.

Manuscriptum translationis germanicae Cod. Pal. Germ. 60, fol. 179v.
University Library of Heidelberg, Germany.

There are more than 100 manuscripts of the *Navigatio Sancti Brendani* (The Voyage of Saint Brendan), and many translations, a fact that attests to the great popularity of the story of the Irish saint's Atlantic expedition. The earliest extant version of the *Navigatio* is dated *circa* 900 CE, and it is thought that the story of his exploits was originally composed in Lotharingia around the 790s CE, that is to say, more than 200 years after his death (Harbison 1991, 37). This is made evident by the fact that, at the close of the eighth century, St. Aengus the Culdee (Óengus mac Óengobann), an Irish bishop, mentioned the voyage in his *Book of Litanies*: "Sexaginta qui comitati sunt Stum Brendanum in exquirenda terra promissionis invoco in auxilium meum" (I invoke unto my aid the sixty, who accompanied St. Brendan in his quest of the Land of Promise) (O'Donoghue 1895, 84). Such an invocation signals that the popularity of the Brendan voyage must have been well-established by the eighth century. It should be noted at this point that, in spite of the fact that the earliest extant text of the *Navigatio* is the aforementioned Latin version from continental Europe, the story is thoroughly Irish, containing several parallels and references to the *Voyage of Bran* and the *Voyage of Máel Dúin*; it is, in short, embedded in the *immrama* tradition of Irish Atlantic voyage tales.[10] The literary theme of the voyage, therefore, is ancient:

> The legend of Brendan the Navigator is a Christianized variation on one of the oldest known literary themes, that of the *Odyssey*, a tradition of which the ultimate origins can be traced back, through a common fund of Indo-European folklore and mythology, by way of the Persian *Thousand and One Nights*, the Irish *immrama*, the Latin, Greek and Sumerian epics, to at least the third millennium B.C. and no doubt beyond. It tells of the fabulous adventures that befall St Brendan and his companions during their seven-year sea journey in search of the Promised Land, and is one of the most widely known voyage-tales of the Middle Ages. (Short and Merrilees 1979, 1)

A short synopsis of each chapter of the *Navigatio* will allow for a better grasp of its overall features:

1. Saint Barrid tells of his visit to the Island of Paradise, which prompts Brendan to go in search of the isle.
2. Brendan assembles 14 monks to accompany him.
3. They fast at three-day intervals for 40 days, and visit Saint Enda for 3 days and 3 nights.
4. 3 latecomers join the group. They interfere with Brendan's sacred numbers.
5. They find an island with a dog, mysterious hospitality (no people, but food left out), and an Ethiopian devil.

---

[10] Although the scholarship is not clear as to which text influenced the others, there are striking parallels among them, such as the inclusion of the three extra passengers (Máel Dúin's foster brothers; Brendan's three extra monks) that perturb the orderly progress of the voyage. In both stories, only when the extra travelers are unloaded can the voyage continue as anticipated.

6. One latecomer admits to stealing from the mysterious island; Brendan exorcises the Ethiopian devil from the latecomer; and the latecomer dies and is buried.
7. They find an island with a boy who brings them bread and water.
8. They find an island of sheep, eat some, and stay for Holy Week (before Easter).
9. They find the island of Jasconius, celebrate Easter Mass, and hunt whales and fish.
10. They find an island that is the "Paradise of Birds," and the birds sing psalms and praise God.
11. They find the island of the monks of Ailbe, who have magic loaves, do not age, and maintain complete silence. They celebrate Christmas.
12. A long voyage after Lent. They find an island with a well, and drinking the water puts them to sleep for 1, 2, or 3 days contingent on the number of cups each man drank.
13. They find a "coagulated" sea.
14. They return to the islands of sheep, Jasconius, and the Paradise of Birds. A bird prophesies that the men must continue this year-long cycle for 7 years before they will be holy enough to reach the Island of Paradise.
15. A sea creature approaches the boat, but God shifts the sea to protect the men. Another sea creature comes, chops the first into three pieces, and leaves. The men eat the dead sea creature.
16. They find an island of 3 choirs of anchorites (monks), who give them fruit, and the second latecomer remains while the others leave.
17. They find an island of grapes, on which they stay for 40 days.
18. They find a gryphon and a bird engaged in battle. The gryphon dies.
19. Journey to the monastery at Ailbe again for Christmas.
20. The sea is clear, and many threatening fish circle their boat, but God protects them.
21. They find an island, but when they light a fire, the island sinks; they realize that it is actually a whale.
22. They pass a "silver pillar wrapped in a net" in the sea.
23. They pass an island of blacksmiths, who throw slag at them.
24. They find a volcano, and demons take the third latecomer down to Hell.
25. They find Judas Iscariot sitting unhappily on a cold, wet rock in the sea, and learn that this is his respite from Hell for Sundays and feast days. Brendan protects Judas from the demons of Hell for one night.
26. They find an island where Paul the Hermit has lived a perfect monastic life for 60 years. He wears nothing but hair and is fed by an otter.
27. They return to the islands of sheep, Jasconius, and the Paradise of Birds.

28. They find the Promised Land of the Saints.
29. They return home, and Brendan dies. (s.v. "Brendan")

But what is the purpose of the voyage? Interestingly, just as Merlin must escape from the coercive power of society, Brendan (Naomh Bréanainn, Munster, c. 484–c. 577), son of Finnlug Ua Alta of the race of Eoghan, "desired to leave the land and his country, his parents and his fatherland, and he urgently besought the Lord to give him a land secret, hidden, secure, delightful, separated from men" (Stokes 1890, 252). Brendan seems to have started off as one more Irish ascetic wishing to lead his spiritual life disconnected from society's temptations. But his journey to find this land quickly turned into an *immram*. Inevitably, this mysterious land must be sought in the preeminent geography for medieval Irish myth, the Atlantic Ocean, whiter Brendan sails with his companions and discovers not a secure island "separated from men," but a myriad of Celtic otherworld islands with very unusual residents.

Yet Brendan's reason for escaping from society is not as clearly delineated as is Merlin's. Ostensibly, Brendan's interpretation of a biblical passage: "And everyone who has left houses or brothers or sisters or father or mother or wife or children or fields for my sake will receive a hundred times as much and will inherit eternal life" (Matthew 19:29 NIV) has been decisive in his travel plans. But his odd construal of what is originally an exhortation to forsake the material possessions of this world reveals an authorial stratagem to align Christian dogma with the ancient literary sea-voyage theme of the *Odyssey* and, most visibly, of the Irish *immrama* tradition.

Besides the socially-sanctioned expedition to further the cause of his religious or social collective, Brendan's voyage is also an exploration of the periphery of the human self, an enigmatic expanse symbolized by the Atlantic Ocean. It is that same exploration, that same quest that in Campbell's "monomyth" requires the hero to return from his adventure as an enlightened mentor, one who has forsaken "this" world in order to achieve unfettered enlightenment:

> When the hero-quest has been accomplished, [...] the adventurer still must return with his life-transmuting trophy. The full round, the norm of the monomyth, requires that the hero shall now begin the labor of bringing the runes of wisdom, the Golden Fleece, or his sleeping princess back into the kingdom of humanity, where the boon may redound to the renewing of the community, the nation, the planet, or the ten thousand worlds. (J. Campbell 2008, 193)

Brendan returns to Ireland with a very specific boon: substantiation for the truth of Christian doctrine. But the conundrum is that Brendan's voyage of enlightenment into the pagan otherworld cosmos should be, by definition, gratuitous and irrelevant. What business does Brendan have in venturing into the unknown, if the Bible contains all the knowledge that Christians need to possess for their salvation? "The believer is not lacking adequate revelation since the inspired Bible itself provides all the revelation necessary for knowing and living as God intends" (Akin 2007, 163). At face value, it would seem absurd for the author to insert Brendan's search for knowledge within the monomyth, and that to achieve this knowledge he should journey not to Jerusalem, but to the fabulous, preternatural otherworld of the druids. It would also seem peculiar that the revelation that Brendan seeks is only available in that "other" druidic world of incalculable vastness, while in "this" world he has ready access to everything he needs in the pages of the Holy Book.

Yet this might not seem so peculiar if we recognize that the saint's expedition was compulsory. To better appreciate the nature of this exigency, we must remember that Brendan is an Irish saint, so apart from its monomyth framework, the quest must take place within a canvas that was expected by the consumers of the story, a backdrop awash with Brendan's native Celtic imagery that constantly breaks through the heavy patina of Christian canonical requirements. This seems to suggest that one of the author's (or authors') critical tasks was to accomplish a sort of thaumaturgy: to denature the story's pagan essence while at the same time allowing for the fact that, in Ireland, the imagery associated with it was as ancient as it was still a fundamental cultural expedient.

Therefore, the cosmos whose relevant traits were conveyed by that imagery was undoubtedly the setting expected by readers of an Irish seafaring story, be they Irish or not. We might imagine the saint as a Christian traveler undertaking a mandatory round-trip within that cosmos, one whose compulsory character recalls Aleksandr Veselovsky's speculations as to whether "each new epoch [works] on images bequeathed from antiquity, being of necessity constrained by their boundaries" (Klinger and Maslov 2016, 227).

Brendan's voyage into the Atlantic, which modern critical assessments would surely assign to the world of fantasy and imaginative virtuosity, transpired more accurately within those boundaries described by Veselovsky, as well as within the range of Irish pre-Christian conceptions of the nature of existence. As such, the voyager's insights were heavily invested in socially systematized images that alluded to age-old concepts regarding the world and our place in it: this is imagery that had traditionally transformed unresponsive reality into a purposeful cosmos for the Irish. The trick was to transform the message and make those images *function* in the service of a different truth, that is, within the context of Christian doctrine.

Hence, Brendan's bizarre experiences occur in labored harmony with Christianity's conceptual truths, and they are narrated in the *Navigatio* with an explicit informative and moralizing purpose that distracts our gaze from the overtly pagan imagery. The medieval mind, unhindered as it commonly was by the need to confirm truth scientifically, responded well to doctrinal representations of reality and truth, so ideational interaction with reality was standard and unexceptional. Because reality was thus mediated, the medieval mind was able to modify its conceptualization of the world: pagandom's inscrutable cosmos became God's unfathomable Creation, that is to say, the filter of collective interpretation was merely adjusted.

The *Navigatio's* ideological cosmos was rooted in classical and medieval texts and maps and in much of Christian and Western mythology; this ideational space was an environment in which much of the world was sited. There was Columbus, for example, who on a voyage of discovery famously reported seeing mermaids (likely manatees) that, unfortunately, were not as beautiful as the Greeks maintained. Spain's "Admiral of the Ocean Sea" still believed that the earthly paradise must lie around the Gulf of Paria, for Pierre d'Ailly, in his *Imago Mundi* (1410; Columbus owned the 1483 edition, on which he wrote countless marginal notes) appeared to give indications that it was in that vicinity (Delumeau 1995, 53-54). To allay any doubts regarding the probity of his perception, Columbus gave a list of notable sources: Isidore, Bede, John Damascene, Strabo, Peter Comestor, St. Ambrose, and John Scotus Eriugena all confirmed the actual existence of Paradise (Flint 1994, 106).

Then there was the Florentine noble and assiduous traveler Giovanni de' Marignolli, who was commissioned by Pope Benedict XII in the mid-fourteenth century to travel to the great Kahn of Cathay's court in an embassy. In his notes, and apparently seriously, Marignolli recounts seeing the Earthly Paradise with its rushing waters on the mainland opposite the island of Ceylon (Abeydeera 1993, 1-23); even Alexander the Great was interested in reaching Paradise (Esposito 1918, 193-205; Lascelles 1936, 31-47).

This brings us to a concept that can further clarify the medieval reading of Brendan's adventures, that of verisimilitude, understood here as the *believability* of anecdotes, reports, descriptions, or accounts. Evidently, what the medieval person believed is very different from what people in subsequent eras have believed, so that claims such as Marignolli's were reasonable within the context of their cultural environment. By definition, and from the medieval perspective, an account's verisimilitude depended not so much on the depiction of material "reality" as on its pertinency to the mental landscape of the times. Free from the demands of plausibility, medieval travel and adventure accounts like the *Navigatio* could be enhanced devices with which to convey deeper truths based on belief. This resulted in the proliferation of texts that communicated *relevant* information, more relevant, that is, than portrayals of physical reality. *Realistic* portrayals would only serve to conceal what *really* counts for the writer and reader behind a complicating, vast volume of extraneous information.

Because the pre-modern imagination did not generally conceive nature (a creation of God or the gods) as impervious to human existence, narrators commonly interpreted reality in terms of human experience and could, on occasion, make use of lyrical analogies to describe it. One example comes from Herodotus: "The Issedones, who appear to have been the same with the Igours, Herodotus informs us, were a civilized nation, dwelling to the far east; beyond them, to the north, the country was impassable owing to the white feathers that were continually falling" (Grahame 1860, 24). Herodotus gives us an excellent example of a dialectic that cultivates the existence of an expedient universe where human sensitivity overrules any "detached" discernment. There is no science to explain snow at that point, and even the word to designate it may have been generally inactive in the vocabulary of Mediterranean peoples; the reader is then given the information in a conventional manner that is easy to decode in accordance with received social covenants and narrative conventions. In this universe, hallowed islands may still be found by people like Brendan, who are pure and uncorrupted by the evils of scientific logic.

The author of the *Navigatio* knows that islands, especially in the vast and unknown Atlantic, hold a special fascination for medieval peoples. In contrast to the well-trodden geography of Western Europe, an island in the great ocean is, in Claude Kappler's words, "by its nature a place where marvels exist for their own sake outside the laws that generally prevail... Ever since Greek antiquity, islands have been favorite places for the most outstanding human and divine adventures" (qtd. in Delumeau 1995, 98).

As is substantiated by the Brendan story, the medieval social imaginary endowed Atlantic islands with considerable symbolic power, allowing them to epitomize concepts such as salvation, protection, righteous seclusion, hope, and redemption; remote islands, in short, allow for a deeper intellectual perspective on mankind and the universe. Accordingly, the *mapamundi* that is formulated from the depictions of a medieval voyager is, in many ways, a *librum vitae hominis* bursting with human lineaments.

Accordingly, if we classify Brendan's adventures as medieval fantastic fiction, we are missing the mark. What we believe today is very different from what Brendan's contemporaries believed. The nature of the descriptions of the places visited and the way in which they are related to the adventures of Brendan and company show that these descriptions of people and landscapes have a subsidiary function in the Brendan stories. Even though these are stories about sailing to distant, mysterious lands, the focal point of interest is the adventure of the Brendanites across a Christian mental landscape, where actions receive their just rewards and punishments in harmony with predictable religious tenets. And it all happens within the realm of what a contemporary of the Irish saint would perceive as verisimilitude. This may not be clear to most readers of the *Navigatio* today: When times change and decoding practices transform, the flow of information from narrator to reader ceases to be seamless and the message can become blurred.

Prince Madoc of Wales, discoverer of America: the medieval myth that crossed the Atlantic

A plaque that was erected in 1953 by the Daughters of the American Revolution in Mobile, Alabama, boldly states: "In memory of Prince Madoc, a Welsh explorer, who landed on the shores of Mobile Bay in 1170 and left behind, with the Indians, the Welsh language" (Curran 2010, 25). The Alabama Parks Department prudently removed it soon after it was first erected.

The life story of Madoc, as that of most mythical characters, is mired in mystery. Purported to be one of the 13 sons of Owain Gwynedd (d. 1170), a king in Wales, there is no mention of him in the most likely places where one would find it, the *Annales Cambriae* and the *Brut y Tywysogion*. There are, nevertheless, two passages in the poetry of Llywarch ap Llywelyn (a.k.a. Prydydd y Moch, poet of the pigs) that seem to suggest to some investigators that a certain Madoc sailed on a voyage of discovery, but nothing in these passages supports such an interpretation. The first of these is in an ode praising Rhodri ab Owain (1135–1195), prince of Gwynedd (r. 1175–1195), a kingdom in northwestern Wales. The poet's allusion, the one taken to refer to Madoc's sailing to America, actually refers to the Battle of Aberconwy (Battle of the Conway Estuary), fought in 1194 between the armies of Llywelyn ap Iorwerth and those of his uncles Dafydd ab Owain and Rhodri ab Owain for control of Gwynedd. The second reference has the name Madog (Madoc), but besides it being a very common name in medieval Wales, the poem relates the poet's efforts to prove himself innocent of having killed Madoc, which makes the subsequent voyage unfeasible.

A third reference appears in a *cywydd* (Welsh traditional poem) by Maredudd ap Rhys in the middle of the fifteenth century. The poet truly loves fishing, and he compares himself to "Madog, right whelp [puppy, offspring] of Owain Gwynedd," who abandoned lands and property to sail on the sea (Sydney Lee 1893, 302). He is also mentioned in the third series of triads, where we are told that Madoc's was the third of three disappearances:

> Three disappearances of the Isle of Britain- (1) Gavran ab Aeddan and his men who went to the sea in search of the Green Isles of the Ocean and were never afterwards heard of, (2) Merddin, the bard of Emrys Wledig and his nine Cylfeirdd, who went to the sea in a house of glass, and nothing farther was heard of them, (3) Madawg, the son of Owain Gwynedd, who went to sea with three hundred men in ten ships, and it is not known whither they went (Jones 1900, 451).

These last two references, while not proving that a Welshman by the name of Madoc discovered the New World, do point to the existence of legends and stories about a hero that ventures forth into the mysterious Atlantic, legends that existed long before Columbus's voyage. These include a manuscript "The Romance of Prince Madoc 1255," written by thirteenth-century poet William the Minstrel, that surfaced in Poitiers in the seventeenth century. Therein Madoc is a "Welshman of noble birth with Viking ancestry and fame as a sailor, who went as a secret emissary to the French court. Later he sailed to search for the Fountain of Youth and to establish a new kingdom of love and music" (Allen 1997, 21). The poem describes what may be the Sargasso Sea, in the middle of the Atlantic, which is likely the assimilation of such information as was currently available about the western ocean. The Madoc story seeped into subsequent works such as *A Brief Description of the Whole World*, of unknown authorship and printed for John Marriott in London in 1620, Thomas Herbert's *Relation of Some Years Travaile* (1626), and Georgius Hornius's *De Originibus Americanis* (1652), adding artificial authority to the claims for a Welsh discovery and settlement of the New World.

Even if Madoc never crossed the Atlantic, his story makes an easy passage, injecting itself into Early American politics. The April 1792 edition of the journal *American Museum or, Universal Magazine* has the anonymous article "Proofs that America was discovered by the Britons" (152-155) where another article by John Williams "An inquiry concerning the first discovery of America, by Europeans" (1791) is quoted at length. The piece includes very interesting passages that suggest geopolitical interests were a cause for the persistence of the Madoc legend, a myth that embeds itself in the discourse of a young United States seeking to expand its borders into Spanish-held parts of North America:

> Madoc, another of Owen Gwyneth's sonnes, left the land in contention betwixt his brethren, and prepared certain ships with men and munition, and sought adventures by sea, sailing west, and leaving the coast of Ireland so far north, that he came to a land unknown, where he saw many strange things.
>
> This land must needs be some parts of the countrey of which the Spanyards affirm themselves to be the first finders since Hanno's time: whereupon it is manifest that that countrey was by Britons discovered long before Columbus led any Spanyards thither.
>
> Of the voyage and return of this Madoc, there be many fables framed, as the common people do use in distance of place and length of time, rather to augment than to diminish; but sure it is, there he was. And after he had returned home, and declared the pleasant and fruitful countries that he had seen, without inhabitants; and upon the contrary, for what barren and wild ground his brethren and nephews did murder one

another, he prepared a number of ships, and got with him such men and women as were desirous to live in quietness, and taking leave of his friends, took his journey thitherwards again. ("Proofs" 1792, 153)

The ethnic makeup of the "first" discoverers of America seems very important to Williams, as he will use it to bolster the idea that they have a legitimate claim to its lands. It should be remembered that "Americans" at this time were essentially descendants of people from Great Britain who had become *politically* separated from Britain; not being Native Americans, Spaniards or Frenchmen, they could only consider their ethnic identity as British. Also as part of the exclusionary discourse, we find the total disregard for the native populations of the continent, which the writer affirms is "without inhabitants."

At a different level, among the "proofs" that the article's title purports to offer is one based on religion: native Americans were already Christian when Columbus made landfall in 1492:

> Therefore it is supposed that [Madoc] and his people inhabited part of those countries; for it appeareth by Francis Lopez de Gomara, that in Acuzamil, and other places, the people honoured the cross. Whereby it may be gathered that christians had been there before the coming of the Spanyards; but because these people were not many, they followed the manner of the land which they came to, and the language they found there. ("Proofs" 1792, 153)

But the writer must be careful not to give the house away to England, with which the newborn United States (in 1792) is still very much at odds. In a long paraphrase, this time from *A Brief Description of the Whole World* (1620), he leaves the ethnic considerations and initiates a *political* evaluation: the facts clearly show that the English *crown*'s claim to North America has no basis in fact:

> I am not ignorant that some who make too much of vain shows, and of the British antiquities, have given out to the world, and written some things to that purpose, that Arthur, some time king of Britain, had both knowledge of those parts (the new world) and some dominion on them; for they find (as some report) that king Arthur had under his government many islands and great countries towards the north and west, which one of some special note hath interpreted to signify America, and the northern parts thereof, and thereupon have gone about to entitle the queen of England, (Elizabeth) to be sovereigne of these provinces by right of descent from king Arthur. But the wisdom of our state has been such as to neglect that opinion, imagining it to be grounded upon fabulous foundations, as many things that are asserted of king Arthur. ("Proofs" 1792, 153)

So the myth that supports the author's point is regarded as an accurate portrayal of historical fact, while the myth that might argue against his interests is dismissed outright.

The myth of Madoc was subsequently reinforced in the United States by folktales of Welsh-speaking Indians and Native American stories of pre-Columbian fort-building white men. John Evans, a Welsh-speaking explorer mapping the upper reaches of the Missouri, where the Welsh-speaking natives were supposed to live, stated unequivocally in a 1797 letter that he saw no signs of anybody speaking Welsh, anywhere. There was an attempt to discredit his story, as he was accused of being a Spanish spy and, because Spain had an interest in keeping this Welsh business under wraps, he could be expected to deny the existence of Welsh speakers in the upper reaches of the Missouri.

It is true that he was imprisoned in 1793 by the Spanish for venturing into Spanish territory around St. Louis. It is also true that, when released in 1795, Evans began to work for the "Spanish Missouri Company, which planned to clear a way to the Pacific Ocean–hence his mapping of the Missouri territory" (Curran 2010, 25). But his spying activities were very hard to prove. Nevertheless, the myth's popularity endured, and even Lewis and Clark "[W]ere still perfectly willing to believe that […] the West might be populated by wooly mammoths or blue-eyed Welsh-speaking Indians–all because Thomas Jefferson's books back in Monticello said so" (Duncan 2004, 66).

So how did John Williams's 1791 story of Madoc, "discoverer of America," first come into being? It appears that in 1584 David Powell, a clergyman in the Welsh Church of England, took it upon himself to publish Humphrey Llwyd's *History of Wales* (*Cronica Walliae a Rege Cadwalader ad annum 1294*; 1559), which was basically a translation of the *Brut y Tywysogion* (Chronicle of the Princes). Calling the work *The Historie of Cambria*, Powell decided to repair the Llwyd text's many "deficiencies," enriching it "with many valuable annotations" (R. Williams 1852, 292). The source of these flourishes is almost certainly popular tradition, which presumably accounts for its charm and popularity and for the "Madoc, voyager to the New World" story. Llwyd's initial account, with Powell's additions, is a likely source for the subsequent torrent of Madoc anecdotes, of which the American 1791 and 1792 articles are a part.

The association of the Madoc myth with early United States political culture is an important one for us because it says something about the nation's intellectual and social landscape at its inception. We'll assume that what a community understands as decent, moral behavior is influential in forming its ethical and political perspectives, its institutions, and its values. There is in Williams, as well as in many other writers of the early post-colonial period in the U.S., an aspiration to deliver an acceptable political compass that could point to the future, but that future had to be righteously defined.

That compass pointed increasingly to the west, an area that was dominated by Spain and contained millions of natives. So this righteous definition needed to subsume the expansionist ideology of a young nation that would demolish peoples and cultures that stood in its way, a nation in which, inconveniently, citizens had a voice in political affairs. As such, it was important to create public consensus and fashion an ideology with a capacity to accommodate, embellish and justify certain agendas that might otherwise prove distasteful to the citizens. Consequently, there are, in discourses like Williams's, veiled political objectives that necessitate the omission of certain inopportune historical facts that could well delegitimize those agendas. The article's mention of a land found by Madoc that was effectively uninhabited, a land to which he laid claim long before the Spaniards, paved the way for a discourse that legitimized and endorsed expansion.

Not that Madoc's was the only myth available to post-colonial America: one of the co-authors of the Declaration of Independence and third President of the U.S., Thomas Jefferson, bought into the *Mayflower* cult and "early on realized the usefulness of the Exodus narrative for American nation-building. He wanted to place the inscription 'the Children of Israel in the Wilderness, led by a Cloud by day, and a Pillar of Fire by night' on the Great Seal of the United States" (Heike 2014, 160). A wilderness is, by definition, an area that is essentially uninhabited and there for the taking. If, moreover, it is God that has given you the right to take it, anything or anyone standing in your way can be righteously removed, as they have no right to stand in the way of God's designs.

The early United States was a nation saturated by mythopoeia. Many glamorized myths like "The First Thanksgiving," "The Pilgrims' Promised Land," or Madoc's, methodically validated foundational accounts that paved the way for political thought and action; these myths could misrepresent the displacement and dissolution of native and other communities as "ethical" processes, thus safeguarding Americans' critical understanding of moral, decent behavior.

Economic and political factors were always at play: while the young United States still felt militarily vulnerable to Spain, it entered into treaties with the natives–such as the Indian Trade and Intercourse Act of 1790–that were supposed to safeguard the Indians against devious white traders. The reality was that there was no need at this point to add to the list of enemies, and the Indian Trade and Intercourse Act not only neutralized some Native American hostilities, but also reinforced the American self-image as that of a moral, decent, and caring people.

But circumstances changed quickly, and as Spain increasingly employed its military resources in fighting insurrections everywhere in the Americas, from Mexico to Argentina, the time came to unveil dormant expansionist policies in the U.S. So it is that the forgers of the nation's political compass very quickly and efficiently put in motion the shameful displacement of native communities (the Georgia Compact of 1802, the Delaware Treaty of St. Mary's of 1818, the Treaty of Doak's Stand of 1820, the Indian Removal Act of 1830…). Something akin to ethnic cleansing became an essential blueprint when formulating a Eurocentric sense of nationhood in the United States. Myth had provided its sturdy pedestal.

The Voyage of Máel Dúin: The Legacy of Syncretism

4.5. Christ Enthroned. *Book of Kells*. Ninth Century.

Trinity College Library, Dublin.

The blond, red-bearded Christ of the *Book of Kells*, surrounded by blond/redheaded figures populating a typically Celtic geometric pattern, is an eloquent image of what happened when Christianity landed in Ireland. Early Christianity on the Atlantic shore exhibits a distinctive syncretism characterized by its acceptance of Celtic culture. Celtic sites such as holy wells and gathering places, events such as festivals, and structures such as royal dwellings were co-opted by proselytizers because of their symbolic power. "The process of conversion by Patrick and others spread gradually and fused with many features of pagan Celtic culture. [...] Thus, even at an early date, the Irish past was being manipulated to effect contemporary opinion" (Finnegan and McCarron 2000, 3-4).

Consequently, the early church established a strong set of practices centered on the sustained appeal to Celtic culture and traditions. It was important to the church that its most symbolic figures become identified with Celtic traditions; this explains why Brendan is an *immram* voyager as much as a saint of the church. Such practices contributed in no small measure to Celtic cultural survival, particularly in Ireland, and were essential in the eventual acceptance of pagan *immrama* stories that were so ingrained in Celtic tradition.[11]

One of these stories is *Immram Curaig Mailduin*, which is conserved incompletely in the *Lebor na hUidre* (at the Royal Irish Academy), in the *Yellow Book of Lecan* (at the Trinity College Library), and in fragments held at the British Museum. The tale, glossed in this text's "Portolan Chart," was redacted in the eleventh century by Aed the Fair, "Now Aed the Fair, chief sage of Ireland, arranged this story as it standeth here; and he did so for the delight to the mind, and for the folks of Ireland after him" (Rolleston 1911, 331). Aed may have copied it from an earlier (c. ninth century) text, but its language and tenor make it reasonable to suppose that it is much older, and it is regarded by Rolleston to be "the earliest [wonder-voyage story] and a model for the rest" (1911, 309).

The voyage of Máel Dúin (Maelduin) is, like Brendan's, a journey through an inner cosmos, through the Celtic otherworld of mystery and fear that lies beyond or after life. Although Rolleston argues that "[i]ts atmosphere is entirely Christian, and it has no mythological significance except insofar as it teaches the lesson that the oracular injunctions of wizards should be obeyed" (1911,

---

[11] Carney (294) fails to include the *immrama* in his study of pre-Christian otherworld literature because he considered them to be firmly established upon biblical and classical prototypes, an opinion largely shared by David N. Dumville, "Echtrae and Immram," 77. While it is true that the *immrama* are the product of ecclesiastical catechizing fervor, it is also true that they build upon pre-Christian modes of mythologizing reality, as is quite evident in this tale.

309), it seems clear that the adventure has echoes of a much earlier, pagan folklore.

As the story goes, Máel Dúin was the son of a warlord called Ailill Ochair Aghra and of a nun that Ailill had raped. Shortly after the rape, a group of raiders from Leix (Loígis, in the midlands region of Ireland) locked him in a church and burned it down with him inside. From the start, then, there are pagan narrative elements that have merged with accretions and alterations emanating from Christian doctrine. Burning the rapist alive inside a church reminds one of pre-Christian rituals such as that of the Wicker Man, where druids burned men alive inside wicker-work images, men who were subjected to an excruciatingly painful death because they were considered wizards, "and fire was chosen because burning alive is deemed the surest mode of getting rid of these noxious and dangerous beings" (J. G. Frazer 2009, 657). Thus, the church building provides a de facto "Wicker Man" that may have conventionalized the story and the practices therein for a community in flux, not wholly pagan anymore, still not quite Christian.

Having given birth, the single-mother nun decided that, given her station, it would be very difficult to rear a child, so she gave Máel Dúin to a queen of the Eóghanachta, a dynasty that dominated southern Ireland from the sixth to the tenth centuries. The queen brought him up as her own child, and Máel Dúin grew up to be a handsome, strong young man who won every physical contest he entered. But as jealousy will rear up its ugly head in tales such as this, a young man from his circle of acquaintances informed him of his indefinite parentage, at which point Máel Dúin stopped eating or drinking with his foster parents the king and queen, pleading to be allowed to meet his biological mother. The monarchs yielded and sent him to see the nun, who told him the story of his birth and of his father's murder at the hands of the marauders. This return to his biological mother has echoes of Celtic, pre-Christian fosterage practices: in the Latin world–the world that brought Christianity to Atlantic shores–adopted children severed all connections to their natural families, whereas the adopted Celt child legally belonged to both families and had obligations to both (Markale 1994, 237). In demanding to see his biological family, Máel Dúin was clearly asserting his rights within the conventions of established Celtic practices.

At first, the young man is content with speaking to his biological mother and visiting his biological father's grave at the Dubcluain churchyard where he died. But at Dubcluain a malicious member of the church community named Briccne convinces him that it is the obligation of a worthy son to avenge his father's murder, even if he was a rapist who died before Máel Dúin was born. Máel Dúin then seeks the advice of a druid named Nuca at Corcomroe (Chorco

Modhruadh, in today's County Clare), who tells him how to find the culprits, but she adds that he must take an exact number of companions: 17.[12]

Scholars have for a long time argued about the meaning of the strange islands that heroes of the *immrama* of early medieval Ireland encounter on their journeys in the vast Atlantic. Máel Dúin's journey features islands where an irritated horse throws rocks at the heroes, where a cat burns one of Máel's foster brothers as punishment for stealing, where a shape-shifter changes form by manipulating its bones, and many more. These islands are places that emanate from a distant past, from a pre-Christian otherworld that co-existed with the world of the living in that strange and limitless expanse of ocean to the west; therein was an adjacent, bizarre reality that might somehow counteract the inanition caused by ordinary reality if one ventured far enough, an uncharted reality that allowed for open flights of the imagination and inner journeys.

In this sense, then, the story of Máel Dúin's voyage is a depiction of a different state of consciousness, like that of U sheen, one in which the individual experiences events in an indistinct, fluid boundary between this world and the otherworld that extends far out into the watery realms. At the outset, these Atlantic islands were to be the stage for the conclusion of a blood-feud that began with his father's murder, so Máel Dúin sails there in order to bring to a close a major unresolved issue in his life. It is here that the syncretism of early Irish Christianity shows most prominently, as the expected violent end to what was essentially a Celtic blood-feud is modified to provide an example of Christian ethics.

---

[12] Nuca's insistence on the number 17 is enigmatic, but it may be due to the number's thaumaturgic attributes. An eminent alchemist of the eighth century C.E. named Geber thought that the number possessed exceptional mystical properties and used it in his quest to turn lesser metals into gold, while Cabalists thought that the path of 17 guided the Righteous to their just rewards. Moreover, the 17th Tarot card is the star, which symbolizes hope and the Magi. The Gospel of John, verse 11, mentions that through Jesus's intervention 153 large fish were caught by the disciples. This number is the result of a cumulative addition of consecutive numbers concluding with 17: 1+2+3+4+5+6…+17=153. This was not lost on St. Augustine, who considered the number 17 very meaningful because of its relationship with 153 and, furthermore, because it was the sum of the 7 gifts of the Spirit and the 10 Commandments; these, by the way, are the two numbers that St. Gregory the Great called "perfect." Then there is 17's mathematical relationship with the *vesica piscis*, or "vessel of fish," a shape formed by the intersection of two circles that have an equal radius with centers on the perimeter of the other. This "fish" shape is symbolic for Christians as the intersection of the heavenly and the material worlds that Jesus represents. Curiously, 17 is the only known prime number that is equal to the sum of its cube (17^3 = 4913, and 4+9+1+3 = 17) and is the only prime that is the average of two consecutive Fibonacci numbers.

Blood feuds were common among the Celts: "That the institution of blood-feud was in existence among the Celts is obvious from the numerous references to it in ancient Irish literature" (Hastings 1908, 720), and this story reflects this fact. But thus handled, the story becomes one of progress towards spiritual enlightenment: at the end, when at last there comes the encounter with his father's killers, rather than take revenge, Máel Dúin, now in Christian garb, forgives them.

Pagan or Christian, the hero's voyage into the Atlantic is a timeless journey that is only loosely attached to physical geography. Venturing into the great ocean, Máel Dúin was sailing into an expanse where he could encounter a more eminent, superior reality, one more meaningful than that of his daily, humdrum existence. So the voyage has to do with the emotional makeup and the inner geography of the hero's self rather than with the incidental manifestations of the physical world.

In engaging the hero's inner geography with the story's audience, its framers needed to take account of that audience's expectations. This means that, to the story's newly Christianized consumers, the murderers' impunity would not seem as perplexing as it would to a pagan audience, who would be fully expecting the criminals to receive their due punishments. So in the extant version of the tale, Máel Dúin's initially pagan emotional response to an affront and his voyage of revenge have been denatured and channeled into a Christian's spiritual journey. Therein, the criminals' impunity is understood as forgiveness, as the ennobling outcome of the hero's edification and enlightenment.

Máel Dúin has journeyed from darkness into the light and can now display the values of mercy and compassion that he did not possess in the initial parts of this *immram*. Nevertheless, the way in which individual characters speak and think resonates unmistakably with the spirit of an earlier folklore: The story's particular conclusion has the feel of a *deus ex machina*, an ending that in the original pagan story would be unanticipated, awkward, and problematic. Sound judgment dictates that Máel Dúin's *immram* must be considered an instance of Christian precepts aggressing and subsuming pagan lore.

The myth, rejuvenated by the Christian scaffolding with which it has reached us, has acquired a rhetorical function: it contextualizes doctrine and promotes its intelligibility against the backdrop of a very ancient and familiar tale. Pagan in appearance, configuration and content–and in all likelihood amply predating the comprehensive adoption of Christianity–the tale's primitive matter makes itself immediately obvious to the keen observer, as its shape-shifters, crystal bridges, river skies that rain salmon, and islands of fire people, thrust up compellingly against the story's doctrinal overlay.

It would be useful to probe, at this point, the reason why the early Christian mission in Ireland understood the world of Celtic myth as a viable medium to transmit its message. Unprocessed, pagan myths were not viewed as feasible agents of Christian truth or doctrine, but strangely enough, their use may have served to remove obstacles that hindered the correct understanding and acceptance of the Christian message. This is because by injecting Christian meaning into the competing pagan culture's conventional folkways the proselytizers were sheathing the church's truth within a protective shell. To recent converts, this truth did not seem so outlandish or alien now: it was more evocative, more familiar, and it seemed almost home-grown. Thus, recognizable pagan myths multiplied the message's illustrative possibilities in a much more synergetic way.

But who were the people responsible for the ancient versions of this story, one that remains among the most seemingly irrational and bizarre tales of pre-modern Europe? They were gifted individuals who understood that for pagan and early medieval people, prophesy, omens, dreams and portents would not have appeared as fabulous or mythic, as they understandably appear to us today. Such portents simply surfaced during important events from the commonplace environs of medieval life. These framers of the story were likely ovates, who spoke with the ancestors and foretold the future, and druids who told of metamorphoses and chimerical beings while performing rituals and bridging the expanse between this life and the unseen geographies of the "other" place.

These were real people who played a part in the decision-making processes of princes and of ordinary folk, and they were ubiquitous in the landscape. So the church was not using "myth" in the modern, trivializing sense of the word; this was not illusory fantasy. Within the early medieval panorama, it was accepted that forces superior to the human being often determined the direction events would take. These forces communicated through ambiguous means such as the extraordinary tales compiled in the Máel Dúin immram, repeated regularly by the bards that roamed the pre-Christian Atlantic shore. The uncertain, confusing and extraordinary nature of the tales symbolizes the indecipherable aspects of life and points to the limits of human understanding. The Christian agenda–an intrusion into the original Máel Dúin oral narrative–articulates an explanatory framework and infuses homiletic correctives into a preexisting, useful, identifiable set of pagan adventures; with these new elements, the hero's actions and decisions are reprogrammed and assigned catechizing functions.

The Máel Dúin *immram*, like so many other *immrama*, is laced with strands of its Celtic, pre-Christian lineage. It is the age-old tale of ancient seafarers venturing into the Atlantic as a quest or in search of the Celtic "Happy Other

World," a place that gradually became identified with the Christian "Earthly Paradise" to which many just souls voyaged before being admitted to Heaven. In essence, it would be idle "to hold that the *immrama* could be essentially based on anything else than [the] Celtic Other-World story" (Brown 1968, 57-58)."[13]

Hy-Brasil (Uí Bhreasail), naughty aliens and the logistics of syncretism

4.6. Ortelius Map of Europe. 1601.

Hy-Brasil and a second island, Demar, to the west of Ireland.

In late December of 1980, Jim Penniston touched the skin of a UFO that landed in Rendlesham Forest, next to an airbase in southern England, and received sixteen pages of binary code piped directly into his brain. Penniston eventually wrote the code down in his notebook. The code turned out to be based on the ASCII convention, so the sender would have had to be conversant in English in order to create the message. This, of course, begs the question: why not just give Penniston the message in English?

---

[13] The process of Christianizing specifically the Celtic "Happy Other World" is seen clearly in both the *Echtra Conlai*, or *Expedition of Connla*, and in the *Voyage of Bran*. The place was very real to the Celts: In the *Pharsalia*, Lucan states that, because of their belief in the "Happy Other World," the Celts were fearless in battle (1.441), and adds that for the Celt death was the middle of a long life (1.458).

While some may be tempted to assume that humorous aliens were playing a trick on innocent humans by making the message more mystifying, it should be pointed out that no one other than Penniston saw this otherworldly craft, and that a guard by the name of Kevin Conde has confessed to creating the "strange" light effects by flashing the lights on his Dodge patrol car while driving in a circle (Pope 2014, 94). But what is interesting to us is that, upon decoding this binary code, the coordinates 52.0942532N 13.131269W were discovered, and they point to one of the locations of the mythical island of Hy-Brasil as it was positioned in several medieval maps (Pope 2014, 241). So either the mischievous space invaders had a penchant for medieval lore, or Penniston was acquainted with one of its most prominent mysteries.

Hy-Brasil has a long history. Placed by over 300 nautical charts in the Atlantic west of Ireland, it was the object of numerous expeditions: St. Brendan set sail for it, and navigators from Bristol claimed to have sojourned there. It is an important feature of Celtic mythology and medieval literature, and as we have seen, it still plays a part in pop culture. Except for the more functional thirteenth-century portolan guides and charts intended to acquaint mariners with coastal areas,[14] medieval charts and maps had a haphazard relationship with the actual geographical areas that they registered. Many of them were more a symbolic, contemplative representation than an accurate rendering, often incorporating Earthly Paradise on top and the Holy Land squarely in the middle, without much regard to proportion. "In medieval world maps, city views, and regional maps, there was little expectation that the map would serve as a mirror of the place represented" (Carlton 2015, 32). Furthermore, and owing to the ethereal nature of the island of Hy-Brasil, the charts placed it in several different places to the west of Ireland, a wandering that contributed, no doubt, to its legendary quality.

It was cartographers from Mediterranean lands that began to place the island in their charts. Circa 1325 Genoese/Majorcan cartographer Angelino Dalorto (or Angelino Dulcert) placed the almost circular island west of Ireland at an approximate latitude of 51° N. The island was subsequently included in several maps such as that of the Pizzigani Brothers (1367) and the Catalan Atlas of 1375. Such charts and maps have been comprehensively studied by H. Winter (1954, 1-12), T. Campbell (1986, 67-94), and J. Kelly (1979, 18-35).

---

[14] "Portolan charts are sometimes viewed as simply the pictorial equivalent of the narrative navigational guides known as portolans, which also began to proliferate in Italy from the latter thirteenth century onward. The earliest surviving example of these portolan guides is the somewhat confusingly named *Compasso di navegare*, now dated to c. 1250 and probably Pisan" (Christopher Kleinhenz, *Medieval Italy*, 762).

Spanish geographers were at the forefront of Hy-Brasil conjecture. Lope García de Salazar (1399–1476), in his *Libro de las bienandanzas e fortunas* (c. 1470), has a badly wounded King Arthur embarking not for Avalon, but for "Brasil," an island that Morgana had enchanted in such a way that it could never be found. García de Salazar also gives the island as round, low-lying, and 25 leagues from Cape Longaneas, which is in Ireland: "Titulo de como Margayna leuo al rey Artur en la varca a la ysla de Brasil e la encanto que no puede ser fallada. ...lo leuo Margayna, su hermana, a la ysla de Brasil, que es a .xxv. leguas del cabo de Longaneas, que es en Erlanda" (Sharrer 1979, 72-73). Martín Fernández de Enciso (c. 1470–1528), in his *Suma de geografía que trata de todas las partidas e provincias del mundo* (1519), states that "Esta Ibernia o Irlanda tiene al Oeste a la isla de Brasil, que está a cincuenta y un grados; es cuasi redonda y tiene de longitud doce leguas y nueve de latitud." That is to say, "This Hibernia or Ireland has, to the west, the island of Brasil, which lies at 51 degrees; it is almost round and has a longitude of twelve leagues and a latitude of nine" (Fernández de Enciso 1519, 111; my translation).

These works were strategically important: It is known that Roger Barlow, the first Englishman to sail to South America (in 1526 from Spain with Sebastian Cabot's expedition), translated Fernández de Enciso's work into English for Henry VIII (C. Williams 2009, 59). For his part, Alonso de Santa Cruz (1505-1572), known for having produced the first map to document magnetic variations from true north (1530), mentions the island of Hy-Brasil in his *Islario general de todas las islas del mundo* (1542), comparing it to its namesake in South America:

> Junto al Lamerich están unos isleos llamados Brasquey, al Poniente de los cuales setenta leguas se halla en la mar cierta isla descubierta por los ingleses, llamada del Brasil, porque en ella nacen árboles de Brasil, aunque no tan fino como lo que se trae a Portugal de la costa del Brasil, en las Indias Occidentales. (Cuesta Domingo 1983, 347)

> Next to Lamerich are certain islets called Brasquey, 70 leagues west of which one finds, in the sea, a certain island discovered by the English called Brasil. It is named in that manner because Brasil trees grow on it, although not as fine as those brought to Portugal from the coast of Brazil, in the West Indies. (My translation)

Hy-Brasil is closely associated with the concepts of the "Isle of the Blessed," "Land of Delight" and "Land of Promise" that made St. Brendan ("the Navigator," c. 484–c. 578), already a septuagenarian, set sail to find it. Furthermore, this mysterious island that is concealed by heavy fog in the ocean, rematerializing (as per a Ballycastle boatman) for only one day every seven years (Freitag 2013, 73), has echoes of a pre-Christian world where the dry-land world of human beings and the liquid "otherworld" were aspects of the same cosmos and possessed an integrated coherence.

In the pagan mental environment that conceived the Isla Encubierta and Hy-Brasil, the individual's conceptualization of the natural world is never entirely limited to utilitarian concerns or dependent on the information provided by the senses: for the medieval mind there is a far-reaching realm beyond the range of the senses that holds a considerable stockpile of implicit knowledge. We have seen this in the Máel Dúin *immram*, for example, where the hero's distinctive moral framework and perception strategies are the product of his assimilation of society's communal codes for perceiving, judging, and acting. Those codes are the source of the hero's supply of implicit knowledge. Not dependent entirely on information provided by the senses, his experiences and his environment emerge as–what might seem to the modern reader–hallucinations; they are imperative reveries in the enactment of an ideological world whose theatricalization is not possible through representations that mimic real experiences in the physical world.

Conceptually, there were two realities at play: the physical and the ideological, but ideological reality embraced the reality of the physical world and cast its events *purposely*, so there could be no fixed perceptual boundary between the two. Accordingly, the Celtic, ancient Irish world acknowledged the natural fluidity and recurring character of the movement between the realm of quotidian perception and that other realm. These two spheres generated a cohesive notional continuity that allowed for back-and-forth journeys as part of the natural arrangement of the universe. This we have seen in Conn's journey to the otherworld to bring back a sacrificial victim and in Arthur's invasion of the otherworld to bring back booty.

With the subsequent prevalence of canonical Christianity, a finer distinction was made between heaven and earth, as the growing stratification and the establishment of hierarchies ossified and stabilized the boundary between the two worlds and inhibited the fluid movement between them. The threat to the church's rigid, systematized metaphysics would make such voyages increasingly rare as the ancient mindset was progressively subsumed by the topical environment. Furthermore, for the early Irish communities, the advance of Christianization gradually aligned ancient ethos with newfangled credenda, increasingly generating and stabilizing stratified metaphysical boundaries. This practice had damaging implications for the conceptual, mythical space that had previously presided over early medieval consciousness in that the power to determine, access, and mediate knowledge passed from a broad range of people that were free from statutory canonical restrictions (druids) to a select group of dogmatists (churchmen).

The concept of fortunate islands like Hy-Brasil, objects of methodical search by Christian explorers and cartographers, betrays an underlying pagan ethos where the ancient fluidity between worlds was assumed. In essence, Christian *invasion* of the Celtic otherworld, however hostile to its persistence, is an implied acknowledgment of that space's continuing consequence for the now-Christian inhabitants of Hibernia.

Mythical landscapes like Hy-Brasil are not vacant lots for abstract intangibles; they are distinct mental constructs, charged with a conceptual substance that reflects a decidedly pre-Christian ethos. Moreover, the medieval imagination saturates those mythical spaces with marvelous elements such as bizarre islands, rivers, mountains, trees, animals, people, dwellings, and events that produce a symbolic cosmos, one endowed with discrete meaning and values that reveal their pagan roots. Accordingly, this serves to structure the world in a manner that positions human existence within it in an acclimatized topography of meaning; therein islands like Hy-Brasil and Isla Encubierta appear and disappear from view, transitioning from this world to the otherworld in an ostentatious display of Celtic inter-world acrobatics. The fact that Christian dogma could not simply ignore, but needed to invade a topography like this reveals the continuing relevance of pagan worldviews in medieval Ireland.

This brings us to consider the way these ocean voyage narratives use language to signify, compose identity, and assemble a due order of common moral values. The Christian/pagan amalgam with which most *immrama* and *echtrai* are forged is not the product of a need to maintain an established community, but rather to steer one, gradually, in an idiosyncratic direction. These hybrid Atlantic adventure narratives like the one where the Celtic Hy-Brasil has metamorphosed into the desired endpoint of Brendan's journeys, the "Isle of the Blessed," were designed to funnel the primordial mythical forces of the community into Christian vessels, not an easy task in a community that had been formed within an ancient and ingrained discursive environment. Accordingly, the outwardly doctrinaire Christian discourse that entrenches itself in these pagan narratives serves to buttress the new ethos and reinforce the new identity paradigms that conform to the relatively new, dominant culture imposed by the church. This discourse is so methodically and comprehensively worked into the narratives that the voice of their pre-Christian origin has become inaudible even to some academics. This methodical incursion into native topographies by saints like Brendan speaks to the enduring vitality of the native/pagan ethos and the need for the church to take it into serious consideration.

Hy-Brasil's transmutation into Brendan's coveted "Isle of the Blessed" suggests that there was a lingering communal recognition, originating in pagan antiquity, of the patterned way (as perceived in the adventures of U sheen, Madoc, Trezenzonio,

Bran, Connla, Amaro, Máel Dúin, Snégdgs, and Mac Ríagla, Brendan) in which one should approach the otherworld and of the marvels that one should expect during the journey. Even subjected to Christian veneers, the Atlantic journeys articulate experience in patterns and categories that are easily identifiable as pagan.

When one considers the difficulties that accompanied the propagation of Christianity in Ireland, the cause for the persistence of the native pagan ethos becomes quite conspicuous. There are times when the dogmata of a new, alien component in a culture cannot be assimilated effortlessly by the community. In the case of early medieval Ireland, where the church's principles had a tenuous hold, they had to be unavoidably infused with elements of the native ethos. What's more, one might question how thoroughly Christian the Irish church actually was, as there is a clear indication of the survival of a pagan ethos, within the church, well into the High Middle Ages. Lanfranc (1010–1089) and Anselm (1033–1109) spoke of their anxiety and concern regarding the Irish church, and Pope Alexander III (1100–1179) called the Irish *gens illa barbara inculta et divina legis ignara* (a barbaric and uncultured nation, ignorant of divine law). Moreover, Bernard of Clairvaux held that the Irish were "Christians in name, pagans in fact" (Gillingham 2000, 146). Edmund Curtis put it this way:

> Among the clergy, [the charges] were: simony and marriage; neglect in places to perform the proper sacraments of baptism and confirmation and to enforce penance; toleration of illegitimacy and uncanonical marriages. Among the laity there were: irregular unions with women, repudiation and changing of wives, and other habits, hinted at rather than named, of pagan nature. (Curtis 2012, 14-15)

But the syncretic nature of Atlantic topographies like those of Hy-Brasil and of narratives like the *immrama* and *echtrai* allowed for at least two diverse modes of interpretation. Because these narratives conflated Christian belief with pagan myth, the Atlantic *beyond* acquired a binary identity, in the sense that it could be experienced optimistically by the proselytizers–as a place where Christian credenda is acted out in a compelling manner–or unpleasantly by erstwhile pagans, as a platform for looking nostalgically at a previous time when the confining and biased social environment upheld by the new religion did not exist. Hy-Brasil, appearing and disappearing at will from maps and charts, evokes the church's inability to solidify an uncontested normative version of its truth, one that could be relevant to people whose ethos was orders of magnitude too complex for the clergymen to overcome effortlessly.

This ethos was of considerable reach, a fact that is considered in previous discussions in this work, in particular those dealing with Spanish Celtic travelers Trezenzonio and Amaro and with the Iberian Celtic populations. The heroes' communally-generated subjective gaze, the common topoi, events, places, beings, and trials and tribulations experienced by Atlantic travelers are witness to the cogency of a shared, traditional cultural milieu that was ubiquitous in Celtic lands along the Atlantic shore. Thus, Spanish immram heroes might have set off into the Atlantic from Spain's coastal regions such as Cantabria (from the Celtic words *kant* > *clach*, meaning rock, boulder, and *briga*, meaning rocky height or outcrop), or Galicia (Gallaecia, the region where a Celtic people called the Gallaeci lived), or Asturias (from the Celtic word *sturr*, meaning strong, a word also associated with many rivers throughout Celtic lands) (Cantó 25 Sept. 2016, n.p.). In short, Hy-Brasil and Isla Encubierta, U sheen, and Trezenzonio share a particular cultural environment that flourished along the Atlantic littoral; they record the conceptual world of a people that participated in a common culture and consequently produced ideas, images, narrative genres and representations of humanity that function ontologically and aesthetically across vast spaces, revealing similar responses to the sundry conditions of human existence.

Conclusion

The early medieval Atlantic was a primordial mythic horizon, it was the mystery of limitless distance that dissipated the tyrannical boundaries of the seaside communities' familiar spatial cosmos, dissolving all laws of temporal continuity and permitting the establishment of a different order of reality, one with transcendent connotations. The Atlantic was a relevant metaphor for that mysterious, immeasurable void that separates mundane existence from the supernatural realm.

Perhaps more accurately, the expeditions of the early medieval imagination into the vast, extrinsic reality of the Atlantic Ocean are symbolic of expeditions towards the inner self, towards realms where axiomatic truths can be the product of subjective insight and not of objective observation. To understand "genuine" truth, the medieval mind needed to liberate itself from the restraints imposed upon it by the consuetudes of its physical surroundings and journey to places where it could touch the eternal, the limitless, and the unfathomable. The Atlantic was the splendid showground for such voyages.

Transcendent, conceptual truths, nestled in the recesses of the inner self, completely saturated ancient and medieval life. They predicated the principles that inspired ethical actions and established the conditions for acquiring knowledge. Codified in religion, they provided standardizing criteria that helped to structure and formalize the social and cultural cosmos. The ubiquitous presence of *consecrated* people–be it druids or priests–in every aspect of pagan and early medieval societies, makes it evident that those truths were not arrived at through discrete, personal experience but are a consequence of the individual's communal circumstances. In these pre-scientific societies, collective conceptual precepts were there to explain reality, provide truth, and prevent the personal disengagement necessary to contemplate the mysteries of existence in an autonomous manner.

Ocean-side ancient and early medieval communities survived in a substantial reality whose salient characteristics were violence, injustice, plagues, wars, hunger, poverty, chaos, and death, a place full of imperfections that could be a burden in the quest to find some transcendent meaning to their existence. As the Celtic conception of the Otherworld was that of a cosmos that was *concurrent* with their physical environment, a cosmos of which the Atlantic was a critical component, it stood to reason that they could observe that otherworld by traveling, while still alive, within the spatial dimensions of *this* world. From the standpoint of Christian theology, however, traveling around in *this* world searching for God's residence would be an extraordinarily pointless endeavor, as the questions of where, how, and why of God and Heaven are answered by faith. Only by faith can the unassailable chasm that opens between this world and the next be negotiated; only through faith can God's unbearable *absence* from this world be explained.

Faith, not a currach, is the vessel in which the believer seeks to know the truth. In a Christian thinker like Augustine one can recognize the standard Christian epistemology in this regard, characterized as *fides quaerens intellectum* (faith seeking understanding); it was further described by Anselm of Canterbury (c. 1033–1109) in his *Proslogion* (II–IV) as *Neque enim quaero intelligere ut credam, sed credo ut intelligam* (I do not pursue understanding in order to believe, but rather, I believe in order to understand). For the pagan Celts, whose otherworld was simultaneous with this solid and quantifiable world, the formula "faith seeking understanding" would have to be altered to "men in boats seeking understanding." This might be a suitable image to describe their distinctive conceptualization of reality, a reality that had ample room within it for the supernatural.

There is a unique "personality" to a culture's particular view of the transcendent, the result of a developmental history that sinks its roots deep in that culture's past. The natural propensity of human conglomerates to standardize their conception of transcendental truths leaves traces in cultural artifacts that, while they may be subsequently re-organized by succeeding dominant faiths in order to fit new cultural models, still bubble up to the surface to remind us of their origin. The Atlantic, with its panorama of strange lands, monsters, miraculous events, and bewildering characters is a major, enduring trace of that resilient, pagan, Celtic culture common to peoples of ancient and medieval Europe's Atlantic shores.

Those seemingly bizarre elements were projections of that culture's specific social and religious concerns, purposely integrated into the conceptualization of their otherworld. The myriad of elements shared by the stories of Trezenzonio, Amaro, and the *immrama* and *echtrai* cannot be explained away as products of some bizarre dysfunctional trait of the Christian imagination; they are powerful and eloquent images of that resilient earlier culture. Moreover, the subsequent conversion of these Celtic stories into Christian evangelizing tales has the peculiar effect of destabilizing the endogenous configuration and value orientation of the original, that is to say, that the Christian protagonist inserted into the Celtic stories becomes an anachronistic subject, as he paradoxically undertakes awkward spiritual adventures through sterilized pagan landscapes whose connection to the eventual Christian message often seems tenuous, contrived and unconvincing.

On the other hand, the pagan Celtic hero setting off into the Atlantic would have entered a transcendental space that is effectively undifferentiated from his familiar space, a place where that recognizable space expands unobstructed into eternity. The difference between the Christian protagonist and pagan hero is that the pagan's ocean, where the Celts unleash their imagination, is uncharted and the opportunities for the mind to expand its spiritual scope are limitless. Christian voyagers injected into *immrama*, on the other hand, are interlopers that find themselves in unfamiliar liminal space, converting it as they move within it into a closed cycle that has predictable edifying stages and a compulsory and predictable dénouement.

Yet the liminal space occupied by the Atlantic is also the stage where medieval anxieties, be they pagan or Christian, are dramatized. The venturing into the ocean, the encounter with bizarre creatures in impossible islands, the time-dilation and uncanny adventures where giants and flying horses seem commonplace, is a journey to the dark recesses of the unconscious and have an underlying cathartic function for the consumer of the stories. This is because the spectacle offered by the *immrama* and *echtrai* upends individual, subjective contemplations that may be unsettling the medieval mind, showing a hero, who embodies the community, doing battle with his own demons and defeating them. Like the hero overcomes his enemies, the anxieties symbolized by these antagonistic creatures are overcome and the mind returns to the communal fold. In a manner of speaking, this was psychogenic rehabilitation for medieval discontents.

So the pagan Celts dealt with anxiety by populating the otherworldly Atlantic, filling it with fantastic lands, beings, and spaces: Trezenzonio, at a moment of spiritual agony, scales Breogán's Tower (Tower of Hercules, Galicia) and detects an island where none should be, recognizing it as "The Great Isle of the Solstice." Ith discovers Ireland while perched atop the same tower in northwestern Spain, and whimsical beings from lands far into the Atlantic reach Europe's coasts and take characters like U sheen on excursions where the finitudes of normal time and space unravel in otherworldly mists. These events are evidence of the endeavor to prevail over spiritual anxieties by colonizing the void and placing spiritual phenomena at the heart of its perplexing vacuum.

Entering the seemingly infinite void of the medieval Atlantic might have given Christian travelers profound trepidations: they could travel forever and never arrive anywhere, as it is beyond the boundaries of the Bible's ecumene. But Celtic heroes seem to be always arriving somewhere while sailing the ocean, turning what was previously an infinite *absence* into a distinctly auspicious dimension of their spiritual world. This characteristic of their symbolic mindscape separates their cosmos from modernity and from Christianity in diverse and profound ways.

As a final commentary, I'll reiterate that scientific discoveries since the advent of the Renaissance have largely relegated mythoi to the realms of pixie dust and ignorance, where they substantially remain despite modern efforts to reclaim their importance. If anything is to be learned from the mythical worlds formed in and around the Atlantic Ocean, it is that the value of myth lies in its fundamental role in shaping human conscious activity and in its effectiveness in casting and reinforcing patterns for communal cohesion and shared belief systems. But belief systems not based on scientific inquiry have been considered an impediment to progress, mostly due to the pernicious actions of believers like Father Niccolò Lorini, who submitted Galileo's writings on heliocentrism to the Roman Inquisition in 1615. As a reaction to such extensive and sustained witlessness, thinkers arose like Francis Bacon, who, notwithstanding his fervent Christian faith, laid the foundations (*Novum Organum,* 1640) for the belief that science is the only path to unveiling the "truth" regarding reality.

To a certain extent, the scientific revolution–set in motion in some measure as a reaction to dogmatic benightedness–has made us believe that there is no end to what we can discover about reality, so we rarely give a second thought to an evident truth: no matter how much science advances toward the understanding of the universe, absolute knowledge is unattainable and will always evade us. There will come a time when we'll need to recognize that we cannot learn anything else about reality, and at that point, we'll be as perplexed by the universe as we were when we started.

In this regard, in his book *The End of Science* (1996), John Horgan famously predicted a time when we would reach the absolute endpoint in our vain attempt to discover reality's ultimate truth. Russell Stannard also speaks of a time when "our descendants reach the stage where they notice that their physics textbooks have not needed updating for the past millennium," and adds that

> Eventually the pursuit of scientific knowledge will come to an end. [...] Technology will continue. But fundamental science itself–the making of fresh discoveries as to how the world is constructed and behaves–that process, almost certainly, will at some stage grind to a halt. (Stannard 2010, 1-2)

I suspect that the "end of science," if it ever comes, is many centuries away. But there is a final knowledge-boundary out there that we cannot cross, and coming to terms with its unassailable existence should make us appreciate our humanity in a clearer light: we are human beings, not gods, because of these limits to our understanding. We will never, in short, be totally acquainted with the reality in which our self-conscious intellect functions. And more importantly, we will never answer the question of purpose, of *why* we are here.

Perhaps, if and when the time comes when they reach the final boundaries of the knowable, our descendants will gaze out into the Atlantic and evoke a time when dreams, hopes, and inspiration fashioned a horizon towards which the spirit could fly, uninhibited and free from the dictates of a finite rational system that pigeonholes our understanding of "reality." Perhaps then, ever-inquisitive human beings will again acknowledge that it may be possible to challenge the void that endlessly assaults our consciousness by recalling that, a long time ago, mythical thought propitiated the detection of a deeper meaning to human existence. At that point, human beings might stop equating science with the endless quest to discover universal truths.

Works Cited

Abercrombie, John. "A Study of the Ancient Speech of the Canary Islands." *Harvard African Studies* 1, no. 1 (1916): 95-129.

Abeydeera, Ananda. "In Search of the Garden of Paradise: Florentine Friar Giovanni de Marignolli's Travels in Ceylon." *Terrae Incognitae* 25, no. 1 (1993): 1-23.

Abreu y Galindo, Juan de. *The History of the Discovery and Conquest of the Canary Islands*. Translated by George Glas. London: R&J Dodsley and T. Durham, 1764.

Adamnán. *The Life of Saint Columba, Founder of Hy*. Edited and translated by William Reeves. Edinburgh: Edmonston and Douglas, 1874.

Adams, Geoff W. *Romano-Celtic Élites and Their Religion*. Armidale, NSW: Caeros, 2005.

Adams Bellows, Henry, transl. *The Poetic Edda*. Mineola: Dover, 2004. First published 1923 by the American-Scandinavian Foundation.

Akin, Daniel L., ed. *A Theology for the Church*. Nashville, TN: B&H Academic, 2007.

Alcaraz, Antonio. *Misterios del Camino de Santiago*. Seville: Punto Rojo, 2014.

Alexander, Dominic. *Saints and Animals in the Middle Ages*. Woodbridge, UK: Boydell Press, 2008.

Allen, John Logan, ed. *North American Exploration*, vol. 1. Lincoln: University of Nebraska Press, 1997.

Amador de los Ríos, José. Historia Crítica de la Literatura Española. Madrid: Joaquín Muñoz, 1865.

Ammianus Marcellinus. *The Roman History*. Translated by C.D. Yonge. London: G. Bell and Sons, 1911.

Andrews, Tamra. *Dictionary of Nature Myths*. Oxford: Oxford University Press, 1998.

"Annals of the Four Masters." CELT: The Corpus of Electronic Texts. The Celt Project. Accessed 18 April 2022, https://celt.ucc.ie/published/T100005A/

Archer, Ian, Caroline Barron, and Vanessa Harding, eds. *Hugh Alley's Caveat: The Markets of London in 1598*. London: London Topographical Society, 1988.

Ardrey, Adam. *Finding Merlin: The Truth Behind the Legend of the Great Arthurian Mage*. New York: Overlook Press, 2008.

Bainton, Roland H. *The Medieval Church*. New York: Van Nostrand, 1962.

Bakunin, Michael. *God and the State*. Mineola: Dover, 1970.

Baragwanath, Emily, ed. *Myth, Truth, and Narrative in Herodotus*. New York: Oxford University Press, 2012.

Bassett, Fletcher S. *Legends and Superstitions of the Sea and of Sailors*. Chicago: Bedford, Clarke & Co., 1885.

Battles, Jan. "The Irish are not Celts, Say Experts." *The Sunday Times*. Sept. 5, 2004, 6.

Beaumont, Douglas. *The Message Behind the Movie*. Chicago: Moody, 2009.
Becker, Udo. *The Continuum Encyclopedia of Symbols*, s.v. "Cup." New York: Continuum, 2000.
Bennett, Michael J. *Belted Heroes and Bound Women: The Myth of the Homeric Warrior-King*. New York: Rowman and Littlefield, 1997.
Bennett, W. Lance. "Myth, Ritual and Political Control." *Journal of Communication* 30, no. 4 (1980): 166-179.
Berger, Peter L., and Thomas Luckmann. *The Social Construction of Reality*. New York: Anchor Books, 1966.
The Bible, English Standard Version. Wheaton, IL: Crossway, 2001.
The Bible, New International Version. Grand Rapids, MI: Zondervan, 1973.
Biddick, Kathleen. "The ABC of Ptolemy. Mapping the World with the Alphabet." In *Text and Territory: Geographical Imagination in the European Middle Ages*, edited by Sylvia Tomasch and Sealy Gilles, 268-294. Philadelphia: University of Pennsylvania Press, 1998.
Blondel, Jacques, and Christelle Fontaine. *The Mediterranean Region: Biological Diversity in Space and Time*. New York: Oxford University Press, 2010.
Bogucki, Peter I., ed. *Encyclopedia of Society and Culture in the Ancient World*. New York: Facts on File, 2007.
Bonnett Reverón, Buenaventura. "La Isla de San Borondón." *Revista de Historia* 2, no. 4 (1927): 227-235.
Boswell, Charles S. *An Irish Precursor of Dante*. London: David Nutt, 1908.
Boswell-Stone, W. G. *Shakespeare's Holinshed: The Chronicle and the Historical Plays Compared*. London: Chatto & Windus, 1896.
"Brendan." *Wikipedia*. Last modified April 18, 2022. en.wikipedia.org/wiki/Brendan#The_Voyage_of_Saint_Brendan_the_Abbot.
Bromwich, Rachel, ed. *Trioedd Ynys Prydein: The Triads of the Island of Britain*. Cardiff: University of Wales Press, 2006.
Brown, Arthur Charles Lewis. *Iwain: A Study in the Origins of Arthurian Romance*. New York: Haskell House, 1968. First published 1903 by Ginn & Co.
Bruce, Christopher W. *Arthurian Name Dictionary*. New York: Garland, 1999.
Burges Watson, Sarah. "Orpheus: A Guide to Selected Sources." Living Poets. Durham University, 2013. https://livingpoets.dur.ac.uk/w/Orpheus:_A_Guide_to_Selected_Sources
Byghan, Yowann. *Modern Druidism: An Introduction*. Jefferson, NC: McFarland, 2018.
Byrne, Aisling. *Otherworlds: Fantasy and History in Medieval Literature*. Oxford: Oxford University Press, 2016.
Caerols Pérez, José J. *Helánico de Lesbos*. Madrid: CSIC, 1991.
Campbell, Joseph. *The Hero with a Thousand Faces*. Novato, CA: New World Library, 2008. First published 1949 by Pantheon.
Campbell, Tony. "Census of Pre-Sixteenth Century Portolan Charts." *Imago Mundi* 38 (1986): 67-94.
Cantó, Pablo. "De dónde vienen los nombres de las Comunidades Autónomas españolas." *El País*. September 25, 2016. https://verne.elpais.com/verne/2016/09/09/articulo/14734346 04_706233.html (accessed June 7, 2022).

Carey, John. "The Church and the Otherworld: Sacred Spaces in the *Matière de Bretagne* and Medieval Ireland." In *Arthurian Literature XXXVI*, edited by Sarah Bowden, Susanne Friede and Andreas Hammer, 13-30. Cambridge: D.S. Brewer, 2021.

Carlisle, Nicholas. *A Topographical Dictionary of the Dominion of Wales*. London: W. Bulmer & Co., 1811.

Carlson, Jon D. *Myths, State Expansion, and the Birth of Globalization*. London: Palgrave Macmillan, 2012.

Carlton, Genevieve. *Worldly Consumers: The Demand for Maps in Renaissance Italy*. Chicago: University of Chicago Press, 2015.

Carne-Ross, D. S. *Pindar*. New Haven, CT: Yale University Press, 1985.

Carney, James. *Studies in Irish Literature and History*. Dublin: Dublin Institute for Advanced Studies, 1955.

Cary, M. and E. H. Warmington. *The Ancient Explorers*. New York: Dodd, Mead and Co., 1929.

Cassirer, Ernst. *An Essay on Man: An Introduction to a Philosophy of Human Culture*. New Haven, CT: Yale University Press, 1944.

Cassirer, Ernst. *The Myth of the State*. New Haven, CT: Yale University Press, 1946.

The Catholic Encyclopedia, s.v. "Miracle." New York: Robert Appleton, 1912.

Cavill, Paul. *Vikings: Fear and Faith*. Grand Rapids, MI: Zondervan, 2001.

Chandler, Richard. *The History of Illium or Troy*. London: James Robson, 1802.

Chil y Naranjo, Gregorio. *Estudios históricos, climatológicos y patológicos de las Islas Canarias*. Madrid: Gaspar y Roig Editores, 1879.

Claster, Jill N. *Sacred Violence: The European Crusades to the Middle East, 1095-1396*. Toronto: University of Toronto Press, 2009.

Cobo, Gabriel Escribano, and Alfredo Mederos Martín. "Ánforas romanas en las Islas Canarias?" *Tabona* 9 (1996): 75-98.

Corning, Caitlin. *The Celtic and Roman Traditions: Conflict and Consensus in the Early Medieval Church*. New York: Palgrave Macmillan, 2006.

Cort Haddon, Alfred. *The Races of Man and Their Distribution*. New York: Cambridge University Press, 1924.

Cosmas Indicopleustes. "The Christian Topography, or, The Opinion of Christians Concerning the World." Tertullian.org. Last modified 2003. https://www.tertullian.org/fathers/ cosmas _01_book1.htm

Cotterell, Arthur. *A Dictionary of World Mythology*. New York: Oxford University Press, 1997.

Cristóbal, Vicente. "Orfeo y otros mitos eróticos en la *General Estoria*" *Cahiers d'études hispaniques médiévales* 38, no. 1 (2015): 65-89.

Cuesta Domingo, Mariano, ed. *Alonso de Santa Cruz y su obra cosmográfica*. Vol. 1. Madrid: CSIC, 1983.

Curran, Bob. *Mysterious Celtic Mythology in American Folklore*. New Orleans, LA: Pelican, 2010.

Curtis, Edmund. *A History of Medieval Ireland: From 1086 to 1513*. New York: Routledge, 2012. First published 1923 by Maunsell & Roberts.

d'Arbois de Jubainville, Marie-Henri. *El ciclo mitológico irlandés y la mitología céltica*. Translated by Alicia Santiago. Barcelona: Edicomunicación, 1996.

D'Emilio, James. "The Paradox of Galicia: A Cultural Crossroads at the Edge of Europe." In *Culture and Society in Medieval Galicia*, edited by James D'Emilio, 1-123. Leiden: Brill, 2015.

Dathome, O. R. *Imagining the World: Mythical Belief Versus Reality in Global Encounters*. Westport, CT: Bergin and Garvey, 1994.

De Vries, Eric. *Hedge Rider*. Green Valley Lake, CA: Pendraig, 2008.

Delumeau, Jean. *History of Paradise: The Garden of Eden in Myth and Tradition*. Translated by Matthew O'Connell. New York: Continuum, 1995.

Detienne, Marcel. "Rethinking Mythology." In *Between Belief and Transgression: Structuralist Essays in Religion, History, and Myth*. Translated by John Leavitt and edited by Michel Izard and Pierre Smith, 43-52. Chicago: The University of Chicago Press, 1981.

Dewey, John. *The Political Writings*. Edited by Debra Morris and Ian Shapiro. Indianapolis: Hackett, 1993.

Dillon, John M., and Lloyd P. Gerson. *Neoplatonic Philosophy: Introductory Readings*. Indianapolis: Hackett Publishing, 2004.

Din, Gilbert C. *The Canary Islanders of Louisiana*. Baton Rouge, LA: Louisiana State University Press, 1988.

Duffy, Séan, ed. *Medieval Ireland: An Encyclopedia*. New York: Routledge, 2005.

Dumville, David N. "Echtrae and Immram: Some Problems of Definition." *Ériu* 27 (1976): 73–94.

Duncan, Dayton. *Scenes of Visionary Enchantment: Reflections on Lewis and Clark*. Lincoln: University of Nebraska Press, 2004.

Dundes, Alan, ed. *The Flood Myth*. Berkeley: University of California Press, 1988.

Dungal. "Hibernici Exulis Carmina." In *Monumenta Germaniae Historia*, 395-402. Munich: Harrassowitz Verlag, 2021.

Durkheim, Émile. *Elementary Forms of the Religious Life*. Translated by Carol Cosman. New York: Oxford University Press, 2001.

Ekrich, A. Roger. *At Day's Close: Night in Times Past*. New York: Norton & Co., 2005.

Eley, Penny. *Partonopeus de Blois: Romance in the Making*. Woodbridge, UK: D.S. Brewer, 2011.

Eliade, Mircea. *A History of Religious Ideas*. Vol. 1: *From the Stone Age to the Eleusinian Mysteries*. Translated by Willard. R. Trask. Chicago: University of Chicago Press, 1978.

Elton, Charles Isaac. *Origins of English History*. London: Bernard Quaritch, 1890.

Encyclopaedia Britannica Online. Accessed May 23, 2022. https://www.britannica.com

Esposito, M. "A Medieval Legend of the Terrestrial Paradise." *Folklore* 29, no. 3 (1918): 193-205.

Evans-Wentz, Walter Yeeling. *The Fairy Faith in Celtic Countries*. New York: Citadel, 1994.

Fanous, Samuel, and Vincent Gillespie, eds. *The Cambridge Companion to Medieval English Mysticism*. New York: Cambridge University Press, 2011.

Farrell Krell, David. *The Tragic Absolute: German Idealism and the Languishing of God.* Bloomington, IN: Indiana University Press, 2005.

Feeling, Durbin. *Cherokee-English Dictionary.* N.P.: Cherokee Nation of Oklahoma, 1975.

Feldman, Burton and Robert D. Richardson, Jr. *The Rise of Modern Mythology, 1680-1860.* Bloomington, IN: Indiana University Press, 1972.

Fernández de Enciso, Martín. *Suma de geografía que trata de todas las partidas e provincias del mundo.* Seville: Jacobo Cromberger, 1519.

Figueira, Dorothy. "Myth in Romantic Prose Fiction." In *Romantic Prose Fiction*, edited by Gerald Ernest et al., 517-526. Amsterdam: John Benjamins, 2008.

Fink, Bruce. *The Lacanian Subject: Between Language and Jouissance.* Princeton, NJ: Princeton University Press, 1997.

Finnegan, Richard B. and Edward McCarron. *Ireland: Historical Echoes, Contemporary Politics.* New York: Avalon Publishing, 2000.

Flanagan, Thomas. *A History of the Church in England.* Vol. 1. London: Charles Dolman, 1857.

Flint, Valerie I.J. "Travel Fact and Travel Fiction in the Voyages of Columbus." In *Travel Fact and Travel Fiction: Studies on Fiction, Literary Tradition, Scholarly Discovery and Observation in Travel Writing*, edited by Z. R. W. M. von Martels, 94-110. Leiden: E.J. Brill, 1994.

Forino, Simona. "Raza y herencia en el exilio." In *Exilio y cine*, edited by María Pilar Rodríguez Pérez, 195-204. Bilbao: Universidad de Deusto, 2012.

Franklin, Anna. *Midsummer: Magical Celebrations of the Summer Solstice.* Woodbury, MN: Llewellyn, 2002.

Frazer, James George, and Robert Fraser. *The Golden Bough: A Study in Magic and Religion.* New York: Oxford University Press, 2009.

Frazer, William O., and Andrew Tyrrell, eds. *Social Identity in Early Medieval Britain.* Leicester, UK: Leicester University Press, 2000.

Freeman, Philip. *Julius Caesar.* New York: Simon & Schuster, 2008.

Freitag, Barbara. *Hy Brasil: The Metamorphosis of an Island.* Amsterdam: Rodopi, 2013.

García Cuartango, Pedro. "El río que los soldados romanos se negaron a cruzar porque temían perder la memoria." *ABC*, May 9, 2022. https://www.abc.es/viajar/destinos/espana/abci-espana-magica-soldados-romanos-negaron-cruzar-porque-temian-perder-memoria-202205091722_noticia.html

Gardiner, Eileen. *Medieval Visions of Heaven and Hell: A Sourcebook.* Milton Park, UK: Routledge, 1993.

Gath Whitley, D. "The Ancient Cornish Serpent Divinity of the Sea." *Records of the Past* 10, May-June (1911): 143-153.

Geoffrey of Monmouth. *The History of the Kings of Britain.* Edited and translated by Michael A. Faletra. Peterborough, Canada: Broadview, 2008.

George, A. R. *The Epic of Gilgamesh: the Babylonian Epic Poem and Other Texts in Akkadian and Sumerian.* Translated by Andrew George. London: Penguin Books, 2000.

Gillingham, John. *The English in the Twelfth Century: Imperialism, National Identity, and Political Values.* Woodbridge, UK: Boydell Press, 2000.

Goodrich, Peter H., and Raymond H. Thompson, editors. *Merlin: A Casebook.* New York: Routledge, 2003.

Grahame, F.R. *The Archer and the Steppe; Or, the Empires of Scythia: a History of Russia and Tartary.* London: James Blackwood, 1860.

Guerra, Ángel, and Michel Segonzac. *Géants des profondeurs.* Versailles: Éditions Quae, 2014.

Hachey, Thomas, and Lawrence J. McCaffrey. *The Irish Experience Since 1800: A Concise History.* London: Routledge, 2015.

Hansen, William F. *Classical Mythology: A Guide to the Mythical World of the Greeks and Romans.* New York: Oxford University Press, 2005.

Haralick, Robert M. *Inner Meaning of the Hebrew Letters.* New York: Rowman & Littlefield, 1995.

Harari, Yuval Noah. *Sapiens: A brief history of Humankind.* New York: Vintage, 2011.

Harbison, Peter. *Pilgrimages in Ireland.* Syracuse, NY: Syracuse University Press, 1991.

Hastings, James et al., eds. *Encyclopedia of Religion and Ethics.* Vol. 2. Cambridge, MA: Harvard UP, 1908.

Haverty, Martin. *The History of Ireland, Ancient and Modern, Derived from Our Native Annals.* Dublin: James Duffy, 1872.

Hazard, Harry W., ed. *A History of the Crusades: The fourteenth and fifteenth centuries.* Madison, WI: University of Wisconsin Press, 1975.

Herodotus. *The Histories.* Translated by A.D. Godley. Cambridge, MA: Harvard University Press, 1920.

Hesiod. *Theogony, Works and Days, Shield.* Translated by Apostolos N. Athanassakis. Baltimore: Johns Hopkins University Press, 2004.

Heuvelmans, Bernard. *Kraken & the Colossal Octopus: In the Wake of Sea-monsters.* New York: Kegan Paul, 2003.

Higginson, Thomas Wentworth. *Tales of the Enchanted Islands of the Atlantic.* London: MacMillan & Co., 1899.

Hodum, Robert. *Pilgrims' Steps: A Search for Spain's Santiago and an Examination of his Way.* Bloomington, IN: iUniverse, 2012.

Hölderlin, Friedrich. *Essays and Letters on Theory.* Translated and edited by T. Pfau. Albany, NY: SUNY Press, 1988.

Holyoake, George Jacob. *English secularism; a confession of belief.* Chicago: Open Court, 1896.

Homer. The *Odyssey.* Translated by George Herbert Palmer. Boston and New York: Houghton Mifflin, 1891.

Horgan, John. *The End of Science.* New York: Basic Books, 2015.

Hourani, George F. *Arab Seafaring in the Indian Ocean in Ancient and Early Medieval Times.* Princeton, NJ: Princeton University Press, 1995.

Huber, Emily Rebekah. *Avalon from the Vita Merlini.* Rochester, NY: The Camelot Project, 2007.

Imperato, Robert. *Early and Medieval Christian Spirituality.* Lanham, MD: University Press of America, 2002.

Irby, Georgia L., ed. *Greek and Roman Cartography*. Hoboken, NJ: Wiley-Blackwell, 2016.
Ireland, Stanley. *Roman Britain*. London & New York: Routledge, 2008.
"Irish Sagas Online." Accessed April 19, 2022. https://iso.ucc.ie/Immram-brain/Immram-brain-names.html
Irving, Washington. *Life and Voyages of Christopher Columbus*. Vol. 1. Philadelphia: David McKay, 1892.
Isidore of Seville. *Isidori Hispalensis Episcopi Etymologiarum Sive Originum, Libri XX*. Vol. 2. Oxford: Oxford University Press, 1911.
James, Grace. *The Moon Maiden and Other Japanese Fairy Tales*. New York: Dover, 2005.
Javierre, José María. *Isabel la Católica: el enigma de una reina*. Salamanca: Ediciones Sígueme, 2004.
Jenkins, Philip. "What Hath Wittenberg to Do with Lagos? Sixteenth-Century Protestantism and Global South Christianity." In *Protestantism after 500 Years*, edited by Thomas Albert Howard and Mark A. Noll, 208-227. Oxford: Oxford University Press, 2016.
Jennings, Andrew, Silke Reeploeg and Angela Watt, eds. *Northern Atlantic Islands and the Sea: Seascapes and Dreamscapes*. Cambridge, UK: Cambridge Scholars Publishing, 2017.
Johnston, Elva. *Literacy and Identity in Early Medieval Ireland*. Woodbridge, UK: Boydell Press, 2013.
Jones, Aneurin. "The Alleged Discoveries of America." *The Cambrian* 20 (1900): 492-497.
Joseph, Frank. *Atlantis in Wisconsin: New Revelations About Lost Sunken City*. Lakeville, MN: Galde Press, 1998.
Joseph, Frank. *Atlantis and Other Lost Worlds: New Evidence of Ancient Secrets*. London: Arcturus, 2011.
Jubb, Margaret. "The Crusaders' Perception of their Opponents." In *Palgrave Advances in the Crusades*, edited by Helen J. Nicholson, 225-244. Basingstoke, UK: Palgrave Macmillan, 2005.
Kant, Immanuel. *Prolegomena to Any Future Metaphysics*. Translated and edited by Gary Hatfield. Cambridge: Cambridge University Press, 2004.
Kapell, Matthew Wilhelm, editor. *Star Trek as Myth: Essays on Symbol and Archetype at the Final Frontier*. Jefferson, NC: McFarland, 2010.
Kappler, Claude. *Monstres, demons, et merveilles à la fin du Moyen Âge*. Paris: Payot, 1980.
Keating, Geoffrey. Dermod O'Connor, ed. *The General History of Ireland... Collected by the Learned Jeoffrey Keating, D.D.* Translated and edited by Dermod O'Connor. London: J. Bettenham, 1723.
Kelly, James E., Jr. "Non-Mediterranean Influences That Shaped the Atlantic in the Early Portolan Charts." *Imago Mundi* 31 (1979): 18-35.
Kent Sprague, Rosamonde, ed. *Older Sophists*. Indianapolis: Hackett, 1972.
Kieckhefer, Richard. *Magic in the Middle Ages*. Cambridge: Cambridge University Press, 2014.

Kierkegaard, Søren. *Concluding Unscientific Postscript to Philosophical Fragments*. Edited and translated by Howard V. Hong and Edna H. Hong. Princeton, NJ: Princeton University Press, 1992.

Kleinhenz, Christopher, ed. *Medieval Italy: An Encyclopedia*. Milton Park, UK: Routledge, 2004.

Kleinschmidt, Harald. *People on the Move: Attitudes Toward and Perceptions of Migration in Medieval and Modern Europe*. Santa Barbara, CA: Greenwood, 2003.

Klinger, Ilya, and Boris Maslov, editors. *Persistent Forms: Explorations in Historical Poetics*. New York: Fordham University Press, 2016.

Knight, Stephen. *Merlin: Knowledge and Power Through the Ages*. Ithaca, NY: Cornell University Press, 2009.

Koch, John T., ed. *Celtic Culture: A Historical Encyclopedia*. Santa Barbara, CA: ABC-CLIO, 2006.

----. and Antone Minard, eds. *The Celts: History, Life, and Culture*. Vol. 1. Santa Barbara, CA: ABC-CLIO, 2012.

Lacy, Norris J. "The Spoils of Annwfn (Preiddeu Annwfn)." *The New Arthurian Encyclopedia*. New York: Garland, 1991.

Lansing Smith, Evans. *The Hero Journey in Literature: Parables of Poesis*. Lanham, MD: University Press of America, 1997.

Larcher, Pierre-Henri. *Historical and Critical Comments on the History of Herodotus*. Vol. 1. London: Whittaker & Co, 1844.

Lascelles, Mary, and N.R. Ker. "Alexander and the Earthly Paradise in Medieval English Writings." *Medium Aevum* 5, no. 1 (1936): 31-48.

Lavezzo, Kathy. *Angels on the Edge of the World*. Ithaca, NY: Cornell University Press, 2006.

Lechner, Peter. *The Life and Times of St. Benedict: Patriarch of the Monks of the West*. London: Burns and Oates, 1900.

Lee, Sang Meyng. *The Cosmic Drama of Salvation: A Study of Paul's Undisputed Writings from Anthropological and Cosmological Perspectives*. Tübingen, Germany: Mohr Siebeck, 2010.

Lee, Sydney, and Leslie Stephen, eds. *Dictionary of National Biography*. Vol. 35. London: Smith, Elder & Co., 1893.

Leighton, Albert C. *Transport and communication in early medieval Europe AD 500-1100*. New York: Barnes & Noble, 1972.

Lewis, Bernard. *Islam and the West*. Oxford: Oxford University Press, 1994.

Livingstone, D. N., and C. W. J. Withers, editors. *Geography and Enlightenment*. Chicago: University of Chicago Press, 1999.

Löffler, Christa Maria. *The Voyage to the Otherworld Island in Early Irish Literature*. Salzburg: Institute for English and American Studies, 1983.

Lorrio Alberto J., and Gonzalo Ruiz Zapatero. "The Celts in Iberia: An Overview." *Journal of Interdisciplinary Celtic Studies* 6 (2005): 167-254.

Loxton, Daniel, and Donald R. Prothero. *Abominable Science!: Origins of the Yeti, Nessie, and Other Famous Cryptids*. New York: Columbia University Press, 2013.

Lucian. *The Syrian Goddess.* Translated by Herbert A. Strong. London: Constable, 1913.
Lupack, Barbara Tepa, and Alan Lupack. *Illustrating Camelot.* Woodbridge, UK: D.S. Brewer, 2008.
Mackley, Jude S. *The Legend of St. Brendan: A Comparative Study of the Latin and Anglo-Norman Versions.* Leiden: Brill, 2008.
Macpherson, James. *An Introduction to the History of Great Britain and Ireland.* London: Becket & DeHondt, 1773.
Mali, Joseph. *The Legacy of Vico in Modern Cultural History.* Cambridge: Cambridge University Press, 2012.
Mallory, J. P., and Douglas Q. Adams, eds. *Encyclopedia of Indo-European Culture.* London: Fitzroy Dearborn, 1997.
----. *The Origins of the Irish.* London & New York: Thames & Hudson, 2013.
Markale, Jean. *King of the Celts: Arthurian Legends and Celtic Tradition.* Rochester, VT: Inner Traditions, 1994.
Marston, William M. et al. *Integrative Psychology: A Study of Unit Response.* Milton Park, UK: Routledge, 1999. First published 1931 by Routledge.
Martin, Christopher. *An Introduction to Medieval Philosophy.* Edinburgh: Edinburgh University Press, 1996.
McCready, William D. "Isidore, the Antipodeans, and the Shape of the Earth." *Isis* 87, no. 1 (1996): 108-127.
McKeon, Richard, ed. *Selections From Medieval Philosophers.* Vol. II. New York: Scribner's, 1930.
Medway, Gareth. *Lure of the Sinister: The Unnatural History of Satanism.* New York: NYU Press, 2001.
Melrose, Robin. *Religion in Britain from the Megaliths to Arthur.* Jefferson, NC: McFarland, 2016.
Menéndez Pelayo, Marcelino. *Orígenes de la novela.* Tome 2: vols. 2-3. Universidad de Cantabria, 2017.
Merino, Roberto. "Larga vida a San Borondón." *ABC Canarias.* March 20, 2011, http://www.abc.es/20110320/comunidad-canarias/abcp-larga-vida-borondon-20110320.html. (accessed April 20, 2022).
Meyer, Ann R. *Medieval Allegory and the Building of the New Jerusalem.* Cambridge, UK: D.S. Brewer, 2003.
Meyer, Kuno, ed. *The Voyage of Bran, Son of Febal, to the Land of the Living.* London: David Nutt, 1895.
Michel, Francisque. *Roman d'Eustache Le Moine Pirate Fameux du XIII Siècle.* Paris and London: Silvestre and Pickering, 1834.
Mitchell-Lanham, Jean. *The Lore of the Camino de Santiago: A Literary Pilgrimage.* Minneapolis: Two Harbors Press, 2015.
Moffat, Alistair. *In Search of Angels: Travels to the Edge of the World.* Edinburgh: Birlinn, 2020.
Moore, Laoise T., et al. "A Y-Chromosome Signature of Hegemony in Gaelic Ireland." *American Journal of Human Genetics* 78, no. 2 (2006): 334-338.
Moreno Martínez, Matilde. *Relatos legendarios: historia y magia de España, desde los orígenes a los siglos de oro.* Barcelona: Castalia, 2007.

Morgan, Kathryn A. *Myth and Philosophy from the Presocratics to Plato.* Cambridge: Cambridge University Press, 2004.

Morris, Mark. *The Anglo-Saxons: A History of the Beginnings of England, 400-1066.* New York and London: Pegasus Books, 2021.

Morris, William. *The Earthly Paradise.* Vol. 1. New York & London: Routledge, 2002.

Most, Glenn W. "Plato's Exoteric Myths." In *Plato and Myth: Studies on the Use and Status of Platonic Myths,* edited by Catherine Collobert, Pierre Destrée, and Francisco J. González, 13-24. Leiden: Brill, 2012.

Nemeth, Charles P. *Criminal Law.* 2nd ed. Boca Ratón, FL, London and New York: CRC, 2012.

Neveux, François, and Claire Ruelle. *A brief history of the Normans: the conquests that changed the face of Europe.* London: Constable & Robinson, 2008.

Newton, Arthur Percival. "Travellers' Tales of Wonder and Imagination." *Travel and Travellers of the Middle Ages.* Edited by Arthur Percival Newton. New York: Knopf, 1950.

Nigg, Joseph. *Sea Monsters: A Voyage around the World's Most Beguiling Map.* Chicago: University of Chicago Press, 2013.

Nutt, Alfred. *Legend of the Holy Grail, With Especial Reference to the Hypothesis of its Celtic Origin.* London: The Folk-Lore Society, 1888.

Nyland, Edo. *Linguistic Archaeology: An Introduction.* Bloomington, IN: Trafford Publ., 2001.

O'Curry, Eugene. *On the Manners and Customs of the Ancient Irish: A Series of Lectures.* Vol. 3. London: Williams & Norgate, 1873.

O'Donoghue, Denis. *Brendaniana: St. Brendan the Voyager in Story and Legend.* Dublin: Browne & Nolan, 1895.

O'Kearney, Nicholas. *The Prophecies of SS. Columkille, Maeltamlacht, Ultan, Seadhna, Coireall, Bearcan, &c.* Dublin: John O'Daly, 1856.

O'Rahilly, T. F. *Early Irish History and Mythology.* Dublin: Dublin Institute for Advanced Studies, 1946.

O'Sullivan, Maurice, and Jack C. Lane. *Florida Reader: Visions of Paradise.* Sarasota, FL: Pineapple Press, 1991.

Otridge, J., et al. *The Annual Register, or, A View of the History, Politics, and Literature for the Year 1808.* London: W. Otridge, 1820.

Ovid. *The Metamorphoses.* Translated by Henry T. Riley. London: Wm. Clowes & Sons, 1899.

Owens, Margaret E. *Stages of Dismemberment: The Fragmented Body in Late Medieval and Early Modern Drama.* Plainsboro, NJ: Associated University Presses, 2005.

Oxford English Dictionary. 2nd edition. Vol. 10. Oxford: Clarendon Press, 1989.

Oxford Reference, s.v. "Tír Tairngire." Oxford: Oxford University Press, 2022. https://www.oxfordreference.com/view/10.1093/oi/authority.20110803104725492 (accessed April 20, 2022).

Paice Macleod, Sharon. *Celtic Myth and Religion.* Jefferson, NC: McFarland, 2012.

Palmer, Martin. *Sacred Land: Decoding Britain's Extraordinary Past Through its Towns, Villages and Countryside.* London: Hachette Digital, 2012.

Palmer, Patricia. *The Severed Head and the Grafted Tongue: Literature, Translation and Violence in Early Modern Ireland.* Cambridge: Cambridge University Press, 2014.

Palsson, Herman and Paul Edwards, translators. *The Book of Settlements: Landnámabók* [IX/X centuries]. Winnipeg: University of Manitoba Press, 1972.

Parkin, Simon. "All Alone in No Man's Sky." Science and Tech. *The New Yorker*, August 10, 2016. https://www.newyorker.com/tech/elements/all-alone-in-no-mans-sky

Partonopex de Blois: A Romance in Four Cantos. Translated by W.M. Rose. London: Longman, 1807.

Pastor Bodmer, Beatriz. *The Armature of Conquest: Spanish Accounts of the Discovery of America, 1492-1589.* Stanford, CA: Stanford University Press, 1992.

Patch, Howard Rollin. *The Other World According to Descriptions in Medieval Literature.* New York: Octagon, 1970.

Paul, Heike. *The Myths That Made America: An Introduction to American Studies.* Bielefeld, Germany: Transcript-Verlag, 2014.

Peattie, Noel. *Hydra and Kraken, Or, the Lore and Lure of Lake-Monsters and Sea-Serpents.* Berkeley, CA: Regent Press, 1992.

Pindar. *Pindarou Epinikoi Nemeonikais.* Edited by J.B. Bury. London: MacMillan, 1890.

Plato. *Theaetetus.* Edited and translated by H.N. Fowler. London: Heinemann, 1921.

----. *Timaeus and Critias.* Translated by A. E. Taylor. London & New York: Routledge, 2013.

Pliny. *The Natural History.* Translated by John Bostock and H. T. Riley. London: George Bell & Sons, 1855.

Plutarch. *On the Failure of Oracles.* Translated by Frank Cole Babbitt. Cambridge, MA: Harvard University Press, 1936.

----. *Plutarch's Morals.* Ed. William W. Goodwin. Boston: Little, Brown and Co., 1874.

Pope, Nick, Jim Penniston, and John Burroughs. *Encounter in Rendlesham Forest: The Inside Story of the World's Best-Documented UFO Incident.* New York: St. Martin's Press, 2014.

Pringle, Heather A. *The master plan: Himmler's scholars and the Holocaust.* Westport, CT: Hyperion, 2006.

Proclus. *Commentary on Plato's Timaeus. Volume 1. Book 1: Proclus on the Socratic State and Atlantis*, edited and translated by Harold Tarrant, New York: Cambridge University Press, 2011.

"Proofs that America was discovered by the Britons," *The American Museum, or Universal Magazine* 11 (1792): 152-155.

Purdy, John. *Tables of the Positions, or of The Latitudes and Longitudes, of Places.* London: James Whittle and Richard Holmes Laurie, 1816.

Rawlinson, George. *The History of Herodotus*, vol. 3. 1920. Frankfurt: Verlag Press, 2022.

Ray, Celeste. "The Sacred and the Body Politic at Ireland's Holy Wells." *International Social Science Journal* 62 (2013): 271-285.

Renard, John. *101 Questions and Answers on Confucianism, Daoism, and Shinto.* New York: Paulist Press, 2002.

Rhys, John. *Lectures on the Origin and Growth of Religion.* London: Williams & Norgate, 1892.

Ribera Llopis, Juan Miguel. "Viajes peninsulares a Ultratumba." *Revista de Filología Románica* 10 (1993): 31-45.

Ristuccia, Nathan. *Christianization and Commonwealth in Early Medieval Europe.* Oxford: Oxford University Press, 2018.

Rodkinson, Michael Levi. *New Edition of the Babylonian Talmud.* New York: New Talmud, 1902.

Roller, Duane W. *Ancient Geography: The Discovery of the World in Classical Greece and Rome.* London: I.B. Tauris, 2015.

Roller, Duane W. *Through the Pillars of Herakles: Greco-Roman Exploration of the Atlantic.* New York: Routledge, 2013.

Rolleston, Thomas William. *Myths & Legends of the Celtic Race.* London: Constable, 1911.

Roseman, Christina H. "Reflections of Philosophy: Strabo and Geographical Sources." In *Strabo's Cultural Geography: The Making of a Kolossourgia*, edited by Daniela Dueck, Hugh Lindsay, and Sarah Porthecary, 27-41. New York: Cambridge University Press, 2005.

Rousmaniere, John. *A Bridge to Dialogue: The Story of Jewish-Christian Relations.* Mahwah, NJ: Paulist Press, 1991.

Rubio Rosales, Jaime. *Nazi Archeology in the Canary Islands.* 6th ed. Durham, NC: Lulu Press, 2013.

Sacred Texts. "Bran." Accessed April 20, 2022. https://www.sacred-texts.com/index.htm

----. "Maelduin." Accessed April 20, 2022. https://www.sacred-texts.com/index.htm

Sacks, David. *A Dictionary of the Ancient Greek World.* New York & Oxford: Oxford University Press, 1997.

Salisbury, Joyce E. *The Beast Within: Animals in the Middle Ages.* London & New York: Routledge, 2011.

Scafi, Alessandro. *Maps of Paradise.* Chicago & London: University of Chicago Press, 2013.

Segal, Erich, ed. *Oxford Readings in Greek Tragedy.* New York & Oxford: Oxford University Press, 2003.

Segal, Robert A. "Greek Myths and Psychoanalysis." In *Approaches to Greek Myth*, edited by Lowell Edmonds, 407-456. Baltimore: Johns Hopkins University Press, 2014.

Seung, T. K. *Nietzsche's Epic of the Soul: Thus Spoke Zarathustra.* New York: Lexington Books, 2005.

Sharrer, Harvey L. *The Legendary History of Britain in Lope Garcia de Salazar's Libro de las bienandanzas e fortunas.* Philadelphia: University of Pennsylvania Press, 1979.

Shaw Sailer, Susan. "Suibne Geilt: Puzzles, Problems, and Paradoxes." *The Canadian Journal of Irish Studies* 24, no. 1 (1998): 115–131.

Short, Ian, and Brian S. Merrilees, eds. *The Anglo-Norman Voyage of St. Brendan.* Manchester, UK: Manchester University Press, 1979.

Sir Orfeo. Adapted by Edward Eyre Hunt. Cambridge, UK: Harvard Cooperative Society, 1909.

Skyes, Edgerton, and Alan Kendall. *Who's Who in Non-Classical Mythology.* New York: Routledge, 2002.

Smith, William, ed. *A Dictionary of Greek and Roman Biography and Mythology.* Boston: Charles C. Little & James Brown, 1876.

Sobecki, Sebastian I. *The Sea and Medieval English Literature.* Woodbridge, UK: D.S. Brewer, 2008.

Spence, Lewis. *The History of Atlantis.* New York: Cosimo Classics, 2007.

----. *The Magic Arts in Celtic Britain.* Mineola, NY: Dover, 1999.

Spiegel, F. "The *Tabernacula* of Gregory the Great." *Anglo Saxon England* 36 (2007): 1-14.

Stang, Charles M. *Apophasis and Pseudonymity in Dionysius the Areopagite: "No Longer I."* New York & Oxford: Oxford University Press, 2012.

Stannard, Russell. *The End of Discovery: Are We Approaching the Boundaries of the Knowable?* New York & Oxford: Oxford University Press, 2010.

Starr, Frederick. *Aztec Place-Names: Their Meaning and Mode of Composition.* Privately printed by the author, 1920.

Stein, Matthew. *When Technology Fails.* Chelsea, VT: Chelsea Green, 2008.

Stephens, Thomas. *Madoc: An Essay on the Discovery of America by Madoc Ap Owen Gwynedd in the Twelfth Century.* London: Longmans, Green & Co., 1893.

Stevens, Anthony. *Ariadne's Clue.* Princeton, NJ: Princeton University Press, 2001.

Stokes, Whitley. *Lives of Saints, from the Book of Lismore.* Oxford: Clarendon Press, 1890.

----. "The Voyage of Snédgus and Mac Ríagla." *Review Celtique* 9, no. 1 (1888): 14-25.

Strabo. *The Geography.* Translated by Horace Leonard Jones. Vol. 2. Heinemann, 1923.

Strassler, Robert B., editor. *The Landmark Herodotus: The Histories.* New York: Anchor, 2007.

Stuart-Glennie, John S. *Arthurian Localities: Their Historical Origin, Chief Country and Fingalian Relations.* Edinburgh: Edmonston and Douglas, 1869.

Suárez, Thomas. *Shedding the Veil: Mapping the European Discovery of America and the World.* Singapore: World Scientific, 1992.

Summers, David. *The Judgment of Sense: Renaissance Naturalism and the Rise of Aesthetics.* Cambridge, UK: Cambridge University Press, 1987.

Thacher, John Boyd. *The Continent of America: Its Discovery and Baptism.* New York: William Evarts Benjamin, 1896.

Thomson, J. Oliver. *History of Ancient Geography.* Cambridge, UK: Cambridge University Press, 1948.

Tolan, John, Gilles Veinstein and Henry Laurens. *Europe and the Islamic World: A History.* Translated by Jane Marie Todd. Princeton, NJ: Princeton University Press, 2013.

Tomlinson, Sally. 2007. "Demons, Druids and Brigands on Irish High Crosses: Rethinking the Images as Temptation of Saint Anthony." PhD diss. University of North Carolina, Chapel Hill.

Tozer, Henry F. *History of Ancient Geography*. Cambridge, UK: Cambridge University Press, 1935.

Twing, Stephen W. *Myths, Models, and U.S. Foreign Policy*. Boulder, CO. and London: Lynne Reinner, 1998.

Uriarte, Cristina G. de. *Literatura de viajes y Canarias: Tenerife en los relatos de viajeros franceses del siglo XVIII*. Madrid: CSIC, 2006.

Van Dale, Johan Hendrik. *Groot woordenboek van de Nederlandse taal*. Utrecht: Van Dale Lexicographie, 2008.

van der Dussen, Willem J., and Lionel Rubinoff, eds. *Objectivity, Method, and Point of View: Essays in the Philosophy of History*. Leiden: E.J. Brill, 1991.

Vasunia, Phiroze. *The Gift of the Nile: Hellenizing Egypt from Aeschylus to Alexander*. Berkeley: University of California Press, 2001.

Vega, C. A. *Hagiografía y Literatura. La Vida de San Amaro*. Madrid: El Crótalon, 1987.

Vere, Aubrey de, ed. "The Children of Lir." *The Catholic World* 33, no. 194 (1881): 185-199.

Vergil, Polydore. *Polydore Vergil's English History*. Edited by Henry Ellis. London: The Camden Society, 1844. First published 1534.

Vespucci, Amerigo. *Letters From a New World*. Edited by Luciano Formisano. New York: Marsilio, 1992.

Villancey, Charles. *A Vindication of the Ancient History of Ireland*. Dublin: Luke White, 1786.

Villanueva, Joaquín Lorenzo. *Phœnician Ireland*. Dublin: Timms, Keene and Wakeman, 1833.

Vishnu-Purana, edited by Manmatha Nath Dutt, Calcutta: Elysium Press, 1894.

Wade, Nicholas. "English, Irish, Scots: They're All One, Genes Suggest." *The New York Times*. March 5, 2007, F1.

Waggoner, Ben. Translator. *The Hrafnista Sagas*. Berkeley, CA: Troth, 2012.

Walter, Philippe. *Tristan et Iseut. Le Porcher et la truie*. New York: Imago, 2006.

Weinstock, Jeffrey Andrew, ed. *The Ashgate Encyclopedia of Literary and Cinematic Monsters*. London: Routledge, 2014.

Wenzell, Timothy. *Emerald Green: An Ecocritical Study of Irish Literature*. Newcastle upon Tyne, UK: Cambridge Scholars, 2009.

Westmoreland, Perry L. *Ancient Greek Beliefs*. San Diego, CA: Lee and Vance, 2007.

Wheelwright, C.A., translator. *Pindar*. London: Colburn and Bentley, 1830.

Whitney, George H. *Hand-Book of Bible Geography*. New York: Carlton & Lanahan, 1871.

White, Pamela, et al. *Exploration in the World of the Middle Ages, 500-1500*. New York: Chelsea House, 2009.

Wilde, Jane. *Ancient Legends, Mystic Charms, and Superstitions of Ireland*. Mineola, NY: Dover, 2006.

Williams, Caroline A., editor. *Bridging the Early Modern Atlantic World: People, Products, and Practices on the Move.* Farnham, UK: Ashgate, 2009.

Williams, Robert. *A Biographical Dictionary of Eminent Welshmen: From the Earliest Times to the Present, and Including Every Name Connected With the Ancient History of Wales.* London: Longman, 1852.

Wilson, Daniel. *The Lost Atlantis and Other Ethnographic Studies.* New York: MacMillan, 1892.

Winter, Heinrich. "Catalan Portolan Maps and Their Place in the Total View of Cartographic Development." *Imago Mundi* 11, (1954): 1-12.

Wormell, Deborah. *Sir John Seeley and the Uses of History.* Cambridge, UK: Cambridge University Press: 1980.

Wright, Thomas. *Biographia Britannica Literaria.* London: Boughton Press, 1842.

"The Wooing of Becfola." The Celtic Literature Collective, accessed April 29, 2022. https://www.maryjones.us/ctexts/becfola.html

Yeats, William Butler. *The Wanderings of Oisin: Dramatic Sketches, Ballads & Lyrics.* London: Fisher Unwin, 1892.

Yonge, Charles Duke, trans. *The Works of Philo Judaeus.* Vol. 4. London: Henry G. Bohn, 1855.

Youngblood, Ronald. *The Book of Genesis: an Introductory Commentary.* 2nd edition. Eugene, OR: Wipf and Stock, 1999.

Ziebart, K. M. *Nicolaus Cusanus on Faith and the Intellect: A Case Study in 15th-Century Fides-Ratio Controversy.* Leiden: Brill, 2014.

Ziegler, Philip. *The Black Death.* New York: Harper, 2009.

Zissos, Andrew, ed. *A Companion to the Flavian Age of Imperial Rome.* Hoboken, NJ: Wiley, 2016.

Zumthor, Paul. "The Medieval Travel Narrative." *New Literary History* 25, no. 4 (1994): 809-824.

Index

A

A Brief Description of the Whole World, geographical reference text of unknown authorship printed in 1620, 209, 210
Ab Urbe Condita, Livy, 18
Aberconwy, Battle of, 208
About the Ocean and the Adjacent Areas, Strabo, 180
Abraham, Hebrew patriarch, 17, 175
Abzû, god of fresh water in Mesopotamian mythology, 24
Achamán, supreme god of the Guanche people of the Canary Islands, 115, 117
Acheron, principal river of Tartarus, the infernal region, 20
Acorán, Gran Canaria, 115
Acuzamil, modern Cozumel, Mexico, 210
Adam, 69, 111, 114, 126
Adamnán, abbot of Iona Abbey, 23, 51, 52, 233
Adelfio, Bishop of Tuy, 192
Adémar de Chabannes, historian and monk in the abbey of St. Cybard, France, 165
Adhan, mother of Merlin in the *Prose Brut*, 106
Adventures of Art son of Conn, 22, 24
Aeaea, mythical Greek island home to Circe, 144
Aed the Fair, chief sage of Ireland, 214
Aegira, city in the Peloponnesus, 174
Aeneas, Trojan hero, son of Trojan prince Anchises and Greek goddess Aphrodite, 106
Aeneid, Virgil, 18
Aengus the Culdee, Saint, 202
Aenon, site where John baptized believers, 20
Aeschylus, ancient Greek tragedian, 161, 246
Aethelbert of Kent, 137
Aethiopica, Marcellus, 118
Africa, xv, 73, 74, 114, 115, 117, 118, 148, 159, 170, 171, 177, 180, 182
afterlife, xii, 20, 31, 40, 48, 49, 52, 62
Agobard, Archbishop of Lyon, 193
Agricola, Gnaeus Julius, 135
ahemon, Guanche word for water, 120
Ahnenerbe, Nazi think tank, 118
Ailill Ochair Aghra, father of Maelduin, 54, 215
Aimon Kondi, indigenous South American god, 120
airgne (slaughters), 139
Akkadian Empire, Mesopotamia, 24, 237
Aksum, Ethiopian kingdom, 159
Al Bakri, Andalusian historian and geographer, 124
Alans, Germanic peoples, 154
Alcántara, Pedro de, 63

Alcuin, Northumbrian scholar and
   clergyman, 91, 92
Aldrin, Buzz, 170
Alexander III, Pope, 149, 224
Alexander romance, 152
Alexander the Great, 206
Alexander VIII, 146
Alfonso X, King of Castile, 17, 132
Algiers, 118
Allthing, Icelandic parliament, 76
Alps, 157
Amaro, Spanish saint, sailed
   across the Atlantic to an
   earthly paradise, 13, 27, 30, 69,
   128, 129, 130, 131, 132, 133,
   134, 224, 228, 246
Ambrose, Saint, Bishop of Milan,
   93, 206
Amergin, chief poet of the
   Milesians, 24, 92
America, 13, 69, 73, 116, 120, 150,
   151, 152, 155, 170, 181, 208,
   209, 210, 211, 212, 221, 239,
   240, 243, 245
*American Museum or, Universal
   Magazine*, 209
Ammianus Marcellinus, Roman
   soldier and historian, 199, 233
Ammon, ancient Egypt's king of
   the gods, 117
an da shealladh, the two sights, 68
*An Leabhar Breac. See Speckled
   Book*, medieval Irish vellum
   manuscript
Anatolia, also known as Asia
   Minor, 158
Andalusia, southern Spain, 124
Angles, Germanic peoples settled
   in Great Britain, 31, 137
Anglica Historia, Polydore Vergil,
   18

Anglo-Saxons, Germanic
   inhabitants of England, 137,
   242
Angrboða, mate of Norse trickster
   god Loki, 75
angst, xii, xiv, 80, 84, 98
Annála na gCeithre Máistrí. *See
   Annals of the Four Masters*,
   compilation of earlier annals,
   spanning from the Deluge
   (2,242 years after Creation) to
   CE 1616
Annales Cambriae, 12th-century
   Latin-language chronicles
   compiled from diverse sources
   in Dyfed, Wales, 105, 208
Annals of the Four Masters,
   compilation of earlier annals,
   spanning from the Deluge
   (2,242 years after Creation) to
   CE 1616, 175, 233
Anselm of Canterbury, Saint, 174,
   224, 228
Antipodes, parts of the earth
   diametrically opposite to
   each other, 73, 159
Antoecians, people that live under
   the same meridian but on
   opposite parallels of latitude, at
   the same north/south distance
   from the equator, 73
Antrim, Ireland, 45, 85, 143
Aodh, son of Lir, 94
Aoibh, daughter of Bodb Derg, 94
Aoife, daughter of Bodb Derg, 95
Aos Sí, supernatural race in Irish
   mythology, 85, 122, 123
Apameia, ancient city in Anatolia,
   180
Aphrodite, mythological Greek
   goddess of sexual intercourse
   and beauty, 25

Index

Apollin, name of a god that medieval Christians believed was worshipped by Muslims, 59
Apollo, Olympian god who presided over religious law, 49, 161
Apollodorus, ancient Greek author, 145
apostasy, 54, 56
Aquinas, Thomas, 81, 93
Aragón, region in Spain, 132, 136
Arawak, indigenous people of South America and the Caribbean, 120
Arbas, sea-monster described by Pliny the Elder in the *Natural History*, 78
Archangel Michael, 48
Arecibo Radio Telescope, 171
Areopagite. See Pseudo-Dionysius the Areopagite
Arfderydd, Battle of, 105, 107, 108
Argentina, 212
Argos, ancient settlement in the Peloponnese, 21, 141
Aridaeus. *See* Thespesius, character in Plutarch's *Moralia*
Aristotle, 48, 72, 123, 174
  Metaphysics, 123
  Meteorology, 72
Armoric coast, northwestern France, 107
Armstrong, Neil, 170
Around the World in Eighty Days, Jules Verne, 170
Art, son of Conn, 22, 23, 24, 52
Arthur, legendary king of the Britons, 26, 29, 108, 113, 154, 191, 210, 221, 222, 233, 234, 235, 241
Arthur, legendary king of the Britons, ancient Celtic inhabitants of Great Britain, 26
Arthuret, location in Cumberland, England, 106
Asia, 38, 114, 128, 129, 130, 147, 149, 151, 152
Assyrians, 24
Asturian monarchy, 13
Asturias, region in northern Spain, 135, 136, 225
Atala, one of the seven regions of Patala in Hindu cosmology, 116
Ater. *See* Achamán, supreme god of the Guanche people of the Canary Islands
Ati, indigenous people of the Philippines, 170
Atlantic, xi, xii, xiii, xiv, xv, 10, 11, 12, 13, 14, 15, 19, 21, 22, 23, 24, 25, 26, 27, 28, 29, 30, 31, 32, 33, 34, 35, 36, 37, 38, 39, 40, 41, 42, 43, 44, 46, 47, 48, 50, 51, 52, 53, 54, 55, 56, 57, 65, 67, 71, 73, 74, 75, 76, 77, 78, 79, 80, 81, 82, 84, 85, 90, 93, 95, 96, 97, 98, 101, 103, 107, 108, 112, 113, 116, 117, 118, 120, 122, 123, 124, 125, 126, 128, 129, 130, 132, 134, 135, 136, 139, 140, 141, 143, 144, 147, 148, 149, 152, 153, 155, 156, 157, 158, 160, 161, 162, 163, 164, 165, 169, 171, 172, 173, 174, 176, 177, 178, 179, 180, 181, 182, 183, 184, 185, 186, 187, 188, 189, 191, 194, 195, 196, 197, 198, 199, 200, 201, 204, 205, 207, 208, 209, 214, 215, 216, 217, 218, 220, 223, 224, 225, 227, 228, 229, 230, 238, 239, 244, 247

Atlantis, 116, 117, 118, 119, 120, 169, 172, 173, 174, 175, 176, 177, 180, 181, 239, 243, 245, 247
Atlas, Catalan (1375), 220
Atlas, first king of Atlantis, 173, 182
*Atl*as, Greek word, 116
Atlas, Mount, 115, 117
Atlas, Titan condemned to hold up the heavens for eternity, 115, 117
Attila, 25
Augustine of Hippo, Saint, 63, 67, 93, 126, 155, 174, 199, 216, 228
Augustine of Kent, Bishop, 137
Aurelius Ambrosius, 140
Aures Mountains, 118
Avalon, 26, 113, 221, 238
axis mundi, 115
Aymara, indigenous people of the central Andes, 170
Aztecs, 116, 245

B

Ba'al Hammon, Chief god of Carthage, 178
Babylon, 37, 65, 130
Babylonian Captivity, 17
Babylonian Empire, 237
beliefs, 24, 37
Bachofen, Johann Jakob, 7
Bacon, Francis, English philosopher and statesman, 5
Baile in Scáil, (The Phantom's Frenzy), echtrae, 43
Bajau, indigenous people of the Philippines, 170
Bakunin, Michael, 4
Balboa, Vasco Núñez de, 149, 150, 151

Balder, Norse god son of the main god Odin and his wife Frigg, 185
Baldr, son of Norse god Odin, 75
Ballafletcher, cup of, 85
Baltic, 30, 71, 157
Banier, abbé Antoine, 5
Bannavem Taburniae, Irish village, 92
Bantry Bay, County Cork, Ireland, 176
baptism, 19, 157, 224
Baralides, holy woman in the fictional nunnery Flor de Dueñas, 133, 134
Barlow, Roger, 221
Barra, island in the Outer Hebrides, 33
Barrid, Saint, 202
Barros, Juan de, 115
Bartolomé de las Casas, fray, 115, 152
Bassarides, lost play by Aeschylus, 161
Bathsheba, 63
Bāxiān, the Eight Immortals, 28
Bé Chuma, sorceress descended from the Tuatha Dé Danann, 51
Becfola. *See* Wooing of Becfola
Becuma, 22, 23
Bede, The Venerable, 206
Beeldenstorm, the Storm of Images, 89
Bellum arterid, also known as the Battle of Arfderydd, 105
Benedict of Nursia, 129
Benedict XII, Pope, 206
Bentayga, sacred mountain of the Guanches, 120
Beowulf, 30
Berbers, 118

Berkeley, George, Bishop of Cloyne, 101
Berlin, 119
Bernáldez, Andrés, 115, 152
Bethlehem, 94
Bible, 20, 25, 48, 63, 68, 91, 120, 123, 130, 153, 154, 155, 156, 157, 158, 159, 160, 171, 175, 187, 195, 205, 229, 234, 246
Binn Ghulbain, 194
Birren, wife of Bith, 175
Bith, Noah's wayward son, 175, 176
Black Book of Camarthen, 104
Black Death, 86, 87, 88, 89, 247
Black Sea, xiii
Blemii, 58
blood-feud, 29, 30, 216, 217
Boadag, Celtic king of the otherworld, 44
Bodb Derg (King Bove), 94
Boeotia, region of central Greece, 49
Bolivia, 147
Bologna, Italy, 87
Bontier, Pedro, 115
Book of Enoch, 48
Book of Fermoy, 22
Book of Invasions, 146, 174
Book of Kells, 213, 214
Book of Leinster, 194
Book of Litanies, 202
Book of Revelation, 133
Book of Settlements, 33, 243
Book of the Dun Cow, 51, 146, 148, 194
Borja, Francisco de, 63
Borrhaus, Martin, 89
Bors, knight in Arthurian legend, 190
Bosch, Hieronymus, 111, 112
Bosphorus, 147

Bougie (Béjaïa), Algeria, 118
Boyne, Battle of the, 146
Boynemouth, County Meath, Ireland, 186
Bran mac Febail, 3, 13, 30, 44, 45, 57, 80, 131, 141, 163, 202, 219, 224, 241, 244
Brân, gigantic Celtic deity, King of Britain, 13, 160, 161, 162, 163, 164, 165, 166
Brânwen, Brân's sister, 162
Breiðafjörður, bay in western Iceland, 83
Brendan, 9, 10, 14, 27, 30, 32, 36, 41, 45, 51, 65, 69, 79, 80, 126, 134, 140, 166, 186, 201, 202, 203, 204, 205, 206, 207, 214, 220, 221, 223, 234, 241, 242, 245
Breogán, king in Spain, ancestor of the Gaels, father of Ith, 121, 122, 123, 124
Breogán's Tower. See Tower of Brigantia
Briareus, Greek mythological giant with a hundred arms and fifty heads, 182
Briccne, pernicious member of the Dubcluain church community, 215
Brigantium, A Coruña, 191
Brigid, pagan goddess, 21
Bristol, England, 220
Britain, 39, See Great Britain
British Isles, 14, 30, 38, 73, 92, 93, 122, 140, 157, 178, 182, 194
British Museum, 214
Britons, ancient Celtic inhabitants of Great Britain, 119, 182, 209, 243
Brittany, northwestern France, 14, 183
Brittonic, xv, 93, 105

Bronze Age, 178
Brú na Bóinne, divine youth Oengus's mansion, 95
Brut y Tywysogion, Chronicle of the Princes of Wales, 208, 211
Brutus of Troy, mythical founder and first king of Britain, 106
Bubi, Equatorial African people, 170
Buile Shuibhne (The Madness of Shuibhne), 104
Bura, city in the Peloponnesus, 174
Burchard of Worms, Bishop of Worms and compiler of canon law texts, 93
Burgos, Spain, 129
Buried Giant of Clonmacnoise, 47
Byblos, city in Lebanon, 161
Byrne, Aisling, xv, 39, 45, 130

C

Cabot, Sebastian, 221
Cadamosto, Aloisio de, 115
Cádiz, Spain, 135, 180, 182
Cadwaladr ap Cadwallon, early medieval king of Gwynedd, Wales, 106
Caesar, Julius, 135, 183, 237
Calderón de la Barca, Pedro, 82
Caledonian Forest, 106
Calpurnius, father of St. Patrick, 92
Calypso, Greek mythological nymph who lived on the island of Ogygia, 144
Cambro-Norman invasion, 187
Camlann, Battle of, 537 CE, 108
Campbell, Joseph, xv, 1, 4, 81, 204
Canary Islands, xiii, xv, 111, 112, 113, 115, 116, 118, 119, 127, 174, 185, 233, 244
Cantabria, region of northern Spain, 225
Cantigas de Santa María, 132
Caribbean, 149, 152
Carlisle, Cumberland, England, 106
Carnagh East, geographical center of Ireland, 39
Carta Marina (1516), Martin Waldseemüller, 149, 150
Carta Marina (1539), Olaus Magnus, 77, 78
Cartas de Relación, Christopher Columbus, 155
Carthage, 48, 178
Carthaginian navigators, 178
Carthaginians, 114
Carwanolow, Cumberland, England, 105
Caspian Sea, 71, 72
Cassirer, Ernst, 8, 10, 235
Castile, Spain, 17, 136
Cath Maige Itha. *See* Mag Itha, battle of
Cath Maige Tured. *See* Mag Tured, battle of
catha (battles), 139
Cathay. *See* China
Catholic, 9, 61, 62, 66, 89, 129, 130, 146, 155, 235, 246
Cattigara, name given by Ptolemy to a port city on the easternmost shore of the Indian Ocean, 151
Cauldron of Renovation, 161
cauldrons, 161, 162, 163, 164
celestial spheres, 48
Céli Dé ascetics, 35
Celtic Church, 48
Celtic Crescent, xii, 15, 28, 137
Celtic cultural substratum, 135, 138

Index

Celtic culture, 13, 68, 119, 134, 147, 162, 214, 228
Celts, 24, 40, 44, 107, 130, 131, 135, 136, 147, 217, 219, 228, 229, 233, 240, 241
Cenophales, creatures with men's bodies and dogs' heads, 58
Centaurs, 58
Ceridwen, enchantress of Welsh medieval legend, 93
Cessair, granddaughter of Noah and mythical leader of the first settlers of Ireland, 175
Ceto, primordial sea-goddess, 145
Chamacoco, indigenous people of Paraguay, 170
Chanson de Roland. *See Song of Roland*, 11th century French epic poem
Charlemagne, 86
Charon, mythological boatman of Hades, 20
Chemnicensis, Andreas Fabricius, 89
Children of Lir, 93, 95, 97, 98, 99, 100, 101, 102, 103, 132, 163, 246
China, 58, 149, 150, 159
Chinese Daoist tradition, 28
Christ, 48, 62, 82, 88, 97, 114, 143, 164, 165, 166, 167, 187, 213, 214
Christendom, xii, 59, 114, 136, 149, 154
Christianity, xii, 19, 24, 29, 30, 31, 32, 37, 38, 48, 52, 56, 77, 85, 88, 90, 125, 129, 135, 136, 137, 157, 158, 166, 167, 170, 176, 205, 214, 215, 216, 217, 222, 224, 229, 239
Christianization, xii, 41, 42, 46, 166, 175, 176, 222, 244
Chronicon, Otto of Freising, 149
Chrysaor, brother of Pegasus, 145

Church of St. Denis, 86
Ciabhán, human lover of the goddess Clídna who brought her to Ireland., 51
Cicero, 48, 124
Circe, Greek mythological enchantress and minor goddess, 53, 54, 143, 185
Clairvaux, Bernard of, 224
Clanna Baiscne, one of the two great clans of the Fianna, 194
Clídna, Irish goddess of love and beauty, 51
Cloud of Unknowing, 81
Clovis, Frankish king, 189
Clyde River, 106
Coaspim River, 58
Codex Alcobacensis, 129
Codex Theodosianus, 183
Coel Hen Godebog. See Coelings
Coelings, British clan, 106
Colaeus of Samos, 144, 177
collective conscience, 14, 40
collective consciousness, 14, 52, 53, 86
collective identity, 2, 17
Colossians, 62
Columba, Saint, 23, 24, 36, 125, 233
Columbanus, Saint, early medieval Irish missionary, founder of monasteries, 35
Columbcille, Saint, early medieval Irish saint and seer, 186, 187
Columbus, 69, 126, 152, 155, 181, 206, 209, 210, 237, 239
Coman of Kinvara, early medieval Irish saint, 56
Comestor, Peter, 206
Commentarii de Bello Gallico, 183
Compert Con Culainn, Birth of Cú Chulainn, 44

composite ethos, 165
Compostela, Santiago de, 129, 136
Comte, Auguste, 6
Concealed Island, also known as San Borondón, 125, 127
Concluding Unscientific Postscript to Philosophical Fragments, Kierkegaard, 90, 240
Conn, father of Art, 22, 23, 24, 52, 222
Conn, grandfather of Cormac mac Airt, 85
Conn, son of Lir, 94
Connacht, Ireland, 55
Connall ua Corra, landowner of Connacht, 55
Connla, hero of the *Echtra Condla*, 44, 219, 224
Constantine, Roman Emperor, 135, 159
contested space, xi, 29, 37, 98, 99, 136
Conti, Natale, 5
Contra Gentiles, 81
Contra Gentiles, Thomas Aquinas, 66
Contributions to the Analysis of Sensation, 6
Copernicus, Nicolaus, 48
coracle, 10, 23, 187
Corbenic, castle housing the Holy Grail in Arthurian legend, 191
Corcomroe, Chorco Modhruadh, in today's County Clare, Ireland, 215
Cormac mac Airt, mythical Irish king, 51, 84, 131, 163, 194
Cornwall, county in southwestern England, 119, 178
Cosmas Indicopleustes, 158, 159, 235
cosmology, 23, 87, 102, 114

County Roscommon, Ireland, 39
County Westmeath, Ireland, 95
courtly love, 189, 190
Covered Sea, 132
Crates of Mallus, 73, 74
Creation, 12, 17, 60, 61, 67, 91, 103, 125, 156, 158, 188, 206
Crimthann Cass, King of Connacht, 43
Crimthann mac Aedh, 47
Crimthann, fox, original name of Saint Columba, 24
Critias, Plato, 120, 145, 172, 243
Croagh Patrick, 21
Crom Cruach, Celtic god, 41
Crónica de Guinea, 115
Crusades, 88, 149, 235, 238, 239
Cruthin, a people of early medieval Ireland, 143
Cú Chulainn, hero and demigod in the Ulster Cycle of Irish mythology, 93, 157, 162
Cuba, xi, 152, 155
cuélebres, mythical Galician dragons, 122, 132
Culhwch ac Olwen, giant, also the title of a Welsh medieval prose work considered one of the earliest extant Arthurian romances, 162
Cumbria, county in northwest England (Cumberland), 105, 106
cura de los Palacios. *See* Bernáldez, Andrés
currach, 15, 56, 188, 228
Cush, biblical land, 130
Cuthbert, Anglo-Saxon saint of the early Northumbrian church, 92
Cylfeirdd, Merlin's companions, 208

Index

Cymraeg, Brittonic subgroup Celtic language of Wales, 105
cywydd, Welsh traditional poem, 208

D

d'Ailly, Pierre, 206
d'Arbois de Jubainville, H., xv, 145, 236
Dafydd ab Owain, Prince of Gwynedd, Wales, 208
Dagda, high god of pagan Ireland, 51, 162
Dáire, ruler of Tír Tairngire, 52
Dál nAraidi, kingdom or confederation of tribes in northeastern Ireland, 104
Dalorto, Angelino, Italian-Majorcan cartographer, 220
Damascene, John (John of Damascus), Christian monk, priest and apologist, 206
Dante, 41, 87, 161, 234
Dardanus, son of Zeus and the Pleiad Electra, 145
Darien Mountains, Panama, 149
Daughters of the American Revolution, 208
David, King of Israel, 17, 63, 190
De Dea Syria. See *Syrian Goddess, The*, Lucian
De Docta Ignorantia, Nicholas of Cusa, 81
De Falsa Sapientia, Lactantius, 159
De genio Socratis, part of Plutarch's *Moralia*, 49
De Iside et Osiride, Plutarch, 172
De Originibus Americanis, Georgius Hornius, 209
De re publica, Cicero, 48

De secretis mulierum, Pseudo-Albertus Magnus, 200
De Sera Numinis Vindicta. See *On the Late Vengeance of the Deity*, Plutarch
Delaware Treaty of St. Mary's, 1818, 213
Delle sette isole Canarie, e delli loro costume, Aloisio de Cadamosto, 115
Demar, mythical Atlantic island, 219
Demetrius, ancient Greek traveler in Scotland, 182
Democritus, Greek pre-Socratic philosopher, 2, 63
Denis of Paris, 161
Dermot, son of Aedh Sláine, 47
Derry, Ireland, 45, 143
Descriptio Mappae Mundi (1128–1129), Hugh of Saint Victor, 58
Detienne, Marcel, Belgian historian and Hellenist, 6, 236
Deucalion, mythical king of Phthia and son of the Titan Prometheus, 145
Devenish Island, island in Lower Lough Erne, County Fermanagh, Northern Ireland, 47
Devil, 55, 82
Devon, county in southwestern England, 119
Dewey, John, American philosopher and psychologist, 91, 236
Diarmait mac Aeda Sláine, High King of Ireland, 47
Diarmait mac Cerbaill, mythical High King of Ireland, 176
Dicuil, early medieval Irish monk and geographer, 34

Ding Dong Mines, Cornwall, 38
Diodorus Siculus, Greek historian, 135
Dionysius of Halicarnassus, Greek historian, flourished during the reign of Emperor Augustus, 145
Dionysus, Greek god of wine and pleasure, 161
Dis, Celtic god of the underworld, sometimes associated with the Roman god of the underworld Dīs Pater or Rex Infernus, 40
Divine Comedy, 87
Divine Providence, 7
Diwrnach the Irishman, owner of a magical cauldron, 162
dogma, 36, 46, 61, 66, 80, 98, 102, 114, 155, 156, 157, 188, 204, 223
Don Quixote, 18, 27
Donn-bó, young Irish warrior whose decapitated head sang after the Battle of Allen, 722 CE, 161
Donnchad, brother of Fiacha, 186
Doré, Gustave, 87
Down, Ireland, 143
doxastic system, 36
doxastic thought, 36
Dracaena draco. *See* drago, autochthonous tree of the Canary Islands
drago, autochthonous tree of the Canary Islands, 112
Dravidian, languages of southern India, 116
Dream of Oengus, 95
druids, 4, 23, 37, 138, 147, 161, 205, 215, 218, 222, 227
Dubcluain, Ireland, 54, 215
Dublin, Ireland, 186
Duff, King of Scotland, 85, 86
Dún na mBarc, Bantry Bay, County Cork, Ireland, 175
Durkheim, Émile, French sociologist, 2, 36, 236
dwarfs, 26, 196
Dyrnwch the Giant, owner of a magical cauldron in the Thirteen Treasures of the Island of Britain, 162

E

Earl of Inchiquin, 175
Early Modern Irish or Gaeilge Chlasaiceach, language, 22
East Anglia, 31
Easter, Christian Resurrection Sunday, 48, 203
Eastern Sea, 28
Ebrauc (Modern York), 106
Ecclesia, 85
Echtra Condla, 43, 219
Echtra Cormaic maic Airt i Tir Tairngiri, 43, 51
Echtra Mac nEchach Muidmedóin, 43
Echtrae Airt meic Cuinn, 52
Echtrae Laegairi maic Crimthann, 43
Echtrae Laegairi, Laegaire's Expedition, 43
Echtrae mac nEchach Mugmedoin, 43
Echtrae Nerai, Adventure of Nera, 43
echtrai, 22, 23, 27, 34, 35, 37, 41, 42, 43, 44, 45, 46, 49, 50, 51, 52, 53, 64, 103, 131, 134, 138, 160, 166, 193, 223, 224, 228, 229
Ectra Airt maic Cuinn, 43
Ecumene, 72, 73, 74

Eden, 69, 112, 126, 128, 130, 153, 155, 172, 191, 236
Edict of Milan (313), 135
effigies, 77, 85, 87
Egypt, 20, 161, 172, 246
Egyptian Maid, 191
Eight Immortals, legendary characters in Chinese mythology, 28
Einstein, Albert, 192
El Cid, legendary Castilian warrior, 146
El divino Orfeo (1663), 82
El Hierro, island in the Canary Archipelago, 124, 127
Electra, Pleiad star-nymph of Mount Saon, loved Zeus and bore him two sons, Dardanus and Iasion, 146
Eliade, Mircea, xv, 4, 19
Elijah, biblical prophet and miracle worker, 48, 187
Elysian Fields, ancient Greek conception of the afterlife, 21, 141
Elysian Plain. See Elysian Fields, ancient Greek conception of the afterlife
Elysium. See Elysian Fields, ancient Greek conception of the afterlife
Emain Ablach, mythical island paradise and home of Manannán mac Lir, 45, 57
Emania, palace residence of the ancient kings of Ulster, 94
Emrys Wledig, also known as Ambrosius Aurelianus, High King of the Britons after Vortigern, 208

Enbarr, magical horse ridden by Usheen and Niam over the Atlantic, 195
Enda of Aran, warrior-king of Oriel, in Ulster, later becomes saint, 202
England, 23, 104, 105, 106, 126, 137, 146, 194, 210, 211, 219, 237, 242
English Channel, 38
English philosopher and statesman, 230
Enkidu, in the *Epic of Gilgamesh*, wartime comrade and friend of Gilgamesh, king of Uruk, 106
Enlightenment, 6, 10, 12, 16, 153, 240
Enoch, biblical patriarch, father of Methuselah, 187
Enyo, one of the three Graiae, 145
Eoghan, Irish lineage, 204
Eóghanachta, southern Irish dynasty, 215
Ephorus of Cyme, ancient Greek historian, 135
epic literature, 139
Epicurus, ancient Greek philosopher, 49
epistemic feedback, 16
Epistola ad Mellitum, 137
Er, evildoer in Plato's *Republic*, 48
Er, Myth of, 49
Eratosthenes, 74, 135, 161
Erin. See Ireland
Eriugena, John Scotus, 206
Escorant, King of Sarras in Arthurian Grail legend, 191
Espinosa, Alonso de, 115
ethea, xi, 24, 36, 41, 53, 101, 128, 153, 165, 177, 180
Ethiopia, 158
Ethiopian devil, 202, 203

Etymologies, 112
Euaemon, mythical king of Atlantis, 120
Eudoxos of Cnidos, Greek astronomer, 48
Eudoxos of Kazikus, ancient Greek sailor, 180, 181
Euphrates, longest river in western Asia, 130
Eurasian continent, 21
Euripides, tragedian of classical Greece, 182
Europe, xiii, xv, 13, 19, 20, 27, 28, 31, 33, 37, 38, 39, 59, 60, 68, 71, 98, 99, 114, 134, 135, 139, 146, 147, 157, 159, 160, 162, 166, 171, 178, 182, 193, 197, 202, 207, 218, 219, 228, 229, 236, 240, 242, 244, 245
Euryale, Gorgon, 145
Eustache the Monk, 193
Euthymenes of Massalia, ancient Greek explorer, 177
evangelists, 86
Evans, John, 211
Eve, biblical first woman, 111, 114
Evnissyen, half-brother of Brân, 162, 163
Extremadura, region in Spain, 135
Ezequiel, Hebrew prophet, 19

F

Fáil, the stone of destiny, 85
Fair Green Isles of the Ocean, 140
fairies, 26, 85, 189
Fang, Equatorial African people, 170
Faroe Islands, 33, 183
Fauna Suecica, Carl Linnaeus, 78
Feni, tribe to which U sheen belonged, 195, 200
Fenian Cycle of Irish mythology, 13, 193
Fenians. *See* Fianna, bands of warrior-hunters in early medieval Ireland
Fer Doirich, druid, 194
Fernández de Enciso, Martín, 16th century Spanish geographer and conquistador, 221, 237
Fernández de Oviedo, Gonzalo, 16th century Spanish soldier and historian, 152, 153
Feyerabend, Sigmund, 16th century Lutheran theologian, 89
Fiacha, oppressor of the men of Ross, 186, 188
Fiachra, son of Lir, 94
Fianna, bands of warrior-hunters in early medieval Ireland, 13, 194
Fibonacci numbers, 216
Fichte, Johann Gottlieb, German philosopher, 7
Field, The (1990), 52
filid, professional, elite poets in ancient Ireland, 161
Finaeus, Orontius, also known as Oronce Finé, French cartographer and mathematician, 151
Finis Terrae, 40
Finn MacCoul and the Bent Grey Lad, 85
Finnian of Clonard, early Irish monastic saint, 56
Finnlug Ua Alta, father of Saint Brendan the Navigator, 204
Fintan. *See* Fintan mac Bóchra, wise seer who accompanied Noah's granddaughter Cessair

to Ireland and only Irishman to survive the biblical Flood
Fintan mac Bóchra, wise seer who accompanied Noah's granddaughter Cessair to Ireland and only Irishman to survive the biblical Flood, 175
Fionn mac Cumhaill, father of U sheen, 194
Fionnuala, daughter of Lir, 94
Fir Bolg, mythical fourth group of people to settle in Ireland, 175
Firth of Forth, estuary in Scotland, 126
Five Lugaids, The, adventure (echtrae) of the five sons of Dáire, 43
fjörulalli, Icelandic sea-monsters, 83
Fled Bricrenn ocus Loinges mac nDuil Dermait, Exile of Dóel Dermait's Sons, 44
flood narratives, 5, 19, 120, 145, 172, 173, 175, 176, 236
Flor de Dueñas, fictional nunnery, 133
Florida, 152, 181, 242
folktale, 32, 149
Fomorians, race of monstrous giants in Irish mythology, 139, 146
Fonseca, Cristóbal de, Spanish writer and mystic, 63
Fontenelle, Bernard de, French scientist and writer, 5, 6
Forfess Fer Fálgae, The Siege of the Men of Fálgae, 44
Forménus, mythical hermit king of Thrace, 66
Fortunate Isles, (Canary Islands), 112, 113

Fountain of Youth, 69, 126, 152, 153, 181, 209
frame-tales, 42
France, xiii, 38, 71, 129, 146, 163, 184, 190, 194
Franco, Francisco, 119
Freud, Sigmund, 3
Freyr, Norse god son of the sea god Njörd, 185
Frigg, Norse goddess, 75
Fuathan, malevolent spirits, 85
Fuente Clara, fountain in the *Periplus of Amaro*, 131
Fursa, early medieval Irish monk, 35
Fursey. *See* Fursa, early medieval Irish monk

G

Gabon, 178
Gaidiar, Son of Mannanán mac Lir, 51
Gailenga, Irish tribe, 197
Galahad, knight of King Arthur's Round Table, 60, 190, 191
Galatae. *See* Celts
Galicia, region in northwestern Spain, 13, 38, 122, 134, 135, 136, 191, 192, 225, 236
Galileo Galilei, 230
Gallaeci, Celtic peoples of Galicia, 225
Gallaecus, Decimus Junius Brutus, Roman general, 40
Galway, Ireland, 39, 143
Gaokerena, tree of immortality, 20
García de Salazar, Lope, 221
Garden of Earthly Delights, 111
Gautreks Saga, 76
Gavra, Battle of, 195, 198, 200

Gavran ab Aeddan, legendary Welsh voyager, 140, 208
Geitey, islet in Iceland, 83
General Estoria, Alfonso X, 17, 235
Genesis, 67, 68, 106, 120, 130, 247
Geographica, Strabo, 38, 73, 135, 173, 245
Georgia Compact of 1802, 213
Gerard of Wales, Cambro-Norman archdeacon and historian, 147, 199
Germany, 71, 164, 201
Gihon, biblical river, 130
Gilgamesh, xi, 20, 97, 106, 173, 237
Ginnungagap, Norse void between the opposite fire and ice worlds, 74
Giraldus Cambrensis. *See* Gerard of Wales
glacial period, 173
God, xi, 9, 20, 25, 29, 30, 33, 41, 42, 51, 56, 61, 62, 63, 64, 65, 67, 69, 80, 81, 82, 84, 85, 86, 88, 89, 91, 92, 93, 98, 103, 107, 111, 123, 124, 129, 130, 131, 137, 154, 156, 165, 181, 182, 187, 188, 191, 203, 205, 206, 207, 212, 227, 233, 237
Godric of Finchale, English hermit, merchant and saint, 92, 163
Goibniu, Irish smith-god, 162
Golden Fleece, 204
Gómara, Francisco López de, 16th century Spanish historian, 115
Gorgons, three mythological monster sisters, 145
Görres, Johann Joseph, 7
Goths, 40, 121
Graiae (Graeae), three sisters in Greek mythology who shared one eye and one tooth, 145

Grail, 85, 191
Gran Canaria, xi, 115, 117, 119
Grand Alliance, 146
Great Britain, xi, 73, 107, 178, 179, 185, 210
Great Isle of the Solstice, xiv, 191, 192, 193, 229
Great Orme Mines, Wales, 38
Greeks, 6, 38, 65, 71, 76, 117, 140, 142, 144, 172, 173, 206, 238
Green Island of the West, 185
Green Islands of the Current, 140
Green Isle, xiv
Green Isles of Floods, 140
Green Isles of the Ocean, 208
Green Meadows of Enchantment, 164
Green Woman, Celtic symbolic creature possibly symbolizing the renewal of nature in spring, 47
Gregory of Nyssa, Saint, 68
Gregory the Great, Pope, 137, 216, 245
Grimm brothers, German academicians and publishers of folklore, 7
Guadalquivir, river in Spain, 135
Guadiana, river in Spain, 135
Guanches, 114, 115, 116, 117, 118, 119, 120
Guatemala, 147
Guaycuru, indigenous people of the Gran Chaco region of South America, 170
Guigemar, Breton lai by Marie de France, 60, 189, 190
Guillaume de Deguileville, French Cistercian monk and writer, 82
Guingamor, Breton lai by Marie de France, 189

Gwales, modern Grassholm Island in Wales, 163, 164
Gwasawg, character associated with Merlin's legend and the Battle of Arfderydd, 108
Gwenddoleu ap Ceidio, British warlord, 106
Gwenddydd, Merlin's twin sister, 106, 107, 108
Gwrgi, British warlord, 106
Gwynedd, kingdom in northwestern Wales, 106, 140, 208
Gwynedd, Owain, father of Prince Madoc of Wales, 208, 245

H

Hades, 40, 185
Hafgufa, medieval Icelandic sea-monster, 78
Hairy Man, Icelandic supernatural creature, 83
Ham, son of Noah, 114, 153
Hamelmannus, Hermannus, 89
Hand-Book of Bible Geography (1871), 157
Hanno, Carthaginian navigator, 178, 209
Happy Other World, 81, 219
Harari, Yuval Noah, 9, 10, 238
Harlech, seaside village in northern Wales, 163, 164
Havilah, biblical land and people, 130
Heaven, 24, 37, 48, 50, 51, 55, 56, 115, 117, 219, 228, 237
Hebrus, present day Maritza River in the Balkans, 161
Hecataeus of Miletus, 71, 72
Hegelian dialectics, 76
Hel, Norse goddess of death, 75

Hel, Norse world of the dead, 74, 75
Helica, city in the Peloponnesus, 174
Hell, 48, 50, 51, 55, 56, 75, 203, 237
Hellanicus of Lesbos, 173
Hellenic archetypal material, 148
Henry II, King of England, 199
Henry the Navigator, King of Portugal, 124
Henry VIII, King of England, 221
Herbert, Thomas, English traveler and historian, 209
Herodotus, 5, 6, 72, 115, 117, 135, 152, 173, 177, 207, 233, 238, 240, 243, 245
Hesiod, 21, 38, 115, 140, 144, 145, 173, 238
Works and Days, 21, 173, 238
Hesperides, Garden of the, 179
Hesperides, goddess nymphs of the night, 115, 145
Himantipodes, man-like creatures who walk with their feet upside-down, 58
Himilco, Carthaginian navigator, 178, 179
Himmler, Heinrich, 118, 119, 243
Hispania, 158
Historia Brittonum, Nennius, 146
Historia del primer descubrimiento y Conquista de las Canarias, 115
Historia General y Natural de las Indias, Gonzalo Fernández de Oviedo, 152
Historia regum Britanniae, Geoffrey of Monmouth, 14
Historical Cycle of Irish mythology, 47
Historie of Cambria, David Powell, 211

history, xv, 5, 10, 12, 13, 14, 15, 16, 17, 18, 33, 87, 106, 119, 121, 146, 147, 152, 161, 169, 173, 174, 175, 176, 199, 220, 228, 238, 242
History of the Indies, Bartolomé de las Casas, 174
History of Wales, Humphrey Llwyd, 211
Hitchhiker's Guide to the Galaxy, Douglas Adams, 171
Hjortspring boat grave, 31
Hockerus Osnaburgensis, Jodocus, 89
Hölderlin, Friedrich, German poet and philosopher, 7, 238
Holly King, Celtic personification of winter, 132
Holy Book, 115, 156, 157, 160, 205
Holy Grail, 27, 242
Holy Island, 126
Holy Land, 220
Homer, 5, 21, 38, 141, 143, 144, 185, 238
Homo sapiens, 9
Homo silvester, 106
Horai, Japanese island of eternal youth, 28
horizon of the fabulous, 169, 170, 171
Hornius, Georgius, German historian and philosopher, 209
Horsehair Grani (Grani Horsehair), a manifestation of Odin, 76
House of Glass, 140
Hrothgar's hall, great mead-hall in *Beowolf* named Herot, 30
Hugh of Saint Victor, Saxon canon regular and prominent theologian, 58

Hume, David, Scottish Enlightenment philosopher, 101
Huns, 154
Huon of Bordeaux, main character in a 13th century French epic poem, 85
Hurmuz, Zoroastrian creator god, 20
Huth, Otto, German archaeologist, theologian and ethnologist, 119
Hvergelmir, well in Niflheim, 75
Hy-Brasil, xiv, 219, 220, 221, 222, 223, 224, 225, 237
Hydrolatry, the worship of water, 19
Hymir's cup, Norse mythological brewing-cauldron, 84

I

Iberian Peninsula, xv, 14, 23, 38, 57, 135, 136, 148, 178, 224
Iceland, 33, 34, 35, 36, 83, 183
Icelandic sagas, 33
Icthyophages, eel-eaters in the *Descriptio Mappae Mundi*, 58
identity, 13, 18, 34, 53, 54, 56, 57, 58, 59, 60, 87, 129, 146, 147, 161, 176, 193, 196, 197, 198, 199, 200, 210, 223, 224
Igours. *See* Issedones
Iliad, Homer, 38
Imago Mundi, 206, 234, 239, 247
Imbolc, pagan festival, 21
Immortal Isle, 28
Immram Brain maic Febail. See Voyage of Bran mac Febail
Immram curaig Maíle Dúin, 42, 214
Immram curaig Úa Corra. See Voyage of the Sons of Uí Chorra

Immram Snédgusa ocus Maic Ríagla. See *Voyage of Snédgus and Mac Ríagla*
immrama, 23, 27, 31, 34, 35, 37, 41, 42, 43, 44, 45, 46, 49, 50, 51, 52, 53, 54, 55, 64, 103, 130, 134, 135, 138, 139, 145, 157, 160, 166, 176, 187, 192, 193, 202, 204, 214, 216, 218, 223, 224, 228, 229
in mari vitae, 82
India, xi, 58, 115, 116, 149, 150, 158, 180
Indian Love Call, song by Slim Whitman (1952), 171
Indian Ocean, 116, 159, 180, 238
Indian Removal Act of 1830, 213
Indian Trade and Intercourse Act of 1790, 212
indigenous Americans, 156
Indochina, 151
Inferno, Dante, 161
Inis Fedaig, otherworld isle, 47
Inis Glora, Irish islet, 89, 93, 95
Introduction to the History of Great Britain, James Macpherson, 185
Iona, small island in Scotland's Inner Hebrides, 125
Ireland, xi, xii, xiii, 3, 13, 19, 21, 22, 23, 24, 31, 32, 33, 34, 38, 39, 41, 42, 43, 44, 46, 47, 51, 52, 55, 57, 73, 86, 92, 95, 98, 104, 105, 121, 122, 123, 124, 126, 132, 139, 143, 144, 146, 147, 148, 157, 161, 162, 163, 166, 167, 171, 174, 175, 176, 177, 178, 183, 185, 186, 187, 193, 194, 196, 197, 198, 199, 200, 201, 204, 205, 209, 214, 215, 216, 218, 219, 220, 221, 223, 224, 229, 235, 236, 237, 238, 239, 241, 243, 244, 246
Irish DNA profile, 147
Irish Mythological Cycle, 93, 195
Irish Protestants, 146
Irish Sea, 164, 166
Iron Age, 19, 31, 125
Irrus Domnannthe, bay in Ireland, 95
Irving, Washington, United States short-story writer and diplomat, 152
Isidore of Seville, Saint, 112, 113, 159, 199, 206, 239, 241
Isla Encubierta, 124, 128, 222, 223, 225
Isla Sirena, also known as San Borondón, 127
Islam, 59, 115, 240
Island of Joy, 45, 57, 143
Island of Paradise, 203
Island of Women, 131, 142, 143
Islands of the Blessed. *See* Isles of the Blest
Islario general de todas las islas del mundo, Alonso de Santa Cruz, 221
Isle of Lesbos, 161
Isle of Lewis, Scotland, 33
Isle of Maidens, 97
Isle of Man, 45, 85, 125
Isle of the Blessed, 144, 221, 223
Isle of the Blest, xiv, 25, 27, 41, 69, 126, 139
Isle of the Sirens, 144
Issedones, ancient people of central Asia, 207
Isthmus of Panama, 149
Italy, 38, 129, 220, 235, 240
Ith, prince of Hispania, son of Breogán, 27, 121, 122, 123, 124, 193, 229

J

James II, King of England, 146
Japan, 28, 149, 150
Japheth, son of Noah, 114, 153
Jasconius, island, 203
Jefferson, Thomas, 211
Jerome, Saint, 174
Jerusalem, 130, 133, 149, 205, 241
Jesus, 46, 61, 62, 68, 69, 81, 85, 91, 191, 195, 216
Jewish apocryphal literature, 48
Jews, 87
Job, principal character of the *Book of Job* in the Bible, 25, 61, 63, 65, 84
Jocelyn of Furness, English Cistercian hagiographer, 105
John II, King of Portugal, 125
John of Fordun, Scottish historian, 105
John the Baptist, 51
Jonah, biblical prophet, 25
Joseph, Frank, United States author and editor, 116
Joshua, leader of the Israelite tribes after the death of Moses, 63
Journey to the Center of the Earth, Jules Verne, 170
Juan de la Cruz, 63
Juan de los Ángeles, 63
Juba II, King of Mauritania, 112, 179
Judas Iscariot, 203
Jung, Carl, Swiss psychiatrist, 3
Justus of Beauvais, Christian martyr whose head continued to speak after decapitation, 161

K

Kabyles, north African Berber group, 118
Kahn of Cathay, 206
Kanne, Johann Arnold, German philologist and linguist, 7
Kant, Immanuel, 61, 239
Keating, Geoffrey, 17th century Irish historian, 175, 239
Kennedy, John F., 170
Kierkegaard, Søren, 89, 90, 91, 240
King of Arran, 54
Kraken, legendary sea-monster, 78, 79, 80, 238, 243
Kronos, Greek god, father of Zeus, 21, 120, 139, 141, 145, 146, 178, 182

L

La Palma, Canary Islands, 128
Lacan, Jacques, French psychoanalyst, 8, 10
Lactantius, early Christian author, 159
Ladra, fictional character that lands in Ireland with Cessair's expedition, 175, 176
Lady of the Lake. *See* Nimue, Lady of the Lake
Lady of the Lake, the Dawn in Geoffrey of Monmouth's version of Merlin, 105
Lakshmi, Hindu goddess of wealth and good fortune and wife of the god Vishnu, 25
Land of Delight, 221
Land of Promise, 51, 131, 202, 221
Lanfranc, Italian jurist and archbishop of Canterbury, 224
Langhorne, village in Wales, 164

Lanzarote, island in the Canary Archipelago, 114
Laois, Ireland, 143
Laplace, Pierre-Simon, 6
las Casas, Bartolomé de, fray, 174
Las Palmas, city in Gran Canaria, 117
Last Supper, 85
Lavezzo, Kathy, xv, 38, 240
Laws, The, Plato, 145
le Verrier, Juan, 115
Leabhar Buidhe Leacáin. See *Yellow Book of Lecan*
Lebadeia, town in Boeotia, central Greece, 49
Lebor Gabála Érenn. See *Book of Invasions*
Lebor na hUidre. See *Book of the Dun Cow*
Legio IX Hispana, 135
Leinster, Ireland, 47, 139, 195, 200
Leix, Ireland, 215
León, region in Spain, 136
Leonites, monk in the fictional monastery of Valdeflores, 133
Levant, 120
Lewis and Clark, expedition, 211
lhiannan-shee, mythical peaceful spirit, 85
Liber monstrorum de diversis generibus, Anglo-Latin catalogue of about 120 fabulous creatures, 7th century, 199
Liber Prodigiorum, Julius Obsequens, 199
Library of Pergamum, 73
Libri Etymologiarum, Isidore of Seville, 199
Libro de las bienandanzas e fortunas, Lope García Salazar, 221

Liddel, Cumberland, England, 105
Life and Voyages of Christopher Columbus, 152
Life of Columba, Adamnán, 23
Life of Solon, Plutarch, 172
Life of St. Kentigern, Jocelyn of Furness, 105
Limia River, 40
liminal spaces, 37, 41, 192
Lindisfarne, 92, 126, 163
Linnaeus, Carl, Swedish physician and botanist, 78
Lir, Irish mythological god and personification of the sea, ancestor figure as father of the god Manannán mac Lir and father/king in The Children of Lir, 93, 94, 96
Litany of Pilgrim Saints, (800 CE), text features details on the adventures of several *immrama* characters, 43
Livy, Roman historian, 18
Llwyd, Humphrey, Welsh cartographer and author, 211
Llyfr Coch Hergest. See Red Book of Hergest
Llywarch ap Llywelyn, medieval Welsh poet, a.k.a. Prydydd y Moch, poet of the pigs, 208
Llywelyn ap Iorwerth, King of Gwynedd in north Wales, 208
Lochan, son of Connall ua Corra, 55
Lochlann, Gaelic word for Norway, 85
Locke, John, English philosopher, 61, 101
Loki, Norse trickster god, 74, 75
London, 11, 137, 162, 163, 209, 233
Longaneas, cape in Ireland, 221

longasa (voyages of exile), 139
Longtown, England, 106
López de Gómara, Francisco, 16th century Spanish historian, 210
Lorini, Niccoló, Florentine clergyman and Preacher General of the Dominican Order, 230
Lough Davra, lake adjacent to the home of the Children of Lir, 95
Lough Derg, lake adjacent to the palace of King Lir, 21, 94
Lough Derravaragh, lake in Ireland, 95
Lough Erne, lake in Northern Ireland, 47, 145
Lough Neagh, lake in Northern Ireland, 45, 145
Lourdes sanctuary, 131
Lucian of Samosata, 118, 161, 241
Lugh Lámfada, warrior-king of the Tuatha Dé Danann, 85, 195
Lughaidh, son of Ith, 122
Lughnasadh, ancient Irish pagan festival, 21
Luigni, Irish tribe, 197
Luis de Granada, 63
Luis de León, 63, 69
Lupercalia, pastoral festival (Feb. 15) of ancient Rome, repurposed as Saint Valentine's Day, 136
lustration, also known as purification, 19
lusus naturae, 11, 52, 80
Lydney Park, Gloucestershire, England., 107
Lyngbakr, medieval Icelandic sea-monster, 78

M

Mabinogi, belonging to the Matter of Britain, the earliest Welsh prose stories, 13, 162
Mach, Ernst, Austrian physicist and philosopher, 6
Macpherson, James, Scottish writer and politician, 185
Macrobius, Ambrosius Theodosius, Roman philosopher and grammarian, 159
Madeira, archipelago in the North Atlantic, 178
Madoc. *See* Prince Madog of Wales
Madog. *See* Prince Madoc of Wales
Madrid, 111, 127, 235
Máel Dúin. *See* Maelduin
Máel Muire mac Céilechair, compiler of the *Book of the Dun Cow*, 146
Maelduin, 3, 14, 29, 30, 32, 36, 54, 131, 166, 202, 213, 214, 215, 216, 217, 218, 222, 224, 244
Mag Itha, battle of, 146
Mag Mell, Delightful Plain of the Celts, 51, 139
Mag Rath, Battle of, 104
Mag Tured, battle of, 146
Magical ships, 184, 189
Magnus Sinus, 150, 151
Magog, mythical ancestor king, appearing in the Table of Nations in *Genesis*, 122
Malo of Aleth, Saint, 36
Malón de Chaide, Pedro, 63
Malory, Thomas, 191
Manannán, sea-god, ruler of the underworld, son of Lir, 45, 51, 84, 93, 131, 142, 143, 144, 195
Manawydan, brother of Brân, 162

Mandeville, 58, 60, 155, 156, 184
Manticores, quadrupeds with the heads of women, 58
Manuel I Comnenus, Byzantine emperor, 149
Mappae mundi, 130, 159
Mar Cuajada, 132
Mar Tapada, 132
Marcellus, writer of the *Aethiopica*, 118
Marcianus of Heraclea, 4th century CE Greek geographer, 118
Mare Tenebrosum, 158
Maredudd ap Rhys, fifteenth century Welsh poet, 208
Marerewana, hero of Arawak flood legend, 120
Marignolli, Giovanni de', medieval traveler also known as John of Marignolli and John of Florence, 69, 126, 155, 181, 206, 233
Mars, planet, 170, 171
Martin, Saint, 188
Mary Magdalene, 92
Massalia, ancient Greek colony in southern France, modern Marseille, 177, 179
Matholwch, King of Ireland, 162
Matthew, Evangelist, 204
Mauritanians, 114
Maurus, Saint, 129
Mayflower, ship, 212
Meath, Ireland, 186
Meðalland, area of southern Iceland, 83
medio orbe, 38
Mediterranean, xiii, xv, 25, 26, 32, 38, 39, 52, 71, 77, 78, 113, 117, 118, 147, 148, 156, 174, 175, 178, 182, 183, 185, 207, 220, 234, 239

Medusa, Gorgon, 145
megalithic structures, 14
Melior, empress in the poem Partonopeus de Blois, 189
Mellitus, first bishop of London in the Saxon period, 137
Memorias, Andrés Bernáldez, 115
Menelaos, king of Mycenaean Sparta, 21, 141
Menéndez Pelayo, Marcelino, 134, 241
Merddin. *See* Merlin
Merlin, 104, 105, 106, 107, 108, 109, 191, 204, 233, 238, 240
Mesolithic, 19
Mesopotamia, 130
metamorphoses, 93, 101, 218
Metamorphoses, Ovid, 242
Metaphysics, 6, 222
Mexico, 150, 170, 212
Micah, prophet, 82
Midacritus, ancient Greek sailor, 178
Middle Ages, xii, 12, 17, 41, 45, 48, 54, 58, 59, 65, 66, 71, 80, 81, 82, 86, 89, 91, 93, 99, 112, 118, 121, 124, 128, 157, 159, 162, 165, 171, 183, 193, 197, 198, 202, 224, 233, 234, 239, 242, 244, 246
Midgard, mythical Norse habitable world, 74, 75
Midsummer Night's Dream, 85
Mikilnefna, Iceland, 83
Miles Espánie. *See* Milesians
Miles Hispaniae. *See* Milesians
Milesians, in the *Lebor Gabála Érenn*, the final race to settle in Ireland, 24, 122, 123, 175
Milesius, mythical king of Spain, 175
Milford Haven, Wales, 164

Milichius, Ludovicus, 89
Mobile, Alabama, 208
Modernity, 82
Mongán mac Fiachnai, historical prince of the Cruthin people, 143
Mongán, son of Manannán mac Lir, 51, 143
Monk of the Little Birds, 28, 132
Monmouth, Geoffrey of, 14, 17, 18, 105, 106, 108, 113, 237
monomyth, 204, 205
Monopods, man-like creatures with one eye and one foot, 58
Monticello, house of Thomas Jefferson in Virginia, 211
Moralia, Plutarch, 49
Mordred, nephew/son of King Arthur, 108
Morgana, sorceress in Arthurian legend, 221
Mount Ida, also known as Phrygian Ida, in western Anatolia, 146
Mount of Olives, 85
mourinhos, inhabitants of underground realms in Galician myth, 122
Moyle, Sea of, ancient name for the narrowest expanse of water between Northern Ireland and Scotland, 95
Mozambique, 149
Muhammad, 59
Muirchertach Mac Erc, possibly a High King of Ireland in the 6th century, 43
Mullet Peninsula, County Mayo, Ireland, 93
mummies, 114, 119
Mummu, Mesopotamian god of mists, 24
Munster, Ireland, 195, 200, 204
Münster, Sebastian, German cartographer and scholar, 149, 150
Musculus, Andreas, German Lutheran theologian, 89
Muslims, 59, 88, 149
Muspellheim, mythical Norse land of fire, 74
Muxía, village in the extreme northwest of Spain, 136
Myrddin Wyllt. *See* Merlin
Mysterious Island, Jules Verne, 170
mysterium fidei, 61
myth, xiii, xiv, xv, 1, 2, 3, 4, 5, 6, 7, 8, 9, 10, 11, 12, 13, 14, 15, 16, 17, 18, 19, 20, 25, 26, 27, 31, 36, 37, 41, 46, 51, 53, 55, 57, 59, 60, 61, 76, 78, 87, 99, 100, 102, 103, 115, 116, 117, 118, 122, 123, 126, 139, 143, 145, 146, 147, 148, 149, 152, 153, 160, 171, 172, 174, 181, 182, 185, 201, 204, 208, 209, 211, 212, 213, 217, 218, 224, 230, 233, 234, 235, 236, 237, 239, 242, 244
Mythological Cycle, 174
mythology, 6, 7, 13, 16, 18, 42, 51, 52, 74, 76, 78, 103, 112, 114, 121, 139, 145, 146, 147, 153, 157, 161, 173, 185, 193, 202, 206, 220

N

narrative envelopes, 57
Nath Í mac Fiachrach, also known as Dathí, fifth century semi-historical Irish king, 66
Natural History of Norway, Erik Pontoppidan, 79

Natural History, Pliny the Elder, 78, 117, 174, 178, 199, 243
Navarra, region in Spain, 136
Navigatio Sancti Brendani, 51, 134, 138, 157, 201, 202, 205, 206, 207, 208
Nechtan mac Collbran, homesick crewmate in the Voyage of Bran mac Febail, 143
Nemed, mythical leader of the third group of people to settle in Ireland, 175
Nemedians, mythical ancient invaders of Ireland, 146
Nennius, Welsh monk, writer of the *Historia Brittonum*, 146
Neptune, Roman god of freshwater and the sea, 122
Nera, hero of the Echtrae Nerai, 43
New Frontier, John F. Kennedy's vision for the future, 170
New Testament, 50
New York, 11
Newton, Percival, 154
Níall Noígíallach of the Nine Hostages, 43
Niam Chinn Óir, spirit maiden and lover of U sheen, 132, 163, 194, 195, 196, 198, 199
Nicasius of Rheims, Bishop of Reims and saint, 161
Nicholas of Cusa, German Catholic cardinal, philosopher, and astronomer, 62, 81
Nicodemus, Pharisee member of the Sanhedrin, 20
Nidaros (Trondheim, Norway), 79
Nietzsche, Friedrich, 96, 244
Niflheim, mythical Norse ice-world, 74, 75
Nile, River, 5, 246

Nimrod, ruler of Babylon, 130
Nimue, Lady of the Lake, 26
Nineveh, ancient Assyrian city, 25
Nisien, brother of Brân, 162
Noah, 20, 114, 153, 175
Nodens. *See* Nud, early name for Merlin
Nodens temple, temple to Zeus/Merlin in Lydney Park, Gloucestershire, England, 107
Norman conquest, 194
Normandy, 165
Norse, 33, 34, 74, 75, 76, 77, 79, 81, 82, 185
Norwegian Sea, 71, 78
Novalis, (Georg Philipp Friedrich, Freiherr von Hardenberg), 7
Novum Organum, Francis Bacon, 230
Nuca, druid, 215
Nud, early name for Merlin, 107
Numidians, 114
Nydam Mose ships, 31
Nyland, Edo, 116

O

Oak King, Celtic personification of summer, 132
Oberon, king of the fairies, 85
objectivity, 16, 90, 91, 100
Obsequens, Julius, writer of the Liber Prodigiorum, 199
Odin, Norse god, 75, 76
Odo, Abbot of Fossé, 129
Odoric of Pordenone, 58
Odysseus, 53, 54, 144, 185
Odyssey, 21, 141, 143, 185, 190, 202, 204, 238
Ogham alphabet, 196

Ogyges, mythological king in ancient Greece, 145
Ogygia, island of the nymph Calypso, 144
Oileach Neid, fortress and seat of the ancient kings of Ulster, 122
Okeanos, 5, 25, 38, 72, 141, 144, 185
Olaus Magnus, Swedish cartographer and clergyman, 77, 78
Old Testament, 65, 114
Olympians, 120
On the Late Vengeance of the Deity, Plutarch, 49
Ora Maritima, (The Sea Coast), Postumius Rufius Festus Avienus, 178
orbis terrarum, 38, 39, 40
Origen of Alexandria, influential Christian theologian, 82
Orkney, 33
Orozco, Alonso de, Spanish Augustinian clergyman, 63
Orpheus, mythical musician and prophet of ancient Greece, 82, 161, 163, 234
Örvar-Odds, twelfth century Icelandic saga, 78
Ossianic Cycle of Irish mythology, 13, 193

Ø

Øster Sottrup, Denmark, 31

O

otherworld, xii, xiii, xiv, 15, 20, 21, 23, 27, 28, 29, 31, 35, 37, 39, 41, 42, 43, 44, 45, 47, 48, 49, 50, 51, 52, 53, 56, 57, 77, 84, 93, 96, 97, 103, 107, 129, 130, 131, 132, 133, 134, 139, 144, 157, 176, 178, 179, 184, 185, 188, 191, 198, 204, 214, 216, 222, 223, 224, 227, 228
Otomi, indigenous people of central Mexico, 170
Otto of Freising, 149
Outer Hebrides, 183
ovates, ancient Irish seers, healers and prophets, 166, 218
Ovid, 93, 178, 179, 183, 242
  Metamorphoses, 93, 178
Oxford English Dictionary, 16
Oxford University, 23

P

Pabbay, one of the Barra Islands of Scotland, 33
Pacific, 28, 149, 150, 170, 211
pagan, xi, xii, xiii, 12, 13, 14, 15, 21, 22, 24, 27, 28, 29, 30, 31, 34, 35, 36, 37, 39, 41, 42, 46, 47, 51, 52, 53, 54, 55, 61, 63, 64, 65, 68, 77, 88, 90, 91, 93, 95, 96, 97, 98, 99, 100, 101, 102, 103, 113, 130, 131, 132, 133, 134, 135, 136, 137, 138, 144, 149, 156, 157, 159, 160, 164, 165, 166, 167, 175, 176, 186, 187, 188, 191, 193, 204, 205, 206, 214, 215, 217, 218, 222, 223, 224, 227, 228, 229
pagan substratum, 30
Papa Stour, Shetland, 33
Papa Stronsay, Orkney, 33
Papa Westray, Orkney, 33
Paparokur, Faroe Islands, 33
Papars, early medieval Irish monks, first people to reach Iceland, 33

Paradise, 13, 28, 45, 48, 51, 69, 81, 82, 111, 112, 113, 126, 129, 130, 133, 134, 181, 193, 202, 203, 206, 219, 220, 233, 236, 240, 242, 244
Partholanus, mythical discoverer of Ireland, 175
Partholón, mythical leader of the second group of people to settle in Ireland, 175
Partonopeus de Blois, medieval French poem, 189, 190, 194, 243
Partonopeus, hero of the poem *Partonopeus de Blois*, 60, 189, 190, 236
Patala, the underworld in Hindu cosmology, 116
Patch, Howard R., xv, 20, 21, 49, 74, 75, 76, 113, 243
Paul the Apostle, 50
Pearl, Middle English poem, 133
pedra de abalar, 136
pedra dos cadrís, 136
Pegasus, mythical winged horse, 145
Pelasgians, inhabitants of Greece before the arrival of the Greeks, 145
Pèlerinage de la vie humaine, 82
Peloponnesus, 174
Pemphredo, one of the three Graiae, 145
Penarddun, wife of Brân, 162
Penglai Shan, Chinese Isle of the Immortals, 28
Penniston, Jim, United States writer and ufologist, 219, 220
Perceval, knight in Arthurian legend, 190, 191
Peredur, British warlord, 106
peregrinatio, 22, 23, 35

peregrinatio pro amore Dei, 22
Pérez de Grado, Hernán, 125
Perioecians, people that live on the same parallel of latitude but on opposite meridians, so midday in one place is midnight in the other, 73
Periplous of the External Sea, Marcianus of Heraclea, 118
Periplus of Amaro, 128, 134, 135, 136, 137, 138
Persephone, mythical Greek goddess queen of the underworld, 117
Perseus, mythical Greek hero and slayer of the Gorgon Medusa, 145
Persian Gulf, 159
petroglyphs, 117
Phaeacians, mythical mariners in the *Odyssey*, 185, 190
Phaedrus, Plato, 63
Philippines, 170
Philo of Alexandria, 174, 247
philosophes, 16
Philosophy, 6, 7, 16, 65, 123, 235, 236, 241, 242, 244, 246
Phoenicians, semitic people from the eastern Mediterranean, 114, 148
Phorcys, primordial sea-god, 145
Picts, ancient people of northern and eastern Scotland, 125, 143
Pilate, Pontius, 91
Pilgrimage Road to Santiago, 136
Pillars of Hercules, 157, 173, 177
Pindar, ancient Theban lyric poet, 140, 141, 173, 182, 235, 243, 246
Pishon, biblical river, 130
Pizzigani Brothers, 14th-century Venetian cartographers, 220

Plato, 5, 6, 48, 49, 63, 67, 71, 90, 117, 120, 145, 172, 173, 180, 242, 243
Pliny the Elder, 78, 112, 117, 135, 174, 178, 180, 199, 243
Pliny the Younger, 174
Plotinus, founder of Neoplatonism, 127
Plutarch, 49, 50, 112, 172, 182, 243
Pluto, mythological ruler of the underworld, 117
Point Peninsula, also Eye Peninsula, Scotland, 33
Poitiers, France, 209
Ponce de León, Juan, 69, 126, 152, 153, 181
Pontoppidan, Erik, Danish Lutheran bishop and author, 79
Porphyry, Neoplatonist philosopher, 127
portolan charts, xiv, xv, 1, 12, 27, 54, 148, 214, 220, 234, 239, 247
Portroe, Co. Tipperary, 176
Portugal, 23, 135, 221
Poseidon, one of the Twelve Olympians and god of the sea, 117, 173, 185
Posidonius of Apameia, 135, 174, 180, 181
Postumius Rufius Festus Avienus, 178
Potitus, grandfather of St. Patrick, 92
Powell, David, 211
Prado Museum, 111
pre-Christian, 19, 29, 34, 52, 91, 95, 96, 98, 121, 134, 136, 138, 158, 160, 165, 205, 214, 215, 216, 218, 221, 223
pre-Columbian, 120, 211
Preiddeu Annwfn, (The Spoils of Annwn), poem in Middle Welsh found in the *Llyfr Taliessin* (Book of Taliesin), 29, 162, 240
pre-literate peoples, 173
pre-modern peoples, 17
prescientific societies, xiii
Prester John, 148, 149, 151, 152, 155, 181
Priests of Sais, ancient Egypt, 172
Prince Madoc of Wales, 13, 14, 140, 163, 208
Proclus of Lycia, 117, 118, 174, 243
Prometheus, Titan and god of fire, 145
Promised Land of the Saints, 204
Prose Brut, collection of medieval chronicles that recount the history of Britain, 106
proselytizers, xii, 29, 32, 37, 46, 53, 97, 100, 101, 102, 131, 134, 160, 167, 176, 214, 218, 224
Proslogion, Anselm of Canterbury, 228
Protagoras, Greek pre-Socratic philosopher and rhetorical theoretician, 90
Protestant movement, 89
proto-Celtic, 23
Psalms, 25
Pseudo-Albertus Magnus, 200
Pseudo-Dionysius the Areopagite, 81
Pseudo-Scymnus, unknown author of work on geography, 135
psychopomp, spirit who guides the souls of the dead, 51
Ptolemy, 48, 72, 112, 150, 151, 158, 180, 234
Pûtika, western sea described in the Zoroastrian Avesta, 20
Pyrenees, mountain range, 136

Pyrrha, wife of Deucalion, 145
Pytheas of Massalia, 73, 76, 179, 180

R

Rædwald, ruler of the East Angles, 31
Randalstown, County Meath, 19
reality, xii, xiii, xiv, 1, 2, 3, 4, 5, 7, 8, 9, 10, 12, 15, 17, 24, 26, 27, 29, 31, 32, 33, 34, 35, 36, 37, 38, 39, 40, 46, 52, 53, 60, 61, 65, 68, 69, 71, 76, 79, 80, 81, 82, 83, 84, 85, 86, 87, 88, 89, 90, 93, 98, 99, 100, 101, 102, 103, 113, 121, 126, 127, 128, 136, 139, 148, 155, 156, 158, 165, 198, 199, 200, 201, 205, 206, 207, 212, 214, 216, 217, 222, 227, 228, 230, 231
Red Book of Hergest, 104, 105, 107
Red Sea, 58, 131, 180
Regino of Prüm, German Benedictine monk and historian, 93
Relation of Some Years Travaile, Thomas Herbert, 209
Renaissance, 27, 229, 235, 245
Rendlesham Forest, England, 219
Republic, Plato, 48
Rhadamanthys, son of Zeus and Europa, 141
Rhea, wife of mythical king Euaemon, 120
Rhiannon, Celtic deity, 163
Rhodri ab Owain, prince of Gwynedd, Wales, 208
rhumb line, 27
Rhydderch Hael, ruler of Alt Clut, a Brittonic kingdom, 108
Rígru Rosclethan, ruler of Tír Tairngire, 52

Ringhorn, mythical Norse ship, 185
River Lethe, 40
River Shannon, 176
Rocks of Scylla, place haunted by the sea-monster Kharybdis, 144
Roland, nephew of Charlemagne, 146
Rollo, conqueror and first Duke of Normandy, 165
Roman Empire, 158, 167, 171
Roman Inquisition, 230
Romans, 40, 61, 112, 114, 120, 183, 238
Romantics, 6
Rome, 38, 39, 47, 57, 112, 129, 130, 149, 158, 159, 171, 199, 244, 247
Rónán Finn, early Irish saint, 104
Ros Bearaigh, forest, 104
Ross, Ireland, 163, 186, 187, 188, 189
Roteiro da viagem, Vasco da Gama, 149
Royal Irish Academy, 22, 214
runes of wisdom, 204

S

Sadbh, mother of U sheen, 194
Sahara, 116
Saint Patrick, 21, 35, 95, 98
Saint Patrick's Purgatory, 21
Saint-Simon, Henri de, 6
Saint-Victor. *See* Hugh of Saint Victor
Salamanca conclave of 1487, 155
Salim, biblical area in western Jordan, 20
Salvation, 81, 85, 91, 188, 240
Samothrace, island in the northern Aegean Sea, 145

San Borondón, also known as Saint Brendan's Isle, mythical phantom island northwest of the Canary Archipelago, 125, 127, 234, 241
San Brandán. *See* Brendan
San Petronio Basilica, Bologna, 87
Sanskrit, ancient Indo-Aryan language, 125
Santa Cruz, Alonso de, Spanish 16th century cartographer and historian, 221, 235
Santa Olalla, Julio Martínez, 119
Saracens, 59
Sargasso Sea, 32, 132, 209
Sarras, land where Arthurian knights were imprisoned, 191
Satan, 81
Saturn, Roman god, 141
Scandinavia, xv, 31, 71, 73
Schelling, Friedrich Wilhelm Joseph, 6, 7
Schlegel, Friedrich, 7
Scientific Bards, Merlin's nine companions, 140
Scipio Aemilianus, Roman general, 48
Scipio Africanus, Roman general, 48
Scotland, xv, 23, 33, 38, 45, 85, 95, 104, 105, 106, 126, 182
Scottish Highlands, 85
Scripture, 61, 68, 103, 155, 159
Scyths, ancient Iranian nomadic people, 154
sea-monsters, 78, 81, 82, 83, 98, 107
Second Battle of Mag-Tuired, 139
Second Sight, 68
Seeley, Sir John, English 19th century historian and political essayist, 16, 247

Ségda Sáerlabraid, son of Dáire and Rígru Rosclethan, 52
Seneca, Lucius Annaeus, 174
Serbs, 9
Serglige Con Chulainn, 43
Severn Estuary, 107
Sgeir, druid, 185
Shakespeare, 85, 234
shape-shifting, 93, 177
Shawia, north African Berber group, 118
Shem, son of Noah, 114, 153
Sheol, Hebrew place of the dead, 25
Shetland Islands, 33
Shuibhne mac Colmáin, King of the Dál nAraidi, 104
Siaburcharpat Con Culaind, The Phantom Chariot of Cú. Chulainn, 43
sianan, ancient Irish ballads, 163, 187
Sicily, 59
Sidhe, fairy mound, 43
sight, 29, 50, 58, 60, 61, 62, 63, 64, 66, 67, 68, 69, 81, 116, 128, 143, 155, 156, 179, 182, 183, 185
Sir Gawain and the Green Knight, 14th-century chivalric romance in Middle English, 161
Sir Orfeo, 13th century Middle English Breton lai, 133, 245
Skarði, area of southwestern Iceland, 83
Skíðblaðnir, mythical Norse ship, 185
skoggra (skogsrået), Mistress of the Forest, 47
Slaughter of Conan's Tower, 146
Snédgus and Mac Ríagla, 31, 163, 187, 188, 224
Socrates, 172

Solomon, King, 190, 191
Solon, ancient Athenian statesman, 172
Somnium Scipionis, 48
Sonchis, ancient Egyptian priest of Sais, 172
Sønderjylland, Denmark, 31
Song of Roland, 11th century French epic poem, 59, 60
Soto, Hernando de, 16th century Spanish explorer and conquistador, 152, 153
Spain, 13, 17, 23, 28, 40, 59, 63, 121, 122, 132, 134, 135, 136, 146, 152, 153, 155, 171, 175, 180, 191, 193, 199, 206, 211, 212, 221, 225, 229, 238
Spaniards, 114, 117, 170, 210, 212
Spanish Carmelites, 63
Spanish Empire, 169, 170
Spanish Missouri Company, 211
Speckled Book, medieval Irish vellum manuscript, 51
Spence, Lewis, 174, 245
Spoils of Annwn, (Preiddeu Annwfn), poem in Middle Welsh found in the *Llyfr Taliessin* (Book of Taliesin), 29
Sri Lanka, 158
Sruth Fada Conn. *See* Irrus Domnannthe, bay in Ireland
St Anne's holy well, 19
St. Brigid's Day, 21
St. John's Day, 132
Star Trek, 170, 239
Star Wars, 170
Starkad, foster son of Horsehair Grani, 76
Steenstrup, Japetus Smith, 78
Sthenno, Gorgon, 145
Stonehenge, 105

Strabo, 38, 73, 135, 144, 173, 179, 180, 206, 244, 245
Straits of Gibraltar, 26, 73, 114, 118, 144, 157, 160, 177, 182
Suma de geografía que trata de todas las partidas e provincias del mundo, Martín Fernández de Enciso, 221
Sumerians, 24, 202, 237
Summa Theologica, Thomas Aquinas, 66
Summum Bonum, Saint Augustine, 63
Sun, xi, 40
Sutton Hoo, 20, 31
Sword of the Strange Hangings, 190
syncretism, xii, 31, 32, 34, 35, 36, 41, 46, 47, 89, 91, 96, 97, 98, 99, 103, 165, 166, 167, 187, 214, 216, 219, 224
Syrian Goddess, The, Lucian, 161, 241
Systema Naturae, Carl Linnaeus, 78

T

Table of Opposites, Pythagoras, 123
Tailkenn (St. Patrick), 95
Tajo, river in Spain, 135
Taliesin, early Brittonic poet, 29, 92
Talmud, Babylonian, 66, 244
Tamar, river, 119
Tamara. *See* Tamarán
Tamarán, Gran Canaria, 119
Taotao Tano, ancestors of the Chamorro people of the Mariana Islands, 170

Tara, ancient seat of power in Ireland, 22, 23, 47, 85
Tara, goddess of fertility in Tibetan Buddhism, 119
Tara, neighborhood in Telde, Gran Canaria, 119
Tarot playing cards, 216
Tartars (Tatars), Turkic-speaking peoples of west-central Asia, 154
Tartessos, ancient civilization in southwestern Spain, 135, 177
Tartessus. *See* Tartessos, ancient civilization in southwestern Spain
Tecla, Saint, 191
Tehom, biblical primordial abyss, 25
Teide Volcano, 115, 178
Telde, Gran Canaria, 119
Ten Commandments, 124
Tenerife, Canary Islands, 115, 116, 128, 246
Teresa of Ávila, 63, 69
Tertullian (Quintus Septimius Florens Tertullianus), early Christian author from Carthage, 93
Tervagant, name of a god that medieval Christians believed was worshipped by Muslims, 59
Tethra, Fomorian ruler of Mag Mell, 139, 145
Thailand, 150
The Lost Empire, novel by Frank Wall, 32
Theaetetus, Plato, 90, 243
Theatrum Diabolorum, 89
Thespesius, character in Plutarch's *Moralia*, 49

Thirteen Treasures of the Island of Britain, 162
Thomas Aquinas. *See* Aquinas, Thomas
Thor, Norse god, 76, 84
Thrace, region in the southwestern Balkan Peninsula, 66
Three disappearances of the Isle of Britain, 208
Tiamat, Mesopotamian goddess of fresh water, 24, 25, 37
Tiber, river in Italy, 158
Tibetan Buddhism, 120
Tibicenas, mythical Guanche hell-hound, 114
Tigris River, 130, 149
Timaeus, Plato, 145, 172, 243
Timarchus, character in Plutarch's *De genio Socratis*, 49, 50
time-dilation, 133, 134, 138, 192, 229
Tír na nÓg, Celtic Land of Youth and otherworld, 45, 195
Tír Tairngire, Land of Promise, otherworld paradise, 51, 84, 242
Tiresias, blind prophet of Apollo, 185
Titania, Queen of the Fairies in Shakespeare's *A Midsummer Night's Dream*, 85
Titans, pre-Olympian gods of Greek mythology, 139, 146
Tochmarc Becfola. *See* Wooing of Becfola, The
Tochmarc Emire. *See* Wooing of Emer, The
tochmarca (wooing), 139
tógbala (conquests), 139
Tomaidm locha Echdach, mythical Irish flood, 145

Tomaidm locha Eirne, mythical Irish flood, 145
Topographia Christiana, Cosmas Indicopleustes, 158
Topographia Hibernica, Gerard of Wales, 147, 199
Torre de Hércules. See Tower of Brigantia
Tounthinna, hill of, 176
Tower of Brigantia, 122
Tower of Hercules. *See* Tower of Brigantia
transparentes, mythical Canary Islands leprechauns, 114
Treaty of Doak's Stand, 1820, 213
Tree of Life, 133, 190
Trezenzonio, 13, 14, 27, 30, 60, 138, 191, 192, 223, 224, 228, 229
Triads. See *Trioedd Ynys Prydein*
Trinity College Dublin, 23, 214
Trioedd Ynys Prydein, 105, 107, 140, 234
Tristan and Iseult, 193
Tristan et Iseut. *See* Tristan and Iseult
Triton, Greek god of the sea, the son of Poseidon and Amphitrite, 178
Trophonius, son of Apollo, 49
Troy, 25, 106, 141, 235
True Story, Lucian of Samosata, 118
Tuath Dé. *See* Tuatha Dé Danann, mythical conquerors of Ireland, *See* Tuatha Dé Danann
Tuatha Dé. *See* Tuatha Dé Danann, mythical conquerors of Ireland
Tuatha Dé Danann, mythical conquerors of Ireland, 51, 52, 94, 174
Tuatha Dé Danann, supernatural race in Irish mythology, 175

Tul Tuinne. See Tounthinna, hill of
Tulach Tuindi. See Tounthinna, hill of
Tutankhamun, Pharaoh, 20
Twenty Thousand Leagues Under the Sea, Jules Verne, 170
twin paradox, 133, 134
Tyre, Phoenician city, 148
Tyre, William of, 88
Tzotzil, indigenous Maya people of southern Mexico, 170

U

U sheen, 13, 14, 28, 30, 65, 132, 163, 193, 194, 195, 196, 197, 198, 199, 200, 201, 216, 223, 225, 229
uatha (adventures inside caves), 139
UFO, 219
Uí Chorra. *See Voyage of the Sons of Uí Chorra*
Uistean, mythical Scottish hero, 85
Ulster, 161
Ultima Thule, 34
unicorns, 58
United States, 210
Universalis Cosmographia, 149
Utnapishtim, character in the *Epic of Gilgamesh*, 173

V

Valdeflores, fictional monastery, 133, 134
Valhalla, Norse mythology's Hall of the Slain Warriors, 75
Van Dale Dutch Dictionary, 16

Varro, Marcus Terentius, Roman scholar and author, 38
Vasco da Gama, Portuguese explorer, 149
Vedas, ancient Hindu scriptures, 106
Veleda, Celtic seeress and prophet, 133
Veneti, ancient people of Brittany, 183
Venice, 25
Vergil, Polydore, British/Italian humanist scholar and priest, 18, 246
Verne, Jules, 170
Versuch einer natürlichen Geschichte Norwegens, 79
Veselovsky, Aleksandr, 19th century Russian literary theorist and historian, 205
Vesica Piscis, symbol of Jesus of Nazareth, 216
Vespucci, Amerigo, 151, 152, 246
Vestmanna, Faroe Islands, 33
Vico, Giambattista, 6, 7, 8, 241
Vikar, legendary Norwegian king, 76
Vikings, 35, 235
Villancey, Charles, 18th century British military surveyor, 147, 246
Virgen da Barca, 136
Virgil (Publius Vergilius Maro), ancient Roman poet, 199
Virgin Mary, 28, 86, 92, 132, 133
Virila, mythical Aragonese abbot, 132
Vishnu Purana, primary sacred text of the Vaishnava branch of Hinduism, 116
Visio sancti Pauli (The Apocalypse of Paul), 50
vision literature, 41, 48, 52, 53
Vita Merlini, Geoffrey of Monmouth, 105, 113, 238
Vitruvius, Roman architect, 38
Vivaldi brothers, 14th century Genoese explorers and merchants, 180
Voltaire, 17
Vourukasha, heavenly sea, 20
Voyage of Bran mac Febail, 42, 43, 57, 131, 141, 143, 144
Voyage of Snédgus and Mac Ríagla, 42, 52, 186, 245
Voyage of the Sons of Uí Chorra, 42, 51, 55, 163
Voyages Extraordinaires, Jules Verne, 170
Vulgate Cycle, early thirteenth century group of Arthurian romances in French prose, 191

W

Waldseemüller, Martin, German cartographer and humanist scholar, 149, 150, 151
Wales, 13, 23, 38, 105, 106, 126, 163, 208, 211, 234, 235, 247
Walkendorf, Erik, Archbishop of Nidaros, 79
waning sun. *See* Holly King
War of the Worlds, Orson Wells radio drama, 171
Wasobiobe, Japanese wise man, 28
waxing sun, 132, *See* Oak King
Wells, Orson, 171
Welsh Triads, 13, 162
Weltanschauung, 8, 39
Wen-tāqqa, Canary Island myth, 115
Werewolf, 93
West Indies, 221

White Island of Atala, xiv, 116
Whitney, George H., 157, 246
Wicker Man, 215
Wilford, Colonel Francis, translator of the *Vishnu Purana*, 116
William III (William of Orange), 146
William Obryen. *See* Earl of Inchiquin
William the Minstrel, 13th century poet, 209
Williams, John, 18th century United States author, 209
Wirth, Herman, 20th century Dutch-German historian and scholar of ancient religions, 118
witches, 86, 89
wood maid, 47
wood wife, 47
Wooing of Becfola, The, 47
Wooing of Emer, The, 43
Wordsworth, William, English Romantic poet, 191

World Above, 122
World Below, 122

Y

Yeats, William Butler, 194
Yellow Book of Lecan, 47, 148, 214
Ymir, mythical Norse primeval giant, 75, 76
Yr Afallennau (The Apple Trees), 107

Z

zeitgeister, 153
Zephyros, Greek god of the west wind, 141
Zeus, 65, 105, 107, 139, 141, 144, 145, 146
Zipangri. *See* Japan
Zoroastrian Avesta, 20
Zurara, Gomes Eanes de, 115

www.ingramcontent.com/pod-product-compliance
Lightning Source LLC
Chambersburg PA
CBHW071347290426
44108CB00014B/1460